Consummate Connecticut:

Day Trips with Panache

Stacy Lytwyn Maxwell

Stacey + Theresa,
I hope you both
enjoy many
wonderful day
Trips everywhere
+ always!

First Edition

Regards,
S. S. Maxwell
2008

Cat Tales PRESS, INC.
Purr-fect Books for Purr-fect People

Greens Farms, CT

www.cattalespress.com

Please help us keep this guide up to date:

Although the author of this guide has tried to make the information presented in this book as accurate and up-to-date as possible, in the world of travel, ubiquitous changes take place constantly. Please send any changes, comments or suggestions to CAT TALES PRESS INC., P.O. Box 382, Greens Farms, Connecticut 06838.

Or email us at: cattalespress@snet.net.

The author, editors and staff at CAT TALES PRESS accept no responsibility for loss, injury or inconvenience sustained by any reader of this book.

**To order extra copies of this book or for information about
CAT TALES PRESS, visit our homepage, www.cattalespress.com.**

Text, photographs, design and maps © 2006 by CAT TALES PRESS, Greens Farms, Connecticut.

Front cover artwork, "The Lamplighter Band on the Library Lawn," is a painting honoring an event hosted by the Wheeler Library in North Stonington. The painting's artist, Connecticut-based, Susan B. Stafford, recalls the inspiration behind her work:

"My husband and I drove my parents down there in his 1947 Cadillac and, along with many other local residents who came with picnic baskets and lawn chairs, we enjoyed a warm summer evening and music from the same era as our car."

This print is one in a series entitled, "A Sense of Community" that highlights places and events in the Stonington area that hold an appeal for visitors and residents alike. The print series is featured on The Wheeler Library web site and can also be viewed in its entirety on Susan's site @ www.susanbstafford.com.

Special Acknowledgment from the Author:

During the core of this project, Editors Patricia Grassi and Laurie J. Stone helped me polish every last detail, and without their unending commitment, this book would not have been possible.

Robin Cummings, a person with sheer artistic talent, also spent endless hours designing a consummate book that only such a mastermind as Robin could!

Printed in the United States of America.

© Cat Tales Press 2006

ISSN: 1558-710X

ISBN: 0-9771230-0-6

First Edition/First Printing

Dedication

For those travelers who have come before me and for those who will follow me and, especially, for those who go alongside me; may you all proceed in the Good Orderly Direction.

•

Thank you all, especially to:

My beloved groom, Robert (Oly, this one is for you)
My beloved children, Marshall and Alexandra
(accept the high and the low of the road and the traveling will be smooth)
My spiritual sister, mentor, friend and everything else, Pat Grassi
(finally *we* did it)
Laurie Stone, forever grateful for your expert editing and perfect eye
Noreen Wilgus, for her guidance and last minute keen eye
Robin Cummings, for her superior artistic and technological abilities
My dear mom, for her many years of encouragement
& to whom I am indebted always
Brother Paul, Diane & Larissa (we can reach for the stars together!)
My heavenly angels (Pop, Mike and all the rest)
The Thursday girls (yes, it's done, and I won't say another word about it)
Easton Public Library Director Bernadette Baldino and her patient
(and I mean patient!) staff
My husband's family, my extended family and the many, many friends
(I hope we always share the same journey)
The state of Connecticut tourism departments, the many attractions and
wonderful places that make this great state—AWESOME!

In gratitude always,

Stacy

Stacy Lytwyn Maxwell

pa·nache
(n) dash or flamboyance in style and action: verve

TABLE OF CONTENTS

IV. SOUTHERN CONNECTICUT

V. SOUTH CENTRAL CONNECTICUT

VI. SOUTHWEST CONNECTICUT

VII. SOUTHEAST CONNECTICUT

VIII. WEST CENTRAL CONNECTICUT

IX. CENTRAL CONNECTICUT

X. NORTHWEST CONNECTICUT

Index

MAPS

Introduction

Connecticut, one of the original 13 colonies, is the consummate state for day trips. Since the total land area measures only 4,845 square miles, motorists can cross the state at any point in less than two hours. Two hours!

Day-trippers will discover a serendipitous New England state in which a turn of the steering wheel unveils changing views in appearance and personality that exude from cities, towns and villages. Combining eight counties and the three largest cities of Bridgeport, New Haven and the state's capital Hartford, explorers will uncover Connecticut's colonial past in the scenic roadways, farmlands, historic village greens and white-steeple churches.

Thirty state forests, comprising 149,352 acres and 93 state parks encompassing 32,960 acres provide generous respite among nature trails, rolling hills, woodlands and streams. In all this green artistry, expect surprises like a hilltop fieldstone mansion at Gillette Castle State Park in Essex. Superbly renovated, actor William Gillette, most known for his stage version of Sherlock Holmes, built the lavish landmark in 1919.

Museums, too, offer an array of exhibitions, some hands-on, that can pique the interest of every age and delve into such subjects as science, history and, of course, everything indigenous to the state (visited a museum devoted to shad fish lately?). Travelers who peruse the galleries will discover timelines that span as far back as the ice age, move through colonial and maritime periods into present-day life and beyond to possible futuristic epochs. Not only do they accommodate a variety of tastes—but also budgets. For instance, the thousands of artifacts at Cheshire's Barker Character, Comic and Cartoon Museum whiz every patron, irregardless of age, back into the nostalgia of childhood without pinching a penny from the piggybank (yes, admission is free).

Day-trippers also have acclaimed restaurants aplenty and eateries where memorable fare can mean a bowl of the award-winning clam chowder at either Hartford's or Branford's U.S.S. Chowder Pot Restaurant; deep-fried clams with the bellies at the ever-popular Lenny and Joe's Restaurant at the Westbrook or Madison location, and a reasonably priced, all-you-can-eat fish fry on Friday at Waterbury's Howard Johnson's, one of a handful of surviving restaurants that in its heyday symbolized an icon to the American motorist.

Off-the-beaten track, Wright's Mill Farm in idyllic Canterbury cooks up the fresh goodness of home on special days. And who can't find room for a teensy-weensy dollop of Italian ice at Micalizzi Italian Ice, one of the best-kept secrets in Bridgeport. West Hartford's Tapas Restaurant has sparked such a craze with its "Almost Famous" salad dressing that customers have it mail-ordered to them all over the world!

Speaking of mom and pop culture, Connecticut also applauds her independently run stores that have stood up to the encroaching big retail establishments. For instance, a sampling of popular bookstores includes R.J. Julia Booksellers, Madison; Millrace Bookstore, Farmington; Just Books and Diane's Bookstore, Greenwich and Hickory Stick Bookstore, Washington Depot.

Additional and distinct excursions in shopping, eating, theater, culture, art, ethnic heritage and nightlife abound when exploring both the urban and rural neighborhoods. Whether spectator or participant, sports enthusiasts can catch nearly every kind of amateur and professional event from golfing to baseball. Students as well as non-students can schedule time to survey the many university campuses, whether it be for a day inhaling botanical wonders at New London's Connecticut College Arboretum, viewing a planetarium show at New Britain's Central Connecticut College, roaming through the University of Connecticut acreage in the rural Storrs section of Mansfield or ambling through prestigious Yale University in New Haven.

In the northwestern corner, two casinos, Foxwoods and Mohegan Sun, have not only unveiled the glitzy face of gaming, but have become destinations within themselves, boasting first-class food, entertainment, hotels, spas, health facilities and other attractions.

Long Island Sound attracts the majority of tourists during the summer, but don't overlook off-season boating and fishing opportunities. Boardwalks trim sweeping beach vistas. Connecticut boasts 21 historic lighthouses. Additional aquatic sites include the Housatonic River, which crosses the western part of the state near the New York State border, and the Thames River located in eastern Connecticut. Bisecting the state, the Connecticut River is New England's longest river, flowing from northern New Hampshire, along Vermont's border and into Massachusetts before emptying into the Long Island Sound in Old Saybrook.

For couples who seek to fire up romance or for singles wanting some solitude, the Litchfield Hills are the ultimate four-season escape. October stains lemon, blush and persimmon hues into the maples, elms, beeches and oaks until the mural oozes with color; a winter chill punctuates the air. Winter contains crystalline beauty and endless ice-skating possibilities. White, powdery snow inspires cold-weather enthusiasts to spend days skiing downhill or cross-country. Beginning in March, fresh, locally made maple syrup refills legions of kitchen pantries. Spring signals a fragrant path made for lazy walks along gardens abloom in daffodils and forsythia. Even amateur artists set up easel in an attempt to capture the summertime colors from bushes of roses, lilac and mountain laurel. Season after season, a trail of antiques stores, wineries, shops, bed and breakfasts and the finest restaurants are ready and waiting—not only in Litchfield County—but in other regions, too.

Connecticut's buzzword is fun. Visitors and locals can revel in seasonal festivals and parades like Stamford's Thanksgiving Holiday Balloon Parade; Norwich's Winterfest Parade; Old Saybrook's Annual WinterFest and Chili Cooking Contest. Other examples include the Eastern Scrabble® Championship, Danbury; Chief Flying Eagle Annual Native American Powwow, Brooklyn; the Shad Festival and Shad Bake, Essex; the Oyster Festival, Norwalk and the Greenwich Concours D'Elegance. Day-trippers wishing to experience the state's signature delights can include an early morning purchase of fresh produce at one of the farmers' markets during the warmer months or listen to a variety of music festivals that waft the summertime air.

Connecticut's multifarious personality shines, thanks also in part to the people who have, and continue to call the Nutmeg State home. The list includes legendary figures, such as Prudence Crandall (state heroine); Nathan Hale (state hero); Harriet Beecher Stowe; Ethan Allen; Benedict Arnold and Mark Twain as well as modern luminaries including Meryl Streep, George H.W. Bush, Whoopi Goldberg, Katharine Hepburn, Mia Farrow, Paul Newman and Joanne Woodward.

Hollywood, too, has left an array of stardust memories on the Connecticut trail. Lucy Ricardo wreaked havoc in Connecticut, specifically Westport, in the final season of *I Love Lucy,* after her TV-land move from New York City. Actor Woody Allen and his crew sprinkled glitz upon Stamford's Town Center when they filmed *Scenes from a Mall* (1991). The village of Mystic heralded in Julia Robert's big motion picture debut when she starred in *Mystic Pizza* (1988). The Lockwood-Mathews Mansion Museum in Norwalk had far more than its minute of fame when it provided the backdrop for the 2004 remake of the 1975 film classic *The Stepford Wives.* Most recently, New London was the setting for the remake of the 1968 film *Yours, Mine & Ours.*

Connecticut monikers are as varied as its features: the Nutmeg State, the Constitution State, the Provisions State and the Land of Steady Habits. And its motto is none other than: "He who transplanted still sustains." State "firsts" include the creation of the first pay phone and the original concoction of the hamburger. Take a day to experience the charm of our great state. Connecticut excursions offer enough panache to appease every traveler, regardless of age, interest or level of curiosity.

TAKE THE LONG WAY HOME

May the road ahead greet you gently at each turn and may you never lose the wonder to travel that extra mile.

Information About *(And How to Use)* **This Book**

Whether you're a lifelong Connecticut resident who wants to uncover the secrets in your own backyard; newcomer relocating; vacationer enticed by our landscape; teacher or youth leader searching for a field trip; business traveler who would like to add a bit of pleasure to the agenda or someone who'd like to enhance his or her stay with friends or relatives while celebrating a significant life event or milestone like a wedding, graduation or reunion, this book (as those clichéd ads proclaim) is for you.

If you are trying to persuade a friend or relative to visit or would like to share our slice of panacea, consider giving her or him a copy of *Consummate Connecticut: Day Trips with Panache*. It provides a bird's-eye view of where we have come from, where we are going and in this case, certainly, where we are now. Like no other guidebook, readers can appreciate a text packed with local color, treasured regional quirks and customs.

The most logical starting point in the book is to begin with the first chapter about Windsor, the state's first established town, originally designated as a trading post in 1633. Then again, perhaps, start with the second chapter about Wethersfield, which is where the first community of settlers convened in 1634. To this day, no one can agree on which town came first. This is just one of the quirks that *Consummate Connecticut* unfolds.

Each chapter (the book highlights 48 cities, towns and villages) includes trivia and interesting slices of historical perspective and idiosyncrasies, such as the Windsor-Wethersfield debate. This way, the day-tripper will not only have a variety of destinations intended for short excursions (two hours or less), but be given a deeper understanding of each place's personality—typically defined by its past.

The third chapter is about Connecticut's undisputed state capital, Hartford, the third established town. The book's chapters proceed, for the sake of geographical clarity, to north central Connecticut and then to the northeastern-most region of what is known as the Quiet Corner; moving southeast to the Mystic/New London vicinity; to the section accurately described by tourism officials as the River Valley and Shoreline; to the posh southwestern Gold Coast into the western elbow of the Housatonic Valley and the Waterbury region and ending deep into the Litchfield Hills.

Each chapter, complemented with maps and photographs, gives an introduction, geographical information and specific, four-season attractions (highlighted in bold) for each town. While writing the book, it was my hope that day-trippers could choose two or three attractions or more, depending on interest and other objectives, and map out a feasible day to embark upon.

The chapters conclude with regional restaurant choices that appease nearly every palate. Make a note that although most restaurants accept credit cards, not all do. There are no specific menu items listed because they tend to change. The general rule is to call-call-call: this way you will not be disappointed.

Each chapter concludes with **Getting There**, **Transportation**, **Additional Information**, **Accommodations** and **Annual Festivals and Events**. The **Getting There** section hones in on a destination's driving directions. For those who may not have a car, the category of **Transportation** lists the available bus, train and airplane services.

If telephone numbers and in most cases, addresses, have not been provided earlier in the chapter, the section, **Additional Information**, lists them. This section also lists the days that attractions are open for business. To eliminate redundancy, the hours of operation and holiday closings have been omitted. As a rule, most places close during the following holidays: Thanksgiving, Christmas, New Year's and Easter. Seasonal attractions tend to be open Memorial Day until Labor Day. Each attraction is unique. It's best to call-call-call.

Although most public places are handicapped accessible, please, again, call before traveling; especially considering constant building renovations. In addition, the state's public buildings prohibit pets. Commonly, the exception to this no-pet rule is specially trained pets for handicapped travelers. Kids, of course, are welcome anywhere (the book highlights many attractions that are particularly children/family friendly)—as long as they don't interfere on another traveler's personal space (or eardrums!). This is the general golden rule for the adult traveler too—please regard others on the road so we can all share in an enjoyable experience.

A list of **Accommodations** is included for day-trippers who wish to extend their visit. Please realize that rates for overnight stays are subject to change. Additionally, room rates don't include state taxes and gratuities. When you call to make a reservation, remember to inquire into details, such as exact room rates and handicapped accessibility. Travelers should also inquire into policies that pertain to such things as smoking and non-smoking areas, children (many bed and breakfast establishments only accept children 12 years old and older), pet-allowances (a growing number of overnight facilities are accepting dogs) and use of credit card as payment; some need a deposit before the actual stay.

Finally, the **Annual Festivals and Events** section is a listing of just that; although not all encompassing, it's quite comprehensive. Assume that, unless noted, many festivals and events charge an admission fee, which changes year-to-year. Call the telephone numbers provided for entrance fees, questions related to handicapped-accessible accommodations and the like. Tourist-related bureaus are also listed to further aid travelers.

Naturally, not every single attraction* and every bit of information in a town—as not every single town in Connecticut—appears in this book. As unfortunate as this is, I, being a former Girl Scout, truly mean when I say—I did my best in an attempt to offer variety insofar as places to go and things to do for a day. Yet, that doesn't mean you can't write us and demand a second book listing additional towns meant for a day-tripper's itinerary. I encourage feedback. Comments from fellow travelers only help me in this journey that for me sometimes takes place in the dark of the night, squinting alone for hours in front of my trusty computer.

I cannot stress the importance of preparedness (remember I was a former Girl Scout). The most important thing is please realize that places close down and relocate and slash or extend their hours, so use this resource as that, a resource; the rest is up to you. In this way, you will be most versed when you learn to:

TAKE THE LONG WAY HOME

— Stacy Lytwyn Maxwell

Please note: none of the attractions, restaurants, accommodations or anything else appearing in the book have paid insertion fees; each merits its own inclusion.

A back road in New Canaan.

I.

NORTH CENTRAL CONNECTICUT
Hartford County
"Heritage River Valley"
Windsor/Wethersfield/Hartford

The Connecticut flag depicts three grapevines representing the earliest state settlements: Windsor (1633), Wethersfield (1634) and Hartford (1635). Most historians agree upon Hartford's, the state capital, settlement date. However, what has been an ongoing debate for more than 200 years is which was settled first: Windsor or Wethersfield? In 1633, English colonists established a trading post in what we know as modern-day Windsor. The first settlers did not arrive until 1635. On the other hand, a community of colonists settled what we know as Wethersfield today in 1634. Some historians insist that Wethersfield precedes Windsor as Connecticut's first town because it was settled as a community (and not a trading post).

To help solve this centuries-old argument and appease the most diehard historians, Windsor holds title as "the oldest town" in the state; Wethersfield has adopted the tag line, "most ancient town."

One certainty is that the reason the early settlers emigrated from the Massachusetts Bay Colony and established these towns was their religious and political dissatisfaction and their quest for fertile farmland.

Today, in the region dubbed by state tourism officials as Connecticut's Heritage River Valley, day-trippers are bound to find historical towns that preserve tradition as well as open space. Approximately nine miles north of Hartford, Windsor delights travelers of all ages with its tobacco barns and shading tents and retro-feel due in part to places like Bart's Drive-In and Windsor Donut Shoppe.

Wethersfield, about five miles south of Hartford, is no newcomer to tourism with its designated Old Wethersfield Historic District. Its interesting mill history also makes for an excellent off-the-beaten-track jaunt for visitors.

Hartford, crowned by its gold-dome state capitol that sits atop a hill in Bushnell Park, provides myriad attractions ranging from museums to theaters and nearly every entertainment venue available to appease the most curmudgeon day-tripper.

What is ascribed as Connecticut's oldest town?

What town's famous murder case at the beginning of the 20th century later inspired the popular play, "Arsenic and Old Lace"?

First Mother Town: **WINDSOR**

Dutch navigator, Adriaen Block, sailed up the Connecticut River in 1614, and historians recorded him as the area's first European explorer. In 1633, Dutch colonists followed suit, and erected a fort and trading post, calling it the House of (Good) Hope in what is presently called Hartford. In the same year, an English Puritan group that had separated from the Massachusetts Bay Colony first launched a trading post and later established a town in what would come to be known as Windsor, Connecticut's oldest town, located at the confluence of the Farmington and Connecticut Rivers. (The state's name is derived from Quinnehtukqut, an Indian name meaning "beside the long tidal river," a reference to the Connecticut River.)

Honoring heritage, the settlers changed the territory's Native American name, Matianuck, to Dorchester, and in 1637, the colony's General Court adopted the English name of Windsor. The Puritans started the tobacco trend in 1640, still prevalent today, with seeds brought from Virginia.

For 100 years, between 1830 and 1930, woolen mills and paper mills dotted the Farmington River and employed many area residents. Still, the backbone of Windsor's economy was brick making and tobacco farming. Due to a decline in demand, brickyards disappeared in the 1960s. Old, brick-laden homes, constructed of Windsor-made bricks, however, have remained.

A Windsor legend involves the notorious case of Amy Archer Gilligan, which later inspired the popular play *Arsenic and Old Lace*. A jury found the elderly woman guilty of poisoning to death residents at her convalescent home. Ultimately, her sentence of hanging was overturned and Mrs. Gilligan served a prison sentence until she was committed to the Connecticut State Mental Hospital, Middletown, where she died in 1962.

Day trips with panache in today's primarily residential town (population 28,000-plus) located some 40 miles inland to the north of Long Island Sound, just north of Hartford, begin on foot. Beneath new walkways, lighting fixtures, building additions and renovations, the historic character of the **Broad Street Green** and the **Palisado Green** prevails. The National Register of Historic Places lists 83 Windsor locations, including many sites clustered near the town greens. The Palisado Green commemorates Dorchester Colony, the early Connecticut settlement where a Palisado (palisade) was built to protect settlers during the Pequot War of 1637. Today, the Founders Monument on the green lists the names of Windsor's earliest settlers. During Halloween season, day-trippers should inquire about the Windsor Historical Society's **Ghost Walks** in proximity of the Palisado Green.

The fourth location of the **First Church in Windsor** (860-688-7229), built in 1794, is at 85 Palisado Avenue. The original congregation started in England in 1630. Today, it is the third oldest Congregational Church in continuous service worldwide. Behind First Church, **Palisado Cemetery**, by the Farmington River, contains what historians believe is the state's oldest tombstone, dated 1644.

Down the street, the 1758 **John and Sarah Strong House** is the headquarters for **Windsor Historical Society**. The house possesses a wealth of 17th-, 18th- and 19th-century furnishings as well as a nationally recognized genealogical research library. The staff toils long hours to provide showcases of regional history within the changing galleries of the **Wilson Museum**. At the hands-on learning center, children can dress in colonial costumes and simulate such novelties as milking cows and cooking an open-hearth meal. The Strong House also preserves the town's first post office and an 18th-century general store that specialized in imported fabrics.

Additionally, the historical society staff offers tours of two nearby properties. At the **Stony Hill School**, 1195 Windsor Avenue, guests can experience a one-room schoolhouse complete with inkwell desks and a potbelly stove that operated from 1850 until 1969. Stony Hill School also doubles as a center for yoga (860-688-9922). The second tour conducted by the society is at the **1765 Dr. Hezekiah Chaffee House**, 108 Palisado Avenue. Antique medical instruments and old pharmaceutical recipes give day-trippers a fascinating glimpse into the life of a country doctor inside the 15-room Georgian Colonial.

The Connecticut Daughters of the Revolution operate the **Ellsworth Homestead** built in 1740. It was the home of Oliver Ellsworth, drafter of the U.S. Constitution and Chief Justice of the Supreme Court, among other things. Marvel at his personal belongings, including a letter from George Washington who visited him in 1789.

A Broad Street landmark is the 6,500-square-foot **Huntington House**, built in 1901, serving as a rotating art exhibit museum. Modeled after a Newport, Rhode Island mansion, the building presents an example of Neo-Classical Revival-style architecture. Inside, a variety of art mediums are unveiled in a dramatic setting of leaded glass and 12-foot ceilings.

A recent newcomer situated east of Broad Street Green is the **Vintage Radio and Communications Museum of Connecticut**. Dedicated to the history of communication, day-trippers can test an array of hands-on radio displays, televisions, telephones, telegraphs and motion picture equipment. Farther east stands the internationally acclaimed Loomis Chaffee School. The original landowner was Joseph Loomis who arrived in Windsor in 1640.

Boaters can explore Windsor through an assortment of public boat launches. Two examples include the **Brissell Bridge Walkway and Boat Launch** and the **Wilson Boat Launch and Bike Path**. Walkers share the **Windsor Center Trail** with hikers, joggers, rollerbladers and bicyclists. Known as **Riverwalk**, the 1.15 mile-long trail is located on a 43-acre site adjacent to the Farmington River at Route 159. The trail also affords boaters direct access to more than 2,000 feet of river. The Riverwalk ties into a second park and another boat launch on Pleasant Street, which, in the future, will be part of a regional trail network.

About five miles northwest, the **Northwest Park and Nature Center** boasts 450 acres of habitat that include more than eight miles of trails for hikers, joggers and cross-country skiers. Property features a self-guided Braille trail for the blind; a nature center with live animals; the **John E. Luddy Tobacco Museum**, an authentic tobacco barn transformed into a museum; a maple sugar house; warming shed and cross-country ski rental center; community gardens; picnic area; world-class soccer fields; a playground and an animal barn. Sample the selection of souvenirs at the gift shop, including Northwest Park Honey, handmade and nature-themed gifts and children's educational toys.

Other Windsor shopping expeditions are just as unique. There is no better cure for a sweet tooth than **KoKo's Candy Store** (860-683-0414), open daily at 645 Poquonock Avenue. Antiques markets include **Union Street Antiques and Collectibles** (860-683-1679; call for days and hours of operation), **Patti's Treasures** (860-687-1682; call for days and hours of operation) and **Central Street Antiques** (860-688-3635; call for days and hours of operation).

Golfers should check into the **Tradition at Windsor** (860-688-2575), an 18-hole, semi-private golf club at 147 Pigeon Hill Road. Golfers can also make note of **Brown's Driving Range** (860-688-1745) at 1851 Poquonock Avenue. During the warmer months, consider catching an act at the **SummerWind Performing**

Arts Center (860-687-9836), 40 Griffin Road. This amphitheater entertainment venue provides a seating capacity of 1,500 under a state-of-the-art outdoor canopy structure as well as 3,500 additional lawn spots.

Whether breakfast, lunch or dinner, the '50s are alive at an area institution located at 55 Palisado Avenue, **Bart's Drive-In Restaurant** (860-688-9035), open daily. Diners can expect exceptionally reasonable prices, a family-owned, friendly eatery and award-winning chili dogs. For old-fashioned donuts visit **Windsor Donut Shoppe** (860-688-8899), located on Broad Street and open daily. For a quick bite, hearty sandwich or gift basket, check out **Beanery Bistro** (860-688-2224), open for breakfast, lunch and dinner daily at 697 Poquonock Avenue.

GETTING THERE:
Windsor is located approximately 20 miles south of Springfield, Massachusetts; 46 miles north of New Haven and approximately 67 miles northwest of Westerly, Rhode Island. Interstate Highway 91 is north/south of Windsor and runs the town's length. Interstate 84 is within 10 minutes.

TRANSPORTATION:
Windsor is located 10 minutes away from Bradley International Airport (860-292-2000) in Windsor Locks. Amtrak commuter trains (800-USA-RAIL) stop in Windsor Center from Springfield to New Haven with connections to Boston and New York. Connecticut Transit Company buses (860-525-9181) serve the needs of commuters throughout Greater Hartford with several routes in Windsor.

ADDITIONAL INFORMATION:
WINDSOR CHAMBER OF COMMERCE.
261 Broad Street. Open all year, Monday through Friday, daily. Call ahead for hours. Situated on the Broad Street Green, this is an advisable starting point providing up-to-date tourism brochures and money-saving coupons. (860) 688-5165.

THE WINDSOR HISTORICAL SOCIETY/JOHN AND SARAH STRONG HOUSE.
96 Palisado Avenue. Open all year, Tuesday through Saturday. General admission is $3.00 adults; $1.00 children 12 and under. (860) 688-3813.

ELLSWORTH HOMESTEAD.
778 Palisado Avenue. Open May 15 through October 15, Tuesday, Wednesday, Saturday. Tours by reservation. (860) 688-8717.

HUNTINGTON HOUSE MUSEUM.
389 Broad Street. Open all year, Tuesday through Sunday. General admission is $6.00 adults and free to children 12 and under. (860) 688-2004.

VINTAGE RADIO AND COMMUNICATIONS MUSEUM OF CONNECTICUT.
33 Mechanic Street. The organization, dedicated to the preservation of vintage communications equipment with an impressive collection on display, has moved recently from West Hartford to this location. At press time, things were still sketchy as far as an official opening date, but Saturdays are the best time to view the collection. Call ahead. General admission is by donation. (860) 243-1447.

WINDSOR PARKS & RECREATION DEPARTMENT.

599 Matianuck Avenue. Call ahead for additional information about park and recreational resources in the town. (860) 285-1997.

NORTHWEST PARK AND NATURE CENTER.

145 Lang Road. Park, nature center and gift shop open all year, daily. Trails open all year from dawn to dusk, daily. Call for upcoming coffeehouse concerts and special events. General admission is free. (860) 285-1886; www.northwestpark.org.

JOHN E. LUDDY/GORDON S. TAYLOR CONNECTICUT VALLEY TOBACCO MUSEUM.

145 Lang Road. Open March 1 through December 20. Call for days and hours of operation. (860) 285-1888.

ACCOMMODATIONS:

HILTON GARDEN INN.

555 Corporate Drive. Located in the Windsor Business Park, atop the highest point in Hartford County, the facility features expansive New England vistas. Amenities in the 57 guestrooms include armchair or small sofa, microwave, refrigerator and coffeemaker. An indoor pool with whirlpool is also available. Rates: $89.95-$109.95. (860) 688-6400.

ANNUAL FESTIVALS/EVENTS

The Central Regional Tourism District, Connecticut's Heritage River Valley, representing 46 communities, provides a gamut of tourism information, which includes seasonal events (800) 793-4480 or (860) 244-8181; www.enjoycentralct.com. For additional festival and event information, contact the Windsor Chamber of Commerce (860) 688-5165.

FEBRUARY

Day-trippers pierced with Cupid's arrow should make note of the **Free Marriage Licenses** available at Windsor Town Clerk's Office on Valentine's Day. (860) 688-5165.

MARCH

Start the morning with a delicious stack of pancakes drenched in maple syrup at the **Pancake Breakfast** at Northwest Park. (860) 285-1886; www.northwestpark.org.

Sheep shearing, sheep dog demonstrations and other hands-on activities are part of the festivities at Northwest Park's **Wild and Wooly Sheep Day**. (860) 285-1886; www.northwestpark.org.

MAY

To commemorate the shad-fishing season, the **Shad Derby** is held the third Saturday in May on the town green. Events include food, crafts, carnival rides and a free parade. The Shad Derby Queen and the renowned Windsor Fife and Drum Corps, an organization designed primarily for young people to preserve the music of the 18th century, are examples of parade participants. For more information, email jaycess@shadderby.com. (860) 688-5165.

The Windsor Lion's Club hosts its annual **Spring Crafts Fair** on the historic Windsor Green. (860) 688-5165.

JUNE
Just For Fun Dog Show. Open to resident and nonresident pets with up-to-date licenses. Winning ribbons for all! (860) 688-5165.

JULY/AUGUST
Weekly summer concerts are held on the town green Thursday evenings from 7 p.m. to 9 p.m. (860) 285-1990. In the event of inclement weather, call the information line, 860-285-1988 for cancellation announcements or alternate site information.

SEPTEMBER
Revolutionary Windsor (biennial) spanning three days and three historic sites; activities include a colonial dance, battle re-enactments between the "invading" British and the "defending" patriots, the Governor's Foot Guard, military demonstrations, an army hospital and military camp demonstrations, colonial crafts and more. (860) 688-5165; info@revolutionarywindsor.com.

OCTOBER
The Windsor Lion's Club hosts its annual **Fall Crafts Fair** on the historic Windsor Green. (860) 688-5165.

To spice up the day, the **Chili Challenge** presents an array of delicious recipes in an event full of fun and entertainment. (860) 688-5165.

DECEMBER
The **Torchlight Parade and Bonfire** is a highly anticipated event that takes place in historical Windsor Center. (860) 688-5165.

A sure-fire way to get into the holiday spirit is to join the **Carol Sing**, which includes the lighting of the Christmas tree on the green and other festivities. (860) 688-5165.

Windsor's Rich Legacy
See pages 12, 15-20

"Tobacco road"

Photos courtesy of John Waiveris,
Invisible Gold, LLC - www.invisiblegold.com

---

*What town touts the state's largest historic district, with
more than 100 buildings built before 1840?*

*What town's favorite legend is about "onion maidens,"
young women who earned money for silk dresses by
havesting red onions while the
men pursued other tasks?*

Second Mother Town: **WETHERSFIELD**

A bronze plaque, showcased on the Broad Street Green, is dedicated to the 10 men from Massachusetts who settled Wethersfield in 1634—and kicked off the "who came first" debate between their town and Windsor (see introduction, Chapter I, **Windsor/Wethersfield/Hartford**).

Regardless of the settlement question, their true struggle was the increasing rift over land with the Pequot Indians. The tribe originally called this region Pyquag, meaning, "cleared land" or "open country." Early settlers renamed the area Watertown and soon after, Wethersfield, from Wethersfield in Essex, England. The most famous battle happened in 1637 when 200 warriors attacked Wethersfield, killing nine colonists and taking two teenage girls hostage. (Later the tribe returned the girls unharmed.)

Situated west of the Connecticut River, until around 1700, Wethersfield prospered from shipbuilding and became the river port for the entire Connecticut Valley, establishing trade connections with places as distant as the Caribbean Islands.

During the 18th century, two pastors serving at the Congregational Church helped educate college-bound young men. Most of these students would later attend Yale, and by the time of the Revolutionary War, Wethersfield had a high population of college-educated residents, which may have begun New England's reputation for genteel culture.

The red onion is the unofficial town symbol of Wethersfield. In fact, the town exported more onions than any other in the country and became known as "Oniontown." According to 18th-century legend, "onion maidens" were young women who earned money for silk dresses by harvesting the red onions while men pursued other tasks. A massive blight wiped the crop out in the 1840s.

Today, the town of Wethersfield with a population of approximately 25,000 covers 13.5 square miles. A Hartford suburb, Wethersfield is home to such watchdog groups as People for the Preservation of Wethersfield Neighborhoods, Wethersfield's Village Improvement Association and Wethersfield Beautification Trust.

Off-the-beaten-track day trips with panache can begin with one of the **Walking Tours of Griswoldville Mills** (860-257-1705), hosted by members of another concerned citizens' group, the Griswoldville Preservation Association. These volunteers host walking tours that explore the remnants and sites where the mills, crucial to the economy in the 1800s, operated. Tours start at 9:30 a.m. the first Saturday of the spring and summer months (rain date is the following Sunday) and meet at the junction of Griswold Road and Country Club Road, located in the southwestern side of town known as Griswoldville.

Day-trippers can discover another echo of the town's past in Old Wethersfield, nestled alongside the Connecticut River in the eastern part of town. The **Old Wethersfield Historic District**, listed on the National Register of Historic Places, is Connecticut's largest historical district and best surveyed on foot.

Broad Street Green meanders about half a mile and tapers at either end. During the early days, livestock shared the stretch as common pasture. In colonial times, the militia trained here and during the revolution, met at the green before leaving for Boston to join the Battle of Bunker Hill. (The **Wethersfield Village Cemetery**, another district landmark, pays homage to many of these soldiers and others who shaped town history.) Concerned citizens saved the tree-lined green from state officials who in 1927 proposed to slice it in half with a Hartford/Middletown route highway. Today, the green remains a meaningful part of Old Wethersfield Village.

Abutting the cemetery and erected in 1761, historical luminaries, such as George Washington and John Adams, were visiting worshippers at the **First Church of Christ** (860-721-7861). Located at 250 Main Street, it's the largest Congregational Church in New England and Connecticut's only Colonial, brick meetinghouse, where audiences congregate to hear seasonal concerts. Historic **Cove Warehouse**, overlooking **Wethersfield Cove**, 10 feet above sea level and 40 miles from Long Island Sound, is located on Main Street's north end. Featured on the town seal, the warehouse, built around 1690, stored goods waiting to be transported downriver. The warehouse, which some say is haunted, is the only structure of its kind that survived after a flood ravaged the town in the late 1600s. Now acting as a museum, interesting exhibits introduce visitors to Wethersfield's 17th- and 18th-century maritime past.

George Washington and Compte de Rochambeau, Commander-in-Chief of the French armies in America, sat in the parlor of the 1781 **Joseph Webb House** as they planned the Battle of Yorktown, the decisive fight that would subsequently end the American Revolution. The original 1760 British wool-flocked wallpaper on the bedroom walls where George Washington slept remains in original form.

Typifying Connecticut River Valley style, the house is one of three restored, 18th-century homes clustered along Main Street that constitute the **Webb-Deane-Stevens Museum complex**, south of the cove area. Owned and operated by the Colonial Dames, period furnishings and décor authenticate the interior of each house.

Silas Deane (1737-1789), a delegate to the first Continental Congress, built the **Silas Deane House**, a two-story Georgian-style structure, in 1766. Observe the house's unusual asymmetrical façade. Delight in the fragrant **Colonial Revival Garden**, planted between the Webb House and the impressive 19th-century **Webb Barn**, a popular venue for private affairs, where occasional summer concerts entertain day-trippers.

Contrasting the Webb and Deane house styles is the **Isaac Stevens House**, built by a leatherworker in 1789. This setting offers a glimpse into middle-class colonial life, which later prospered during the Federal Era.

Across the street from the museum complex, the **Buttolph-Williams House** is the oldest dwelling in Wethersfield. Owned by the Antiquarian and Landmarks Society, the Webb-Deane-Stevens Museum staff manages the house. Circa 1720, it exemplifies Early Americana and provided author Elizabeth George Speare's setting for her young adult novel, *The Witch of Blackbird Pond*.

Also across the street from the Webb-Deane-Stevens Museum complex is the **Wethersfield Museum at Keeney Memorial,** operated by the **Wethersfield Historical Society**. Inside, the *Legendary People, Ordinary Lives* exhibit brims with more than 100 artifacts and helps re-create town history. Ever-changing galleries promote the works of local artisans. A first-floor museum shop, stocked with books and gift items, benefits the Wethersfield Historical Society. Peruse the host of regional travel brochures at the **Wethersfield Visitor's Center,** positioned in front of the Keeney Memorial. The Wethersfield Historical Society, located down the street in the **Old Academy**, also offers day-trippers travel-related maps and other printed materials. An on-premises **genealogical and research library** accommodates scholars.

Adjacent to the Wethersfield Museum, *Colonial Homes Magazine* (April 1996) featured the elegant **Hurlbut-Dunham House**, constructed in brick and representative of Georgian-style architecture. The home touts an impressive array of early 20th-century accessories, including original Rococo Revival-style wallpaper, painted ceilings and cornices, plus the many furnishings and personal belongings of previous residents Howard and Jane Dunham, a prominent couple in the region.

Day-trippers who are bent on exploring nature in Wethersfield have 617 acres of town-owned parks and recreation areas at their disposal. **Cove Park** at the cove contains more than 110 acres including a popular boat launch. Old Wethersfield's **Standish Park**, off Main on Garden Street, boasts more than 10 acres of land with sports fields, tennis courts and children's playgrounds. In the park's northwest corner, **Mikey's Place** is a wheelchair-accessible playscape for children.

Driving west from Old Wethersfield, still under expansion is **Heritage Way**, offering approximately two miles of hiking and biking trails. The Pitkin Community Center property, Greenfield Street, allots easy access to the trail. Within walking distance of the **Eleanor Buck Wolf Nature Center** is 110 acres of **Wintergreen Woods** that leads to **Folly Brook Pond** and **Quarry Park** in Rocky Hill.

For poetry-in-motion, it's worth it to stay until early evening to experience the **Wethersfield Library's** (860-721-2985) once a month program, **Closet Poets**. Expect unstructured but entertaining performances by published and unpublished poets.

Nature abounds indoors at Eleanor Buck Wolf Nature Center with live animals, mammals, birds, reptiles and special exhibits that teach environmental principles. The **Owl's Nest** gift store helps shoppers find nature-themed gifts and souvenirs. Old Wethersfield's Main Street is plentiful with additional shopping opportunities like **Heart of the Country** (860-257-0366), open Monday through Saturday, brimming with gifts, home accessories and charm. For a splash of color and fragrance, seven days a week, anytime of year, **Comstock Ferre and Company** (800-733-3773; 860-571-6590) is a handsome garden center that was established in 1820, making it the oldest, continuously operating seed company in the country!

Tom's Trains of Connecticut (860-529-6157; call for days and hours of operation) and an award-winning florist and gift shop, **A Victorian Garden** (860-563-8414; call for days and hours of operation) are two other interesting shopping options along the Silas Deane Highway. Day-trippers can enjoy breakfast, lunch or dinner at the ever-popular **Wethersfield Diner** (860-529-9690), open daily. Main Street eateries, as copious as the neighboring shops, range from the casual atmosphere of **Village Pizza** (860-563-1513) for lunch and dinner daily to the elegant surroundings of **Mainly Tea** (860-529-9517), next door. Reservations are essential at this tea parlor, open Thursday, Friday and Saturday for lunch and, of course, afternoon tea. Historic **Village Tavern** (860-563-5277) cooks up traditional American fare with a tropical twist for lunch and dinner Tuesday through Sunday; Sunday brunch.

GETTING THERE:
Wethersfield is located 12 miles south of Windsor; 30 miles south of Springfield, Massachusetts and five miles south of Hartford. The Berlin Turnpike and Interstate 91 connect Wethersfield to the regional highway system. Major roads, such as the Silas Deane Highway (Route 99) and Ridge Road, are extensions of the Hartford road system, an example of early suburban development.

TRANSPORTATION:
Wethersfield is located about 19 miles from Bradley International Airport (860-292-2000), Windsor Locks. Connecticut Transit Company buses (860-525-9181) serve the needs of commuters throughout Greater Hartford with five Wethersfield routes.

ADDITIONAL INFORMATION:
COVE WAREHOUSE.
Main Street. Open mid-May through mid-October, Saturday and Sunday; call for occasional extended hours. General admission is $1.00 adults; free to children 16 and under and to historical society members. (860) 688-3813; www.wethhist.org/sites.html.

WEBB-DEANE-STEVENS MUSEUM.
Main Street. Open May 1 through October 31, Wednesday through Monday; closed Saturday and Sunday, November 1 through April 30. Inquire about family programs and special seasonal events. General admission for a three-house tour is $8.00 adults; $7.00 seniors; $4.00 children and free to children 5 and under. (860) 529-0612; www.webb-deane-stevens.org.

BUTTOLPH-WILLIAMS HOUSE.
249 Broad Street. Open May 1 through October 1, Wednesday through Monday; closed Saturday and Sunday, November 1 through April 30. The Webb-Deane-Stevens museum tour includes admission to the Buttolph-Williams house or call for separate ticket pricing. (860) 529-0612; www.wethhist.org/sites.html.

WETHERSFIELD MUSEUM AT
KEENEY MEMORIAL/WETHERSFIELD VISITOR'S CENTER.
200 Main Street. Open all year, Tuesday through Sunday. Gallery admission is $3.00 adults; free to children 16 and under; Wethersfield residents and historical society members. (860) 529-7161.

WETHERSFIELD HISTORICAL SOCIETY/ GENEALOGICAL AND RESEARCH LIBRARY.
Old Academy. 150 Main Street. Open all year, Tuesday through Friday and by appointment. The society offers adult group tours, including bus tours, Old Wethersfield walking tours and house tours. The historical society also provides up-to-date tourism brochures. General admission to the Old Academy building is free. (860) 529-7656; www.wethhist.org.

HURLBUT-DUNHAM HOUSE.
212 Main Street. Open mid-March through mid-May, Thursday through Sunday; Saturday through Sunday, November and December or by appointment. House tours originate at Keeney Memorial at 200 Main Street. General admission is $3.00 adults; free to children 16 and under and to historical society members. (860) 529-7656; www.wethhist.org/sites.html.

WETHERSFIELD PARKS & RECREATION DEPARTMENT.
505 Silas Deane Highway. Call or visit, Monday through Friday, to pick up additional park and recreational information. (860) 721-2890.

ELEANOR BUCK WOLF NATURE CENTER.
Millwoods Park, 156 Prospect. Open all year, call for days and hours of operation. Inquire about family programs and special seasonal events. General admission is free. (860) 721-2953.

ACCOMMODATIONS:
CHESTER BULKLEY HOUSE BED & BREAKFAST.
184 Main Street. Three of the five guestrooms in this Greek Revival home built in 1830 have private baths. The other two rooms share a bath. Host Thomas Aufiero furnishes the premises in period antiques to enhance the Early American décor that features wide pine floors and hand-carved woodwork. Rates: $95, shared bath; $125, private bath. (860) 563-4236.

ANNUAL FESTIVALS/EVENTS
The Central Regional Tourism District, Connecticut's Heritage River Valley, representing 46 communities, provides a gamut of tourism information, which includes seasonal events (800) 793-4480 or (860) 244-8181; www.enjoycentralct.com. For additional festival and event information, contact the town manager at (860) 721-2801.

JUNE
Wethersfield Festival celebrates Old Wethersfield's colonial past. Three-day weekend events include Revolutionary War encampments and battles, concerts, lantern-light tours, an antiques show, international food and crafts fair, children's crafts and games and trolley and walking tours. Most events are free. (860) 721-2975.

American Heritage Festival showcases popular lantern-light tours of vintage American homes by reservation only. (860) 721-2975.

Eleanor Buck Wolf Nature Center Annual Tag Sale is a bargain hunter's utopia and also helps benefit the center. (860) 721-2953.

JULY
Special programs and activities fill the day at the **Annual Historic Gardens Day** held at the Webb-Deane-Stevens Museum. (860) 529-0612.

SEPTEMBER
Sponsored by the Chamber of Commerce, the **Wethersfield Cornfest** is held at the Broad Street Green in Old Wethersfield. The day's agenda includes food, entertainment, craft fair and business expo.

SEPTEMBER/OCTOBER
Scarecrows Along Main Street amounts to scarecrows of all sizes and styles that make a colorful addition to Old Wethersfield's Historic District. (860) 529-9013.

OCTOBER
More than 100-juried crafters are presented along with food booths, farmers' market and children's activities at the **Fall Craft Fair** at Cove Park. (860) 529-7656.

NOVEMBER
The **Annual Antiques Show** at Pitkin Community Center, 30 Greenfield Street, highlights nearly 50 antiques dealers. (860) 529-7656.

DECEMBER
A seasonal favorite to start the morning for young and old is **Santa's Pancake Breakfast** held at Pitkin Community Center, 30 Greenfield Street. (860) 529-7656.

All are welcome to the annual **Holiday Caroling** at Broad Street Green in Old Wethersfield. (860) 529-7656.

Old Wethersfield

See pages 8, 22-23, 25-26

Folk art illustration of Old Wethersfield by the masterful hand of acclaimed artist Katie Berry.

Folk art illustration and photo courtesy of Katie Berry, www.katieberry.com

*In what city did Mark Twain live and later publish
"The Adventures of Tom Sawyer"; the first typewritten
manuscript submitted to a publisher?*

*In what city can you find Cedar Hill Cemetery, final
resting place of such luminaries as actress Katharine
Hepburn and Horace Wells, a dentist who discovered
nitrous oxide (laughing gas) and whose gravestone is
inscribed with the following words:
"There shall be no pain"?*

Third Mother Town: **HARTFORD**

In 1636, three years after Dutch colonists erected the House of (Good) Hope, a fort and trading post, (see introduction, **Windsor** chapter), Reverend Thomas Hooker and Reverend Samuel Stone led a group of about 100 English colonists who had abandoned their Newtown settlement (now Cambridge) in Massachusetts in search of greater religious freedom and a better life.

They established Hartford in 1637, making it the third Connecticut settlement after Windsor and Wethersfield. The name honors Herefordshire, England, the birthplace of Reverend Stone, who, like Hooker, was a teacher of the church and whose name was first inscribed on the Indian deed to Hartford (the modern-day city's Native American name was *Suckiaug*) in 1636.

For more than three centuries, situated on the west side of the Connecticut River, the city prospered in shipbuilding and river trading (two entities that also fueled neighboring Wethersfield's economy), claiming ports as far away as the West Indies and the Mediterranean.

Yankee perseverance, resourcefulness, manufacturing astuteness, literary genius and sometimes-offbeat choices led Hartford to become a metropolis of many "firsts." For example, in 1639, a collaborative committee of men, including Reverend Hooker, penned the Fundamental Orders, which established an independent government separate from England and bound together the three mother towns of Windsor, Wethersfield and Hartford. Historians have classified the Fundamental Orders as the first constitution (and many say the foundation for the American Constitution).

In 1687, unlike other colonies, the General Court of Connecticut refused to relinquish to the English crown the Royal Charter, a declaration of the colony's independence that settlers modeled after the Fundamental Orders. Colonists hid the charter in a Hartford oak tree (this is why Connecticut is designated the "Constitution State"). Legend goes that a storm destroyed the historic Charter Oak in 1857 and, today, people like to think that the many trees that grow on the state capitol grounds and in Bushnell Park are its descendents. Visitors can view the original charter showcased in a frame crafted from the original Charter Oak at the Museum of Connecticut History. Additionally, city officials erected a monument at the intersection of Charter Oak Avenue and Charter Oak Place, in proximity to the once standing Charter Oak.

27

In 1764, Thomas Green published the *Connecticut Courant,* known today as the *Hartford Courant,* which is the oldest, continually published newspaper in America—another first. During the revolution, the *Courant* helped incite the colonies to rebel against the British. The rest, as the cliché goes, is history.

Hartford in the mid-to-late 1800s grew rapidly; its booming economy driven by publishing, insurance, banking, river trading and manufacturing industries. Hartford dentist Horace Wells discovered nitrous oxide (laughing gas) as a dental anesthetic in 1844. His grave at Hartford's Cedar Hill Cemetery immortalizes his discovery with the words, "There shall be no pain."

Interesting trivia connects Wells to Robert Louis Stevenson's 1876 novel, *Dr. Jekyll and Mr. Hyde,* saying that the author's main character was inspired by Wells who self-tested his revolutionary medicine and as a result of his inebriated state ended up assaulting New York City prostitutes. Visitors can see a sculpture of Wells by T.H. Bartlett in Bushnell Park.

During the 1800s, Hartford was a publishing center with Samuel Clemens, best known as Mark Twain, the first writer ever to submit a typewritten manuscript, *The Adventures of Tom Sawyer,* to a publisher. During the early part of the 20th century, Hartford was where native Katharine (Houghton) Hepburn fought for women's suffrage, women's right to vote, and was a forerunner of such organizations as Planned Parenthood. Her daughter Katharine Hepburn, who would become an iconic actress, was also born here and later buried in the Hepburn family plot at Cedar Hill Cemetery.

Throughout the remaining years, the state's capital and third largest city after Bridgeport and New Haven respectively, with a current-day population of more than 120,000, has certainly experienced a range of urban highs and lows. Day-trippers who seek panache will realize the influence Hartford has, not only on Connecticut, but also throughout the world.

A day trip that soars 527 feet above ground atop **Travelers' Tower** (860-277-4208), the headquarters for Travelers Insurance, is a trip quite apropos in a city dubbed "Insurance City" where the insurance industry was born in 1794 after a homeowner's policy against fire was drafted. An elevator ride, plus 100-stair climb, ascends to a bird's-eye city view. Located in downtown (just one of 17 distinct city neighborhoods), off Main, the pink Westerly granite structure, crowned with an 81-foot-high gold pyramid-shaped roof and copper-coated cupola, once had the notoriety of being the tallest building in New England. Since 2000, the outside of the building's 21st floor has been the official abode to Amelia, an adult female peregrine falcon.

Southward on Main, Hartford's earliest settlement was where the **Old State House** stands today in the middle of downtown's main transportation center, first called Meeting House Yard, later Meeting House Square. This vicinity (where the settlers wrote the first constitution) served as a meeting place, marketplace and contained everything from jails to pillories. Forty-five years before the famous Salem witch trials, Alse Young, originally from Windsor, was the first person in the colonies accused of witchcraft and later hung in 1647 at the same site where the Old State House stands today. It was also the location of the first meeting between General George Washington, Commander-in-Chief of the American armies, and the Compte de Rochambeau, Commander-in-Chief of the French armies in America (see **Wethersfield** chapter).

Designed by Charles Bulfinch, who was America's first nationally recognized architect, the Old State House is commemorated as the first and oldest in the nation. The city held the trials of the Amistad men (see **New Haven** chapter) and Prudence Crandall (see **Canterbury** chapter) at the Old State House.

Those who tour the restored 1796 landmark will encounter things like an original portrait of George Washington. On the building's second floor, for a more whimsical display, **Joseph Steward's Museum of Curiosities** features oddities like a two-headed calf and a set of ribs from a whale. The collection belonged to Mr. Steward, who was a predecessor to P.T. Barnum (see **Bridgeport** chapter) and portrait painter-in-residence at the Old State House. His hunger for the exotic prompted him to amass peculiar objects, many of which, historians believe, he purchased from transient seamen.

The Old State House maintains a well-stocked visitor's information center and is a perfect starting point into the city. Currently operated by the Hartford Historical Society, visitors can anticipate a future interactive children's exhibition gallery. The Old State House also serves as a backdrop for in-season farmers' markets, special events and shows. Check out the sculpture of Thomas Hooker by Frances L. Wadsworth (1950), located outside.

An assortment of galleries and aesthetic spaces has ranked Hartford among the top-20 art lover's cities in the *Places Rated Almanac*. The best-known art museum is the **Wadsworth Atheneum**. Approximately one and one-half blocks south from the Old State House, arts patron Daniel Wadsworth founded it in 1842, and it is America's oldest, continuously operating public art museum. Acclaimed as one of the top-10 art museums in the country, it was also the first American museum to acquire art by Salvador Dalí, Joan Miró, Caravaggio, Frederic Church, Piet Mondrian, Balthus and Joseph Cornell. The museum's collection includes more than 50,000 sculptures, paintings, textiles, furnishings and accessories, spanning more than 5,000 years, from the ancient Egyptian to the contemporary period. The largest art library in Connecticut, a museum shop, theater and café open for lunch also constitute the Wadsworth campus.

Be sure and view Alexander Calder's three-story-tall sculpture **Stegosaurus**, sandwiched outdoors between the Wadsworth Atheneum and the 1915 beaux arts-style Hartford Municipal Building. A smaller version of the dinosaur, named *Little Stego*, sold at auction for 3.4 million dollars.

Center Church (860-249-5631; call for days and hours of operation), corner of Gold and Main Streets, offers indoor tours from May through December. A classic temple design, including Louis Tiffany windows, Congregationalists built the church in 1807. One of the founders of Hartford, Thomas Hooker, helped start the parish itself that dates from 1632. The **Ancient Burying Ground**, also known as the Center Church Cemetery, in the churchyard of Center Church, is a menagerie of granite and brownstone headstones, some dating back to the 1600s. Some believe Hooker himself is buried here. The original **Founders Monument** on the cemetery grounds, a brownstone obelisk listing the names of the city's founders, had deteriorated. However, day-trippers today can witness a replacement monument carved from Connecticut granite and dedicated in 1986.

What would a Hartford day trip be without touring downtown's **Connecticut State Capitol**? One of Hartford's most distinguished sites—"Moorish" is how one tour guide describes it—a building infused with Gothic, classical and Second Empire styles, crowned with an unmistakable gold dome, was completed (conjuring up mixed reviews) in 1878 and is listed as a National Historic Landmark. The nice thing about joining a capitol tour (weekday tours include the adjacent **Legislative Office Building**) is hearing lore about the resident ghost of William Buckingham (Connecticut Governor 1858-1866; look for his statue), who some believe still roams the halls!

Revolutionary War hero Nathan Hale's statue and Revolutionary War General Lafayette's actual bed are other interesting capitol artifacts. The Hall of Flags is a sprawling exhibit of Connecticut flags that have returned from historical battlegrounds ranging from the Civil War to the present-day colors of the War on Terror. In the same vicinity, yes, the gravestone preserved under glass is Revolutionary War Major General Israel Putnam's actual cemetery marker (see **Brooklyn** chapter). The most important theme of the building is how an ordinary citizen can change the course of history by proposing a bill that may turn into a law. Watching "live government in action," when the state Senate and House of Representatives are in session, may just inspire judicial ideas from a visiting day-tripper.

The capitol grounds spill over to **Bushnell Park**, corner of Elm and Jewel Streets. More than 125 tree species grow in the 41 acres at America's oldest public park (1850). Here's another first: Hartford became the first city in the world to vote for this land purchase with the purpose of creating a public park, thanks to the persistence of Reverend Horace Bushnell. Park designers were from the firm of Frederick Law Olmsted, owned by the Hartford-born landscape architect who was responsible for Central Park in New York City. Warmer weather means rides on the 1914 Stein & Goldstein **Bushnell Park Carousel**. Another park landmark is the 1947 Tudor-style **pump house**, previously housing art exhibits. Other impressive features include the **Corning Fountain**, a tribute to the original Native American inhabitants. The 100-foot-tall, 30-foot-wide medieval-style **Soldiers and Sailors Memorial Arch** at the Trinity Street entrance, constructed in 1884, honors Hartford's Civil War soldiers, and is the first permanent and triumphal memorial arch in America (another first!). Park trivia includes accounts of **Park River** that once streamed along the park's north side. However, excess flooding caused early 20th-century residents to bury part of the river underground (call **Huck Finn Adventures**, 860-693-0385 for information about **Lost Park River excursions**).

Facing the state capitol is the **Museum of Connecticut History**. The museum, located alongside the 1910 **Connecticut State Library** and **State Supreme Court** building, houses Memorial Hall, a restored beaux arts-style gallery and a nationally known historical and genealogical library. The multi-faceted historical focus of the changing and permanent museum galleries include: state government, military and industrial history. Noteworthy is the permanent display of the 1662 Colony of Connecticut Royal Charter (see introduction, above).

The Colt collection memorializes Hartford firearms manufacturer Samuel Colt, who among other things, invented and patented the first revolving cylinder for firearms. As a side note, his wife, Elizabeth, was responsible for starting Hartford's public library, the first one (yes, another first!) in the country.

Before departing the capitol area, book a one-hour tour of the **Governor's Residence**. The 1909 Georgian Revival mansion has been home to Connecticut's governors since 1945 and is a particularly popular attraction when it is dressed up in its December holiday attire.

Moving westward, the **Connecticut Historical Society** (CHS), which concentrates on the state's heritage, was established in 1825, making it the nation's seventh oldest historical society. Collections include more the 200,000 prints and photographs, with 35,000 objects, showcasing 17th- and 18th-century furniture; costumes and textiles; portraits and landscapes; tavern and trade signs; decorative arts; toys and tools. Expansion plans, slated to be completed in 2008, will facilitate, among other things, hands-on exhibitions, library, auditorium, classrooms, media resource lab, restaurant and gift shop.

Less than one mile south from the CHS, day trips to the **Mark Twain House & Museum** leave little room for much else, except, perhaps, a jaunt to neighboring **Harriet Beecher Stowe House**. More than 100 years ago, Twain's High Victorian, 19-room house, the largest on the block, with a sheen of gaudiness in its painted brick, standing stately under a slate roof and six chimneys, changed the landscape of the Nook Farm section of town as well as the notoriety of the surrounding city. A National Historic Landmark since 1963, many people still don't realize that, yes, Twain (legal name: Samuel L. Clemens) was born and raised in Missouri, but later moved to Hartford. This is where for 17 years (1874 to 1891) he lived in what neighbors dubbed, "the curious house that Mark built."

The home was the actual setting for the 2002 PBS two-episode, four-hour documentary directed by Ken Burns about the master folk writer.

"We never came home from an absence that its face did not light up and speak out its eloquent welcome—and we could not enter it unmoved," Twain once wrote about the house in which he spared no expense.

One-hour guided tours explore the quarters where Twain wrote some of his masterpieces including *Tom Sawyer*, *Huckleberry Finn* and *Life on the Mississippi*. Restored to perfection, Louis Comfort Tiffany originally decorated the interior, drawing from Indian, Middle Eastern, Japanese and North African influences. Although the house has had several incarnations since the Mark Twain family lived there, much of the Clemens's furniture remains and the family's ghosts still echo throughout the rooms.

The accompanying Museum Center that opened in 2003 helps further define the man and his legend. The gift shop supplies unique gifts and collectibles ranging from a Mark Twain "Delmonico" bust to coffee mugs inscribed with Mark Twain quotes and Tom Sawyer caricatures.

Twain built his house in 1874 on Farmington Avenue, across from the home of world-famous Harriet Beecher Stowe. Today, the interior of Harriet Beecher Stowe's house, where she lived from 1873 to 1896, is tidily preserved. The exterior is also intact, flourishing with Victorian gardens in the summer. Original paintings, period furniture and first editions of Stowe's 1852 abolitionist classic, *Uncle Tom's Cabin*, fill the Victorian "cottage." To tour both historical homes in a day allows the sojourner to experience the bigger picture of the post-civil war era through two small, but utterly fascinating lives.

Two other historical houses, both owned by the Antiquarian and Landmarks Society (860-247-8996; call for days and hours of operation and admission fees), include the **Butler-McCook Homestead**, 396 Main Street, dating back to 1782 and the 1854 **Isham-Terry House**, 211 High Street.

Off-the-beaten track day trips include the **Menczer Museum of Medicine and Dentistry** (860-236-5613; call for days and hours of operation and admission fees) at 230 Scarborough Street, on Hartford's northwest corner, with collections that emphasize dental instruments, equipment, furnishings, and portraits from the 18th, 19th, and 20th centuries, and commemorate the life of Horace Wells and the history of anesthesia.

Garbage is prized (and admission free) at the Connecticut **Resources Recovery Authority Visitor's Center** (860-247-4280), 211 Murphy Road, in which 6,500 square feet contain exhibits that teach visitors everything there is to know about managing the state's solid waste.

Horse lovers should saddle up at the **Ebony Horsewomen Equestrian Center** (860-293-2914), 337 Vine Street. Instructors offer private and group lessons (English or Western) at this 693-acre park that includes a 6,000-square-foot indoor riding area. The center, boasting a variety of activities, is also a favorite among spectators.

The construction of Interstate 91 (officially opened in 1958) cut the city off from the Connecticut River. To remedy the situation, since 1981, Riverfront Recapture (860-713-3131), a private, non-profit organization has not only restored public access to the water, but also cleaned up the mighty Connecticut. This park system has more than 6.5 miles of shoreline, with abundant boat launches. It also has over eight miles of trails and walkways and more than 90 acres of developed and undeveloped land. Warmer-weather visitors can expect a variety of live entertainment under a high-tech canopy with lawn amphitheater seating up to 2000 people.

Another state endeavor is **Adriaen's Landing**, a 33-acre site that overlooks the Connecticut River. Named in honor of Dutch navigator, Adriaen Block, the first European to explore and sail up the Connecticut River in 1614, the prized jewel of the project is a 540,000-square-foot Connecticut Convention Center. Other recent developments include a 409-room **Hartford Marriott Downtown** (860-249-8000); entertainment; retail and cultural venues and residential units and Rentschler Field (860-610-4700), a 40,000-seat stadium in East Hartford.

Day-trippers who are searching for golf have two public courses to choose from: **Goodwin Golf Course** (860-956-3601), a 27-hole course, located on Maple Avenue and **Keney Golf Course** (860-525-3656), an 18-hole course, located on Tower Avenue.

Bookworms will find a roster of booksellers, including the **Gallows Hill Bookstore** (860-297-5231; call for days and hours of operation), 300 Summit Street at Trinity College, hosting many local authors. A welcoming staff and comfy chairs entice patrons to stay longer than planned.

Places Rated Almanac has ranked Hartford among the top-25 cities for arts and culture. Whether professional, semi-professional or amateur theater, day-trippers are afforded a plethora of matinees or evening performances. Many theatrical shows have gone to Broadway. A sampling of performing venues includes the **HartfordStage** (860-527-5151; www.hartfordstage.org), **Bushnell Center for the Performing Arts** (888-824-2874; www.bushnell.org), **Hartford Children's Theatre** (860-249-7970; www.hartfordchildrenstheatre.org), **Austin Arts Center** at Trinity College (860-297-2199; www.austinarts.org) and **Charter Oak Cultural Center** (860-249-1207; www.charteroakcenter.org).

For a hip night out, purchase tickets to hear national and lesser-known live music acts ranging from rock to reggae performed at **Webster Theater** (860-525-5553; www.webstertheatre.com), 31 Webster Street. One of the oldest existing buildings in the city, to see the renovation of the art deco-style, onetime movie cinema alone is worth the visit. The **Meadows Music Centre** (203-949-1222; www.meadowsmusic.com/main.html) is another popular venue to enjoy many nationally known live bands. Whether hearing a panel of your favorite authors or discussions about "Extreme Politics," the **Connecticut Forum** (860-509-0909), 750 Main Street, encourages the free exchange of ideas in myriad subjects and topics. Presented four times annually (ticket prices vary), sign up for a free online newsletter, www.ctforum.org.

The city's many visual art venues hold **Open Studios** (860-371-3924) every May and December. During this event, the city offers shuttles to many museums and private studios, which include the now defunct **Colt Manufacturing Company**, a commercial space for artists. Colt's revolver inventor Samuel Colt designed the building crowned with a blue, star-spangled onion dome after he toured Russia and Turkey in the 1800s.

In Hartford's Parkville section where the Portuguese Bakeries on Park Street coax daytime wanderers to halt in their tracks and taste homemade goodies, **Real Art Ways (RAW) Center for Contemporary Culture** (860-232-1006; www. realartways.org), 56 Arbor Street, presents an impressive calendar of visual arts exhibits, special movie screenings and live arts events. RAW, housed in a converted onetime-typewriter factory, allows *real* people to sink their teeth into art forms aplenty.

Parkville neighborhood restaurants are a United Nations-style cornucopia. Two family-owned and homey Portuguese restaurants on Park Street that buzz with loyal locals are **Patio Da Rainha** (860-233-7488) and **O'Camelo Restaurant** (860-321-8067), both open daily. Still on Park, try the **King & I** (860-232-5471) for Thai and **Mango Tree** for Vietnamese (860-523-5477), both open for lunch and dinner Monday through Saturday. At number 2027, **George's Restaurant and Pizzeria** (860-232-5568), another family-owned establishment, has been serving fresh, tasty pizza and Italian-style meals for more than 40 years.

Local vendors in white trucks sell hot dogs, wraps and the like on Elm Street in the Capitol area. Stationed on the corner of Clinton and Elm, the novel idea of cooking inside a movable bus is how **Bon Appetit Xpress** attracts the on-the-go breakfast and lunch crowd. (While noshing, keep an eye out for the Governor and other dignitaries zipping up and down past the vendor trucks.)

Breakfast and lunch crowds also have the option of hyped-up "fast food" served in an art deco-ish ambiance at **Global Gourmet** (860-278-4466), 960 Main Street. No question about it: Hartford knows good food! Amelia Simmons published America's first cookbook here in 1796. Today, the city's hundreds of restaurants will match any palate. Just a sampling of the ethnic delights: African American, Middle Eastern, Latin American, Caribbean, Ethiopian, Greek, Indian, Irish, Italian, Jamaican, Asian, Polish, Ukrainian, Portuguese and West Indian, and more. For a taste of Rome, try Hartford's "Little Italy," situated along Franklin Avenue. Anyone can direct visitors to the **Omar Coffee Company** (800-394-6627; 860-296-4313), which has been a Franklin Avenue institution since 1939.

Three and four-star city restaurants (call for days and hours of operation) include: **USS Chowder Pot IV** (860-244-3311); southern specialties at **Black-Eyed Sally's** (860-278-7427 [RIBS]; www.blackeyedsallys.com); Italian cuisine at **Peppercorn's Grill** (860-547-1714); an array of fresh fish and pasta selections at **Max Downtown** (860-522-2530; www.maxrestaurantgroup.com) and **Carbone's** (860-296-9646; www.carbonesct.com), an Italian restaurant that has become an area institution. Note: **Pierponts Restaurant** (860-522-4935) at the Goodwin Hotel (see **Accommodations**) at 1 Haynes Street is an elegant dining option for breakfast daily, lunch (Sunday brunch), Monday through Friday and dinner, Monday through Saturday. In the heart of Hartford's Italian neighborhood at 329 Franklin Avenue, anytime of day is a good time to stop in for a pick-me-up at **Mozzicato DePasquale Bakery and Pastry Shop's Caffe** (860-296-0246), which highlights a full liquor and coffee bar. Open daily, the shop is a frequent winner of various reader-choice polls. Before saying "Arrivederci," take home some pastries, cakes, cookies or breads.

GETTING THERE:
Dubbed the Gateway to New England, Greater Hartford is located at the crossroads of Interstate Highways 91 and 84, midway between New York and Boston.

TRANSPORTATION:
Downtown Hartford is located 20 minutes from Bradley International Airport (860-292-2000) in Windsor Locks. Union Station Transportation Center, a multi-model transportation center in downtown Hartford, provides scheduled Amtrak service (800-USA-RAIL). Nonstop bus transportation (860-247-5329) to every major northeast city also runs regularly to and from Union Station.

ADDITIONAL INFORMATION:
GREATER HARTFORD CONVENTION & VISITOR'S BUREAU.
31 Pratt Street, 4th Floor. The staff offers up-to-date brochures and special-events information (see below). (860) 728-6789 or (800) 446-7811.

GREATER HARTFORD TOURISM DISTRICT.
31 Pratt Street. Another good resource for up-to-date-travel information. (860) 244-8181 or (800) 793-4480.

TRAVELERS' TOWER.
1 Tower Square. Tours run May through October, Monday through Friday. Tours to the tower's observation deck on the 27th floor are every half-hour. Walk-ins are welcome, but it is advisable to call ahead for individual tours. Group tours by appointment. No wheelchair access for the observation deck tours. General admission is free. (860) 277-4208.

OLD STATE HOUSE.
800 Main Street. Open all year, Monday through Saturday. Call in advance for group tours and special events. Completely handicapped accessible. General admission is free. (860) 522-6766; www.ctosh.org.

WADSWORTH ATHENEUM MUSEUM OF ART.
600 Main Street. Open all year, Tuesday through Sunday. General admission is $9.00 adults; $7.00 seniors (62+); $5.00 students and free to children 12 and under and free until noon on Saturday for everyone except during special fund-raising events. (860) 278-2670; www.wadsworthatheneum.org.

STATE CAPITOL.
210 Capitol Avenue. Open all year, Monday through Friday; open Saturday, April through October. Guided one-hour tours, sponsored by the League of Women Voters, are run hourly beginning at 9:15 a.m. Advance reservations required for groups of 10 or more. Small gift shop located in the legislative building (not open Saturday). Handicapped accessible. General admission is free. (860) 240-0222.

BUSHNELL PARK.

Corner of Elm and Jewel Streets. Open all year, daily. Park carousel (860-585-5411), operates May through October, Tuesday through Sunday. Rides are 50 cents. For a list of park tours and special-entertainment-events schedule throughout the year, call (860) 232-6710.

MUSEUM OF CONNECTICUT HISTORY.

231 Capitol Avenue. Open all year, Monday through Saturday. General admission is free. (860) 757-6535; www.cslib.org/museum.htm.

GOVERNOR'S RESIDENCE.

990 Prospect Avenue. Open all year by appointment only. Call for December weekend open house schedule. General admission is free. (860) 566-4840.

CONNECTICUT HISTORICAL SOCIETY.

One Elizabeth Street at Asylum Avenue. Open all year, Tuesday through Saturday. General admission is $6.00 adults; $3.00 seniors (60+); $3.00 students/children and free to children 5 and under and free on the first Saturday and Sunday of every month. (860) 236-5621; www.chs.org.

MARK TWAIN HOUSE & MUSEUM.

351 Farmington Avenue. Open all year, daily; closed Tuesdays in the month of November and during the months from January to April. The first floor of the house is wheelchair accessible. Call the visitor's center to reserve library time. Free parking. To arrange tours for visitors with special needs, call (860) 247-0998, ext. 130. Free brochures available by e-mailing name and address to info@marktwainhouse.org. General admission is $16.00 adults; $14.00 seniors (65+); $12.00 students; $8.00 children and free to children 5 and under. (860) 247-0998, www.marktwainhouse.org.

HARRIET BEECHER STOWE CENTER.

77 Forest Street. Stowe's house (1871), Visitor Center (1883 carriage house), another area landmark, the Katharine Seymour Day House (1884) and a museum gift store are open all year, Tuesday through Saturday; Mondays, Memorial Day through Columbus Day and December. Research library is open by appointment. General admission is $6.50 adults; $6.00 seniors (65+); $2.75 children and free to children 5 and under. (860) 522-9258; www.harrietbeecherstowe.net.

ACCOMMODATIONS:
THE GOODWIN HOTEL.

One Haynes Street. The 124 guestrooms exude turn-of-the-18th-century luxury and charm in a décor of rich wood furnishings, sleigh beds and marble baths. Amenities include business services, indoor pool, fitness center and valet parking garage and on-site restaurant (see above). Rates: $119-$329. (860) 246-7500; (800) 922-5006; www.goodwinhotel.com.

HILTON HARTFORD HOTEL.

315 Trumbull Street (at the Civic Center Plaza). After a recent 34-million-dollar renovation, the hotel ranks as a four-star property with the distinction of being

connected by a skywalk to the Civic Center, allowing guests easy access to sporting and special events and concerts. There are 392 guestrooms and suites; amenities include indoor swimming pool, fitness center and lounge. (860) 728-5151.

MARK TWAIN HOSTEL

131 Tremont Street. Consider an option you might not have thought about. Located amidst an array of Victorian mansions in the west end, book one or more of the 42 beds in dorm-style quarters. The house has fully equipped kitchen, common rooms and laundry facilities. Rates: $18-$54. (860) 523-7255; (800) 909-4776.

ANNUAL FESTIVALS/EVENTS

The Central Regional Tourism District, Connecticut's Heritage River Valley, representing a total of 46 communities, provides a gamut of tourism information, which includes seasonal events (800) 793-4480 or (860) 244-8181; www. enjoycentralct.com.

CONNECTICUT EXPO CENTER

265 Reverend Moody Overpass. More than 30 annual events, such as the **Connecticut International Auto Show**, the **Connecticut Flower and Garden Show**, **Festival for Kids** and the **Northeast Fishing and Hunting Expo** are held throughout the year at Connecticut's largest exhibition facility. (860) 493-1300.

HARTFORD CIVIC CENTER

One Civic Center Plaza. Connecticut's largest sports and entertainment facility, which is managed by Madison Square Garden in New York City. Home to the **Hartford Wolf Pack**, AHL affiliate of the New York Rangers, the **Big East Conference Women's Basketball Championship**, the **NCAA Division I Women's Basketball Championship East Regional** and the home away from home for the **University of Connecticut Men's and Women's basketball** programs. Annual events include the **Original Connecticut Home Show** and **Latino Expo**. (860) 249-6333.

JUNE

An array of food samples from area restaurants and a host of entertainment are scheduled at **Taste of Hartford**, Constitution Plaza in downtown Hartford. (860) 920-5330.

JULY

Special programs and activities fill the day at the **Annual Historic Gardens Day** held at the Harriet Beecher Stowe Center. (860) 522-9258; www.harrietbeecherstowe. net.

Greater Hartford Festival of Jazz at Bushnell Park. (860) 722-6231.

AUGUST

Mark Twain Days are held at Bushnell Park, Charter Oak Landing & Riverfront Plaza, the Mark Twain House and the Harriet Beecher Stowe House. Re-enactors bring to life Twain's literary works from jousting to fencing to storytelling. Other events include concerts, a crafts fair, bamboo-pole fishing and fence whitewashing. (860) 713-3131; www.marktwainhouse.org.

OCTOBER

Greater Hartford Marathon. All races start and finish in Bushnell Park. Open to all ages. Preregistration required. Fee. (860) 652-8866.

The **Thomas Hooker Day Parade and Festival** celebrates Thomas Hooker, Hartford's founding father, with food, colorful costumes and entertainment for all ages. Parade begins on Main Street in downtown Hartford. (860) 525-7537.

NOVEMBER

Hartford's **Festival of Lights** marks the start of the official holiday season. Festivities begin the day after Thanksgiving on Constitution Plaza with traditional Christmas caroling, holiday lights and Santa who arrives in a neon sled atop Fleet Building's rooftop. (800) 446-7811.

Winter Brew Festival at Trinity College. Students in theater and dance departments present directing, playwriting and performance project finals. Free. (860) 297-2199.

DECEMBER

On December 31, Hartford marks New Year's Eve with **First Night** celebrations throughout the city, which include fireworks shot over the Connecticut River. (800) 446-7811.

Hungry?
See page 33

*X-press breakfast & lunch
on-the-go in Hartford.*

Connecticut Historical Society
See pages 30-31

Amistad Exhibit

NORTH CENTRAL CONNECTICUT
Hartford County
"Heritage River Valley"
West Hartford/Farmington/Simsbury

These Hartford County towns that tourism officials dub "Connecticut's Heritage River Valley" are serene day-escapes overflowing with wonderful surprises. Opulent and affluent West Hartford, Farmington and Simsbury brim with rich history, architecture, arts, entertainment and culture. History fans can see some of the first dictionaries at the birthplace and childhood home of America's first linguist Noah Webster in West Hartford. Hot air ballooning is a popular mode of transportation to explore the hills, flora, woodlands, reservoirs and the Farmington River and Farmington Valley Greenway. For sightseeing that doesn't abut the clouds but offers utterly breathtaking views of the valley, hike atop Heublein Mountain in Simsbury. No matter what angle you look at things, be prepared for sheer delight!

According to legend, what settlement donated what would amount to 30,000 dollars today to help General George Washington's troops in 1777?

What town has achieved consistent top ranks from "Connecticut Magazine's" annual "best of" town polls?

Tried & True: WEST HARTFORD

From the approximate 100 colonists who seceded from Newtown (now Cambridge), Massachusetts and settled Hartford (see **Hartford** chapter), in 1636 under the leadership of Reverends Thomas Hooker and Samuel Stone, another small group separated and moved west in what was still part of the Hartford settlement. Initially, settlers referred to the former Indian plantation as West Division. Named West Hartford in 1806, officials incorporated the town in 1854.

During the winter of 1777, General George Washington and his troops suffered through harsh, freezing weather, food shortages and the hardships of Valley Forge while the British occupied nearby Philadelphia. Legend goes that West Division donated what would amount to 30,000 dollars today (safely delivered on horseback over hundreds of miles through wilderness) to help the patriot cause!

Modern-day West Hartford, with a population hovering around 61,000, has been ranked in past years by *Connecticut Magazine* as number one for its public school performance and number two for its overall lifestyle qualities among similarly populated towns. Day-trippers can experience this robust, suburban community's surroundings, which include three historic districts (consisting mostly of private homes), **Buena Vista**, **Boulevard** and **West Hill**; plus safe neighborhoods touting superior shopping and dining districts.

Day Trips with *Panache* ················

Day trips with panache can begin at any one of the three West Hartford universities: the **University of Hartford** (860-768-4100), **St. Joseph College** (860-660-1000) or the **University of Connecticut**, West Hartford campus (860-570-9214), where concerts, art galleries, live theater, sporting events and museum exhibitions are always on the roster—many of which are free. The **Hartt School Concert Series** (860-768-5566), for instance, at the University of Hartford, entertains audiences throughout the year. Another interesting UH venue is the **Museum of American Political Life** (860-768-4089), which, in addition to changing exhibits, hosts a collection of U.S. presidential memorabilia.

Beyond the many buildings and busy thoroughfares on the east side of **Goodman Green**, a narrow triangle at the busy intersection of Farmington Avenue and West Main Street, stand remnants from colonial times. Northwest of North Main Street and Farmington Avenue, **Veterans Green's** park-like atmosphere lends itself to day-trippers who choose to "brown bag" a lunch or snack. At 968 Farmington Avenue, enthusiasts should browse the well-stocked shelves at locally owned and operated **Bookworm** (860-233-2653; call for days and hours of operation).

Historical day trips convene downtown at the **Noah Webster House Museum of West Hartford History**, South Main Street, and the West Hartford Historical Society's headquarters. Inside the 1770s saltbox, hailed as the birthplace and childhood home of Noah Webster, author of the first American dictionary, guides clad in period costumes lead tours and invite guests to practice such activities as flax processing and wool carding.

Within this National Historic Landmark museum, Mr. Webster's story unfolds. Pièces de résistance include his desk, two personal clocks and the early editions of *Webster's Dictionary of the American Language.* (His first *American Dictionary of English Language* was published in 1828 when he was 70, containing 70,000 definitions and taking more than 27 years to compile!) Museum store shoppers can purchase anything from a facsimile of the original *Blue-Backed Speller* (his pre-dictionary wordbook that sold 24 million copies in his lifetime) to colonial toys, arts and crafts.

Since its humble beginnings as a single-room children's museum in 1927, the **Science Center of Connecticut,** located one mile north from the house museum, has become a favorite family trip. Allot at least two hours for hands-on experimentation that explores the fun side of science, nature and technology.

At the center, test-drive a gravity-powered, LEGO ® brick car. Forecast the weather. Saunter inside Conny, a life-size sperm-whale model, which also happens to be Connecticut's official state animal. Catch a featured show at the **Gengras Planetarium**. View more than 50 species of reptiles, birds and mammals (the government confiscated many of these former illegally held pets; others were injured in the wild) at the **United Technologies Wild Life Sanctuary**. Consider making plans to roam through the science center's affiliate, the **Roaring Brook Nature Center** (860-693-0263), a wildlife sanctuary in Canton within a 30-minute drive.

Weather permitting, golfers can experience the **Rockledge Golf Club** (860-521-6284). Located at 289 South Main Street, the 18-hole course is open to the public. Another golfer's utopia is **Buena Vista Golf Course** (860-521-7359), a nine-hole, executive-style public course at 37 Buena Vista Road.

For a Sunday matinee or weekend evening show, reserve tickets for an upcoming production at **Park Road Playhouse** (860-586-8500; www.parkroadplayhouse. org). The community theater at 244 Park Road, an area that has undergone urban renovation, was established in 1997 as the City Repertory Company, Inc. It produces works by a host of playwrights ranging from Neil Simon to William Inge. For an extraordinary time, inquire about upcoming theatrical performances and special events at the **American School for the Deaf** (860-570-2307), 139 North

Main Street. (Day-trippers can also schedule an appointment to view the on-site museum that chronicles the first school for the deaf established in 1817 and also the birthplace of American Sign Language.)

Classical music enthusiasts can order tickets for one of four reasonably priced shows (September to May) at the **West Hartford Symphony Orchestra** (860-521-4362; www.whso.org), a community-based orchestra formed in 2002.

In the southern end of West Hartford, history buffs will delight in viewing the **Sarah Whitman Hooker House**, an 18th-century mansion that started as a one-room building back in 1715. The Sarah Hooker Society restored the house, which immortalizes the memory of the wife of Thomas Hart Hooker, a descendant of the Reverend Thomas Hooker (see above). Inside the house, some of the most impressive features include extensive furnishings, porcelain collections and portraits of Revolutionary War Tories under house arrest (which Mrs. Hooker herself guarded!) at the house between 1775 and 1776.

At 56 Buena Vista Road, public ice-skating is available all year at the **Veteran's Memorial Ice Skating Rink** (860-521-1573; call for days and hours of operation). The indoor rink has undergone a complete renovation. Also in the south end of town are three eclectic art galleries: **Saltbox Gallery**, **Clubhouse Gallery** and the **Little Red Schoolhouse**; run by the West Hartford Art League (860-521-3732; call for days and hours of operation).

Miles of natural habitat unroll in the eastern section of town. **Westmoor Park** (860-232-1134), 119 Flagg Road, is a four-season wonderland that encompasses 162 acres of woodlands and nature trails. Free to the public, the environmental, agricultural and horticultural education center (call for days and hours of operation), offers exhibits, hands-on learning, a heated greenhouse, seasonal gardens and barnyard animals.

Summer meanderings are not complete without a visit to nearby **Elizabeth Park**, when more than 14,000 bushes representing 900 different varieties of roses bloom in what historians record as the first municipal rose garden in the United States. A bequest from Charles H. Pond, a wealthy Hartford industrialist and political leader, started the park (named after his wife, Elizabeth) in 1903. The **Pond House**, the park's restaurant, is a popular stop for lunch and dinner.

The entrance to the **West Hartford Reservoir** is on the north side of Route 4 (Farmington Avenue), leading into the **Talcott Mountain Reservoir** (860-278-7850; www.themdc.com/talcottmountain.htm). With more than 3,000 acres of woodlands, 30 miles of paved and gravel roads greet joggers, bicyclists, hikers, horseback riders (with permit) and dog walkers. There are also wheelchair-accessible picnic groves. In the winter, day-trippers can enjoy cross-country skiing and snowshoeing.

Approximately one mile from the reservoir and beginning at the intersection of Farmington Avenue (Route 4) and South Main Street is **West Hartford Center**, a popular shopping hub. More than 140 specialty shops, boutiques, coffee shops, cafes and restaurants share space with tree-lined walkways and brick sidewalks. One food choice at the center is **Bricco Restaurant** (860-233-0220), serving lunch (Monday through Saturday) and dinner daily. This is a bistro-ish nook for those who have a yen for seasonal Italian/Mediterranean cuisine. A sampling of Farmington Avenue lunch or dinner favorites includes (call for days and hours of operation): **Harry's Pizza** (860-231-7166); **Max's Oyster Bar** (860-236-6299) and **Butterfly Chinese Restaurant** (860-236-2816). **Quaker Diner** (860-232-5523; call for days and hours of operation), an area legend since 1931 at 319 Park Road, the eatery is known for its homemade and ample meals. **Tapas** (860-521-4609; www.tapasonline.com) at 1150 New Britain Avenue, open for lunch and dinner daily, is consistently voted in local newspapers as the area's best Greek and vegetarian restaurant.

GETTING THERE:

West Hartford is located about three miles west of Hartford and approximately 31 miles from Springfield, Massachusetts. Interstate Highway 84 is the main highway to West Hartford. Routes 4 and 6 are the main roads. Interstates 84, 91 and I-291 connect West Hartford to the regional highway system.

TRANSPORTATION:

West Hartford is located 20 miles from Bradley International Airport (860-292-2000) in Windsor Locks. Downtown Hartford's Union Station Transportation Center, a multi-model transportation center, provides scheduled Amtrak service (800-USA-RAIL) and other services. Connecticut Transit buses (860-525-9181) offer West Hartford routes.

ADDITIONAL INFORMATION:

NOAH WEBSTER HOUSE MUSEUM OF WEST HARTFORD HISTORY.

227 South Main Street. Open all year; call for days and hours of operation. The museum is handicapped accessible. Inquire about family programs. Admission is $5.00 adults; $4.00 seniors, AAA members and students; $3.00 children and free to children 5 and under and to museum members. (860) 521-5362; www. noahwebsterhouse.org.

SCIENCE CENTER OF CONNECTICUT.

950 Trout Brook Drive. Open all year, Tuesday through Sunday. Call for days and hours of operation. Wheelchair access is limited to outside area; there are no elevators or ramps inside the science center. Call for general admission prices. (860) 231-2824; www.sciencecenterct.org.

SARAH WHITMAN HOOKER HOUSE.

1237 New Britain Avenue. Open all year, Monday and Wednesday or by appointment. Call for hours of operation and for general admission prices. (860) 523-5887; www. west-hartford.com/Profile/HistoricInfo/SarahWhitmanHooker.htm.

ELIZABETH PARK.

Prospect and Asylum Avenue. Open all year, Monday through Friday. Inquire about gardening lectures and other special events. Tours of the facility are free. (860) 231-9443. Pond House Café and Hall (860) 231-8823.

ACCOMMODATIONS:

WEST HARTFORD INN.

900 Farmington Avenue. The 50 renovated guestrooms in this family-operated business are a short walk from West Hartford's center. Amenities include cable TV, three smoking rooms, workout room and free parking. Rates (including continental breakfast): $103-$119. (860) 236-3221; www.westhartfordinn.com.

ANNUAL FESTIVALS/EVENTS

The Central Regional Tourism District, Connecticut's Heritage River Valley, representing 46 communities, provides a gamut of tourism information, which includes seasonal events (800) 793-4480 or (860) 244-8181; www.enjoycentralct. com. For additional festival and event information, contact the Leisure Services Department (860) 523-3159 or the West Hartford Chamber of Commerce (860) 521-2300.

APRIL

West Hartford's **YMCA Healthy Kids Day** is a day full of activities for both children and adults. (860) 521-5830.

JUNE

Experience arts and crafts, entertainment and activities for all ages at **Celebrate! West Hartford**. (203) 523-3226.

Summer Garden Tours are held by the West Hartford Garden Club. (860) 523-3238.

JUNE/JULY/AUGUST/SEPTEMBER

A **summer concert series** enlivens the atmosphere at the north lawn of the rose garden at Elizabeth Park. (860) 231-9443; www.elizabethpark.org.

AUGUST

Wolcott Park hosts a **Family Concert Series**. (860) 232-1134.

SEPTEMBER

The town hall offers the **Annual Labor Day Concert**. (860) 523-3100.

DECEMBER

Join the Friends of Elizabeth Park at their **Annual Game Dinner**. (860) 231-8823; www.elizabethpark.org.

Science Center of Connecticut

See page 39

Rufus, the resident Bobcat was dropped off in a cat carrier and left inside Conny, the whale!

The museum's mascot, Conny, a 45-foot-sperm whale made of concrete by the CT Cetacean Society.

Photos Courtesy of the Science Center of CT

What river town was once known as the
"mother of all towns"?

What town boasts comely estates that include an
ex-boxing champion's 52-room, 48,000-square-foot mansion
that hit the market for more than four million dollars?

River Treasure: **FARMINGTON**

Early settlers purchased "Tunxis Sepus," which translates "at the bend of the little river," from the Tunxis Indians. In 1645, settlers incorporated a farming town and aptly named it Farmington. The largest deeded settlement at the time, proportioned to 165 square miles, the territory extended north to what we know today as Simsbury, south to what is now called Wallingford, northwest to Indian-occupied "Mohawk country" and northeast to Windsor. Even when communities started to separate, Farmington was affectionately dubbed the "mother of towns."

A group of the Tunxis Tribe remained at "Indian Neck" on the east bank of what is now the Farmington River. Although the tribe adopted English culture and lifestyle, settlers segregated them from village life and by the end of the 18th century most of the Indians had sold their land to settlers and relocated to New York State.

In the 1800s, plans for the Farmington Canal, an inland waterway connecting a 17-town region and extending from New Haven to Northampton, Massachusetts, were short-lived, superseded by a railroad line. Meanwhile, the western portion of Farmington attracted industry while the northern village of Unionville was born, the site of paper mills and factories manufacturing such commodities as wooden screws, clocks, cutlery and nuts and bolts.

Modern-day Farmington is part of the Connecticut Freedom Trail, dedicated to the history of the African Americans' struggle for freedom. After their capture, imprisonment and eventual release by the Connecticut Supreme Court in 1841 (see **New Haven** chapter), Farmington abolitionists employed, educated and housed the freed Africans who had taken part in the famous revolt upon the slave ship "La Amistad."

By mid-19th century, an influx of immigrants; first, Irish and English, then Italians, Slovaks and others arrived in Farmington to work, particularly in the Unionville factories, until the infamous flood of August 1955 demolished Unionville center and downstream neighborhoods. Today, Farmington, located about 10 miles southwest of Hartford in the mid-western portion of Hartford County, is a residential hub of approximately 23,000. This river town boasts comely estates (ex-boxing champion Mike Tyson owned a 52-room, 48,000-square-foot mansion that last sold for more than four million dollars), while the buildings like that of Miss Porter's School, the late Jacqueline Kennedy Onassis's alma mater, add to the charm of Main Street, a one-mile stretch designated as a "scenic highway" and the center of Farmington Village.

Housing and commercial developments have edged into the main thoroughfare of Farmington Avenue (Route 4). The east side harbors many new industrial parks, condominiums and the University of Connecticut Health Center, Farmington's largest employer. In the historic Unionville section, despite modern commercialization, Victorian-style homes and small manufacturers like Sanford and Hawley Lumber Company serve as reminders of Unionville's past.

Offsetting the growth spurt, the Farmington Land Trust has preserved 258 acres of open space. An additional 350 town-owned acres, just off Route 4, can be found in the **Winding Trails Recreation Area** (860-677-8458). Although this is a members-only outdoor arena comprised of 13 miles of well-marked hiking trails, the public can cross-country ski and attend special events (see **Annual Festivals/ Events**).

Defunct canal lines and abandoned rail beds have been resurrected into the **Farmington Valley Greenway and the Farmington River Trail**, operated by the **Farmington Valley Trails Council** (860-658-4065), a volunteer group. Day trips with panache can begin on these paved trails, which are 10-feet wide, wheelchair accessible, and promote outdoor recreation, such as walking, jogging, biking and inline skating. When council volunteers finish construction, the multi-use trails will total 38 miles and link five central Connecticut towns—Farmington, Avon, Simsbury, East Granby and Suffield. Presently, hikers can explore historic buildings, canal locks, town paths, iron bridges, stone arches and other interesting artifacts. When the **Farmington Canal Heritage Trail**, the umbrella project encompassing the trail system, is complete in its entirety, it will stretch 87 miles from New Haven to Northampton, Massachusetts.

Main Street's **Day-Lewis Museum**, with its gambrel roof and clapboard exterior, is owned by Yale University. Operated by the Farmington Historical Society, focused upon Native American culture, artifacts include arrowheads and knives discovered during an on-site archaeological dig in the 1970s—an incredible feat; uncovering more than 10,000 years worth of human existence!

Day-trippers are also welcome Tuesdays or by appointment to 71 Main Street at the **Farmington Historical Society** (860-678-1645) to view a document collection and artifacts representative of Farmington's village past. While there, request a walking tour guide and site map of the Freedom Trail in Farmington, which records many homes (privately owned today) and sites that mark Farmington's abolitionist movement.

East of Main, the **Stanley-Whitman House**, a National Historic Landmark, connects day-trippers to 1700-era Farmington when the house's High Street address was known as Back Lane. Guides dressed in period costumes show off this circa 1720 house with its massive central chimney and superior 18th-century furnishings. Patrons can also join a historic village or graveyard tour.

Beyond the array of painstakingly landscaped estates, there's more hidden treasure tucked away at 35 Mountain Road. The **Hill-Stead Museum**, another National Historic Landmark, owns a venerable collection of French Impressionism by such artists as Claude Monet, Édouard Manet, Edgar Degas, James McNeill Whistler and Mary Cassatt. Once the private home of Theodate Pope, a turn-of-the century architect who bequeathed it to the town. In this 1901 Colonial Revival-style mansion, the artwork is preserved in the original 36 period rooms, accessorized with antiques.

Day-trippers are also encouraged to set up an easel on the mansion's 152-hilltop acres, which include sunken gardens designed by Beatrix Farrand, made famous by the summer poetry readings staged there. In the museum shop, for a unique remembrance, purchase prints and note cards featuring reproductions of Hill-Stead's Impressionist paintings.

For some downtime, head to **Farmington Miniature Golf and Ice Cream Parlor** (860-677-0118). Located on Farmington Avenue (Route 4), many architectural obstacles including a castle and perfectly manicured grounds create the 18-hole course. To complete the visit, an old-fashioned ice cream parlor equipped to make mouth-watering sundaes awaits the warmer-weather sojourner.

To experience a tranquil journey down the **Farmington River**, call **Huck Finn Adventures** in Collinsville, (860-693-0385). Or see the Farmington Valley from an airborne perspective: **KAT Balloons** (860-678-7921) and **A Windriders Balloon** (860-677-0647) are two Farmington companies offering hot-air ballooning excursions throughout the year.

Refined tastes are sure to be appeased listening to the **Farmington Valley Symphony Orchestra** (860-409-3702; www.fvsoct.org). Directed under the expert care and passion of John Eells, Director of Music at Miss Porter's School, the orchestra performs in the vicinity throughout the year. For off-the-beaten-track excursions, the staff at the **Farmington Library** (860-677-6877; www. farmingtonlibct.org) actively promotes a variety of musical programs, art exhibits and author appearances.

The side streets of Farmington Village are a shopper's haven. Horticulture lovers should see the garden varieties offered by **Haworth's Florist and Greenhouse** (800-429-6788) at 43 Garden Street. Book lovers shouldn't miss independently owned **Millrace Bookstore** (860-677-9662; www.millracebooks.com) at 40 Mill Lane. The outdoor waterfall further inspires a good read. Downstairs, in this building that has the distinction of being Farmington's first gristmill dating back to the 1640's, it is a good idea to reserve a table at **Grist Mill Café** (860-676-8855) at 44 Mill Lane. Located directly on the Farmington River, the restaurant exudes exemplary white linen table settings and freshly prepared lunch (Sunday brunch) and dinner selections offered daily.

For another ultimate romantic setting, reserve your spot for seasonal outdoor dining by Farmington River at **Ann Howard's Apricots** (860-673-5405). The New American, continental, award-winning cuisine, served for lunch and dinner daily, can be experienced either in the formal (jackets required, no jeans) dining room upstairs or in the informal English-style pub below.

The 525,000-square-foot **Westfarms Mall**, on the Farmington/West Hartford town line, is a shopper's paradise that offers a range of casual food choices. Consider lunch or dinner at **Rainforest Café** (860-521-2002). This dining adventure includes "animatronic" jungle animals, a 700-gallon-saltwater tropical fish tank and a fiber optics "Starscape" consisting of shooting stars and changing constellations and simulated rainforest thunder and lightening.

Future chefs prepare lunch Monday through Friday for the public at the **Connecticut Culinary Institute** (860-677-7869), 230 Farmington Avenue. While on the Avenue, delay final departure in order to peruse the **Farmington Crafts Common** (860-674-9295), open Tuesday through Sunday, showcasing the multimedia works of some 200 artisans. Don't forget to visit the café for a snack.

GETTING THERE:

Farmington is located about 10 miles southwest of Hartford and 36 miles from Springfield, Massachusetts. Interstate 84 is the main highway to Farmington. It's located on Route 10 with Routes 4 north and 6 south.

TRANSPORTATION:

Farmington is located approximately 22 miles from Bradley International Airport (860-292-2000) in Windsor Locks. Downtown Hartford's Union Station Transportation Center, a multi-model transportation center, provides scheduled Amtrak service (800-USA-RAIL) and other services. Connecticut Transit buses (860-525-9181) offer Farmington routes.

ADDITIONAL INFORMATION:

STANLEY-WHITMAN HOUSE.

37 High Street. Open all year; call for days and hours of operation. The museum is handicapped accessible. Inquire about the research library on premises, special events, lectures, hands-on programs and open-hearth cooking programs. Historic village and graveyard tours are by appointment at least two weeks in advance. Admission is $5.00 adults; $4.00 seniors; $3.00 children and free to children 5 and under and to museum members. (860) 677-9222.

THE DAY-LEWIS MUSEUM.

158 Main Street. Open March through November, except August; Wednesday afternoons and by appointment. Call for general admission price. (860) 678-1645.

HILL-STEAD MUSEUM.

35 Mountain Road. The museum shop and home are open all year, Tuesday through Sunday. The first floor of the museum is wheelchair accessible. Inquire about special programs and events. Admission is $9.00 adults; $8.00 seniors; $7.00 students, $4.00 children and free to children 5 and under and to museum members. (860) 677-4787; www.hillstead.org.

ACCOMMODATIONS:

THE FARMINGTON INN.

827 Farmington Avenue. The inn was built after the Revolutionary War and is one of the Classic Hotels of Connecticut, a local hotel group that also owns and operates the Simsbury Inn (see **Accommodations, Simsbury** chapter). The 72 rooms, which include 13 executive suites, feature regional artwork, canopied beds, European linens, down mattresses, marble bathrooms, and modern amenities. A complimentary booklet, *The Farmington Lady*, introduces guests to the area's favorite ghost. Rates (including continental breakfast): $109-$129. (860) 677-2821; www.farmingtoninn.com.

HOMEWOOD SUITES BY HILTON FARMINGTON.

2 Farm Glen Blvd. Two-room suites are available with separate living and sleeping areas and fully equipped kitchens. Amenities include complimentary van service within a five-mile radius of the hotel, business center, meeting rooms, indoor pool and fitness room. Rates: $99-$149. (860) 321-0000.

ANNUAL FESTIVALS/EVENTS

The Central Regional Tourism District, Connecticut's Heritage River Valley, representing 46 communities, provides a gamut of tourism information, which includes seasonal events (800) 793-4480 or (860) 244-8181; www.enjoycentralct. com. For further festival and event information, call the Farmington Valley Visitors Association (860) 676-8878; (800) 4-WELCOME or the Chamber of Commerce (860) 676-8490 or the Farmington Town Hall (860) 675-2300; www.farmington-ct.org.

MARCH/APRIL

The **Annual Butterfly Quilt Opportunity** is a two-month raffle for which participants can purchase tickets and try to win an exclusive, hand-stitched quilt. Proceeds help educate the public about the disease of lupus and towards finding a cure. Sponsored by Farmington's Medical Health Center and the Lupus Foundation of America, the winner does not need to be present at drawing to win. (860) 953-0387.

APRIL

Kids delight in the **Annual Easter Egg Hunt** held on the grounds of the Farmington Miniature Golf & Ice Cream Parlor. (860) 677-0118.

MAY/JUNE/OCTOBER

One of the largest outdoor crafts fairs in the state is the **Farmington Polo Grounds Crafts Fair,** held annually on the Farmington Polo Grounds (off Route 4). The event features more than 200-juried professional artists and crafts people. (860) 871-7914; (860) 745-5071.

JUNE/SEPTEMBER

Professional as well as amateur antiques dealers attend the **Farmington Antiques Weekend**, one of the largest shows in Connecticut with more than 600 quality dealers. The event is held the second weekend in June and Labor Day weekend on the Farmington Polo Grounds. Fine food concessions are also available. (860) 677-7862; www.farmington-antiques.com.

JUNE

Riversplash involves activities geared for all ages that are organized at numerous Farmington River sites. (860) 658-4442.

JULY

A much-anticipated event is the **Annual Farmington Horse Show** at the Farmington Polo Club. (860) 676-8490.

The **Farmington Horse Show & Wild Animal Petting Zoo** at Farmington Polo Grounds, attracts visitors far and wide. (860) 677-8427.

Special programs and activities fill the day at the **Annual Historic Gardens Day** held the Hill-Stead Museum. (860) 677-4787; www.hillstead.org.

AUGUST

See men and women, individual and relay teams, compete in the **Annual Farmington Valley Off-Road Triathlon** (860-677-8458) at Winding Trails Recreation Facility.

Connecticut's oldest Native American gathering is the **Annual Connecticut River Powwow** held at the Farmington Polo Grounds. Highlights include a native village, music, dance, storytelling, crafts and food. (860) 684-6984.

SEPTEMBER
The **Ye Olde Publick Fair** is a living 18th-century history fair at the Stanley-Whitman House. Activities range from open-pit cooking to colonial tradesmen demonstrations (like candle dipping) to colonial music and dance. Barnyard animals are also part of the extravaganza. (860) 677-9222.

NOVEMBER/DECEMBER
Do not miss the Farmington Heritage Sightseeing tours of the annual **Ancient Evening Graveyard Walking Tours** through two ancient graveyards in the village of Farmington. A colonial-style dinner concludes the evening. (860) 677-8867.

Up-Close Encounters with the Farmington River Via Huck Finn Adventures
See page 45

Photos Courtesy of Huck Finn Adventures

What river town did Indian warriors burn to the ground; only for some of the original settlers and a new pioneer group to rebuild and resettle one year later?

Where was the first copper coinage in America?

Cozy & Tranquil: SIMSBURY

During Simsbury's earliest history, the Massacoe Indians reaped a bountiful livelihood from the area's verdant valley, bordered by two, low mountain ranges, teeming with wildlife, abundant rivers and virgin pine forest. Settlers, appearing from Windsor as early as 1664, arrived with the main objective of stripping pitch and tar from the pines for shipbuilding. Between 1648 and 1661, the Native Americans gradually traded off what was known as the Massacoh Plantation by the settlers. Incorporated in 1670, the colonists renamed Simsbury after Symondsbury, Dorset, England, believed to be the homeland of many of the first settlers.

However, territorial tensions between the Indians and colonists mounted. As a result, King Philip's War, so called from the name of the war's leader, Indian chief Metacom whom the English named Philip, erupted in 1675. Colonists fled as Philip's warriors burned and pillaged Simsbury. The following year after the conflict ceased, some former settlers and a new group of pioneers rebuilt the settlement. One hundred years later, this tenacious spirit reappeared in those patriots (approximately 1,000) who became Revolutionary War soldiers.

Resourcefulness was another quality Simsbury's earliest inhabitants shared. In 1705, copper discoveries jumpstarted a sense of ingenuity when Dr. Samuel Higley minted, among the first in America, copper coins from 1737 to 1739 in Simsbury. (Today, Higley coins are a prized collector's item!) During the Revolutionary War, what was once the first site of a copper coinage in America became the infamous **Old-New Gate Prison**, a major tourist attraction in what is East Granby today.

Dr. Higley also pioneered the manufacture of steel created from native Simsbury iron, starting America's first operating mill in 1728. By 1836, Simsbury's workers manufactured the first safety fuse in America.

Modern-day Simsbury, with a land area covering nearly 35 square miles, traversed by the Farmington River, still boasts many of the same natural resources the Massacoe Indians cherished. Twenty-seven minutes northwest of Hartford, with a population just over 23,000, commercialization has, for the most part, bypassed the town. Fertile farms and varied topography stretch along both sides of the river and roll into the West Simsbury hills.

Day trips with panache are well worth the mile-and-a-half climb up to **Heublein Tower**, the valley's most visible—up to 50 miles away—landmark. Just off Route 185, **Talcott Mountain State Park's** entrance leads to the hiking trail that winds 165 feet above the 1,000-foot mountain range once frequented by Mark Twain. The Farmington River and several quaint towns below weave a charming mountainside tapestry where, on a clear day, you can catch a bird's-eye view across Massachusetts, New Hampshire and Long Island Sound.

Renovated and open to the public is the 1914 Bavarian-style tower atop Talcott, which the Heublein family of Hartford, famed business moguls, built as a summer retreat. The large opening in Talcott Mountain is called **Metacomet Ridge**, also known as King Philip's cave. According to legend, this is where the Indian sachem Metacom (Philip) sat watching Simsbury burn in 1675.

"Experts only" whitewater aficionados frequently travel to **Tariffville Gorge**, located at the gap in Talcott Mountain. Once a water source power for early Tariffville village industries, it is currently a site of national canoe and kayak competitions, including **national and Olympic trials**, **New England Championship competitions** and **National Canoe Poling competitions**.

Equestrian types should reserve a riding lesson or call ahead for a schedule of upcoming horse shows at **Folly Farms Stables** (860-658-9943) on 75 Hartford Road near Route 185. This sophisticated, full-service equestrian center caters to both beginner and expert riders.

Back onto Route 185, any local can point out the state's largest and oldest tree, the Pinchot Sycamore, possibly three centuries old, which grows on the banks of the Farmington River in the Weatogue section. Southward, minutes away, the **Old Drake Hill Flower Bridge** (860-658-3255) spans 183 feet. In the early 1990s, a concerned residents' group revamped this 19th-century, metal-truss bridge (defunct in 1992), and reopened it to pedestrian traffic. Suspended 18 feet over the Farmington River, it serves as Simsbury's centerpiece, especially in the summer when it's adorned with hundreds of flower boxes and baskets donated by community members. This is a great spot for swimming or launching a boat. A preferred backdrop for wedding photographs, it's also a romantic spot for picnics.

Nearby, **East Weatogue's Historic District**, nestled among the town's newer homes, features some of Simsbury's oldest Colonials. In-season farmers' markets emerge: **Rosedale Farm** (860-658-6348) advertises the "sweetest sweet corn." **Hall's Farm Roadside Stand** (860-658-4511) sells organic produce and prized pumpkins.

The first stop on Route 10, which leads toward the town center, should be **Arts Exclusive Gallery/Visitor's Center** on Hopmeadow Street, named in remembrance of the hops that once grew in Simsbury. Sharing space with Webster Bank in a turn-of-the-century brownstone building, 2,500 square feet and 20-foot-high walls highlight approximately 600 original works of art. Philip M. Janes has run Arts Exclusive, one of the oldest galleries in New England, for more than 25 years. His dual role as Director of the Simsbury Visitor's Center is not surprising; with his town expertise, he could easily be called honorary mayor! In the gallery's foyer, approximately 70 different brochures help travelers plan a perfect day.

Discover some of the town's earliest history at the **Phelps Tavern Museum and Homestead**, operated by the Simsbury Historical Society. Sprawled on two acres, this complex includes the 18th-century **Captain Elisha Phelps** house and a **1670 meetinghouse**. Special exhibits enhance period rooms and interactive galleries that bring to life the tavern's days as an inn from 1786 to 1849.

A few doors down, the **Free Library's Simsbury Genealogical and Historical Research Library** has an extensive collection of materials for serious researchers. Art buffs will enjoy 19th-century paintings and artifacts.

Visitors are welcome to watch international stars and up-and-coming hopefuls work at the **International Skating Center of Connecticut**, Hopmeadow Street. The largest ice-skating rink complex in the state, this excellent facility is also open to the public for ice-skating.

There are plenty of upscale stores in the center of town, including the quaint stretch of **Simsburytown Shops**. Theatergoers may be interested in the **Theatre Guild of Simsbury's** (860-658-0666; www.theatreguildsimsbury.org/sponsors. html) annual November performance. This non-profit organization, formed in 1972 by a group of Simsbury residents, presents Broadway-style musicals at the Simsbury High School Auditorium. Whether Broadway's musical hits or barbershop classics, the **Farmington Valley Chorus**, composed of amateur female singers, has enchanted audiences for more than 30 years. Call for a schedule of upcoming performances (860-485-9541; www.singfvc.org). While in the area, consider a free July concert at **Simsbury Farms Recreational Complex**. The **Simsbury Community Band** (860-651-3081; www.simsbury.k12.ct.us/scb/scb. htm), a non-profit organization formed in 1974, also performs annual concerts throughout town.

For rural charm, follow Route 309 past the rocky hillsides and fields surrounding West Simsbury's farms. Since 1786, the 270-acre **Tulmeadow Dairy Farm** (860-658-1430) has been offering—among other things—legendary fresh ice cream. **Flamig Farm** (860-658-5070) entertains audiences of all ages with its petting zoo. Also on the farm's roster are regular pig roasts, country music concerts and a super-scary Halloween hayride.

Golfers should check out **Simsbury Farms** (860-658-6246; www. simsburyfarms.com), one of the state's most picturesque public golf courses. This onetime apple orchard also offers three swimming pools, tennis courts, children's playgrounds and skating rink.

At 77 West Street, romantic lunches (all-you-can-eat Sunday brunch) and dinners are the norm at **Hop Brook Tavern** (860-651-7757; www.hopbrooktavern. com). A classic menu is served in a distinct atmosphere created by a renovated 300-year-old gristmill and waterfall.

Back in the center of town, excellent food choices include **Metro Bis** (860-651-1908; www.metrobis.com). This American bistro offers old-world Parisian fare for lunch (Sunday brunch) and dinner daily. **Evergreens** (860-651-5700; www.simsburyinn.com), located at the Simsbury Inn (see **Accommodations**), serves a classic breakfast, lunch and dinner daily. At Simsbury 1820 House (see **Accommodations**), the **1820 Café** (860-658-7658; www.simsbury1820house. com) prepares a seasonally varied menu for dinner daily.

Sakimura (860-651-7929) on Wilcox Street serves fresh Japanese lunch Tuesday through Friday and dinner, Tuesday through Sunday. Also nearby is **One-Way Fare** (860-658-4477). This onetime railroad station (1870), listed in the National Register of Historic Places, features family-friendly dining available for lunch (Sunday brunch) and dinner daily.

GETTING THERE:

Simsbury is located 12 miles north of Farmington and 28 miles southwest of Springfield, Massachusetts. Interstate highways 91 and 84 are accessible to Simsbury. Routes 185 and 10 are two of the main roads.

TRANSPORTATION:

Simsbury is located 13 miles from Bradley International Airport in Windsor Locks. Downtown Hartford's Union Station Transportation Center, a multi-model transportation center, provides Amtrak service (800-USA-RAIL) and other services. Connecticut Transit Commuter Express (860-525-9181) offers Simsbury routes.

ADDITIONAL INFORMATION:
TALCOTT MOUNTAIN STATE PARK/HEUBLEIN TOWER.
Route 185. The Heublein tower/museum is open mid-May through August, Thursday through Sunday; September through October, daily. General museum admission is by donation. (860) 424-3200. (860) 424-1158. Seasonal telephone number to gift shop: (860) 677-0662.

ARTS EXCLUSIVE GALLERY/VISITOR'S CENTER.
690 Hopmeadow Street (Route 10). The gallery and visitor's center are open all year, Tuesday through Sunday. General admission is free. Gallery: (860) 651-5824; visitor's center: (860) 658-4000.

PHELPS TAVERN MUSEUM AND HOMESTEAD.
800 Hopmeadow Street. The museum and gift shop are open mid-May through Columbus Day weekend, Tuesday through Saturday. Admission is $6.00 adults; $5.00 seniors; $4.00 children; free to children 5 and under. (860) 658-2500; www.simsburyhistory.org/phelps-tav.-mus.html.

SIMSBURY GENEALOGICAL AND HISTORICAL RESEARCH LIBRARY.
749 Hopmeadow Street. Open all year, Thursday through Saturday. General admission is free. (860) 658-5382.

INTERNATIONAL SKATING CENTER OF CONNECTICUT.
1375 Hopmeadow Street. Skating rink, pro shop and café open all year. Call for special event performances, Olympic-level workout schedule and public ice-skating schedule and rates. (860) 651-5400; www.isccskate.com.

ACCOMMODATIONS:
SIMSBURY INN.
397 Hopmeadow Street. Listed as one of the Classic Hotels of Connecticut, the inn is owned by a local hotel group that also owns and operates the Farmington Inn (see **Accommodations, Farmington** chapter). The inn is the largest in town and boasts 100 French country-style guestrooms and an on-site restaurant (see above). The premises, managed by a congenial staff, are smartly designed. Rooms include full, modern amenities; plus an indoor pool and Jacuzzi on premises. Rates (including continental breakfast): $149-$169. (860) 651-5700; www.simsburyinn.com.

SIMSBURY 1820 HOUSE.
731 Hopmeadow Street. This is a gracious country inn, complete with gambrel roof and veranda. Built in 1820 and restored to its original grandeur in 1985, it is listed on the National Register of Historic Places. The 32-room inn, providing full, modern amenities and restaurant (see **1820 Café**, above), was once home to Gifford Pinchot, Father of the American Conservation Movement, in whose memory the Simsbury sycamore (see above) was named. Rates: $149-$169. (860) 658-7658; www.simsbury1820house.com.

MERRYWOOD BED & BREAKFAST.

100 Hartford Road. Deep in the woods of six groomed acres lies an elegant Colonial Revival house filled with European furnishings and such unique accessories as 18th-century Indian robes. There are a total of two guestrooms and one suite at Merrywood with full, modern amenities. Rates (including candlelit, full, country breakfast): $150-$175. (866) 637-7993. (860) 651-1785; www.merrywoodinn. com.

LINDEN HOUSE.

288/290 Hopmeadow Street. An 1860, restored Victorian set among Talcott Mountain's unspoiled views. The house's six guestrooms each have a private bath, telephone and cable television; four have working fireplaces. Rates (including full breakfast): $140-$150. (860) 408-1321.

ANNUAL FESTIVALS/EVENTS

The Central Regional Tourism District, Connecticut's Heritage River Valley, representing 46 communities, provides a gamut of tourism information, which includes seasonal events (800) 793-4480 or (860) 244-8181; www.enjoycentralct. com. For further festival and event information, call the Farmington Valley Visitors Association (860) 676-8878; (800) 4-WELCOME or the Simsbury Chamber of Commerce (860) 651-7307.

MAY

The **Chamber Music Festival of Simsbury** complements the larger scale outdoor performances of the summertime Talcott Mountain Music Festival. Performances are held at Simsbury High School. (860) 676-8878.

Call for date and location of **springtime performances of the Simsbury Light Opera Company**, one of the oldest non-profit light opera companies in the nation. Talented, amateur performers showcase a major production annually at Simsbury High School. (860) 651-0809.

Colonial cooking, troop's drills, troop's muster, fiddlers, fife and drum corps are just some of the day's activities at the **Day of Muster** held on the grounds of Phelps Tavern Museum and Homestead. (860) 658-2500.

JUNE

The **Iron Horse Half Marathon** for runners is a scenic, flat two-loop course that begins and ends on Iron Horse Boulevard. (860) 652-8866.

JUNE/JULY

The **Talcott Mountain Summer Music Festival**, the popular summer music series, is held at the Simsbury Meadow, off Iron Horse Boulevard in the center of town. (860) 246-8742, ext. 300.

JUNE/JULY/AUGUST

The Farmington Valley Music Foundation performances of the **Summer Carillon Concert Series** are held at the Simsbury United Methodist Church. (860) 651-9962.

Simsbury Summer Theatre is held at the prestigious Westminster School in the northern end of the town center. (860) 658-4444.

Simsbury Women's Club Annual Arts & Crafts Festival is held on Iron Horse Boulevard in the center of town. (860) 651-7307.

Septemberfest is a three-day event, sponsored by the Chamber of Commerce, which showcases area businesses and restaurants, as well as community and social organizations. Entertainment for all ages is also featured all day. (860) 651-7307.

OCTOBER
Herald in the season with the **Tower Toot & Fall Festival** at Talcott Mountain State Park, Heublein Tower. (860) 677-0662.

NOVEMBER
Simsbury Historical Society's **Annual Antiques Show** is a much-anticipated, quality exhibition that is held the first weekend of November. More than 65 dealers from New England and mid-Atlantic regions display their wares during this two-day event. (860) 658-2500.

DECEMBER
Flamig Farm hosts its **Annual Breakfast with Santa and the Grinch**. Frosty and the elves also make an appearance. (860) 658-5070.

NORTHERN CONNECTICUT
Hartford County
"Heritage River Valley"
East Windsor/Windsor Locks/Suffield

One- and two-lane roads stretch open to travelers. Part of the Central Regional Tourism District, East Windsor, Windsor Locks and Suffield are sandwiched between the city of Hartford and the Massachusetts state border. Many adults who grew up here remember summers spent working on tobacco farms, helping harvest a crop, which these days plays a less vital but still important economic role. For residents or visitors, the tobacco barns, quaint farms and stately Colonials evoke a sense of nostalgia.

A cable car ride at the Connecticut Trolley Museum stirs enthusiasm in young and old alike. Also, popular with all ages is a visit to the New England Air Museum in Windsor Locks, northeast's largest aviation museum. Whether day-trippers spend a couple hours or more, fun, pure and simple, is the buzzword.

What settlement sent soldiers to fight in the Revolutionary War as well as supplied cattle and cloth to the patriot cause?

What town is one of the best for viewing black migratory ducks, and in what town would you likely bump into members of the Connecticut Butterfly Association?

Classic Farm Country: **EAST WINDSOR**

Attracted by the valley's flat terrain and fertile soil, a group of Windsor settlers migrated and began farming on the east bank of the Connecticut River in the mid-1600s. What the Puritans knew as East Windsor first included what we know today as Ellington and South Windsor. Although East Windsor became a separate town in May 1768, Ellington did not secede until 1786 and South Windsor followed suit in 1845.

The more than four and a half miles of the Connecticut River abutting East Windsor helped add shipbuilding to its economic history. During the Revolutionary War, the town supplied militia as well as cattle and cloth for the patriot cause.

Today, East Windsor, covering an area of 26.8 square miles, has a residential population just a smidgeon under 10,000. Apart from light industry and commerce, the town's rural charm is prevalent in its five villages: Broad Brook, Melrose, Scantic, Warehouse Point and Windsorville.

Anglers who desire a day trip with panache can cast a line from the banks of the Connecticut River at **Volunteer Park**, South Water Street. The **Scantic River** and its tributaries, plus **Broad Brook Pond** are two other public-fishing outlets.

Scantic River is also a bird lovers' hot spot, especially to espy black migratory ducks. Southwest on Tromley Road, the **John Flaherty Field Trail Area** attracts four-season day-trippers. Weather permitting, the trail area provides excellent ground for cross-country skiers. During milder weather, fragrant wildflowers attract throngs of butterflies. Typically, not far behind are members of the Connecticut Butterfly Association, the first organization in the state devoted exclusively to the study, observation, appreciation and preservation of butterflies and moths.

At 115 Scantic Road is the **East Windsor Academy Museum**, also the headquarters for the East Windsor Historical Society (860-623-3149). Open only on Sunday mornings, proceeds from the society's numerous fund-raising campaigns have helped renovate the onetime schoolhouse. Showcased inside are, among other things, Native American artifacts, early textile machinery, farm implements, weapons and military uniforms. Visitors can also peek inside a vintage barbershop and tobacco shed that complement the property.

Less than three miles from Scantic Road and by far the most popular attraction in East Windsor is the **Connecticut Trolley Museum**, Route 140. The Connecticut Railway Association operates the museum complex sprawling on 17 acres. Founded in 1940, this is the nation's oldest incorporated organization dedicated to the preservation of the trolley era—once so prominent in East Windsor's heyday.

The association owns over 70 pieces of rolling stock that dates back to 1869 and includes passenger and freight streetcars, interurban cars, elevated railway cars, service cars, locomotives, passenger and freight railroad cars. Approximately half the collection is stored in barns where guests can gauge trolley restoration efforts.

The visit's highlight is aboard a three-mile roundtrip streetcar ride. Hear the volunteer conductors' nostalgic stories about such things as the many marriage proposals that transpired on these vehicles! Competing with glitzy amusement park giants, trolley survival has been tough going, but devoted volunteer staff members have not only endured, but have moved forward (much like the antique cars) through what must surely total millions of volunteer hours and a love so great, they probably hear trolley bells in their sleep!

The **Connecticut Fire Museum**, adjacent to the trolley museum, holds a glistening fire truck collection dating from 1850 to 1967. This small building, resembling a hangar, also contains an impressive display of fire-fighting equipment and related memorabilia.

The Warehouse Point vicinity indulges any shopper's desire for style and charm. Day-trippers who seek breakfast or lunch should stop at **Good Mornings** (860-623 5056), 44 Bridge Street, open daily. A popular 24/7 area institution, **East Windsor Diner** (860-627-0124) has been going strong for more than 30 years on South Main Street. The family-owned operation offers homemade cooking at reasonable prices, breakfast anytime, an early-bird and children's menu and the fresh taste of Omar Coffee, a local favorite (see **Hartford** chapter). South Main's **Nutmeg Restaurant** (860-627-7094; www.nutmegrestaurant.com) attracts diners near and far with its daily fine dining lunch/dinner menu (Sunday brunch). For listening pleasure, musicians perform after dinner, Friday and Saturday. Named after a Revolutionary War officer, **Jonathan Pasco's** (860-627-7709), 31 East Main, open daily, provides a late 18th-century restaurant ambiance. A continental, American dinner menu (Sunday brunch) has achieved a loyal following.

GETTING THERE:
East Windsor is located midway between Hartford and Springfield, Massachusetts. Two major highways, U.S. 5 and I-91, traverse the western part of town. Interstate Highway 84 is within 10 minutes.

TRANSPORTATION:
East Windsor is located 10 minutes away from Bradley International Airport (860-292-2000) in Windsor Locks. Amtrak commuter trains (800-USA-RAIL) stop in Windsor center from Springfield to New Haven with connections to Boston and New York. Connecticut Transit buses (860-525-9181; Enfield-Somers/Windsor Locks Express) provide arrivals and departures at Warehouse Point.

ADDITIONAL INFORMATION:
CONNECTICUT TROLLEY MUSEUM.
58 North Road (Route 140). Call for days and hours of operation, April through December; closed January 1 through March 31 or open by appointment. Admission is $6.00 adults; $5.00 seniors; $3.00 children and free to children 2 and under. (860) 627-6540; www.bera.org.

CONNECTICUT FIRE MUSEUM.
58 North Road. Open during the summer months; call for days and hours of operation. General admission to the Connecticut Fire Museum is free with Connecticut Trolley Museum admission. (860) 623-4732.

ACCOMMODATIONS:
BEST WESTERN COLONIAL INN.
161 Bridge Street. Conveniently located near Interstate 91, the inn offers 121 guestrooms. Amenities include outdoor pool, whirlpool and on-premises restaurant and lounge. Rates: $69-$99-plus. (860) 623-9411.

ANNUAL FESTIVALS/EVENTS
The Central Regional Tourism District, Connecticut's Heritage River Valley, representing 46 communities, provides a gamut of tourism information, which includes seasonal events (800) 793-4480 or (860) 244-8181; www.enjoycentralct.com. For additional festival and event information, contact the town of East Windsor, (860) 627-6662 or the East Windsor Town Hall, (860) 623-8122.

MAY
Join the many other spectators at Warehouse Point for the **Annual Memorial Day Parade and Town-wide Weekend Festivities**. (860) 627-6662.

OCTOBER

For fun and games, a visit to the pumpkin patch and unlimited trolley rides, go to the Connecticut Trolley Museum during the **Annual Pumpkin Patch Day**. (860) 627-6540; www.bera.org.

The Connecticut Chapter of the March of Dimes presents the **Annual Chef's Auction of Greater Hartford** at East Windsor's La Renaissance, a banquet and catering facility. The evening is full of celebrities, food and silent and live auctions. (860) 290-5440.

NOVEMBER

Revay's Garden and Gift Shop, 266 North Road, presents the arrival of **Teddy the Talking Tree** who comes from the deep woodlands to visit. (860) 623-8012.

NOVEMBER/DECEMBER

The Connecticut Trolley Museum offers unlimited rides during **WinterFest** on an electric sleigh or in a closed, heated trolley as travelers enjoy more than 6,000 lights decorating the premises. (860) 627-6540;www.bera.org.

Connecticut Trolley Museum
See page 56

*It's worth the trip...
all aboard!*

Photos Courtesy of Connecticut Trolley Museum

What did people call Pine Meadow for nearly 200 years
before officially naming the Connecticut town?

What town encompasses one of the smallest areas
in the state and owns one of the oldest
Connecticut weekly newspapers?

Historic Canal Heritage: **WINDSOR LOCKS**

Meandering on the west bank of the Connecticut River, 12 miles north of Hartford, the original Windsor settlers encountered the territory we now know as Windsor Locks and purchased the land parcel from native Indians in 1634. Through those early years, following the Connecticut River Valley trend, tobacco was the principal cash crop.

In 1829, the town constructed a canal with locks, incorporating a hydraulic lift system that allowed canal water to fill up, enabling riverboats to sail through the otherwise impassable shallow rapids of the Connecticut River. Thus began a new trade route between the northern settlements and western Massachusetts. In honor of the successful economic impact of the canal, the community changed the original town's name Pine Meadow to Windsor Locks, nearly 200 years after English settlement. Officials incorporated the town in 1854. Additionally, engineers implemented a trolley car system served by the Hartford and Springfield Street Railway to run alongside the canal. After the advent of the railroad, the canal functioned as a power source for area mills. Today, the mills and trolleys are mere memories.

Leading to the west of East Windsor, the canal still parallels the river. With a population just above 12,000 residents, Windsor Locks is primarily a suburban community, still a small-scale tobacco producer, attracting a solid base of industry including aerospace. This town, one of the state's smallest, owns one of the oldest Connecticut weekly newspapers, the *Windsor Locks Journal*.

Constructed in 1941, **Bradley International Airport**, the second largest airport in New England, comprises about one-sixth of the town's 9.2 square miles. The airport boasting numerous terminal, concourse and roadway improvements, located on Route 75, is an advisable starting point for a day trip with panache. A host of brochures describing area attractions, accommodations and restaurants is available in the airport's visitor information area. Also, look for the *Airport News*, containing airport-related, tourism and business news, plus restaurant reviews.

At the airport headquarters is the **New England Air Museum**, the largest aviation museum in the northeastern United States. It offers more than 75,000 square feet of exhibit space. The exhibitions in the military hangar and the connecting civil aviation hangar account for more than 80 aircrafts and nearly 153 engines; plus a host of uniforms and other memorabilia. The 58th Bomb Wing (a significant bombardment group of World War II) is one of the museum's most recent exhibits.

Witness the Silas Brooks Balloon Basket (1870), the oldest surviving aircraft in the United States. View a Gulf War fighter plane. Marvel at the Exambian, one of the largest flying boats ever built, took nearly 10 years to restore, and is the museum's crown jewel.

Other museum holdings include helicopters, jets and trophy-winning race cars. Another exhibit is devoted to Ukrainian-born Igor Sikorsky, founder of Sikorsky Aircraft, located in nearby Stratford. Milder weather allows visitors to tour the outside storage yard full of other interesting aircrafts. During Open Cockpit Weekends, visitors can role-play their favorite aviation heroes.

About four minutes away, across from the National Army Guard, Perimeter Road, is the **Connecticut Fire Academy** (860-627-6363). Throughout the year, day-trippers can view the monument accompanied by an eternal flame memorializing Connecticut firefighters who died in the course of duty.

About six minutes due east is the **Noden-Reed House and Barn**. Operated by the Windsor Locks Historical Society since 1976, a 22-acre town park (and nature trails) surrounds the Victorian 1840 house and 1826 adjacent brick barn. Listed on the National Register of Historic Places, legend has it that the site was home to Connecticut's first Christmas tree in 1777. As the story goes, a Hessian soldier, held captive during the Revolutionary War, was the first to introduce this Christmas custom from his homeland to the colony. The house collection exudes a sense of country motifs, including old jugs, bottles, wooden utensils and hand-stitched quilts. Barn accessories include sleek horse and buggy carriages and farmer's tools.

Go-kart enthusiasts are familiar—or should be—with **Kart Trak** (860-623-3377; www.karttrak.com), the state's only indoor racing course. The facility is open Tuesday through Sunday on 62 Lawn Acre Road, about eight minutes from the airport.

Anglers can take advantage of shad runs at the head of the tidewater navigation of the **Connecticut River** just below the **Enfield Dam**. Rumors circulate about the creation of a fishing-access park alongside the bike canal. The local bait and tackle shop is **Joe's** (860-623-7980), 12 Dickerman Avenue.

Meanwhile, directly off Route 159, bikers and walkers can experience nearly six miles of level terrain through the canals and locks of the **Windsor Locks Canal**, situated along the historic Connecticut rapids. With plenty of interesting birds and other wildlife on route, horses that once pulled the boat traffic through the canal used the Toe Path, as locals call it today.

Back around the airport hub, there are a multitude of Chinese take-outs and fast-food establishments, including a McDonald's on Ella Grasso Boulevard (named for Connecticut's popular former governor) boasting a replica of an airplane as its roof décor and, indoors, an aircraft photograph display. On the Ella Grasso Turnpike strip, **Skyline Restaurant** (860-623-9296) specializes in Italian-American cuisine for lunch and dinner daily. Open for dinner daily, **Albert's Restaurant & Cigar Bar** (860-292-6801) offers a wide selection of after-dinner cigars. Breakfast, lunch and dinner are available daily at **Concorde's** (860-627-5311), stationed directly inside the Sheraton Hotel (see **Accommodations**), offering a menu with a seafood emphasis; swordfish being one of the specialties.

GETTING THERE:

Windsor Locks is located midway between Hartford and Springfield, Massachusetts. Two major highways, U.S. 5 and I-91 traverse the eastern part of town. Interstate Highway 84 is within 15 minutes.

TRANSPORTATION:

Windsor Locks has its own major airport, Bradley International Airport (860-292-2000). Amtrak (800-USA-RAIL) services Windsor Locks. Connecticut Transit buses (860-525-9181) serve the needs of commuters throughout Windsor Locks.

ADDITIONAL INFORMATION:

NEW ENGLAND AIR MUSEUM.

Bradley International Airport, Schoephoester Road, Route 75. Open all year, daily. Call to inquire about special events. An on-premises research library (call for hours of operation) is open for both members and non-members of the museum every Tuesday and the second and fourth Saturday of each month. Admission is $8.00 adults; $7.00 seniors; $4.00 children, and free to children 5 and under and to museum members. (860) 623-3305; www.neam.org.

NODEN-REED HOUSE AND BARN.

58 West Street. Open May through October, Wednesday and Sunday and by appointment. Inquire about special events. (860) 627-9212.

ACCOMMODATIONS:

(There are approximately eight national chains of hotels/motels, most within five minutes of Bradley International Airport.)

SHERATON BRADLEY INTERNATIONAL AIRPORT HOTEL.

1 Bradley International Airport. There are 237 guestrooms providing full, modern amenities. Other amenities include health club, indoor pool and on-premises restaurant, Concorde's (860-627-5311; see above). Rates: $99-$159. (860) 627-5311; (877) 422-5311.

ANNUAL FESTIVALS/EVENTS

The Central Regional Tourism District, Connecticut's Heritage River Valley, representing 46 communities, provides a gamut of tourism information, which includes seasonal events (800) 793-4480 or (860) 244-8181; www.enjoycentralct. com. For additional festival and event information, contact the Windsor Locks Chamber of Commerce (860) 623-9319 or the town clerk's office, (860) 627-1444.

JUNE

Sponsored by the Connecticut Council of Car Clubs, enthusiasts hold the **Auto Show and Aircraft Exhibit** at the New England Air Museum that highlights antique, classic, special interest, sports cars, and street rods. (860) 623-3906; (860) 526-5729; www.neam.org.

JULY

Volunteers organize Windsor Lock's **Firemen's Carnival** annually during a designated date and place. (860) 627-1444.

What town was the subject of a bitter land dispute between
Massachusetts and Connecticut that lasted for nearly two centuries?

What town did the inventor of the Graham Cracker hail from?

Timeless Masterpiece: SUFFIELD

Colonial people called the heavily timbered route between Springfield, Massachusetts, and Windsor, Connecticut, the Hampton path. Local Indian encampments were primarily around Congamond Lake and the Manatuck Mountains. In 1670, Major John Pynchon, a Springfield fur merchant, paid the Indians 30 pounds for the land by then recognized as the Stony Brooke Plantation. The Commonwealth of Massachusetts incorporated the settlement, which included Springfield, in 1674. At that time, the pioneers changed the name of the territory to "Suffield," a derivative of "Southfield," a geographic identity of the land. For nearly two centuries, Suffield became a subject of bitter land disputes between the two colonies until 1803, when it fell under the jurisdiction of Connecticut.

Following the Connecticut River Valley trend, tobacco was the chief crop. Suffield entrepreneurs built the first cigar factory in the United States in 1810. At different times the town was home to two paper mills, a distillery-cider mill, a cotton mill, a water spring rumored to be curative and called "the Pool" (at the end of Poole Road), a one-half mile horse race track and the town's own newspaper, the *Impartial Herald*. One famous resident born in West Suffield in 1794 was Sylvester Graham, an American reformer and Presbyterian minister. He goes down in history for his invention of—you guessed it—Graham Crackers!

These days, although tobacco farming has diminished, in warmer weather, the appearance of white tents on shade-grown tobacco fields and tractors hauling broadleaf tobacco to awaiting barns remains tradition. Today, Suffield, covering 43.1 square miles, with a residential population of about 11,500, also boasts dairy and agricultural farms, numerous 4-H Clubs and the Helena Bailey Spencer Tree Fund, which plants and cares for trees along the town's highways.

Bordered on the east by the Connecticut River and the west by the Congamond Lakes, day trips with panache follow a walking map of **Suffield's Main Street** (Route 75), compliments of the Suffield Historical Society and the Antiquarian and Landmarks Society, which the town hall distributes.

The 4.3-mile Route 75 stretch is part of the Suffield Historic District, designated a State Scenic Highway. Seeped in charm, shaded by more than 100 dogwood and other trees, lined by 18th- and 19th-century Colonial and Victorian homes, the bulk of Main Street includes a green that meanders gently from the northwest to the southeast.

Examples of buildings dotting the Suffield Green include the **First Congregational Church**, **Second Baptist Church** and the **Kent Memorial Library**, containing the **Spencer Historical Room** that has amassed an outstanding collection of source materials, records, and documents pertaining to north central Connecticut. **Suffield Academy**, the prominent boarding school designed for high school-age boys and girls, located on a 350-acre campus, anchors the town green to the west.

Two notable museums in this central locale of specialty retail shops are great for day trips. Listed on the National Register of Historic Places, the **Alexander King House**, on the corner of Kent Avenue, is the museum of the Suffield Historical

Society. Built in 1764, the center-chimney mansion drawing distinction with its long porch was the home of a prominent physician. Among the period furnishings, other interesting exhibits emphasizing local history are a rare collection of tobacco and cigar-related memorabilia, surgical instruments from the Civil War era, and collections of flasks, bottles and Bennington Pottery.

Farther north on Main is the **Phelps-Hatheway House**, operated by the Antiquarian and Landmarks Society and the Suffield Historical Society. Under the umbrella of a 300-year-old sycamore and surrounded by gardens abloom in the summer, the interior of the house, first built in 1760, represents three periods of 18th-century architecture. The interior ranges from modest rooms to those of lavish proportion, illustrating the accumulation of wealth of real estate tycoon Oliver Phelps. The white clapboard Colonial also showcases some of the earliest examples of Neo-Classical-style architecture in the Connecticut River Valley and rare patterned French wallpaper in its original condition.

Interesting to note is that in the 1950s, before the house became a museum, historians removed one of the entire rooms and sold it to the Winterthur Museum in Delaware. In exchange, the Winterthur staff built and installed an exact room replica (of the one removed) back into the house!

From Main Street to High Street, approximately three-fourths of the route has been designated as the Hastings Hill Historic District. Day-trippers should note the examples of Greek Revival and early 18th-century architecture. In addition, the **First Baptist Church**, organized by Joseph Hastings in 1769, is the earliest Baptist Church in Hartford County and one of the first in Connecticut. Hastings's gravestone stands north of the church.

Day-trippers who prefer riding horses should check out the full-service equestrian facilities in the area: **Echo-Ridge Training Center** (860-668-5393) and the **Wishing Rock Farm** (860-668-2307). Golfers also have options: **Airways Golf Course and Country Club** (860-668-4973) and **Vic Svenberg's Total Practice Center** (860-668-5700), a full-practice driving range.

For more than 50 years, the **Suffield Players** (800-289-6148; www.suffieldplayers. org), a community theatrical group, have been entertaining theatergoers with a variety of contemporary plays and musicals. The troupe stages three annual performances at Mapleton Hall, located in the northeast corner of Suffield, a carefully restored and preserved building dating back to 1883.

Outdoorsy types do not have to look far for recreation. **West Suffield Mountain**, which includes Talcott Mountain and the Heublein Tower (see **Simsbury** chapter); dominates Suffield's town center. Mountain Road provides a picturesque motorist's tour of the area; its highest point above sea level measures 710 feet. **Over the Mountain Cemetery**, located on Phelps Road, presents a menagerie of interesting colonial gravestones.

The most popular trail, the Metacomet, meanders along the mountain's crest and is a blue-blazed Connecticut Forest & Parks Association Trail. **Spencer Woods**, owned and maintained by the Suffield Light Conservancy, is accessible at the junction of Route 168 and Phelps Street. The westerly climb is a relatively easy 1.54-mile hike through the northern section of the Metacomet Trail and leads about 150 feet to the top of the ridge with panoramic valley views awaiting. Embark on the miles of other trails at the **Farmington River Canal** and **Windsor Locks Canal Trail**, which runs from Windsor Locks to Suffield.

In the winter, cross-country skiing is also available to the public at **Lewis-Farm Wildlife Sanctuary**. For public picnicking, cross-country skiing, hiking and permit-only camping, try **Jesse F. Smith Memorial Forest** and **Stony Brook Park**.

The **Congamond Lakes** are accessible via Route 168, and are located on the Connecticut and Massachusetts border. Summer activities include boating, canoeing, fishing and swimming. **Connecticut River** forms Suffield's eastern border with plenty of fishing areas at the end of Canal Road.

"Pick-your-own" farmers' markets, such as **Kuras Farms** (860-668-2942), 1901 Mountain Road in West Suffield, are a summer tradition.

For a cappuccino, bagel or roll, try **Atlas Coffee House** (860-668-7230), located on Bridge Street, which is open past dinner hour, and features musicians, poets and the like on random Saturday nights. **Suffield Pizza and Family Restaurant** (860-668-7774) is a good option for lunch and dinner daily on Bridge Street.

The gamut of eateries located on Mountain Road include **Chang's Gourmet Cuisine** (860-668-9889), open for lunch and dinner daily; **Francescos** (860-668-0200), offering Italian cuisine for lunch and dinner, Tuesday through Sunday (no lunch Sunday); **Zanto** (860-668-2421), also providing an Italian-style menu for lunch and dinner daily (no lunch Sunday), and **Suffield Inn** (860-668-0219), a family-style restaurant specializing in seafood and steak, serving lunch and dinner, Tuesday through Sunday.

GETTING THERE:

Suffield is located about four miles north of Windsor Locks; 13 miles south of Springfield, Massachusetts and 18 miles north of Hartford. The town is easily accessible from Interstate Highway 91. Route 168 is Suffield's major east-west connector and it travels over West Suffield Mountain.

TRANSPORTATION:

Suffield is located about 10 minutes away from Bradley International Airport (860-292-2000) in Windsor Locks. Downtown Hartford's Union Station Transportation Center, a multi-model transportation area, provides scheduled Amtrak service (800-USA-RAIL) and other services. The Hartford Express (Granby-Bloomfield Express) offers limited weekday rush hour service in Tariffville, about 10 miles from Suffield, with connecting routes to the town of Suffield (860) 525-9181.

ADDITIONAL INFORMATION:

DR. ALEXANDER KING HOUSE.

232 South Main Street (Route 75). Open May through September, Wednesday and Saturday. General admission is by donation. (860) 668-5256; www.suffield-library.org/localhistory/king.htm.

HATHEWAY HOUSE.

55 South Main Street. Open mid-May through mid-October, Wednesday, Friday, Saturday and Sunday. Call for general admission price. (860) 668-0055; (860) 247-8996; www.suffield-library.org/localhistory/hatheway.htm.

ANNUAL FESTIVALS/EVENTS

The Central Regional Tourism District, Connecticut's Heritage River Valley, representing 46 communities, provides a gamut of tourism information, which includes seasonal events (800) 793-4480 or (860) 244-8181; www.enjoycentralct.com. For additional festival and event information, contact the Parks & Recreation Department at (860) 668-3896 or the Suffield Chamber of Commerce at (860) 668-4848.

MARCH
Suffield Business Showcase & Taste of Suffield is sponsored by the Chamber of Commerce and is a showcase of local businesses and restaurants. (860) 668-4848.

MAY
The weekend after Mother's Day, the Suffield Garden Club sponsors a **May Market**, accented with house and garden tours. (860) 668-4897.

JUNE
The **Annual Suffield Firemen's 5K Race, Run and Non-Competitive Walk**, begins on South Grand Street at West Suffield Center. (860) 668-0505.

JUNE/JULY/AUGUST/SEPTEMBER/OCTOBER
Look for **Farmers' Markets** held on Saturday at the Suffield Town Green. (860) 668-4848.

JULY
Sponsored by the Suffield Firemen's Association, the **Firemen's Carnival** includes amusement rides, Firemen's Parade and fireworks. (860) 668-4848.

JULY/AUGUST
Concerts on the Green are held every Wednesday throughout the month at the gazebo on the town green. (860) 668-3862.

SEPTEMBER
Comprising the largest weekend event of the year, thousands of people visit the **Suffield on the Green** activities, which include food and games. (860) 668-4848.

Runners from around the state and beyond look forward to the **Annual 10K Road Race and 2.3 Mile Fun Run**. For location and further information call, (860) 668-3896.

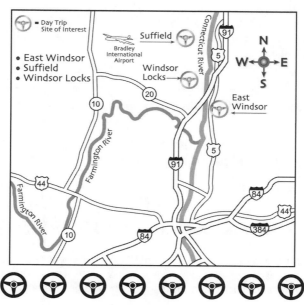

II.

NORTHEAST CONNECTICUT
Tolland County
"Quiet Corner"
Coventry/Storrs/Mansfield

Coventry begins, as tourism officials dub, "the Gateway to Northeastern Connecticut's Quiet Corner." A 27-town region, encompassing more than 745 square miles, represents the "Quiet Corner," part of the Quinebaug and Shetucket Rivers Valley National Heritage Corridor, barely touched by the mass modernization of the surrounding region. The towns of Coventry and Mansfield, including the village of Storrs, home of the University of Connecticut's main campus, are located in Tolland County; within a 10-mile drive of each other.

The National Park Service recognizes Coventry and Mansfield along with 19 other Connecticut and out-of-state towns as the "Last Green Valley," representing the last 1,085 square miles of undeveloped land (foliage seekers make note!) recognizable from an aircraft or satellite between Boston and Washington, D.C.

Day trips to these Connecticut treasures unlock historic mill villages, farmlands, old stonewalls, a world-renowned herb farm, cozy bed and breakfasts, antiques shopping, a vineyard, a public beach and state boat launch on Coventry Lake, also known as Lake Wangumbaug. Nature seekers have a host of other naturalist opportunities at Mansfield Hollow Lake and State Park. Adults or children with a sweet tooth needn't go farther than tasting the homemade ice cream at the University of Connecticut's Dairy Bar. In the mood for nostalgia? Catch a flick at one of the last surviving drive-in movie theaters in the state. The Quiet Corner adds punch to the cliché, "Have a good day!"

What settlement did a Mohegan sachem will to colonial settlers?

What town is famed for its 19th-century glassmaking; the glass pieces today, prized by collectors?

Herbal Bouquet: COVENTRY

Situated in valleys of rolling hills (think artist's paintbrush, canvas and easel), historians believe early pioneers named present-day Coventry after the English town of Coventry. Joshua, sachem, and third son of the famous Mohegan chief, Uncas, bequeathed the land to early settlers as a sign of friendship. The Connecticut State Library in Hartford preserves the will records. After some land disputes between Indian tribe members and early settlers, Coventry was incorporated in 1712.

Colonial maps, dating as early as 1708, reveal area allotments for a school, church and gristmill operations on Mill Brook. By the 1800s, at least 17 working mills enhanced the local economy beyond an agriculture-based town. Coventry's manufactured items included wool, cloth, cotton yarn and sewing silk, an especially prevalent product in Mansfield (see **Storrs/Mansfield** chapter).

The Coventry Glass Factory, one of many factories operating during the 19th century, is another example of historic heritage leaving a permanent, distinguishing mark on the town. Today, spread over about 37 square miles, on the Willimantic River, Coventry (locals pronounce it CAH-ven-tree) is about 34 minutes from Hartford, boasting a population of 11,500.

Day trips with panache begin on historic South Street, off Routes 44 and 6, which was, along with Cross Street, the town's first road. Even though Nathan Hale never stepped inside South Street's **Nathan Hale Homestead**, listed on the National Register of Historic Places, the site is a popular addition to any day's itinerary. Out of the more than 100 Coventry men who served in the Revolutionary War, most famous was the onetime, Connecticut schoolteacher, Nathan Hale, who is the official state hero. Centuries of history books have immortalized the army captain's final words: "I only regret that I have but one life to lose for my country."

His family built the South Street house in 1776, the same year the British hanged 21-year-old Hale for being a spy in what's now New York City. However, Hale had spent his childhood in a former (now demolished) house that had been at the same site.

The homestead, operated and managed by the Antiquarian & Landmarks Society, is a showcase of original family furnishings and mementos down to Hale's shoe buckles and his shadow portrait traced over a door, said to be the only existing picture of him.

The homestead stands on 12 acres of fields and forests, vegetable and period flower gardens, crisscrossed with original stonewalls, all nestled near the 500-acre **Hale State Forest**, of which 400 acres once belonged to the Hale family. For a nominal fee, hikers, horseback riders and interested wayfarers can pick up a map in the 18th-century barn, which doubles as the homestead's gift shop. Before final exit, view the video about Hale's life. (His historical impact makes it understandable why he serves as state hero!)

Just west of Nathan Hale Homestead on South Street is an early 18th-century farmhouse, along with assorted outbuildings, the **Strong-Porter House**, formerly owned by Captain Hale's maternal ancestors. Also listed on the National Register of Historic Places, the five-room house contains local history exhibits. The **Coventry Historical Society** (860-742-9025; www.coventrycthistoricalsociety.org) runs the house museum. The society itself is headquartered in the **Elias Sprague House** (circa 1821), 2187 South Street, another dwelling listed on the National Register of Historic Places, located west of the Nathan Hale Homestead.

What could be more American than the **Nathan Hale Ancient Fifes and Drums** (www.bobcastillo.com/nathan.htm)? Started in 1965, this is not only a remarkable performing group, but also the official owners of two other South Street buildings, the Blacksmith Shop and the Weaver Shop; on occasion, there is talk to renovate and open the sites to the public.

Approximately one mile north on Silver Street is **Caprilands Herb Farm**. Lots of speculation surrounded the 50-acre farm after proprietress Adelma Grenier Simmons died in 1997 at the age of 97. A worldwide celebrity in her own right; Simmons was to modern-day herbs in North America what Alexander Graham Bell was to the telephone. In 1929, she established what historians today consider America's oldest herb farm, Caprilands—named after the goat farm that had previously stood on the Silver Street property. ("Capri" means "goat" in Latin.) Because of its herbal patroness, Coventry has become synonymous with Caprilands and tourists from all over the world visit "America's herbal farm stand."

Capriland's more than 30 herb gardens, representing about 300 varieties of herbs, rouse every sense. Likewise, day-trippers still partake in a series of lectures-luncheon programs that Mrs. Simmons once hosted in her greenhouse and 18th-century farmhouse. In addition, guests can purchase dozens of "herbal bibles" by the prolific author along with other herbal-themed specialties at the farm's gift barn.

Within a two-mile radius of Caprilands, there are two other establishments associated with high-quality herbs. From April 15 to October 1, the greenhouse and fields are open at **Topmost Herb Farm** (860-742-8239; www.topmostherbfarm. com). Check out the farm's array of interesting lectures and special events. Open all year are **South River Herbals Shop and Education Center** (860-742-1258; www. southriverherbals.com) offering special events and classes (soap making anyone?) for both adults and children.

In addition, open year-round, within a three-minute drive from Caprilands, is **Edmondson's Farm** (860-742-6124; www.edmondsonsfarm.com) at 2627 Boston Turnpike. This family-owned fruit, produce and herb farm boasts greenhouses and gardens along with country gift and floral shops. Expect pick-your-own fruit and vegetables in the summer and hayrides pulled by a tractor and horse in the fall.

Traveling eastbound, the **Museum of Connecticut Glass** is located on Route 44 at North River Road in the **John Turner House**, earlier home of 19th-century glassblower, John Turner. Also managed and maintained by the Coventry Historical Society, the museum, dedicated to the preservation and research of historical glass, showcases free-blow and mouth-blow styles and many other glasswares including a variety of bottles and other glass products made at the Coventry Glass Factory during a span of nearly 37 years. Opened sporadically, the building denotes the **Coventry Glass Factory Historic District**. A number of 19th-century houses near the site of the long-ago demolished Coventry Glass Factory (c.1813-1845) forms the district listed on the National Register of Historic Places.

Although hours are limited, while in this vicinity, day-trippers may want to include a stop at the **Brick School House** at Merrow Road at the intersection of Goose Lane. Another property managed and maintained by the Coventry Historical Society, the schoolhouse, built between 1823 and 1825, provided pupils with a one-room district school until 1953. In 1976, historians restored and accessorized the building with mid-19th-century furnishings. South about two miles, crossing back over Boston Turnpike, the road takes day-trippers to another laudable listing on the National Register of Historic Places, **Coventry Village**. **Coventry Lake**, (AKA **Wangumbaug Lake**), well known by water-sports enthusiasts, paints a dramatic backdrop. Eighteenth-century houses, modeled in Colonial, Greek Revival, Italianate and Queen Anne-styles, take center stage around the triangular-shaped **Coventry Green**. Hundreds of thousands of daffodils bloom every spring and are just one gift bestowed by the Coventry Village Main Street Partnership, a non-profit volunteer organization founded in 1993. This civic group coordinates and promotes community projects in and around the village.

Another not-for-profit community group is the Preservation Committee (860-742-6917) founded in 1999. The committee's handiwork of cleaning up weathered and littered gravestones can be viewed by day-trippers in **Nathan Hale Cemetery**, where volunteers have spruced up approximately 25, 18th-century stones. The committee offers walking tours of the Lake Street cemetery, home to more than 175 gravestones from the colonial period. (No one can overlook the imposing granite monument dedicated to Hale!)

The **Visitor's Center** (860-742-1085) on Main Street (Route 31) furnishes tourists with brochures, postcards and pertinent area information. Souvenir shoppers can also purchase cookbooks ($10 each): *Exclusively Broccoli, Exclusively Blueberry, Exclusively Rhubarb, Exclusively Pumpkin* and *Exclusively Corn* published by the Coventry Historical Society.

While at the center, pick up a self-guided walking tour brochure of Millbrook Walkway, located just outside the center. On route, view the stone ruins of Tracy Shoddy Mill. Downtown is a concentration of antiques centers and specialty shops. One of the largest sources for antiques in the vicinity (Route 44 and Boston Turnpike) is **Memory Lanes Countryside Antiques Center** (860-742-0346; www.memory-lanes.com/memory-lanes/memorylanes/default.htm), a multi-dealer shop lodged in more than 5,000 square feet.

Wine connoisseurs may want to journey off-the-beaten track to **Nutmeg Vineyards Farm Winery** (860-742-8402; call for days and hours of operation), a cottage-size winery at 800 Bunker Hill Road, featuring wine tasting and vineyard walks. Additionally, golfers have a choice of two public courses in Coventry: **Skungamaug River Golf Club** (860-742-9348; www.skungamauggolf.com/index.htm) on Folly Lane and **Twin Hills Country Club** (860-742-9705), Route 31.

One popular Main Street eatery for lunch and dinner daily includes the homemade goodness of **Bea's Country Kitchen** (860-742-7255). Don't forget to say "hi!" to Bea. South Coventry's **Bidwell Tavern** (860-742-6978) at 1260 Main Street offers a pub-style lunch and dinner menu daily in an ambiance that only a 1822-Colonial tavern, complete with overhead beams and wood-planked floor, can extend. Day-trippers can enjoy the woodstove in the winter or summertime dining on the deck. Just look for the horse (not real) outside. In North Coventry at 3444 Main, **Dimitri's Pizza Restaurant** (860-742-7373) provides a perfect family atmosphere for lunch and dinner, Tuesday through Sunday.

GETTING THERE:

Coventry is located 34 minutes from Hartford and 25 minutes from the University of Connecticut and Interstate 84. Interstate 395 connects to numerous routes that reach the town of Coventry.

TRANSPORTATION:

Coventry is located approximately 33 miles from Bradley International Airport (860-292-2000) in Windsor Locks. Downtown Hartford's Union Station Transportation Center, a multi-model transportation center, provides scheduled

Amtrak service (800-USA-RAIL) and other services. The Willimantic-Coventry Commuter Bus Arrow Line (800-243-9560) serves the Coventry area.

ADDITIONAL INFORMATION:

NATHAN HALE HOMESTEAD.
2299 South Street. Open mid-May through mid-October, Wednesday through Sunday or by appointment. The grounds, first floor of the museum and the gift shop are handicapped accessible. General admission is $4.00 adults; $4.00 youth (up to 18) and students with valid ID and free to children 6 and under and to Antiquarian & Landmarks Society members. (860) 742-6917; www.hartnet.org/als/nathanhale.

STRONG-PORTER HOUSE MUSEUM.
2382 South Street. Open mid-May through mid-October on the first and third weekends of the month. Call for hours of operation and for general admission prices. (860) 742-9025; www.coventrycthistoricalsociety.org.

CAPRILANDS HERB FARM.
534 Silver Street. Open all year, daily. The staff serves high tea April through December, Sundays at 2 p.m. June through October the luncheon-lecture program is conducted in the farmhouse Saturdays at noon. Reservations for high tea and luncheons are required. Free entrance to the grounds. Fee for lecture, luncheons and teas. (860) 742-7244; www.caprilands.com.

BRICK SCHOOL HOUSE.
Merrow Rd. Open mid-May through mid-October, Sundays. General admission is free. (860) 742-9025; www.coventrycthistoricalsociety.org.

COVENTRY LAKE.
Offers swimming, motor boating, canoeing, water-skiing and ice fishing in the winter. A public beach is open from mid-June until Labor Day. **Patriot's Park** consists of 17 acres by the lake that features a community center and lodge available for group rental. It also features a playscape, pavilion, band shell picnic area with grills and free parking. Call (860) 742-4068.

ACCOMMODATIONS:

SPECIAL JOYS BED & BREAKFAST/DOLL AND TOY SHOP.
41 North River Road. Both the solo traveler and traveling couples will encounter sweet dreams—among a throng of antique dolls and toys inside this pink, Cape Cod-style home turned Victorian. The three guestrooms, each with private entrance and two with private baths, are immaculately crisp and detailed with Victorian-style accessories. Note: Proprietress Joy Kelleher also runs the museum/shop, displaying such treasures as Steiff dolls and animals, French fashion dolls, toy furniture and vintage doll clothes, and opens it free to day-trippers, Thursday through Sunday. Rates (including country breakfasts served in the conservatory): $55-$70. (860) 742-6359; www.antiquing.com/shops/specjoy.

BIRD-IN-HAND B & B.

2011 Main Street (Route 31). A former tavern, this 1731 Colonial offers four bedrooms, three with fireplaces, private baths and full breakfast. Children over 10 welcome. Rates (including full breakfast): $90-$150 per night, double occupancy. (860) 742-0032; www.thebirdinhand.com.

ANNUAL FESTIVALS/EVENTS

Mystic Country/CONNECTICUT representing 42 communities, provides a gamut of tourism information, which includes seasonal events (800) 863-6569 or (860) 444-2206; www.ctquietcorner.com or www.mysticcountry.com. For additional festival and event information, contact the Coventry Visitor's Center, (860) 742-1085; the Tolland County Chamber of Commerce (860) 872-0587; the Booth & Dimock Memorial Library (860) 742-7606 and/or the Coventry Recreation Department (860) 742-4068.

JANUARY

Stew and Story Night has become an annual sellout event hosted by the Coventry Historical Society. Everyone sits around the fireplace and enjoys a hearth-cooked meal as readers share stories. (860) 742-9025.

A **Family Ice Fishing Derby** (weather permitting) is held at Lake Wangumbaug-Coventry Lake. Prizes for all children under 16 years old. For further info, call the DEP Fisheries Division at (860) 424-FISH or (860) 663-1656.

MAY

A **Mother's Day Garden Talk, Tour and Tea** are held Mother's Day at the Nathan Hale Homestead. (860) 742-6917.

Approximately 60 dealers participate in the **Coventry Doll and Toy Show**, sponsored by the Lion's Club and held at the high school on Route 31. Showcased are antiques and collectible dolls, toys, bears and miniatures. (860) 742-6359.

MAY-OCTOBER

The **Coventry Regional Farmers' Market** is held every Sunday in front of the Coventry Glass Museum, Route 44 and North River Road. (860) 742-1085.

JUNE-AUGUST

In season, a free **Summer Concert Series** is held every Wednesday at Patriot's Park. (860) 742-4068.

JUNE

Consider a **Father's Day Tour** of the Nathan Hale Homestead, which includes cannon-firing demonstrations and other special events. (860) 742-6917.

The Connecticut Herb Association sponsors the **Herbfest at Topmost Herb Farm**. Vendors, children's activities, food and informative talks honor Mother Earth. (860) 742-8239.

Food and games begin **CoventryFest** and nighttime fireworks displays end the festival, held at Patriot's Park, 124 Lake Street. (860) 742-4068.

JULY
Explore the **Nathan Hale Antiques Festival** at the Nathan Hale Homestead, an outdoor antiques show featuring house tours, lectures and other programs. (860) 742-6917.

One of the most popular events of the year is the **Colonial Encampment and Muster** at the Nathan Hale Homestead, featuring the Nathan Hale Ancient Fife & Drums. (860) 742-6917.

SEPTEMBER
The Coventry Historical Society invites the public to its **Election and Proposed Budget Meeting** along with a potluck supper and a roster of entertainment. (860) 742-9025.

OCTOBER
Walking Weekend—Quinebaug-Shetucket Heritage Corridor Region constitutes the 35-town region in Northeastern Connecticut and South Central Massachusetts. Ninety guided walks explore the historical, natural and cultural resources of the "Last Green Valley." (866) 363-7226.

DECEMBER
The Coventry Historical Society holds its **Annual Christmas Party** and invites the public to attend the potluck supper and enjoy an evening of entertainment. (860) 742-9025.

The Coventry Historical Society conducts **Coventry Christmas House Tours**. (860) 742-9025.

A **Lantern-Light Tour** from Strong Porter Museum to Nathan Hale Homestead, featuring historical vignettes, is cosponsored with the Antiquarian & Landmarks Society. (860) 742-6917.

Special Joys
See page 70

A joyful end to a joyful day....

Photos Courtesy of Special Joys B & B

In what American town was the first brass cannon cast?

What town led the country in 19th-century silk production?

Hooray Huskies: **STORRS/MANSFIELD**

Mansfield's first settlers arrived from the Massachusetts Bay Colony around 1692, living in what's now the Mansfield Center area. They purchased the Indian tract of land, "Naubesatuck," incorporating the town in 1703. The Anglo-American name origin is debatable; perhaps named after Major Moses Mansfield, a prominent landowner, or in honor of Lord Mansfield, Chief Justice of England.

In this early farming community, sawmills and gristmills sprang up along rivers. Gradually, the town expanded to include small industries: tanneries, ironworks, a small shoe factory and a cannon foundry where artisans cast the first brass cannon in America.

Roughly 1760, native son Nathaniel Aspinwall started a mulberry orchard and began raising silkworms. By the 19th century, entrepreneurs built America's first silk mill in Mansfield, and the town led the country's silk production. Unfortunately, a mulberry tree blight around 1840 destroyed local raw silk production for good.

In 1881, a land grant from Mansfield brothers Augustus and Charles Storrs helped establish Storrs Agricultural College and changed the face of the town forever. Since the 20th century, the University of Connecticut, the town's chief industry, has been located in what is known as the Storrs section of Mansfield. The university, with 26,000 students enrolled at the main campus, is currently undergoing a 20-year, 2.8-billion-dollar renovation. Officials consider it the most ambitious publicly funded building program for any public university in the nation.

The town of Mansfield is in the center of eastern Connecticut. About nine miles long and five miles wide, the area comprises hills, valleys, forests, streams and wetlands. The town's three principal rivers: the Willimantic, Fenton, and Mount Hope are part of the Thames River (named after the famous English river, but pronounced phonetically) system that reaches Long Island Sound at New London.

Three prominent areas define the town: the original settlement of Mansfield Center (population about 1,000), Storrs (approximately 10,000 residents) and Mansfield Depot (approximately 10,000 residents). Mansfield Four Corners, Gurleyville, Atwoodville, Mount Hope and Spring Hill are boroughs of Storrs. Listed on the National Register of Historic Places are Mansfield Center, Spring Hill, Gurleyville and sections of the university.

Day trips with panache begin with touring the original settlement of Mansfield Center and examining the old **Mansfield Center Cemetery** on the east side of Route 195. Designated as the oldest cemetery in Tolland County, listed on the National Historic Register, witness the many uniquely carved 18th-century gravestones.

Since 1999, the town of Mansfield has been in the process of strengthening its downtown identity. Plans include developing more commercial establishments and a town green.

Driving eastward from Mansfield Center, a favorite jaunt for naturalists is the 2,472-square-mile **Mansfield Hollow Dam and State Park**. Located in the park is Mansfield Hollow Lake, also known as Naubesatuck Lake, an artificial lake created by the dam, its primary water source is the Natchaug River—waters abundant with bass and northern pike. Day-trippers can also enjoy the park's hiking trails and in wintertime, ice fishing, snowshoeing and cross-country skiing. A private company occupies the restored **1882 Kirby Mill**, down the river from the Mansfield Dam.

To visit the only other existing mill, **Gurleyville Gristmill**, take Chaffeeville Road to Stone Mill Road, within four miles of Mansfield Center. Additionally, the mill, circa 1830, is the state's only remaining stone gristmill. Displayed inside are a gamut of 19th-century machinery and tools, photographs and other artifacts. The mossy surroundings and cool temperatures of the surrounding park make it a perfect hideaway on a particularly hot day.

Route 195 leads to the Storrs area and the main attraction of Mansfield. An advisable starting point for the day-tripper exploring the **University of Connecticut** is the **Lodewick Visitor's Center**, operated by staff and student volunteers. This tourism library includes maps, pamphlets and booklets highlighting major and off-the-beaten track, local attractions.

During the day, visitors' parking is available in the metered lots in front of Storrs Hall on Glenbrook Road or in the North Parking Garage. In addition, free shuttle buses run throughout the campus. In the evening and on weekends, although any campus lot or parking garage will accommodate visitors, shuttles do not operate.

The university provides myriad live theater, cultural and musical venues; professional or student-sponsored productions, which are available for audiences in a variety of forms like children's matinees. The main stages include: **Jorgensen Center for the Performing Arts** (860-486-4226), **Jorgensen Theatre (Connecticut Repertory Theatre)** (860-486-1628) and the **von der Mehden Recital Hall** (860-486-2260). All theaters present weekday and weekend programs throughout the year.

A variety of **sporting events** (860-486-2724) are another favorite pastime. On the subject of sports, the **Ice Rink** (860-486-3808), located on Stadium Road, is open to the public a few hours a day and sporadically on weekends throughout the year.

Leaving the visitor's center, campus day trips with panache begin heading towards Hillside Road and the **William Benton Museum of Art**, which has completed its new addition, including the Gilman Gallery. At this state-of-the-art museum, visitors will encounter changing fine art exhibits, European and American paintings, drawings, prints and sculpture from the 16th century to present. There is also a gift shop and café on premises.

During weekdays, day-trippers are also welcome to peruse the changing exhibits of contemporary art by faculty, alumni and nationally and internationally known artists at **Atrium Gallery** (860-486-3930), located in the fine arts building on the west side of the campus.

Hillside Road is also the new residence for the **Connecticut State Museum of Natural History**, which includes the new **Connecticut Archaeology Center**. The redefinition of this museum means extensive exhibits focusing on the fields of archeology and anthropology with an eye on natural history. The museum collection documents more than 11,000 years of Connecticut history and is the single largest repository of Connecticut Native American, colonial and industrial artifacts in existence.

Outside campus attractions, the **Mansfield Historical Society Museum**, Storrs Road, provides an interesting collection of furnishings, costumes, photographs and many historical artifacts housed in the former town office building and 1843 Old Town Hall.

At the UConn Depot Campus on Weaver Road is the **Ballard Institute & Museum of Puppetry**, brainchild of master puppeteer Frank Ballard who created his first puppet at the age of five. He developed the nation's first college degree program in puppetry at UConn (UConn along with the University of West Virginia are the only two institutions of higher learning that offer puppetry as an academic major), starting the university's museum in 1962. The museum galleries feature changing exhibits from a collection of more than 2,000 puppets, plus a hands-on room for young children.

Day-trippers who arrive with children should pick up *Follow the Animal Trail, a Children's Guide to the Animals at UConn's Storrs Campus*, at the visitor's center or in any of the animal barns that are open to the public. Certainly, not confined to families, self-guided tours of the UConn Animal Barns (860-486-1088; open daily) are an interesting day trip for all ages. On view are cows at the Frances E. Osborne Kellogg Dairy Center along with a variety of sheep, horses and pigs. See cows milked daily at 1 p.m.

Expert and neophyte horticulturists should visit the **UConn Greenhouse** (860-486-4052), a nationally recognized facility growing more than 5,000 kinds of plants within a 12,000-square-foot greenhouse (plus a 300-square-foot "fern" room), nursery and outdoor gardens.

While in the vicinity, taste the freshness at the **UConn Dairy Bar** (860-486-2634), Horsebarn Road, legendary for its Jonathan Supreme Ice Cream and featuring 25 flavors of ice cream and frozen yogurt.

Before leaving the UConn campus, don't forget to purchase an array of official "Connecticut Husky" merchandise at the **HuskyShop at the UConn Co-op**, (860-486-3537), the official bookstore for the University of Connecticut.

Another shopping option is eastern Connecticut's largest indoor-outdoor flea market facility at the **Mansfield Drive-In Theatre and Marketplace**. An area institution since 1954, this also happens to be Connecticut's only three-screen, drive-in movie theater featuring first-run, family films.

At a cost of about 170 million dollars, day-trippers can expect a new Storrs Center outlet for shopping, eating and simply roaming. It will be built adjacent to the UConn campus, off Storrs Road (Route 195), across from the university's Fine Arts Center.

Dining fare on Storrs Road alone offers a bounty of choices for lunch and dinner including: **Chang's Garden** (860-487-1688); **Angellino's Restaurant** (860-450-7071), offering generous portions of seafood and Italian-style cuisine; **Paul's Pizza** (860-429-6001); **Husky Bean Café** (860-429-2244); the **Blue Oak Café** and **Abigail's Lounge** at the **Nathan Hale Inn & Conference Center** (860-427-7888; see **Accommodations**). Also serving breakfast, along with lunch and dinner and specializing in upscale pub-style meals is the **Nutmeg Grille** (860-486-3421), and serving breakfast, lunch and dinner and open weekdays only is **Altnaveigh Inn** (860-429-4490; see **Accommodations**), which offers fine dining with a Sunday brunch.

GETTING THERE:

Mansfield-Storrs is located approximately 27 miles outside Hartford. The town is easily accessible from Interstate Highways 395 and 84, which connect to numerous routes that reach town.

TRANSPORTATION:

Mansfield-Storrs is located approximately 55 minutes away from Bradley International Airport (860-292-2000) in Windsor Locks. Downtown Hartford's Union Station Transportation Center, a multi-model transportation center, provides scheduled Amtrak service (800-USA-RAIL) and other services. The Bonanza Bus, Peter Pan Lines (860-389-1531 or 800-243-9560) services the UConn campus daily.

ADDITIONAL INFORMATION:

MANSFIELD HOLLOW DAM AND STATE PARK.

Bassett Bridge Road. Open daily, the area is closed at sunset except for fishing. A state-owned boat launch is located adjacent to Bassett Bridge Road. The park's picnic areas and sports field are handicapped accessible. Swimming, water skiing and windsurfing are prohibited. For further information, call the Mansfield Hollow Dam and Park (860-423-5603), or the Mansfield Parks and Recreation Department. (860) 429-3321; www.dep.state.ct.us/stateparks/parks/mansfield.htm.

GURLEYVILLE GRISTMILL.

Stone Mill Road. Open late May through mid-October, Sundays, and by appointment. General admission is by donation. (860) 429-9023.

LODEWICK VISITOR'S CENTER.

University of Connecticut. 115 North Eagleville Road. Open all year, daily. Group and individual campus tours are available by appointment. (860) 486-4900; www. visitors.uconn.edu.

WILLIAM BENTON MUSEUM OF ART.

245 Glenbrook Road. Open all year, Tuesday through Sunday. Closed during some college recesses. General admission is free. (860) 486-4520; www.benton.uconn.edu.

CONNECTICUT STATE MUSEUM OF NATURAL HISTORY AND CONNECTICUT ARCHAEOLOGY CENTER.

2019 Hillside. The museum and center are open all year, Monday through Friday and Sunday. Call to inquire about the current events calendar. General admission is free. (860) 486-4460; www.cac.uconn.edu.

MANSFIELD HISTORICAL SOCIETY MUSEUM.

954 Storrs Road. Open June through September, Thursday and Sunday. Suggested donation is $1.00. (860) 429-6575; www.mansfield-history.org.

BALLARD INSTITUTE AND MUSEUM OF PUPPETRY.

Weaver Road (Off Route 44). Open late-April to early November, Friday through Sunday. Admission is $3.00 adults; $2.00 children, senior citizens and students with valid ID. (860) 486-4605; www.sp.uconn.edu/~wwwsfa/bimp.html.

MANSFIELD DRIVE-IN THEATRE AND MARKETPLACE.

At the junction of Routes 21 and 32. The theatre and marketplace are open every Sunday, indoors and outdoors, rain or shine. Closed January, February and the first part of March. Handicapped-accessible bathrooms. General marketplace admission is $1.00 and $2.00 for parking. Call for general admission movie prices. (860) 423-4441; www.mansfielddrivein.com.

ACCOMMODATIONS:

BEST WESTERN REGENT INN.

123 Storrs Road. Directly in Mansfield Center, 87 modern guestrooms are offered for travelers. Amenities include an indoor swimming pool and fitness center. Rate (including continental breakfast): about $86.50/per night. (860) 423-8451.

ALTNAVEIGH INN.

957 Storrs Road. Two rooms with private baths offer perfect New England charm in a 1734 country inn, which also houses a restaurant (see above). Rates (including continental breakfast): $75. (860) 429-4490; www.altnaveighinn.com.

THE FITCH HOUSE.

563 Storrs Road. This 1836 Greek Revival-style mansion decorated with period antiques and listed on the National Register of Historic Places offers gracious bed and breakfast accommodations. Three guestrooms contain complete modern amenities and two bathrooms. Children over 13 are welcome. Rates (including full, country breakfast): $110-$125. (860) 456-0922; www.fitchhouse.com/index.html.

NATHAN HALE INN & CONFERENCE CENTER.

855 Bolton Road. Located in the heart of the UConn campus, the Colonial-style inn offers 100 deluxe guestrooms. Modern amenities include extensive business services, indoor heated pool, fitness room, Jacuzzi and on-premises dining (see above). Rates: $149-$179. (860) 427-7888; www.nathanhaleinn.com.

ANNUAL FESTIVALS/EVENTS

Mystic Country/CONNECTICUT representing 42 communities, provides a gamut of tourism information, which includes seasonal events (800) 863-6569 or (860) 444-2206; www.ctquietcorner.com or www.mysticcountry.com. For a listing of UConn events, 24 hours, call the hotline at (860) 486-2106.

MARCH

International Women's Day is a celebration in honor of women in the arts worldwide. Films, exhibits, food and performances are on the day's roster at UConn, Storrs campus. (860) 486-4900.

APRIL
APRIL
Latin Fest is a night of Latin music and dancing in Storrs. Call (860) 486-4226 for location and admission price.

MAY
Connecticut Canoe & Kayak Day, full of fun and instruction, is held annually at Mansfield Hollow State Park. (860) 456-0558.

For children under 16 (accompanied by adult), is the **Annual Kids Fishing Derby** held at Bicentennial Pond. (860) 429-3014.

SEPTEMBER
The **Family Weekend** includes a street fair and other special activities at the Storrs campus, UConn. (860) 486-4900.

OCTOBER
The Connecticut Archaeology Center and the Museum of Natural History hosts the **Annual Connecticut Archaeology Expo**. The event features hands-on activities for children and families as well as presentations by experts in the field, demonstrations of ancient technologies, displays and information from archaeological and historical organizations, vendors and food. (860) 486-5690.

DECEMBER
Festival of Lights marks a celebration of faith and spirituality, communities, culture and winter season. (860) 486-4900.

The **Annual Victorian Christmas Weekends** are popular events held at Fitch House with special activities, holiday shopping, guided tours and special meals. (860) 456-0922.

Join the **Pottery Trail** that visits the Connecticut towns of Storrs, Brooklyn, Danielson and Woodstock and examine the studios of regional, professional artists and potters. (860) 779-6383.

Ballard Institute &
Museum of Puppetry
See page 75

Only one of UConn's gems!

Photo Courtesy of Eastern Regional Tourism District

NORTHEAST CONNECTICUT

Windham County
"Quiet Corner"
Canterbury/Brooklyn/Putnam/Woodstock

These Quiet Corner towns—Canterbury, Brooklyn, Putnam and Woodstock—have the distinction of sharing the Route 169 address, which many expert travelers describe as Connecticut's most distinct and scenic road after the Merritt Parkway, the most scenic highway in the state and one of the most scenic in the nation. In fact, the Federal Highway Administration designated the 32.1-mile, Quiet Corner route as a Connecticut State Scenic Road and a National Scenic Byway. In other words, bring a camera and extra film!

Voted one of the top-10 scenic roads in the country (wow!) by *Scenic America*, the neighboring towns on this stretch, beginning at Lisbon and ending at Woodstock, transform the sightseer back through time. New England churches with towering steeples, manicured town greens, copious stonewalls, barns with grain silos, pastures of apple orchards and farms that grow acres of corn dot the gentle landscape of rolling hills. It is little wonder that during fall foliage season, some motorists who did not reserve hotel rooms well in advance camp out in their cars alongside a road to catch a glimpse of nature's masterpiece.

As rumors circulate about Native American-owned casinos eventually claiming a parcel of this "part of the woods," (the two Connecticut casinos are approximately a half-hour away), the Quiet Corner, meanwhile, boasts the largest number of campgrounds in the state and more than 40 bed and breakfasts and country inns. Fall foliage is a yearly showstopper. Seasonal hay and sleigh rides plus agricultural fairs are tradition. Blackberries are sold in the summer months and goat's milk all year; both on the honor system. Day-trippers can visit a real, live bison farm in Brooklyn, Putnam's charming antiques shops or Woodstock's prestigious Roseland Cottage, a National Historic Landmark. Serene countryside, abundant dairy farms and interesting history greet visitors at every turn.

In what town did the founder of Cleveland, Ohio, come from?

What town is home to Connecticut's famous heroine?

Distinctly Genteel: **CANTERBURY**

In 1684, what we presently call Canterbury was part of a large land parcel (extending south to what we know as Norwich today), which Captain James Fitch obtained from the Indian sachem Oweneco. Fitch, one of the major 17th-century speculators at the time, established the area in 1690. In 1699, about 30 families petitioned Governor Jonathan Winthrop to incorporate what was then called Quinebaug Plantation, comprised of land on both sides of the Quinebaug

River. Finally in 1703, colonists living on the western banks of the river separated from what is known as Plainfield today (located on the east bank) and incorporated their town. English settlers changed the name of the region (which at the time also included what we know today as the towns of Pomfret and Brooklyn) from its Native American name, "Peagscomsueck" to Canterbury in honor of Canterbury in Kent, England.

The town's most famous native son was Moses Cleaveland (1754-1806), a prominent lawyer, soldier and legislator who as a surveyor traveled to the Western Reserve in Ohio eventually to found what would become the town of Cleveland (the spelling of the name changed from "Cleaveland" to "Cleveland" over time). Day trips with panache begin at a plaque on Route 169 (also known as South and North Canterbury Road), north of the Canterbury Green, which marks the birthplace of Moses Cleaveland, in a town with a current residential population of about 4,700 and a total land area of almost 40 square miles. This is an advisable stop to capture some of the most breathtaking views (reserve at least one day during fall foliage!) in a town that still lives up to its agricultural past—even its town seal depicts a plow and harvest.

Cleaveland's family buried him alongside many of the town's early settlers like James Fitch, in what we today call **Cleaveland Cemetery**; formerly the Old Church Burying Ground north of the green on Route 169. Day-trippers may be interested in viewing the large boulder that city officials from Cleveland, Ohio, erected at the cemetery gate in his honor. The National Register of Historic Places lists **Canterbury Center**, which includes North Canterbury, South Canterbury and Westminster Roads. The most unobservant person cannot mistake the homes styled in Georgian, Federal and Colonial architecture.

This Quiet Corner town owns two greens, both within the historic district. **Canterbury Green**, about one and a half acres, further characterizes the charm of Route 169. Over the years, the Canterbury Historical Society has been in the process of restoring and renovating the circa **1850 Centre Green District Schoolhouse** at 8 Library Road, near the intersection of Routes 14 and 169. Periodically, the society opens up the schoolhouse for day-trippers.

Meeting House Green, also known as **Westminster Green**, is located on Route 14 (Westminster Road), intersecting Route 169. Its hilltop location makes it one of the highest-elevated greens in the state. Making it among the oldest area institutions and the green's centerpiece, worshippers have held continuous services since 1770 at the **Westminster Congregational Church**, which is located next to the cemetery. Early settlers used the stone pillar in front of the church as a public whipping post!

At the junction of Routes 14 and 169 is a wonderful example of Federal-style architecture. Operated by Hartford's Connecticut Commission on Arts, Tourism, Culture, History and Film, the house belonged to Prudence Crandall, official Connecticut State Heroine. In 1832, Ms. Crandall opened the school in order to educate the daughters of wealthy town residents. Ms. Crandall's admittance of a young black woman, however, started a controversy that redefined the school as New England's first academy for black women. Unfortunately, two years after it opened, a stream of racial prejudice from townsfolk prompted the school to close down.

The **Prudence Crandall House Museum** is credited today as being a National Historic Landmark and listed as part of the Connecticut Freedom Trail and the Connecticut Women's Heritage Trail and includes three period rooms, a reference library (by appointment) and gift shop. Changing exhibits focus on black history, abolitionism and women-related subjects.

About five miles off Route 169, deep in the woods, it is not unusual to discover a sea of out-of-state license plates belonging to day-trippers who are loyal followers of **Wright's Mill Farm** (860-774-1455; www.wrightsmillfarm.com) at 63 Creasey Road. High on a hill, within a spaciously restored and modern barn, thematic lunches and dinner buffets celebrating holidays and special events entice travelers all year. A friendly and gracious staff at this family-owned business makes certain everyone feels like one big, happy family. Mealtime musical performances add to the festivities. The 250-acre farm is also a paradigm of New England's changing seasons: hayrides and seasonal pumpkin patch in the fall; cut-your-own Christmas trees, Silo Christmas Shop and horse-drawn sleigh rides in the winter and miles of walking trails to enjoy the changing flora all year. When weather permits, experience the remains of the defunct Joe Wright's old mill complex (and the farm's namesake), a nearly 300-year-old, 20-acre millpond with 100-foot-high mill—a popular backdrop for many weddings.

When Wright's Mill isn't hosting a meal, consider **Brom's Place Restaurant** (860-546-9409), a favorite eatery at Westminster Road serving breakfast, lunch and dinner (Sunday brunch) daily.

GETTING THERE:
Canterbury is approximately 17 miles east of Mansfield. The town is easily accessible from Interstate Highway 395, connecting to I-95 and I-84 and from Massachusetts Turnpike, I-90.

TRANSPORTATION:
Canterbury is located approximately 13 miles outside of Danielson (CT) Airport. Approximately 13 miles from the Rhode Island border; T.F. Green Airport in Warwick is about 43 miles away. Additionally, Canterbury is approximately 53 miles east of Bradley International Airport in Windsor Locks and 47 miles from Worcester (MA) Municipal Airport. Downtown Hartford's Union Station Transportation Center, a multi-model transporation center, provides scheduled Amtrak service (800-USA-RAIL) and other services. The Bonanza Bus, Peter Pan Lines (860-389-1531 or 800-243-9560), located in the town of Danielson, services the vicinity.

ADDITIONAL INFORMATION:
PRUDENCE CRANDALL HOUSE MUSEUM.
At the junction of Route 14 and Route 169. Call for days and hours of operation. The museum's first floor is handicapped accessible. General admission is $3.00 adults; $2.00 seniors; $2.00 children and free to children 5 and under. (860) 546-9916; www.chc.state.ct.us/crandall%20museum.htm.

ANNUAL FESTIVALS/EVENTS
Mystic Country/CONNECTICUT representing 42 communities, provides a gamut of tourism information, which includes seasonal events (800) 863-6569 or (860) 444-2206; www.ctquietcorner.com or www.mysticcountry.com. For additional festival and event information, contact the Canterbury Town Clerk (860) 546-9377.

FEBRUARY
A popular romantic Canterbury gathering is the **St. Valentine's Dinner and Dance** at Wright's Mill Farm. (860) 774-1455; www.wrightsmillfarm.com.

MAY
Canterbury Heritage Days is a celebration at Manship Park, less than a mile east of Route 169. The day's activities include Civil War reenactments, rare-breed animals, food and entertainment. (680) 546-6932.

Another popular celebration is **Mother's Day Brunch** at Wright's Mill Farm. (860) 774-1455.

JUNE
For a memorable day, join the **Father's Day Celebration** at Wright's Mill Farm. It features a display of classic cars and motorcycles and entertainment. (860) 774-1455; www.wrightsmillfarm.com.

OCTOBER
Oktoberfest means a full, German-style buffet and live entertainment at Wright's Mill Farm. (860) 774-1455; www.wrightsmillfarm.com.

NOVEMBER
Celebrate Thanksgiving in style and attend the **Annual Thanksgiving Dinner** at Wright's Mill Farm. (860) 774-1455; www.wrightsmillfarm.com.

DECEMBER
The **Holiday House Tour** hosted by the Canterbury Historical Society guides visitors through numerous historical homes and buildings brimming in their holiday best. (860) 546-9346.

Enjoy the tastes, sights and sounds of the season during the **Annual Christmas Brunch Buffet** offered December weekends at Wright's Mill Farm. (860) 774-1455; www.wrightsmillfarm.com.

Prudence Crandall House Museum
See page 80

A tidy, little house with a huge personality.
Photos Courtesy of the Prudence Crandall House Museum

---

*What town touts the oldest, continuously operating,
annual agricultural fair in the country?*

*What town center displays a memorial containing
the remains, sealed in a sarcophagus, of Major
General Israel Putnam?*

Slice-of-Peach Pie: **BROOKLYN**

Officials did not incorporate the town of Brooklyn, covering 28.7 square miles today, from Pomfret and Canterbury (see **Canterbury** chapter) until 1786. In the early 1800s, entrepreneurs built mills along the Quinebaug River that formed its eastern boundary. The textile industry became prominent in the districts of West Wauregan and East Brooklyn. What has to this day brought the most notoriety to Brooklyn is the oldest, continuously operating agricultural fair in the country (see **Annual Festivals/Events**), started by the Agricultural Association, which formed around 1820.

Prominent 19th-century homes attest to the early economic stability of the town. Brooklyn residents (totaling some 6,710 today) contributed to many war efforts in history—you can't go too far without bumping into a monument honoring these veterans.

Today, the eastern section of Brooklyn serves as its commercial hub; dominant fixtures include sawmills and producers of electrical goods. A rural character, emphasized by a few remaining dairy farms, still permeates other parts.

In the center is **Brooklyn Green**, listed on the National Register of Historic Places; intersecting streets divide it into four sections. Among the Colonial-style houses dotting the green, the most impressive landmark is the 1771 meetinghouse.

Day trips with panache, especially for history hounds, begin on Route 169 (Canterbury Road), at the south-end green featuring another outstanding landmark. In 1888, in commemoration of the famous Revolutionary War Major General's life, residents erected the larger-than-life **bronze statue of Israel Putnam** riding a horse. His family's farm was located in a section of Pomfret that later became part of Brooklyn. After the war, Putnam came back to Brooklyn and during his later years operated a tavern. He died in town, laid to rest in the town's cemetery until fans mutilated his marble marker to the point where, in 1888, experts removed this true Connecticut folk hero's remains and sealed them in a sarcophagus built into the foundation of the equestrian statue. The original town cemetery stone is on view under glass in the north alcove of the Connecticut State Capitol (see **Hartford** chapter).

Other members of the Putnam family are buried in the **Old Brooklyn Burying Ground**. Also known as **South Cemetery** containing excellent examples of 18th-century gravestones, it is located about a half-mile south from the town center on Canterbury Road.

Across the street from Putnam's statue is the headquarters of the **Brooklyn Historical Society** (860-774-7728), which displays General Putnam's memorabilia. Visitors can also tour the adjacent **Daniel Putnam Tyler's law office**. Maintained by the historical society, the furnished interior re-creates the years 1822 to 1875, when the great-grandson of the Revolutionary War hero, Israel Putnam, practiced law here.

Within about a one-mile radius and available for tours is **Putnam Elms**, a spacious farmhouse. Although many of the elms surrounding the property have disappeared, the house, built in 1784, has remained in the Putnam family for nearly 200 years. The Colonel Daniel Putnam Association, an organization consisting primarily of family descendents, operates and maintains the house museum.

At the intersection of Routes 169 and 6 is the **New England Center for Contemporary Art**. The collection includes about 80 Native American photographs taken from 1896 to 1930 by Edward Curtis. Four minutes away, heading southeast, at 19 Purvis Road visitors can learn the difference between a buffalo and bison at **Creamery Brook Bison Farm** (860-779-0837; www.creamerybrookbison.com). The 125-acre working farm was an *Editor's Pick* by *Yankee Magazine's Travel Guide to New England*. Don't leave without perusing the on-premises store (closed Sundays), which includes an array of books further depicting these wooly creatures.

The **Quinebaug River** furnishes a host of outdoor activities. For walking enthusiasts, the **Quinebaug River Trail** is accessible from Day Street. Day-trippers who prefer to fish can obtain licenses in late April at the town hall or at the **Brooklyn Trading Post** (860-774-7468), while canoers have the advantage of a launch site on Route 205.

Tennis fans will find public courts, which are lighted for night use, located behind the Brooklyn Recreation Office on Prince Hill Road, less than a half mile from Route 169. Visitors in search of unique shopping can stop at the **Lion and the Lamb** (860-779-0568), and browse the many books, gift items and collectibles, Tuesday through Saturday.

Providence Road and Route 6 offer a variety of Chinese take-out and fast-food establishments for hungry day-trippers. At 18 Providence, the **Calabash Coffee Company and Café** (860-774-8263), which redefined the old Brooklyn Academy Boy's School building, not only offers worldwide coffees, but breakfast and lunch, Wednesday through Sunday. Check out the local artwork for sale. For a one-of-a-kind dining experience, call ahead for reservations at the **Golden Lamb Buttery** (860-774-4423; call for days and hours of operation), located in the bucolic setting of a 250-acre farm on Wolf Den Road. Sing-a-longs, hayrides and live music complement an evening of fine food.

GETTING THERE:
Brooklyn is approximately 44 miles east of Hartford and six miles north of Canterbury. The town is located at the intersection of two scenic routes, 169 and 6. Brooklyn is easily accessible from Interstate Highway 395, connecting to I-95; I-84 and from Massachusetts Turnpike, I-90.

TRANSPORTATION:
Brooklyn is located approximately four miles outside of Danielson (CT) Airport. Approximately eight miles from the Rhode Island border; T.F. Green Airport in Warwick is about 38 miles away. Additionally, Brooklyn is approximately 55 miles

east of Bradley International Airport in Windsor Locks and 40 miles from Worcester (MA) Municipal Airport. Downtown Hartford's Union Station Transportation Center, a multi-model transporation center, provides scheduled Amtrak service (800-USA-RAIL) and other services. The Bonanza Bus, Peter Pan Lines (860-389-1531 or 800-243-9560), located in the town of Danielson, services the vicinity.

ADDITIONAL INFORMATION:
DANIEL PUTNAM TYLER LAW OFFICE.
Route 169. Open Memorial Day through Labor Day, Wednesday and Sunday. General admission is free. (860) 774-7728.

PUTNAM ELMS.
191 Church Street. Open July through mid-October, Wednesday, Saturday and Sunday. General admission is $5.00 adults; $3.00 students and free to children 12 and under. (860) 774-1567; www.putnamelms.org.

NEW ENGLAND CENTER FOR CONTEMPORARY ART.
7 Putnam Place. Open all year, Saturday and Sunday. General admission is free. (860) 774-8899; www.museum-necca.org.

ACCOMMODATIONS:
FRIENDSHIP VALLEY B & B.
60 Pomfret Road. Listed on the National Register of Historic Places and also a stop on the Underground Railroad, this 1795 Georgian, country house inn is impeccably styled in Victorian décor. Nestled on 12 acres, innkeepers named the six guestrooms, each with private bath, in honor of the five previous families who lived in the home. The Benson Room was named after the abolitionist George Benson who, despite widespread opposition, offered refuge at the house to Prudence Crandall during her trial (see **Canterbury** chapter). Crandall, in turn, gave the house its name to show appreciation for the kindness bestowed on her. Rates (including full, country breakfast): $140-$170. (860) 779-9696; www.friendshipvalleyinn.com; inquire about *Britain with Beverly Tours*, planned and offered by innkeeper Beverly Yates (Rusty is her co-partner at the inn), whose passion is all things British.

ANNUAL FESTIVALS/EVENTS
Mystic Country/CONNECTICUT representing 42 communities, provides a gamut of tourism information, which includes seasonal events (800) 863-6569 or (860) 444-2206; www.ctquietcorner.com or www.mysticcountry.com. For additional festival and event information, contact the Brooklyn Town Clerk (860) 779-3411.

APRIL
Sponsored by the Southern New England Agility Club, **Show n' Go** features "dog-filled days" at the Brooklyn Fairgrounds. Activities include herding, dog freestyle-dancing, canine good citizen tests, rescue organization raffles and food. (800) 863-6569.

JUNE
Creamery Brook Bison Farm hosts the **Chief Flying Eagle Annual Native American Powwow**, constituting a weekend full of music and dance. (860) 267-7695.

The East Coast Antique Tractor Club, Nutmeg Chapter, sponsors an **Annual Truck Show and Flea Market** at the Brooklyn Fairgrounds, Route 169. The day's activities include entertainment, food; proceeds benefit charity. (800) 863-6569.

AUGUST
The Brooklyn Fairgrounds are home to the **Brooklyn Fair**, which has been an annual event since 1852, making it the oldest, continuously operating agricultural fair in the United States. The Windham County Agricultural Society, which organizes the event, offers a host of exhibits, competitions, historical displays and the like. (800) 863-6569; www.brooklynfair.org/index.html.

SEPTEMBER
Yankee Yesteryear Car Club holds its **Annual Auto Meet and Flea Market** at the Brooklyn Fairgrounds, Route 169. Refreshments and food are on sale throughout the day. (860) 774-6465.

OCTOBER
The **Village Green Fall Festival** takes place at Federated Church on Route 6. Visitors can expect a flea market and crafts, baked goods and food. (860) 774-9817.

Held at Putnam Elms, the day's activities at the **Halloween and Harvest Festival** include 19th-century music, tales and demonstrations. (860) 774-1567.

DECEMBER
The **Sugar Plum Fair**, featuring seasonal crafts and gifts, homemade baked goods, silent auction, white elephant sale and luncheon, is held at Federated Church on Route 6. (860) 774-9817.

Creamery Brook Bison Farm
see page 84

Where all things wooly and wonderful roam.

Photo Courtesy of Eastern Regional Tourism District

**What town was named after a famous
Revolutionary War hero?**

**In what town has the historical society retained
its original Native American name?**

Antiques & Treasures: **PUTNAM**

Rehobeth, Massachusetts, emigrants, Captain John Sabin and Richard Evans, first settled what we call Putnam in 1693. The Native Americans called the area "Aspinock." Quinebaug River (as called today) divided the territory until Captain Sabin and his sons built the first town bridge in 1722. Officials incorporated Putnam, named in honor of Revolutionary War hero General Israel Putnam, in 1855. (The historical society still maintains the name of Aspinock.)

The town prospered and grew from textile mills fed by the abundant river supply. In 1806, workers constructed one of the first cotton mills in the country. However, a flood devastated Putnam in 1955. Although suffering its share of setbacks, Putnam has rebuilt and reinvented itself into a desirable town for residents, businesses and visitors. Most of the defunct mill buildings are now private businesses in this 20.3-square-mile town (population about 9,000). Likewise, Industrial Park, a 171-acre commercial development, has enticed numerous industries and businesses into Putnam.

A driving force behind the town's cultural renewal was Jerry Cohen, a transplanted Californian. In 1990, Cohen opened the **Antiques Marketplace** (860-928-0442; www.antiquesmarketplace.com), a multi-dealer shop, in the former C.D. Bugbee Department Store building and helped Putnam earn its "Antiques Capital of New England" moniker. Today, antique hunters swarm from all over the country to visit this town, which is about 10 miles south of Massachusetts and about six miles west of Rhode Island, and peruse what amounts to about 20 upscale antiques shops. Day trips with panache begin at 109 Main Street (Route 44), the Marketplace's address, billing itself as the largest antiques store in New England, displaying wares from more than 300 dealers. In the center of the district, 26 Front Street, browse the quality antiques at **Jeremiah's Antique Shoppes** (860-963-2671; open Wednesday through Sunday). Then indulge the taste buds at **Jimmy Stewart's Ice Cream Parlor** (860-963-2671; open Friday through Sunday), a full-service ice cream and soda fountain—a rare treat these days!

Walking eastbound, get a spot of tea Wednesday through Monday at **Mrs. Bridges' Pantry** (860-963-7040; www.MrsBridgesPantry.com.), which is a unique combination tearoom and store selling British-themed gifts, gourmet food items and candy. Open daily is **Wonderland Books** (860-963-2600) next door. Exceptional books, including many written by local writers, fill the premises. The gift and greeting card assortment add to the wonderment.

Day-trippers can enjoy weekend matinees in the heart of downtown at **Bradley Playhouse** (860-928-7887;www.bradleyplayhouse.org), 30 Front Street. The playhouse provides an eight-show season that features live theatrical productions ranging from comedy to drama to children's productions; plus dinner packages.

In proximity of the train station, the **Aspinock Historical Society** (860-963-0092; call for days and hours of operation) has converted a train's boxcar to house the **Gertrude Warner Boxcar Museum and Education Center**, honoring the onetime Putnam resident, grade school teacher and author of the *Boxcar* children's book series.

For outdoor meanders, pedestrians and bicyclists have numerous options, including **Rotary Park**, Kennedy Drive, in downtown. A 1.32-mile **River Trail**, which is a million-dollar construction project along the east bank of the Quinebaug River, connects to the East Coast Greenway. Historical markers, interpretative plaques, a 200-foot-long footbridge and **Upper Cargill** and **Lower Cargill Falls** (named after a onetime mill owner, Benjamin Cargill) are trail highlights. Near the falls, there is a boat launch area and day-trippers interested in fishing the river should obtain a license at the town hall.

Dining options on Main Street include **Vine Bistro** (860-928-1660), specializing in American cuisine, and open for lunch and dinner, Tuesday through Sunday. For casual lunch and dinner fare daily, consider **Courthouse Bar and Grille** (860-963-0074), located in the old courthouse building.

GETTING THERE:

Putnam is approximately 46 miles northeast of Hartford and 13 miles north of Brooklyn. The town is located near the intersection of two scenic routes, 169 and 44. Putnam is easily accessible from Interstate Highway 395, connecting to I-95; and I-84 and I-384 and also from Massachusetts Turnpike, I-90.

TRANSPORTATION:

Putnam is located approximately nine miles outside of Danielson (CT) Airport. Approximately 37 miles from the Rhode Island border; T.F. Green Airport in Warwick is about 40 miles away. Additionally, Putnam is approximately 55 miles east of Bradley International Airport in Windsor Locks and 27 miles from Worcester (MA) Municipal Airport. Downtown Hartford's Union Station Transportation Center, a multi-model transporation center, provides scheduled Amtrak service (800-USA-RAIL) and other services. The Bonanza Bus, Peter Pan Lines (860-389-1531 or 800-243-9560), located in the town of Danielson, services the vicinity.

ACCOMMODATIONS:
THE COLONNADE B & B.

255 E. Putnam Road. A bucolic setting provides a serene backdrop for this 1860 Greek Revival-style home characterized by its spacious porches. Three guestrooms with private bathrooms allot for a variety of options for the single traveler, couples and families. Children 8 years old and older are welcome. Rates (including full, country breakfast): $90-$125. (860) 963-2569; www.colonnadebandb.com.

ANNUAL FESTIVALS/EVENTS

Mystic Country/CONNECTICUT representing 42 communities, provides a gamut of tourism information, which includes seasonal events (800) 863-6569 or (860) 444-2206; www.ctquietcorner.com or www.mysticcountry.com. For additional festival and event information, contact the Putnam Recreation Department at (860) 963-6811.

MAY
Rotary Club members sponsor the **Fishing Derby** at Rotary Park. (860) 963-2121.

JUNE
The **Annual Strawberry Social**, sponsored by the Aspinock Historical Society on the society grounds, features a day of entertainment and food. (860) 963-0092.

JULY
Fireworks display and concert, sponsored by the Putnam Recreation Department, is held at Rotary Park, Kennedy Drive. (860) 963-6811.

JULY-AUGUST
Warm temperatures mean it's time for the **Summer Concert Series** at Rotary Park. (860) 963-6811.

AUGUST
Rubber Duckies race on the Quinebaug River for fun and prizes during the **Annual Rubber Duckie Race** at Rotary Park, Kennedy Drive. Additional festivities include music, food and games. All proceeds support individuals with mental retardation and related disabilities in Northeastern Connecticut. To "adopt" a duck, call (860) 928-1951.

SEPTEMBER
Family Day features activities and entertainment for the whole family. (860) 963-6811.

OCTOBER
Enjoy fun for all ages at a **Halloween Haunted House**. (860) 963-6811.

NOVEMBER
Holiday lights illuminate Putnam and the town celebrates the season with a **Dazzle Light Parade** the day after Thanksgiving. (860) 963-6811.

DECEMBER
Be on the lookout for all the bold colors and holiday pomp during the **Christmas Home & Business Decorating Contest**, a town-wide event sponsored by the Recreation Department. (860) 963-6811.

What town has nearly 75 percent of its land as open space?

What town boasts the second oldest, continuously operating agricultural fair in New England and one of the oldest in the country?

Copacetic Corner: **WOODSTOCK**

In 1686, Massachusetts Bay Colonists settled Wabaquasset Indian land, which is Woodstock today. First, the settlers named it New Roxbury, after their Massachusetts township, and it remained like many other Connecticut colonies under Massachusetts providence. It was later renamed Woodstock after Woodstock, Oxfordshire, England. Woodstock seceded from Massachusetts in 1749 and became part of Connecticut Colony.

Captain, later General, Samuel McClellan led 184 Woodstock men to fight for the patriot's cause in the Revolutionary War. The general's house, which now houses **McClellan Elms Antiques**, (860-928-0885; www.mcclellanelmsantiques. com) is at the corner of Route 169 and Stone Bridge Road, across from South Woodstock Common. **South Woodstock Common**, one of two town greens, is trimmed in old shade trees and exudes a picture-perfect town; one reason why Woodstock continuously achieves the top-10 list in *Connecticut Magazine's* index of the *Best Small Towns.*

Witnessing a brief run in textile manufacturing during the 19th century, Woodstock residents (current population 7,750) have fought to preserve its rural character and, today, open land stretches over nearly 75 percent of the town's 61.8 square miles. During summer and fall, the farms and orchards offer day-trippers a sweet odyssey of produce: strawberries, blueberries, raspberries, apples, peaches, pears, pumpkins and the like.

Woodstock is the site of the Old Quasset School, which educated pupils from 1745 to 1946, and is listed as the oldest, continuously run one-room schoolhouse in the United States. Connecticut's northeast-corner town also boasts Woodstock Airport, a small South Woodstock facility accommodating charter and private aircrafts. Thirty minutes from Sturbridge Village, Massachusetts, and 90 minutes from Boston, the town is also home to the Woodstock Fair (see **Annual Festivals/Events**). The fair started in 1858 and is the second oldest (after Brooklyn's Agricultural Fair; see **Brooklyn** chapter) in New England and one of the oldest agricultural fairs in the country. Day trips with panache begin by viewing Woodstock's historical exhibits (open weekends May through December) in **Palmer Memorial Hall** on Route 169, operated by the **Woodstock Historical Society** (860-928-1035; woodstockhistor-icalsociety.org). Stock up on paintings and lithographs of Woodstock, books and handmade gifts at the gift shop behind the hall.

Also behind the yellow brick, historical society building is **Palmer Arboretum**, a small but inviting park for short walks where you can't help but notice the plant and shrub variety. Across the street, the edifice painted coral pink belongs to the

Roseland Cottage-Bowen House, situated directly on South Woodstock Common, Route 169. The house was built as a summer cottage for native son, newspaper publisher Henry C. Bowen in 1846, a descendent of Henry Bowen, one of the 13 original (1686) Woodstock settlers. Complete with pointed arches and stained glass windows, the building exemplifies Gothic Revival-style architecture. Maintained by the Society for the Preservation of New England Antiquities, listed as a National Historic Landmark, the interior still contains Bowen's original furnishings. The centerpiece of the two acres surrounding the home is a breathtaking boxwood parterre. Henry Ward Beecher, General John Charles Fremont, President Ulysses S. Grant and President Benjamin Harrison rambled through these grounds as guests of Bowen during his famed Fourth of July celebrations. During these summer galas, the revelers bowled in the (1846) carriage barn that today constitutes one of the oldest surviving bowling alleys in the country. Today, musical summer concerts on the lawn grace the air.

Another legacy from the Bowen family is the **Woodstock Golf Course** (860-928-4130), a nine-hole public course located on Roseland Park Road. A second public course is the **Harrisville Golf Club** (860-928-6098), an 18-hole course at 125 Harrisville Road.

Nature lovers can drive west from North Woodstock onto Route 197 until they reach Route 171, which leads to the **Bigelow Hollow State Park** entrance and the adjoining **Nipmuck State Park** (860-346-2372; 860-424-3200). Both areas provide an 18-acre pond with boat launch ramp and more than 9,000 acres of recreation opportunities including miles of hiking trails, picnic tables, restroom areas, cross-country skiing and snowmobile trails as well as fishing and scuba diving areas.

Hot air balloon day-trippers congregate at Chace Building Supply on Route 171. **Brighter Skies Balloon Company** (860-963-0600; 800-677-5114; www. brighterskies.com) affords some of the best views of Northeastern Connecticut.

At 848 Route 171 is the **Taylor Brooke Winery** (860-974-1263; www. taylorbrookewinery.com; open May through December, Friday through Sunday), a small but impressive husband- and-wife-team operation. You will find many Taylor Brooke wines sold in local stores and served at nearby restaurants like the **Inn at Woodstock Hill** (see below).

Opera lovers can obtain tickets at the **Hyde Cultural Center** (860-928-2946), Route 169, home of Opera New England of Northeastern Connecticut.

One of the best Woodstock souvenirs is something from the garden, whether fresh produce at Route 169's **Woodstock Orchards** (860-928-2225; open seasonally, daily) or fresh flowers from **Plantaholic Nursery** (860-963-1103; call for days and hours of operation) at the junction of Routes 197 and 169. For the most novel gift, consider an alpaca (yes, they are live animals!) from **Southwood Alpacas**; by appointment only (866-SWD-CRIA; www.southwoodalpacas.com).

Holiday lovers have two stores to splurge in: Route 169's **Christmas Barn** (860-928-7652; open July through December, Tuesday through Sunday) and **Mary's Christmas Shop** (860-928-6807) at "the Blacksmith Shop," off Route 169. For a light breakfast, lunch or early dinner, on Route 171, try **Cinnamon Tree Bakery** (860-928-2234; call for days and hours of operation). Another option for breakfast or lunch on Route 169 is **Sweet Evalina's** (860-928-4029 call for days and hours of operation). For breakfast all day, try **JavaJive** (860-963-1241; open daily), a coffee shop that's always perking! Reservations are recommended for lunch (Sunday brunch), Tuesday through Saturday, and dinner daily at the elegant and award-winning **Inn at Woodstock Hill** (860-928-0528; see **Accommodations**).

GETTING THERE:

Woodstock is approximately 47 miles east of Hartford and five miles northwest of Putnam. The town is located on scenic route 169, about six miles south of the Massachusetts border. Woodstock is easily accessible from Interstate Highways 395 and 84 and from Massachusetts Turnpike, I-90.

TRANSPORTATION:

Woodstock has its own small airport (see above chapter) and is located approximately 14 miles outside of Danielson (CT) Airport. T.F. Green Airport in Warwick, Rhode Island, is approximately 45 miles away. Additionally, Woodstock is approximately 55 miles east of Bradley International Airport in Windsor Locks and 28 miles from Worcester (MA) Municipal Airport. Downtown Hartford's Union Station Transportation Center, a multi-model transporation center, provides scheduled Amtrak service (800-USA-RAIL) and other services. The Bonanza Bus, Peter Pan Lines (860-389-1531 or 800-243-9560), located in the town of Danielson, services the vicinity.

ADDITIONAL INFORMATION:

ROSELAND COTTAGE-BOWEN HOUSE.

Route 169. Open June 1 through October 15, Friday through Sunday. Tours leave on the hour; last one is at 4 p.m. General admission is $8.00 adults; $7.00 seniors; $5.00 children and free to children 5 and under and to SPNEA members and Woodstock residents. (860) 928-4074; www.historicnewengland.org.

ACCOMMODATIONS:

INN AT WOODSTOCK HILL.

94 Plaine Hill Road. Listed on the National Register of Historic Places, John Truedell constructed the main house for William Bowen (see **Bowen House**, **Roseland Cottage**, above chapter) in 1816. Waverly fabrics, numerous fireplaces and four-poster beds accent the 16 guestrooms, each with private bath. Consider booking a family reunion at the guest cottage with three private bedrooms and bath. Amenities include high-speed Internet service in every room and smoking and non-smoking rooms and an on-site restaurant (see above). Rates (including continental breakfast): $130-$200. (860) 928-0528; www.woodstockhill.net.

B & B AT TAYLOR'S CORNER.

880 Rte. 171. Listed on the National Register of Historic Places, this completely restored 18th-century, center-chimney farmhouse, complete with English gardens, boasts three guestrooms with private bath and features a host of antiques. Children 12 and older welcome. Rates (including weekday continental breakfast and full, country breakfast on weekends): $95-$140. (860) 974-0490; (888) 503-9057; www. taylorsbb.com.

ELIAS CHILD HOUSE.
50 Perrin Road. Deep in the woods of Woodstock is this bed and breakfast, which started its history in the early 1700s with a simple one-room frame. Today, the house, decorated in period antiques, offers one suite and two guestrooms, each with fireplace and private baths. Canine guests and children 8 years old and older welcome. Rates (including continental breakfast): $105-$135. (860) 974-9836; (877) 974-9836; www.eliaschildhouse.com.

BEAVER PINES CAMPGROUND.
Route 198. This small, family-owned campground surrounded by the Nipmuck State Forest provides campers a range of sites from remote areas for tents to level sites with electric and water hookups for trailers. Pets welcome. Call for daily, weekly and seasonal rates. (860) 974-0110; www.beaverpinescampground.com.

ANNUAL FESTIVALS/EVENTS
Mystic Country/CONNECTICUT representing 42 communities, provides a gamut of tourism information, which includes seasonal events (800) 863-6569 or (860) 444-2206; www.ctquietcorner.com or www.mysticcountry.com. For additional festival and event information, contact the Woodstock Town Clerk (860) 928-6595.

MAY
Woodstock Fairgrounds, Routes 169 and 171 in South Woodstock, hosts the **Windham County Dog Show** in which dogs from around the region are exhibited. (800) 863-6569.

JULY
The East Woodstock Congregational Church on the Town Common holds a **Jamboree** every Fourth of July. The day's activities include a parade, children's games, silent auction, hayrides, food, which includes a chicken barbeque lunch and entertainment. (800) 863-6569.

Special programs and activities fill the day at the **Annual Historic Gardens Day** held at the Roseland Cottage-Bowen House. (860) 928-4074.

Woodstock Memorial Day 6.2 Mile Road Race congregates at the Woodstock Academy at the town green. (800) 863-6569.

Fairvue Farms holds the **Annual Horse and Farm Show**, rain or shine, at 199 Route 171, with free balloons, posters and samples of ice cream and dairy products, plus activities for the whole family, such as hayride tours. (860) 928-9483.

SEPTEMBER
Labor Day weekend means three days of fun and entertainment at the **Woodstock Fair**, a harvest celebration held at the Woodstock Fairgrounds, Routes 169 and 171 in South Woodstock. (860) 928-3246.

One of Woodstock's most popular shopping weekends is the **Annual Shop Hop**. Held the first weekend in September, town merchants offer everything from special discounts to refreshments to door prizes. (800) 863-6569.

OCTOBER

The weekend after Columbus Day, Roseland Cottage is the setting for an annual **Fine Arts & Crafts Festival**. Artisans display a variety of handmade crafts and original artwork. (860) 928-4074.

DECEMBER

Woodstock Common stages **Woodstock's Annual Winter Festival**. Festivities include tree lighting, special activities for adults and children and food and crafts. (860) 928-4074.

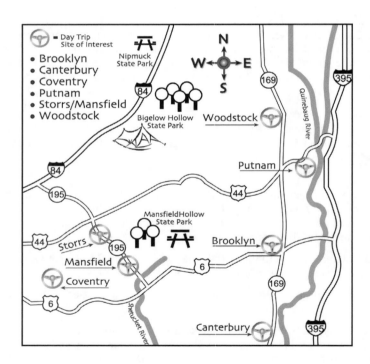

III.

SOUTHEAST CONNECTICUT

New London County

"Mystic Country/CONNECTICUT"

Norwich/Ledyard/Montville/North Stonington/ Stonington/Mystic

Located in the southeastern part of the state, anchored between the Connecticut River Valley and the state of Rhode Island, for more than 30 years, Connecticut's tourist hotspot has been Mystic with its historical seaport and state-of-the-art aquarium. These days, many residents grumble that the gambling empires of Foxwoods Resort Casino and Mohegan Sun Resort Casino have done little more than fatten local roadways (predominantly Route 2) with traffic.

State tourism officials have labeled this region "Mystic Country/ CONNECTICUT" hoping to market the city of Norwich and its slumbering villages along with the neighboring seacoast towns and casino glitz. Move away from the ca-ching of the slot machines, and you will discover quiet landscapes lined with well-preserved, 18th- and 19th-century architecture; seascapes overflowing with rich history—and never-ending stories associated with the last surviving fishing fleet in the state! Lest we forget a number of idyllic town greens; one of the area's most spectacular old-time Christmas parades, Norwich's annual Winterfest Parade, and even a professional baseball team!

In what city did Benedict Arnold, onetime patriot and ally of George Washington and who later became a traitor, hail from?

During the turn of the century, in what city did more millionaires live than anywhere else in New England?

New England Rose: **NORWICH**

During 1659, a group of Saybrook men, led by Major John Mason and Reverend James Fitch, purchased from Mohegan chief, Uncas, a virgin pocket of land located at the confluence of the Shetucket and Yantic Rivers. In return, the colonists helped the Mohegan Tribe in its fight against its Pequot enemies. Early pioneers settled around a three-mile area (what is now Norwichtown Green, north of the current downtown) under the name Mohegan, about 15 miles from what we today know as Long Island Sound. These days, a handful of homes dating back to the 1660s marks this period in history, as does the town's annual celebration of Historic Norwichtown Days (see **Annual Festivals/Events**).

In 1668, settlers established a wharf at Yantic Cove. Hence, during the Revolutionary War, Norwich evolved into the state's second largest and wealthiest port; New Haven being the first. The city also boomed from mills powered by the abundance of river sources. By the mid-19th century, only New Haven and Hartford exceeded Norwich's residential population.

Many of the city's historical accolades can be measured through its partial list of "firsts": first survey for the first turnpike in America, 1670; first chocolate mill, 1770; first traitor, Norwich-born Benedict Arnold (who helped the British in 1780); first typewriter, 1843; first cork cutter, 1855 and first party game manufactured as "Sillyettes," 1927.

By the turn of the 19th century, as a result of textile mills, more millionaires lived in Norwich than anywhere else in New England; many of their mansions still apparent around Norwichtown. However, as the 20th century progressed, a bridge that linked Groton and New London bypassed the town, luring motorists away. When the Great Depression further squelched Norwich's economy, the mills became silent. Paradoxically, during the 1930s, Norwich earned the title of "Christmas City" in recognition of its festive street decorations—a Yuletide tradition that continues to this day.

Fortunately, the "Rose of New England," which was nicknamed in the 19th century by Litchfield native and abolitionist Henry Ward Beecher (dad to Harriett; see **Hartford** and **Litchfield** chapters), who compared the hilly terrain to rose petals, is again in full bloom. The city mirrors the zest of nearby New London with its rejuvenation projects and new commercial developments like Artspace, residences for working artists. Additional development plans involve the creation of **Occum**, an award-winning riverfront park and **Norwich Heritage Discovery Center**, a concentration of interactive exhibits helping visitors learn about local history and culture. Planned restoration projects include the 1855 **Wauregan Hotel** and the 19th-century **Cassidy House**, home of the first Surgeon General of Connecticut. In addition, enterprising individuals are converting historical sites like Ponemah Mills in the surrounding village of Taftville into commercial properties. The **Chelsea District**, also known as downtown Norwich, alone has two renovated community theaters, the **Spirit of Broadway** (860-886-2378; www.spiritofbroadway.org) and the **Norwich Art Council's Donald Oat Theater** (860-887-2789; www.norwicharts.org/donald_oat_theater.htm).

A municipal project costing 9.3 million dollars, the **Thomas J. Dodd Memorial Stadium** (860-889-2854), home of professional baseball team Norwich Navigators, debuted in 1995. The **Norwich Municipal Ice Rink** (860-892-2555; www.norwichrink.com), a not-for-profit facility hosting amateur and professional skaters as well as hockey teams and skating clubs, also opened to the public in 1995.

Day trips with panache begin by experiencing the bold architecture in the city selected as New England's winner of the *Prettiest Painted Places in America* by a panel of judges from the Paint Quality Institute. At the **Norwich Tourism Office** (860-886-4683; www.norwichCT.org), 77 Main Street, pick up a *Walking Guide to Historic Washington & Broad Streets* or *Walking Guide to Historic Broadway*

& *Union Street*, which will help you maneuver through a city that is home to two historical societies, and listed 42 (yes, 42!) times on the National Register of Historic Places. Norwich also has more than 500 (yes, 500!) homes representing various eras and designs of architecture. (Day-trippers should be on the lookout for a marker a few blocks from the green designating the location of Benedict Arnold's birthplace; the house no longer exists.) Browse the novel souvenirs like t-shirts and "Benedict Arnold" mugs that the tourism folks offer.

The **Norwich City Hall** (860-823-3732) on Broadway also supplies a visitor's information booth open during office hours. Once inside, catch a glimpse of Abraham Lincoln's 1860 election campaign banner housed inside this restored, 1870 French Second Empire-style building. The **Norwich Arts Council** (860-887-2789; www.norwicharts.org), its office and gallery located at 60 Broadway, just south of the city hall, is a powerful force behind Norwich's revamped façade.

Chelsea Parade, located within a National Register Historic District, its large, triangle-shaped green—one of four greens in Norwich—is at the intersection of Broadway and Washington Street. In 1783, residents erected a 27-foot, six-inch Civil War Monument at the southern end of the green of a Union soldier mounted on an octagonal granite base surrounded by a metal fence. Inside the fence, community members buried a time capsule in 1959, indicated by a stone marker. Those day-trippers who are around in 2059 can plan to see the time capsule unearthed!

The Parade's centerpiece is the **Norwich Free Academy**. Established in 1856, this academy is a privately endowed public high school, the second largest in the state. The **Slater Memorial Museum**, headquartered in an impressive three-story, Romanesque Revival-style building, was a gift to the city and presented as a museum in 1886 by the prominent Slater family. More than 100 years later, it is one of only two fine art museums in the United States located on a high school campus. The museum, carrying one of the largest plaster collections in the world, is comprised of more than 150 castings of Greek, Roman and Renaissance figures, including Michelangelo's Pieta. Slater's complementary exhibit, *Art of Five Continents*, features fine art from North and South America, Europe, Asia and Africa. Don't forget to allot time with the wee ones at the Gaultieri Children's Gallery.

The **Converse Art Gallery** is adjacent to the museum and features changing, temporary exhibitions almost exclusively devoted to contemporary arts and crafts. Stroll behind the art gallery to Rockwell Street and witness pastoral **Mohegan Park** and the glorious **Rose Gardens** where summer concerts performed by the Norwich City Band sweeten the air. This two-acre garden features 2,500 rose bushes in 120 varieties, fully bloomed in June, with most continuing to blossom throughout the summer.

In proximity, across the street on Sachem Street is the **Royal Mohegan Burying Ground**, Uncas's final resting place, situated near the falls of the **Yantic River** where naturalists will discover the famed **Indian Leap**, a popular fishing spot. Per legend, the gorge is where Uncas jumped to escape the Narragansetts. The Mohegans, in turn, pushed the warring tribe members to their deaths here, marking the Narragansetts' final battle with the Mohegan Tribe.

Proceeding northwest, past William Backus Hospital, is the **Norwichtown District**. This suburb features examples of 17th- and 18th-century architecture including the **Leffingwell House Museum** (860-889-9440; www. leffingwellhousemuseum.org), operated and maintained by the Society of the Founders of Norwich and located at the intersection of Route 2 and 348 Washington

Street. Beginning as a humble two-room house in 1675, the home's expansion began in 1701. The house is open to day-trippers seasonally and by appointment. View an interesting collection including fine silver, clocks and children's toys.

Tiptoe through the moon faces on the tombstones and a paradoxically eerie but beautiful mix of 17th- and 18th-century headstones at **Old Norwichtown Burial Ground**, off Town Street. Benedict Arnold's mother, Hannah, is buried here. (Her traitor son's body is buried in England.) The Norwich Tourism Office offers a detailed brochure of the grounds. Those with a penchant for the past should make way to the 1660 **John Baldwin House** on West Town Street that houses the ever-popular **Books, Etc.** (860-889-5990), which specializes in topics of local history.

Day-trippers can wind down the day and make a beeline downtown to picnic near the **Marina at American Wharf** at **Howard T. Brown Memorial Park** (860-887-2789; www.norwichct.org/visitors/map). Those without picnics can enjoy the view while dining on lunch or dinner daily (May through October) at **Americus on the Wharf at the American Marina**. Other food choices throughout the city include pizza, fast-food style restaurants and ice cream shops. **Olde Tymes Restaurant** (860-887-6865; www.oldetymes.com, see web page offerings) is a popular jaunt for breakfast, lunch or dinner daily. For creative and upscale hotel dining, breakfast, lunch and dinner, try **Kensington's Restaurant at the Spa at Norwich Inn** (see **Accommodations**) that seasonally offers outdoor dining. Dinner theatergoers should reserve seats at the **Majestic Rose Dinner Theater** downtown (860-889-6300).

During summer weekends, day-trippers can become acquainted with the harbor and surrounding waters, sailing on one of the **Norwich cruise boats** (877-248-6964).

Note that 15 miles away from Norwich, hikers and bikers who are on the lookout for a variety of terrain should stop at **Pachaug State Forest** (www.//dep.state.ct.us/stateparks/forests/pachaug.htm), just off Interstate 395 in Voluntown. This is the largest state forest in Connecticut with a total of 24,000 acres rambling into five towns and nearly every brook has evidence of old mill sites and dams.

GETTING THERE:

Norwich is approximately 15 minutes from Mohegan Sun Resort Casino and 15 minutes from Foxwoods Resort Casino; 35 minutes from Mystic. Norwich is easily accessible from Interstate Highway 395, connecting to I-95 and I-84.

TRANSPORTATION:

Norwich is located 15 miles away from the Groton-New London Airport, which serves a growing demand of business commuters and leisure travelers. T.F. Green Airport in Warwick, Rhode Island, is 50 miles in driving distance. Additionally, Norwich is 54 miles east of Bradley International Airport in Windsor Locks and 62 miles from Worcester (MA) Municipal Airport. Southeast Area Transit (SEAT) bus service (860-886-2631) serves various points in Norwich.

Norwich also plans to construct a transportation center, which would provide access to the area by bus, passenger rail, and possibly high-speed ferryboats.

ADDITIONAL INFORMATION:

For a complete listing of development projects and updates, call the Norwich Community Development Council at (860) 887-6964.

SLATER MEMORIAL MUSEUM.

108 Crescent Street. Open all year, Tuesday through Sunday. The museum's first floor is handicapped accessible. Guided tours are available. General admission is $3.00 adults, $2.00 seniors and free to children 12 and under and to Friends of Slater Museum. (860) 887-2506; www.norwichfreeacademy.com/slater_museum/.

ACCOMMODATIONS:

Norwich offers a number of chain-hotel options like **Courtyard by Marriott** (860-886-2600; www.marriott.com/property/propertypage/GONCY) and **Ramada Hotel** (860-889-5201) for day-trippers who want to extend their visits.

THE SPA AT NORWICH INN.

607 West Thames Street. Located 10 minutes away from the **Norwich Public Golf Course** (www.norwichgolf.com), 103 rooms combine country-inn classic elegance with a full complement of spa treatments and exercise classes. This world-class spa features 32 treatment rooms and a 25-meter indoor pool. Guestroom amenities include bathrobes, CD players and nightly turndown service; villas offer kitchens, fireplaces, private balconies, and upscale restaurant (see listing above). The renovated 1929 Georgian-style luxury inn is rich in character and history. Rates: $225 and up. (860) 886-2401; (800) ASK-4-SPA; www.thespaatnorwichinn.com.

ANNUAL FESTIVALS/EVENTS

Mystic Country/CONNECTICUT representing 42 communities, provides a gamut of tourism information, which includes seasonal events (800) 863-6569 or (860) 444-2206; www.ctquietcorner.com or www.mysticcountry.com. For additional festival and event information, contact the Norwich Tourism Office (860) 886-4683; www.norwichct.org/ or toll-free at 1-888-4-NORWICH.

FEBRUARY

Day-trippers can enjoy food like a variety of sweet potato delicacies and pies as well as entertainment at the **Sweet Potato Festival**. (860) 887-4888.

APRIL

Art lovers haven't missed the annual **Connecticut Artists Juried Exhibition**, showcased at the Converse Gallery, in more than 60 years! (860) 887-2506.

MAY

Community Appreciation Day is held at the Howard T. Brown Park. Activities include games, contests, prizes, moonwalk and food. (860) 886-4683.

The **Memorial Day Parade** proceeds from Little Plain to Chelsea Parade. (860) 886-4683.

JUNE/JULY/AUGUST
The Brown Park Gazebo at Norwichtown Green hosts **Free Summer Music concerts**. Call the Norwich Arts Council, (860) 887-2789.

JUNE
Rose City Day involves children's activities and "The Rose City Challenge," a road race open to the public. (860) 823-4247.

Railroad Heritage Day features a two-hour ride through scenic Shetucket Heritage Corridor. Train leaves the Old Norwich Railroad Station located at 10 Railroad Place. (860) 887-3289.

JULY
The **Eastern CT Antique Auto Show** is the largest antique and classic car show in the state, which is held on the grounds of Dodd Stadium, Stott Avenue. Hundreds of cars and antique farm equipment are featured. (860) 464-7373.

AUGUST
Norwich Grange Fair is an annual fair promoting agriculture with activities, such as exhibits, silent auction, raffle, bake sale and arts and crafts. (860) 859-3265.

SEPTEMBER
Held at Brown Park, **Taste of Italy** promotes Italian heritage with culinary cuisine, games, art exhibits and fireworks. (860) 889-1369.

Held at the Holy Trinity Greek Orthodox Church, the **Grecian Festival** celebrates Greek ethnicity with food and music. (860) 887-1458.

Historic Norwichtown Days feature historic re-enactments of our country's early beginnings. Handicraft demonstrations, lectures and discussions are organized throughout the weekend. (860) 376-3170.

More than 16 dealers feature gem and mineral displays, silent auctions and jewelry-making procedures at the **Thames Valley Annual Gem & Mineral Show** at Norwich Tech School. (860) 889-2803.

Family Day features food and games at Mohegan Park. (860) 823-3782.

NOVEMBER
Norwich hosts several interesting guided walks during the **Walking Weekends** that include 35 towns of the Quinebaug and Shetucket Rivers Valley National Heritage Corridor. (860) 963-7226.

The classic production of **Nutcracker on Ice** is presented annually at the Norwich Ice Rink. (860) 892-2555.

The Converse Gallery holds the **Annual Craft Sale**. Baked goods and coffee are also available. (860) 887-2506.

DECEMBER
The annual parade starts at Chelsea Parade grounds to kickoff **Winterfest**. Float trophies are awarded. (860) 892-1813.

**What town kicked off Connecticut's
Native American-casino craze?**

**What town is home to the world's largest gaming facility,
not to mention one of the most impressive Native American
history museums anywhere?**

High-Rollin' History:
MASHANTUCKET/LEDYARD

Around 1500, the Pequot and Mohegan Indian Tribes uneasily shared and inhabited central and eastern Connecticut. Before the arrival of Europeans in the 1600s, both nations had become warring enemies. In 1620, the Pequot (translated as the "destroyers") with about 6,000 members, dominated the region. By 1637, however, tribal wars and a smallpox epidemic had reduced this number to 3,000. Tensions between English settlers and the Pequot mounted until the Mohegans, the Narragansett and the English settlers formed an alliance and annihilated most of the Pequot Tribe during the infamous Pequot War in 1637. Centuries later, the 1910 census would calculate only 66 Pequots.

Descendents of the original Pequots constitute some 1,150 members of the Eastern Pequot Tribal Nation comprised of the Mashantucket or Western Pequot Tribe of Ledyard and the approximate 600-member Paucatuck Eastern Pequots and Eastern Pequot Tribes. The latter group, although recognized by the state, have fought for federal recognition for many years; having lived and shared the Lantern Hill Reservation in North Stonington (totaling about 247 acres) for more than 300 years.

Meanwhile, today's approximate 550-member Mashantucket Tribe, on the other hand, owns some 2,500 acres; a small portion of this was reacquired from the government through the Mashantucket Indian Land Claims Settlement Act of 1983.

Situated on the Thames River estuary, the Ledyard area totals just over 40 square miles. The northern half of Groton's submarine base is also located there. The Mashantucket Pequot Reservation lies within three miles of Ledyard Center. Overall, a suburban community, Ledyard has an estimated residential population of 15,600.

First settled in 1653, Ledyard was not incorporated from Groton until 1836. Residents named the town after Colonel William Ledyard, a Revolutionary War commander who historians say had given up his life during a battle against the British at Fort Griswold in Groton.

Present-day, casino-hype aside, Ledyard's historical sense shines through and visitors can experience it in such pleasant day trips as the **Gales Ferry Historic District**. There, the National Register of Historic Places honors an assortment of 18th-century farmsteads. In addition, the **Ledyard Historical Society** (www.

town.ledyard.ct.us/culture.htm) owns and maintains the **Gales Ferry One-Room Schoolhouse** (860-464-2865; call for days and hours of operation). The school's Hurlutt Road location is an enchanting setting (dating back to 1868) where visitors can come to browse local artwork and crafts. The **Historical Room at Bill Library** (860-464-9912), also overseen by the society, invites budding and professional scholars (by appointment) to peruse volumes of local historical and genealogical materials.

The **Nathan Lester House and Farm Tool Museum** (860-464-8540; inquire about special demonstrations and events), maintained by the Town of Ledyard through the Historic District Commission, is open to day-trippers on Tuesday, Thursday and weekends from Memorial Day through Labor Day. Inside the six-room house, visitors can discover furnishings dating from the Victorian Age, all the way back to the 1700s in this 1793 farmhouse. Two adjacent barns showcase colonial-period tools, a milk wagon, sleighs and a horse-drawn snowplow.

Boasting a strong maritime history, the Ledyard riverfront continues to attract anglers and water-sport adventurers. **Stoddard Hill State Park** is a 55-acre recreational area situated at the foot of a rocky, wooded knoll on Thames River. Summer day trips with panache, especially for water lovers, begin swimming and sunning at the park's public beach. Boaters will find launch ramps; fishers have their own access platform.

On Route 214, near the town center is **Ledyard Water-Powered Up-Down Sawmill Park** (860-464-8740; 860-464-8888; call ahead). This unique mill on the 11-acre, town-owned property is a day-tripper's favorite, especially during the spring and fall when there is ample water. Cap the day off with lunch to enjoy at the picnic area.

As Mohegan Sun affected Montville, **Foxwoods Resort Casino** (800-FOXWOOD; www.foxwoods.com), less than about 15 miles away, has brought worldwide notoriety (and congested traffic) to this once obscure region since it first opened in 1992. This Mashantucket-owned, gigantesque structure surging above the farmland draws up to 70,000 (no, this is not a typo!) patrons a day and grosses more than one billion dollars annually. The world's largest gaming palace, it has, among other things, six casinos, 6,400 slot machines, 354 table games and the world's largest bingo hall. When it comes to tribal members, big is not big enough: after unveiling a 300-million-dollar-Rainmaker-casino extension, which includes the **Hard Rock Café**, patrons can look forward to developers completing a 700-million-dollar expansion in summer 2008. Developer's plans include a new 825-room hotel tower, 5,000-seat theater, 1,500 more slot machines and what amounts to more than two-million additional square feet. Hard to imagine how this resort casino's roots sprouted with a humble, austere bingo hall that opened for high-stakes bingo gaming in 1986.

Today, day-trippers who have a yen to extend the day have a nighttime entertainment assortment at Foxwoods, ranging from top-headline acts to champion boxing events; the Foxwoods Arena being the largest venue. Jazz, comedy, blues and professional DJs are examples of things that keep the atmosphere at the **B.B. King Dance & Night Club** electrified.

For respite and relaxation, day-trippers can reserve a host of services offered at **The Grand Salon & Spa** (www.foxwoods.com/Resort/SalonSpa). Located on the ninth floor of the Grand Pequot Tower, after a relaxing massage or other body treatment, visitors have a comprehensive beauty care menu.

Golfers can be shuttled a half-hour away to Rhode Island, taking advantage of Foxwoods' nearby course (401-539-0300; www.foxwoodsgolf.com/Directions.aspx), which includes a clubhouse, PGA-staffed pro shop and the **Fountain View Grille**. Closer to home, Foxwoods more recently unveiled **Lake of Isles** (888-475-3746; 860-312-2101; www.lakeofisles.com) with private and public courses designed by golf course architect Rees Jones. Located in North Stonington, and surrounding a 90-acre lake with a 50,000-square-foot clubhouse, day-trippers can anticipate a year-round teaching and practice facility and eight, four bedroom luxury villas. (Look for high-profile golf tournaments in the future.)

Foxwoods shoppers have 12,000 square feet of concourse to mosey through. Retail establishments sell everything from Native American-themed artifacts to children's games to sundries with store names, such as **Kidstuff**, **Indian Nations**, **Two Trees Inn Gift Shop** and **Jewelry Kiosk**.

Dining options, ranging from buffet-style to gourmet specialties, are as varied as the shopping experience. Among the restaurants are **Golden Dragon Café** (www.foxwoods.com/Dining/Casual/Menus/GoldenDragonCafe.htm), the **Bistro**, **Cedars Steak House** and **Sports Bar**.

However, what some believe is the true jackpot in town and less than a half-mile away from the casino, is the **Mashantucket Pequot Museum and Research Center**. Hundreds of millions of casino dollars built the world's largest and most comprehensive Native American museum and research center in 1998. Plan to spend the greater part of the day mesmerized by more than 85,000 square feet of permanent dioramas, interactive-computer programs and exhibits that depict 18,000 years of art and culture.

The journey begins with an escalator ride guiding day-trippers down into a simulated 18,000-year-old glacial crevasse. Highlights of the tour include a re-created, life-size, Indian summer village highlighted with poly-resin sculptures of nearly unclad native people. For adults and older children, the day's climax is watching the movie documenting the Pequot Massacre of 1637, which nearly brought demise to the native tribe. Changing exhibits, live performances and special events pour even more magic into the day.

GETTING THERE:

The Mashantucket area is approximately two hours from Boston, MA, and more than three hours from New York City; about 25 minutes away from Mohegan Resort Casino. The region is easily accessible from Interstate Highways 395, 95, 84 and also from Massachusetts Turnpike, I-90, which connects to I-395.

TRANSPORTATION:

The Mashantucket area is located approximately 25 minutes from the Groton-New London Airport and T.F. Green Airport in Warwick, Rhode Island, is approximately 45 miles away. The area is 61 miles southeast of Bradley International Airport in Windsor Locks. Southeast Area Transit (SEAT) bus service (860-886-2631) serves various points in and around Mashantucket. Numerous motor coaches serve Foxwoods Resort Casino.

ADDITIONAL INFORMATION:
The Mashantucket Pequot Tribal Eastern Area Office (860) 572-6100 will assist visitors with any questions about area attractions.

STODDARD HILL STATE PARK.
Route 12, Ledyard. Open all year, 8 a.m. to sunset. The park is located five miles south of Norwich. (860) 444-7591; www.friendsctstateparks.org/parks/stoddard_ hill.htm.

MASHANTUCKET PEQUOT MUSEUM AND RESEARCH CENTER.
110 Pequot Trail, Mashantucket. Open all year, daily, last admission is at 4 p.m. General admission is $15.00 adults, $13.00 seniors, $10.00 children and free to children 6 and under. Call about group rates. (800) 411-9671; www.pequotmuseum. org.

ACCOMMODATIONS:
GRAND PEQUOT TOWER.
Route 2. More than 800 deluxe guestrooms and suites offer world-class surroundings and a host of amenities. Other features include complimentary valet service, indoor pool, health spa and sauna and business center. Rates: $175-$315-up. 800-FOXWOOD; www.foxwoods.com.

GREAT CEDAR HOTEL.
Route 2. These 300 elegant, amenity-rich guestrooms and suites sit atop one of the resort's action-paced gaming rooms. Rates: $190-$275. (800) FOXWOOD; www. foxwoods.com.

TWO TREES INN.
240 Lantern Hill Road. Another Mashantucket Tribe-owned property located across the street from the casino. Designed in country-style ambience, the 260 guestrooms and suites include full, modern amenities. On site are also an indoor pool and fitness room; a 24-hour shuttle to the casino is available for guests. Rates: $125-$210. (800) FOXWOOD; www.foxwoods.com.

MARE'S INN B & B.
333 Colonel Ledyard Highway. Approximately seven and one-half miles from Foxwoods, five guestrooms with private baths and fireplaces await the sojourner. Pets are welcome by prior arrangement. Rates (including full breakfast): $100-$175. (860) 572-7556.

ABBEY'S LANTERN HILL INN.
780 Lantern Hill. Within walking distance to Foxwoods, but nestled within the countryside, take downtime in one of the five guestrooms and suites or private cottage, boasting private entrances, fireplaces and Jacuzzis. The innkeepers have incorporated their own elegance and contemporary flair throughout the inn's décor. Dog friendly, too! Rates: $89 to $140. (860) 572-0483.

ANNUAL FESTIVALS/EVENTS

Mystic Country/CONNECTICUT representing 42 communities, provides a gamut of tourism information, which includes seasonal events (800) 863-6569 or (860) 444-2206; www.ctquietcorner.com or www.mysticcountry.com. For additional festival and event information, contact the Ledyard Town Hall (860) 464-3203; www.town.ledyard.ct.us. Also, call Foxwoods Resort Casino (800-FOXWOOD; www.foxwoods.com) for information about hundreds of concerts and special events.

APRIL

The **Annual Spring Egg Hunt** at Ledyard Fairgrounds is a big hit with children. (860) 464-9122.

JULY

The **Powwow Festival** at the Mashantucket Pequot Museum is an odyssey of color and culture. On hand are Native American artisans, souvenirs and food. (800) 411-9671; www.pequotmuseum.org.

SEPTEMBER

An old-fashioned, town-wide event features traditional fair rides at the **Ledyard Fair,** full of food and entertainment at Ledyard Fairgrounds. (860) 464-9122; www.ledyardfair.org.

OCTOBER

The **Annual Fall Thanksgiving Celebration** at the Mashantucket Pequot Museum gives thanks with a variety of Native American demonstrations and entertainment venues. (800) 411-9671.

DECEMBER

Shoppers should mark their calendars for the **Winter Moon Native American Market** at the Mashantucket Pequot Museum. It offers thousands of Native American arts, crafts and souvenirs. (800) 411-9671.

The **Annual Light Parade and Carol Sing** is a town-wide activity. The town provides refreshments in exchange for canned-food donations for the food bank. (860) 886-0329.

Mashantucket Pequot Museum and Research Center
see pages 103-104

*The place...
the people...
the adventure;
History Comes
Alive!*

Photo Courtesy of
Steve Dunwell, Photography, Inc., MPMRC

Photo Courtesy of
Jeff Goldberg, Esto, MPMRC

What village was named after a well-liked Indian sachem?

What town is home to one of the world's largest and most profitable casinos and offers some of the oldest attractions related to Native American culture?

High-Rollin' Country Roads:
MONTVILLE/UNCASVILLE

Approximately halfway between Norwich and New London with a residential population of more than 17,000 is the town of Montville. Characterized by rolling hills and green pastures, it sprawls along 45 square miles. Located on the west side of the Thames River, the town includes the village of Uncasville as well as Mohegan, Chesterfield and Oakdale. Although speculation surrounds the origin of Montville's name (the town was incorporated in 1786), Uncasville was named after Mohegan sachem Uncas, well-known Indian ally of the colonists.

Early on, Montville became synonymous with its river mills. However, during the height of colonization, as English settlements expanded, Uncas and his tribe relocated to the town's Shantok region. By the 18th century, the adjacent village of Shantok raged with territorial conflicts between the Mohegans and neighboring Rhode Island's Narragansett Tribe.

The Mohegan (meaning "wolf") Tribe overcame various strife through the centuries. Its major feat was gaining federal recognition, which it finally accomplished in 1994, albeit the Connecticut Colony recognized the sovereignty of the Mohegan Tribe in the Treaty of 1638. In 1995, the tribe reacquired 240 acres of the northernmost Mohegan reservation land, lost in 1872 due to corrupt state practices. Today, the Mohegan Tribe owns 409 acres of federal-trust land in both Montville and Norwich and a potential to gain future federal property.

The **Mohegan Reservation** is adjacent to the village of Uncasville, sharing the western bank of the Thames River. Also located on the Thames River are historical **Fort Shantok State Park** and its ancient burial grounds. These days, the Mohegan village, a backbone of the Mohegan culture, constitutes a National Registered Historic Landmark, where day trips with panache begin. Be forewarned that this is sacred land and ground disturbance, such as littering or picnicking on any part of Shantok, is a federal offense. The piled up stones, serving as a cairn (in the shape of a wigwam), is the **Leffingwell Memorial**, in honor of the lieutenant and his English relief force from Saybrook that had saved the fort from attacking Narragansetts in 1645.

Three generations of Mohegan women from the Tantaquidgeon family founded Uncasville's **Mohegan Church**, now filled with historic documents and artifacts, in 1827. Members have conducted tribal meetings and festivities here ever since. The Tantaquidgeon family also founded the **Tantaquidgeon Museum** in 1931, today, constituting the oldest Indian-run museum in America. The modest fieldstone building, still run by the same family, presents Mohegan and other Woodland Indian artifacts, including a teepee and traditional baskets woven from oak and ash, dating back more than 200 years.

Of course, what has brought worldwide fame to their area is the **Mohegan Sun Resort Casino** (888-226-7711; www.mohegansun.com). The casino portion alone in this 34-story glass and steel hotel complex is an astounding site jutting out above the green forest nestled along Thames River, featuring more than 300,000 square feet of gaming fun, including over 6,000 slot machines, table games, poker and horseracing games. Operated by the 1,500-member Mohegan Tribe, this is one of the world's largest—a tad shy in size of neighboring Foxwoods—and one of the most profitable casinos.

Open 24/7 for serious day- and night-trippers, beyond gambling, this is a destination oasis boasting the world's largest planetarium dome, **Kids Quest/Cyber Quest** family entertainment facility, a 10,000-seat arena (where the **Mohegan Wolves** [860-443-1900] play arena football) and 300-seat cabaret, both billing world-renowned celebrities and entertainment.

Day-trippers searching for a relaxing massage or specialized treatment at the 20,000-square-foot **Elemis Spa** should book a reservation well ahead of their scheduled day of arrival. No matter what is on the day-trippers' agenda, plan on a walk through the Mohegan Sun complex just to experience the architecture and beauty of its stunning onyx and glass design.

Shoppers and souvenir hunters have a diversified selection of stores that include **Lux, Bond & Green** (860-862-9900 www.lbgreen.com/StoreMoheganSun. aspx?cookie=0), **Yankee Candle** (860-889-5333; www.mohegansun.com/ shopping/index.jsp), **Clay Pipe** (860-862-8297; www.mohegansun.com/shopping/ other_shops.jsp#essentials), **Everything Under the Sun** (860-862-7499; www. mohegansun.com/shopping/other_shops.jsp#everything) and **Trading Cove** (860-862-8268; www.mohegansun.com/shopping/specialty_shops.jsp#trading).

The many restaurant options range from **Big Bubba's BBQ** (860-862-9800; www.mohegansun.com/dining/casual_big_bubbas.jsp) to **Michael Jordan's 23.sportcafe** (860-862-2300; www.mohegansun.com/dining/casual_michaels_ 23sportscafe.jsp), **Jasper White's Summer Shack** (860-862-8600; www. summershackrestaurant.com) and **Rain** (888-226-7711; www.mohegansun.com/ dining/gourmet_rain.jsp).

GETTING THERE:

Montville is approximately 105 minutes from Boston, MA, and two and a half hours from New York City; about 25 minutes away from Foxwoods Resort Casino. The region is easily accessible from Interstate Highways 395, 95, 84 and from the Massachusetts Turnpike, I-90, connecting to I-395.

TRANSPORTATION:

The Montville area is located approximately 20 minutes from the Groton-New London Airport and T.F. Green Airport in Warwick, Rhode Island, approximately 56 miles away. The area is 43 miles southeast of Bradley International Airport in Windsor Locks. Southeast Area Transit (SEAT) bus service (860-886-2631) serves various points in and around Montville. Numerous motor coaches serve Mohegan Sun Resort Casino.

ADDITIONAL INFORMATION:
The Mohegan Tribal Office (860) 862-6100 will assist visitors with any questions regarding Montville and its attractions.

FORT SHANTOK STATE PARK.
Fort Shantok Road, Montville. Open all year, sunrise to sunset.

MOHEGAN CHURCH.
Located off Route 32, Uncasville. Located on Mohegan Hill. The church is open to the public by appointment. The public is also invited to the Congregationalist Protestant services, Sunday at 9:30 a.m. Closed summers.

TANTAQUIDGEON MUSEUM.
1819 Norwich-New London Turnpike. Open limited days and times; call for days and hours of operation. The museum's first floor is handicapped accessible. General admission is $3.00 adults, $2.00 seniors, $2.00 children and free to children 5 and under. (860) 546-9916.

ACCOMMODATIONS:
MOHEGAN SUN RESORT CASINO.
1 Mohegan Sun Boulevard. The 34-story, 1,200-room hotel houses the largest ballroom in the northeast and state-of-the-art meeting rooms. Hotel rooms feature triple-sheeted bedding of Egyptian cotton. Amenities include a business center, indoor pool, fitness center, cable television and modem hookups in guestrooms. Rates: $175-$375-up. (888) 226-7711; www.mohegansun.com/hotel_spa/index.jsp.

ANNUAL FESTIVALS/EVENTS
Mystic Country/CONNECTICUT representing 42 communities, provides a gamut of tourism information, which includes seasonal events (800) 863-6569 or (860) 444-2206; www.ctquietcorner.com or www.mysticcountry.com. For additional festival and event information, contact the Montville Town Hall (860) 848-3030. Also, call Mohegan Sun Resort Casino (888-226-7711) for information about myriad concerts and special events.

APRIL
Divers can find new and used scuba gear at the **Scuba Swap Meet** at the Polish-American Club in Montville. Raffles and a silent auction are also part of the festivities. (800) 863-6569.

JULY
Make note of the **Classic Auto Show** on the rooftop of Mohegan Sun Resort Casino that features prizes and giveaways. (508) 428-8055.

Summertime means there must be a **Southeastern Connecticut Mustang Club** Saturday Night Cruise at Mohegan Firehouse, Route 32 in Uncasville. (800) 863-6569.

The **Annual Pillar Polkabration** is the longest running polka festival in America. The Mohegan Sun Resort Casino hosts the day of dance and food. (860) 848-8171; (888) 226-7711.

AUGUST

The third weekend of August is devoted to the Mohegan Tribe's annual **Green Corn Festival**, which is also known as "**The Wigwam**." Dancing and storytelling are presented, clam chowder and succotash are served and tribal artwork is featured at Fort Shantok. (860) 862-6277 or 1-800-MOHEGAN.

The **Montville Agricultural Fair** is a day full of competitions, livestock exhibitions and entertainment. It is held on Old Colchester Road across from Montville High School. (860) 848-3030.

Shop at Mohegan Sun Resort Casino
See page 107

What Connecticut town is the only one that
faces the Atlantic Ocean?

What town is home to the last surviving
commercial fishing fleet in the state?

Serene Sojourns:
STONINGTON/NORTH STONINGTON

The modern-day Stonington area, located between the Thames and the Pawcatuck Rivers, used to belong to the Pequots who referred to the territory by two names: Pawcatuck and Mistack. Settled in 1649 by the Massachusetts Bay Colony, it was renamed Southertown in 1658, due to its southerly location. By 1666, settlers finally dubbed the region "Stonington," because of many failed attempts to farm the hilly countryside's rocky soil.

Residents incorporated the borough of Stonington, the oldest in Connecticut, in 1801. The community of Stonington not only includes this borough, but also parts of Mystic (see **Mystic** chapter), Old Mystic, Pawcatuck and Wequetequock, which was the first region of settlement. The town of North Stonington was separated from Stonington in 1724 and incorporated in 1807. Today, this inland town has a population of nearly 5,000. The primary industry, following in the steps of its ancestors, is dairy farming.

Stonington, Connecticut's easternmost coastal town, less than six miles from the Westerly, Rhode Island border, is situated on the only Connecticut harbor that directly faces the Atlantic Ocean. Stonington has a residential population of just over 17,000. Visitors will get a healthy dose of everything nautical including peninsulas, islands, coves and marshes along Stonington's rocky shoreline. Especially on a clear day, espy Fisher's Island and Long Island on the southwest and Block Island on the southeast. The early borough of Stonington prospered through sealing, whaling and shipbuilding, besides remaining home to the last surviving commercial fishing fleet in the state.

During the Revolutionary War, Stonington townsfolk succeeded in putting the kibosh on British forces twice, once in 1775 and again in 1814. Community members display two 18-pound cannons that helped defend Stonington during both these incidents in the center of town at **Cannon Square**. Throughout the 20th century, Stonington became a popular retreat for city dwellers and travelers seeking respite. A popular trend, for the most part, that remains today.

Day trips with panache commence with a stroll through **Stonington Borough** where the land juts out into Little Narragansett Bay. The commercial fishing fleets hurling in their daily fish and lobster catches create a feeling of anticipation and excitement. Discover the well-preserved, 18th- and 19th-century homes with exceptional examples of Colonial Federal and Greek Revival-style architecture and flower gardens lining the narrow streets. Images of famous poet and native son, James Merrill who immortalized Water Street in his poem by the same name, come to mind.

A pamphlet entitled, *Historic Walking Tour of Stonington*, best identifies a mile of this region. Pick up this map, along with an array of other helpful tourist information, at the **North Stonington State Welcome Center** (see **Additional Information**). At 101 Main Street, the Friends program at **Wheeler Library** (860-535-0383) has arranged for free and discounted passes for day-trippers to such area attractions as the Denison Pequotsepos Nature Center and Mystic Seaport (see **Mystic** chapter) and the Wadsworth Atheneum (see **Hartford** chapter). While at the library, inquire about any special library events or concerts open to the public. (The depiction on this book's front cover illustrates an example of one of the past outdoor concerts!)

In the borough, summers are synonymous with a refreshing swim at **Dubois Beach**. **Dodson Boatyard** (860-535-1507; www.dodsonboatyard.com) is a popular harbor and stopover for pleasure boats and yachts. A farmers' market on the town dock, Saturday morning, featuring fruit, flowers, seafood and other native goods, signals harvest time from June until October.

Near Dubois Beach at "the point" in the village, embark on the winding stairway in the **Old Lighthouse Museum**, an imposing stone structure. At the top, day-trippers can encounter a bird's-eye perspective of the harbor as well as views of Fisher's Island, New York and Watch Hill, Rhode Island. Six rooms of nautical and historical exhibits (including the retelling of Stonington's participation in two major colonial battles; see the beginning of this chapter) complement the visit to the museum. Old Lighthouse Museum draws about 13,000 visitors a year. Operated by the Stonington Historical Society, contractors built the lighthouse in 1823, the first to be established by the U.S. Federal Government.

The historical society's sister property is the **Captain Nathaniel B. Palmer House**, the crown of the borough that draws a nearly perfect imaginary line connecting to Stonington point. Two brothers, Captains Alexander Smith Palmer and Nathaniel Brown Palmer, "the Yankee skipper who discovered Antarctica," built this 16-room Victorian mansion in 1852. Inside, their journey unfolds through an array of intriguing seafaring artifacts, whimsical initials carved in old glass windows and a cupola in which one can soak up the sun of Stonington Harbor or eavesdrop on the village below.

Heading north, at 523 Taugwonk Road is **Stonington Vineyards** (860-535-1222; www.stoningtonvineyards.com), where day-trippers can ramble through 58 acres proving stony soil is only good for grapes! Watch the process that produces more than 15,000 gallons of wine annually. Leave with a bottle of Seaport White or Seaport Blush from the gift shop. Open daily, hosts give free wine cellar tours at 2 p.m.

Back in the village, shoppers have more than 30 antiques stores and boutiques to probe. On Water Street is **Devon House Antiques** (860-535-4452) featuring English, Irish, French and country-style furniture, accessories and gifts. **Cumulus** (860-535-0491) specializes in handcrafted jewelry and gifts, plus ceramics and glassware. At 17 High Street, the **Book Mart** (860-535-0401) is a favorite hiatus to indulge in good reads. Take the time to turn off Route 2 (what locals call "Casino Road"!) in North Stonington to browse **Raspberry Junction** (860-535-8410; www.raspberryjunction.com/crafters.html), a premier arts and crafts center offering more than 250,000 handcrafted items from more than 300 artisans across America.

Two favorite eateries located on Water Street are **Water Street Café** (860-535-2122), a whimsical little café that's big on contemporary-American flavor, serving lunch and dinner daily; and **Noah's** (860-535-3925), with its homey atmosphere complemented by an array of homemade foods, serving breakfast, lunch and dinner daily. **Skipper's Dock** (860-535-0111), 66 Water Street, provides free dockage to patrons. Open for lunch and dinner daily all year, the restaurant wins rave reviews from expert critics and local diners alike for its fresh food and scenic atmosphere year after year.

Leave 'carb counters home before entering **Custy's International Buffet** (860-599-1551; www.custys.com) on nearby Route 2, and don't forget to wear loose clothing when pigging out at "the World's Most Famous Buffet." Open Wednesday through Sunday (double check off-season dates), all-inclusive adult buffets, under $65, mean unlimited trips to the food station to load up on lobsters, Black Angus steaks, seafood and every decadent dessert and side dish imaginable. Pineapples dipped in chocolate, anyone?

Randall's Ordinary (860-651-5700; www.randallsordinary.com/dining.asp), located at the Inn at Stonington (see **Accommodations**), serves breakfast, lunch and dinner daily and features open-hearth cooking. Listed on the National Register of Historic Places, the stop was once on the Underground Railroad and, today, servers costumed in 18th-century attire greet visitors.

While in North Stonington, consider a tour of **Jonathan Edwards Winery** (860-535-0202; www.jedwardswinery.com), 74 Chester Main Road, which showcases wines from Napa Valley. Occasional receptions are held in the on-premises art gallery.

Day-trippers seeking outdoor adventure cannot miss Pawcatuck's **Barn Island State Wildlife Management Area** on Palmer Neck Road. Open year-round, it's great for hiking, wildlife and bird watching, fishing, boating, canoeing and kayaking (there is a public launch) and windsurfing.

Other popular Pawcatuck stopovers include **Adam's Garden of Eden** (860-599-4241) that carries garden specialties and unique gifts. At **Cottrell Brewing Company** (860-599-8213; www.cottrellbrewing.com; call for days and hours of operation), a small family-run brewery since 1997, sample Old Yankee Ale. During the summer, adults and children of all ages can catch some old-fashioned fun at **Maple Breeze Park** (860-599-1232; call for days and hours of operation), a small but charming amusement park.

GETTING THERE:

The Stonington area is within three hours or less from New Haven and Hartford, CT, Boston, MA, Providence, RI, and New York City; about 18 miles southeast of Mohegan Sun Resort Casino. The region is easily accessible from Interstate Highway 95, which connects to I-84 and also from Massachusetts Turnpike, I-90, which connects to I-395.

TRANSPORTATION:

The Stonington area is located approximately 13 miles from the Groton-New London Airport. T.F. Green Airport in Warwick, Rhode Island, is approximately 41 miles northeast. The area is 72 miles southeast of Bradley International Airport in Windsor Locks. Stonington is within three hours or less of major transportation centers in New Haven and Hartford, CT, Boston, MA, Providence, RI and New York City. Southeast Area Transit (SEAT) bus service (860-886-2631) services Mystic Village, located within the town of Stonington. In addition, Amtrak (800-USA-RAIL) is also located in Mystic.

ADDITIONAL INFORMATION:

NORTH STONINGTON STATE WELCOME CENTER.
I-95 southbound between exits 92 and 91. The tourism center is open 24/7. State tourism guides are on duty during the day. (860) 599-2056.

OLD LIGHTHOUSE MUSEUM.
7 Water Street. Open May through October, Tuesday through Sunday; also open Monday, July and August. General admission (which also includes a tour to the Captain Nathaniel B. Palmer House, see listing below) is $5.00 for adults, $3.00 children and free to children 5 and under. (860) 535-1440; www.stoningtonhistory. org/light.htm.

CAPTAIN NATHANIEL B. PALMER HOUSE.
40 Palmer Street. Open May through October, Tuesday through Sunday. General admission (which also includes a tour of the Old Lighthouse Museum, see listing above) is $5.00 for adults, $3.00 children and free to children 5 and under. (860) 535-8445; www.stoningtonhistory.org/palmer.htm.

ACCOMMODATIONS:

THE INN AT STONINGTON.
60 Water Street. Located directly on the waterfront in Stonington Borough and named *Travel and Leisure* Magazine's *Inn of the Month*, yachts have their own pier at their disposal. Many of the 18 guestrooms, complete with outside decks, provide views of Stonington Harbor and Fisher's Island Sound. All rooms feature full, modern amenities and include fireplaces, oversized, luxurious bathrooms; most have Jacuzzis. There is also an on-premises exercise room available. Rates (including continental breakfast): $135-$395. (860)535-2000; www.innatstonington.com.

ANOTHER SECOND PENNY INN.
870 Pequot Trail. This historic 1710 Colonial features two guestrooms and one suite providing full, modern amenities including luxurious bathrobes. Hearth-cooking classes are available during the cooler months. The innkeepers welcome children 8 and older and some pets. Rates (including a five-course breakfast menu): $80-$195. (860) 535-1710; www.secondpenny.com.

RANDALL'S ORDINARY.
Route 2, North Stonington. In 1685, John Randall II built the original house, which was expanded in 1720 and completed in 1790. Operated today by the Mashantucket Pequot Tribe, the 15 guestrooms and suites at the ordinary (an old word for "tavern") feature full, modern amenities, including handicapped-accessible rooms, an on-premises restaurant (see above) and a lovely, quaint flavor within 200-plus emerald-green acres. Ghost seekers may opt to book Room 12 at the inn and see if the original owner "pays a visit." Rates (including full breakfast): $150-$350. (860) 599-4540; www.randallsordinary.com/lodging.asp.

ANTIQUES AND ACCOMMODATIONS.
32 Main Street, North Stonington. Antiques brim from nearly every interior corner of this Victorian-style compound comprised of three historic houses. Five guestrooms and suites offer private baths; some Jacuzzis and fireplaces. Rates (including candlelit breakfast): $110-$249. (860) 535-1736. (800) 554-7829; www. antiquesandaccommodations.com.

ANNUAL FESTIVALS/EVENTS

Mystic Country/CONNECTICUT representing 42 communities, provides a gamut of tourism information, which includes seasonal events (800) 863-6569 or (860) 444-2206; www.ctquietcorner.com or www.mysticcountry.com. For additional festival and event information, contact the Stonington Town Hall (860) 535-5000.

MAY
Stonington Vineyards is home to the **Spring Wine & Food Festival**. (860) 535-1222.

JUNE
A **Wine Festival** is held at Jonathan Edwards Winery in North Stonington. (860) 535-0202.

JULY
Stonington Vineyards hosts a summer **Wine & Food Festival** on its premises. (860) 535-1222.

Going for more than 41 years, the **North Stonington Fair**, one of the most recognized in the state, is a must. Sample at least one of four days chockfull of events in which farm life is the main focus. View tractor and animal pulls and competitions. Purchase award-winning vegetables, arts and crafts, fruits and baked goods. Enjoy entertainment and food throughout the day. (800) 863-6569.

AUGUST
A longtime tradition in Stonington is the **Blessing of the Fleet**. Festivities include a solemn religious observance in remembrance of anglers lost at sea as well as a blessing for the safety and prosperity of active anglers today; a parade and concert. (800) 863-6569.

Adam's Garlic Fest features gourmet garlic treats, handicrafts and a farmers' market. Adam's Garden of Eden is located at 360 N. Anguilla in Pawcatuck. (860) 599-4241.

Take part in old-fashioned fun at the annual **Village Fair** that attracts crowds from everywhere. (800) 863-6569.

SEPTEMBER
The **Country Fair** is another old-fashioned, fun festival that is an annual pilgrimage for many to the area. (800) 863-6569.

OCTOBER
The **Harvest Wine & Food Festival** at Jonathan Edwards Winery features wine, gourmet food, vendors, arts and crafts, music and a grape-stomping contest. (860) 535-0202.

---

*What Connecticut village falls under the
jurisdiction of two different towns?*

*What Connecticut village boasts the
largest maritime museum in North America?*

Maritime Merriment: **MYSTIC**

Immortalized by its booming 19th-century wooden shipbuilding industry, Mystic possesses a fascinating maritime history and picturesque setting on the east bank of the Mystic River. When tourists think Connecticut, usually Mystic, especially in the summer, comes to mind.

Called "Misstuck," meaning "great tidal river," by the Pequot Indians, modern-day Mystic has its own zip code, fire department and post office, but officials classify it as a village rather than a town. Geographically, it forms a horseshoe over the Mystic River that falls half in Groton and half in Stonington. Citizens on the east side of the river are part of Stonington's government; those on the west are under the jurisdiction of Groton.

Mystic's residential population totals approximately 4,000. Less than three miles north, the village region of Old Mystic has another approximately 3,200. Day trips with panache unfold with a stopover at the "Scenic Overlook," a designated alcove before Exit 90 North on Interstate Highway 95. Observe dozens of ship masts pierce the skyline as vessels bob over the billowy river below, part of the exhibit at **Mystic Seaport: The Museum of America and the Sea**. Between 1783 and 1919, artisans built more than 1,400 wooden sea vessels along the Mystic and Thames Rivers (west of Mystic), creating a major shipbuilding center. Today, many devoted volunteers and staff keep this nautical past alive at the 17-acre Mystic Seaport, a former shipyard, touted as North America's largest maritime museum.

Situated along the Mystic River, Mystic Seaport opened in 1929, making it one of the state's first major tourist attractions. Actual remnants salvaged from nearby shipyards went into building this re-creation of an 1800s New England whaling and shipbuilding village. Today, the living history museum features hundreds of ships, more than 60 buildings, exhibits, a planetarium, art gallery, gift shop, eateries and a lighthouse replica of Nantucket Island's Brant Point Light. A closer examination reveals a notable vessel collection that represents the art of wooden shipbuilding, a craft nearly forsaken since the advent of fiberglass and steel. A bodacious example is the Charles W. Morgan, which was actively whaling until 1921 and is today a National Historic Landmark, not to mention, America's last surviving wooden whale ship.

For a closer look (May through October) and superb photo opportunities of the **Morgan Point Lighthouse** in the neighboring village of Noank, book a river excursion or charter cruise on the 1908 **Steamboat Sabino** (860-572-5351). Docked at the seaport as a working exhibit, the Sabino is the last coal-fired steamboat in operation in the United States.

Less than one mile north is the other acclaimed area attraction, **Mystic Aquarium and Institute for Exploration**, with renowned animal research, rescue and rehabilitation programs and facilities. Opened in 1973, this non-profit marine life center, boasts more than 30 indoor and outdoor exhibits containing thousands of mammals, fish and invertebrates.

African black-footed penguins, beluga whales, jellyfish and a 30,000-gallon coral reef delight visitors. Learn about ocean exploration and marine archaeology through interactive programs and exhibits. View one of the daily, live shows featuring four California sea lions at the Marine Theater where you will not only be mesmerized by "search and rescue" feats performed by a retired "Navy Seal," but also witness how a whopping 845 pounds doesn't infringe upon the ballerina-style of 18-year-old sea lion Coco! No one leaves without learning the most popular question posed at the theater: what is the difference between a sea lion and a seal? Before heading out, sail into the **Waterfront Café** next door to the gift shop and refuel with a hot dog or veggie burger.

Nearby the aquarium, **Olde Mistick Village** (860-536-4941; www. oldmysticvillage.com) with more than 60 retail shops is reminiscent of 1720 New England. Surroundings include ponds, picket fences, stonewalls, waterwheels and during the summer, hear concerts. Pick up tourism information, coupons and the like at **Mystic and Shoreline Visitor Information Center** (860-536-1641), building 1D in Olde Mistick Village.

One charming Olde Mistick Village shop is **A Taste of New England** (860-572-4896; 888-572-4896) that sells unique gifts, souvenirs, collectibles, antiques and gourmet foods. Warning: one taste of fudge and you'll be hooked! At building 58 is **Haight Vineyard** (800-577-9463), sister to Litchfield County's main winery by the same name, specializing in apple wines. Art lovers can browse through hand-blown glass and paintings at **Go Fish** (860-536-2662) in Olde Mistick Village. Opposite Olde Mistick Village and the aquarium are the **Mystic Factory Outlets** (860-443-4788), where 24 national brand factory outlets offer everything from clothes to kitchenware.

From Coogan Boulevard, Route 27 leads to Old Mystic, less than two miles in distance. On route, the **Indian & Colonial Research Center** is a treasure trove for serious and budding historians, anthropologists and genealogy researchers. The main building was originally Mystic National Bank (notice the barred windows) completed in 1856. Inside, display cases contain Eastern Woodlands and Southwestern Native American artifacts, such as pottery, beadwork, textiles and stone tools. The old bank vault stores colonial manuscripts.

Make a note that at 129 North Stonington Road, **B.F. Clyde's Cider Mill** (860-536-3354) opens on August 1 with an assortment of hard ciders, apple wines, jams, maple syrup, fudge and local produce. From Labor Day into December, this famous sweet cider is pressed fresh daily from what is the largest and oldest (1881) steam-powered cider press in New England. The sixth generation of the Clyde family operates this National Historic Landmark. Other fall specialties include home-baked pies and breads, gourds, Indian corn, pumpkins, candy apples and fresh Johnnycake meal ground at the circa 1920 gristmill.

In historical **downtown Mystic**, the famous Mystic River bascule drawbridge connects the Stonington side of the village to the Groton side. Built in 1922, it is the oldest of its type in the country. Opening everyday in the summer at quarter past the hour, beginning at 7:15 a.m. until 7:15 p.m., it helps distract impatient tagalong companions who accompany serious shoppers on Route 1.

You'll require ample time when perusing Mystic's boutiques and shops; call for days and hours of operation. Check out "bearaphernalia" at **Good Hearted Bears**, (860-536-2468); **Shells Galore 'N More**, (860-536-8060); **Bank Square Books** (860-536-3795); **N.L. Shaw and Company** (860-572-5838) carrying antiques and estate jewelry and **Southern Exposure** (860-572-1007) offering American-themed merchandise.

A good starting point on the Mystic art trail is the **Mystic Art Association Museum and Gallery** (860-536-7601). Celebrating nearly a century of art, the gallery, open all year, daily, features permanent, changing exhibits and a roster of classes and special events; the facility also extends perfect river views.

Cruising, sailing and fishing are other daytime expeditions that leave from downtown throughout the summer. For instance, **ARGIA** (860-536-0416), an authentic replica of a 19th-century, gaff-rigged sailing schooner at 15 Holmes Street, offers a variety of day-trip voyages. Call for a cruise schedule for downtown's **Mystic Whaler** (1-800-697-8420; 860-536-4218), a windjammer vessel that was originally built in 1967 and rebuilt in 1993. For deep-sea fishing, try **Lorna Anne Fishing Charters** (860-423-9121; www.lornaannecharters.com) at Mystic Shipyard East.

Open daily, **Mystic Depot Welcome Center LLC** (860-572-1102) at 2 Roosevelt Avenue on Route 1, carries brochures, maps and other tourism-related information on the many day-tripping options in and around the area. Another way to get around Mystic other than car is on a bicycle or moped, which day-trippers can rent at **Mystic River Rental Bait & Tackle** (860-572-0123), 15 Chiles Street. Other store rentals include kayaks, canoes, rowboats, fishing poles as well as bait and tackle sold; plus, a series of guided tours for landlubbers and river enthusiasts are offered.

One of the major undertakings of the **Mystic River Historical Society** is the **Portersville Academy** (860-536-4779; www.mystichistory.org; call for days and hours of operation), which is located at 74 High Street off West Main Street. Housed in an 1839 Greek Revival schoolhouse, admission is free. Peruse changing exhibits, sit at an antique desk and imagine how life was more than 100 years ago.

For an additional dose of colonial Mystic, travel less than two miles northeast to the **Denison Homestead Museum**. Located on 200 acres of meadows and woodlands, George Denison, grandson of early settlers Captain George and Lady Ann, built the house in 1717 for his bride Lucy Gallup. The original furnishings, collections and artifacts from the Denison family in the house represent the period from 1717 to 1941. Today, 11 generations later, the Denison Society owns and maintains the homestead as a museum.

The society rents its property across the street for a dollar a year to the **Denison Pequotsepos Nature Center**. Spend the day bird watching, hiking, cross-country skiing in the winter or simply enjoying nature in this 200-acre preserve. For an enhanced hands-on encounter with native wildlife, enter the natural history museum. The indoor exhibits allow for close encounters with live frogs, fish, snakes and turtles. Visitors also get a hoot out of the wildlife sanctuary that provides outdoor flight enclosures for several species of hawks and owls; all indigenous to southern New England. Purchase a handmade birdhouse or walking stick at the **Trading Post** gift shop as a souvenir. The nature center also operates Peace Sanctuary on River Road. Try to make a special trip in May when nearly 400 pink lady's slippers bloom.

Open seven days all year, for frolicking fun throughout the year, take the family or your sweetie for a spin on the 36-foot carousel at Mystic's **Carousel and Fun Center** (860-572-9949), 193 Greenmanville Avenue. Visitors will also find plenty of other indoor amusements like train rides, kiddy play maze and arcade games. Remember to bring enough money to spend at the gift shop.

Hunger pangs are easy to soothe. One of the newer establishments already receiving rave reviews for its fusion of local ingredients like Stonington Scallops is **RiverWalk Restaurant** (860-536-5220), 14 Holmes Street, open all year, lunch daily, and dinner Thursday through Sunday. In season, dine outdoors while being serenaded by the sounds of Mystic River. Downtown Mystic is also home to **Mystic Pizza** (860-536-3700; www.mystic-pizza.com.) where Hollywood crews filmed the 1988 movie by the same name. Open for lunch and dinner daily, it remains a popular—be prepared for long lines in the summer—restaurant with tourists. In the heart of downtown, at 4 Pearl Street, encounter the **Harp and Hound Pub** (860-572-7778), a favorite among locals and visitors. Whether lunch, dinner or after-hours, this lively place, open Thursday through Sunday, features an authentic Irish-style menu and large selection of Irish and Scottish malts, plus Irish ales on tap.

Two other popular choices at the junction of Route 1 and Route 27 are **Sea Swirl** (860-536-3452), an award-winning clam shack open March through October and serving breakfast, lunch and dinner and **Christine's Flood Tide Restaurant** (860-536-8140), located at the Inn at Mystic (see **Accommodations**). This upscale restaurant serves breakfast, lunch (Sunday brunch) and dinner daily and specializes in French, continental cuisine.

Located at the north entrance of Mystic Seaport is **Seamen's Inne Restaurant & Pub** (860-572-5303). Open for lunch and dinner daily; and weekend breakfast, the restaurant is reputed for its casual, fine New England dining menu. At 20 Coogan Boulevard is **The Mooring** (860- 572-0731), specializing in seafood, it is open for lunch and dinner daily. Located at the Hilton Mystic (see **Accommodations**), it was voted *best hotel dining* by *Connecticut Magazine*.

GETTING THERE:

Mystic is within three hours or less from New Haven and Hartford, CT, Boston, MA, Providence, RI, and New York City; about five miles west of Stonington. The region is easily accessible from Interstate Highway 95, which connects to I-84 and from Massachusetts Turnpike, I-90, which connects to I-395.

TRANSPORTATION:

Mystic is located approximately nine miles east of the Groton-New London Airport and T.F. Green Airport in Warwick, Rhode Island, is approximately 44 miles northeast. The area is 68 miles southeast of Bradley International Airport in Windsor Locks. Mystic is within three hours or less of major transportation centers in New Haven and Hartford, CT, Boston, MA, Providence, RI, and New York City. Southeast Area Transit (SEAT) bus service (860-886-2631) services Mystic Village. In addition, Amtrak (800-USA-RAIL) is also located in Mystic.

ADDITIONAL INFORMATION:

MYSTIC SEAPORT: THE MUSEUM OF AMERICA AND THE SEA.
75 Greenmanville Avenue. Open all year, daily. Inquire about special programs and events for all ages. General admission is $17.00 adults; $16.00 seniors; $9.00 children and free to children 5 and under and to Mystic Seaport members. (860) 572-5315; (888) 9seaport; www.mysticseaport.org.

MYSTIC MARINELIFE AQUARIUM.
55 Coogan Boulevard. Open all year, daily. Inquire about special programs and events for all ages. General admission is $16.00 adults; $15.00 seniors; $11.00 children and free to children 2 and under and free to Mystic Marinelife Aquarium members. (860) 572-5955; www.mysticaquarium.org.

INDIAN & COLONIAL RESEARCH CENTER.
Route 27, Old Mystic. Open April through November, Tuesday, Thursday and Saturday. Hours are limited. Also, open by appointment to members and "serious" researchers. General admission for research is free the first visit and then $5.00 for subsequent visits; admission is always free to members. (860) 536-9771.

DENISON HOMESTEAD MUSEUM.
Pequotsepos Road. Open May through October, Thursday through Monday and by appointment. General admission is $4.00 adults; $3.00 seniors; $3.00 students; $1.00 children under 12 and free to members. (860) 536-9248.

DENISON PEQUOTSEPOS NATURE CENTER.
120 Pequotsepos Road. Open all year, daily. General admission is $6.00 adults; $4.00 seniors and $4.00 children under 12 years old. (860) 536-1216; www.dpnc.org/index.html.

ACCOMMODATIONS:
Mystic boasts a fabulously diverse, charming and original line of accommodations ranging from classic inns like **Whaler's Inn** (860-536-1506; 800-243-2588); **Steamboat Inn** (860-536-8300; www.steamboatinnmystic.com); **Taber Inne Suites** (860-536-4904; 866-466-6878; www.taberinne.com) and the **Old Mystic Inn** (860-572-9422; www.oldmysticinn.com) to charming bed and breakfasts like **Brigadoon B & B** (860-536-3033) to campgrounds like **Seaport Campground** (860-536-4044; www.seaportcampground.com) in Old Mystic and facilities that also include a cottage-for-rent at **Harbour Inne** (860-572-9253; www.harbourinne-cottage.com). For complete lodging selections, click on www.visitmystic.com.

INN AT MYSTIC.
Junction Routes 1 and 27. Listed on the National Register of Historic Places, overlooking Mystic Harbor, this is a two-story resort complex with 67 guestrooms, suites, efficiencies and on-premises, upscale restaurant (see above). Many of the rooms on this 15-acre, hillside location provide ocean views, balconies, wood-burning fireplaces, oversized bathrooms, whirlpools, canopied queen- and king-sized beds. Lauren Bacall and Humphrey Bogart honeymooned here, and the inn hasn't lowered its standards since! Rates: $75-$295. (860) 536-8140; www.innatmystic.com.

HILTON MYSTIC.

20 Coogan Boulevard. The 182 guestrooms and five suites with Jacuzzis allow day-trippers perfect respite after a long day of touring. Complete, modern amenities include soundproof rooms, Sony Playstation in every room, heated indoor swimming pool, fitness center and on-premises restaurant (see above). Rates: $125-$279-up. (800) HILTONS; (860) 572-0731; www.hiltonmystic.com.

ANNUAL FESTIVALS/EVENTS

Mystic Country/CONNECTICUT representing 42 communities, provides a gamut of tourism information, which includes seasonal events (800) 863-6569 or (860) 444-2206; www.ctquietcorner.com or www.mysticcountry.com. For additional festival and event information, contact the Mystic and Shoreline Visitor Information Center (860) 536-1641; www.mysticinfo.com.

MAY

Lobsterfest means that New England lobster dinners are served, along with hot dogs, every Memorial Day weekend at Lighthouse Point by the Rotary Club of Mystic. (860) 536-1641.

JUNE

Watch small boats at Mystic Seaport's annual **Small Crafts Weekend**. (888) SEAPORT; www.mysticseaport.org.

Mystic Seaport sponsors the annual **Sea Music Festival** as musicians perform from the decks of the ships. (888) SEAPORT; www.mysticseaport.org.

Day-trippers can receive hoards of educational information on organic foods and gardening while getting to know the grounds of the nature center at the **Pequotsepos Solstice Celebration**. Food, live music and entertainment are also on the agenda. (860) 536-1216; www.dpnc.org/index.html.

JULY

Experience an old-fashioned 1870s **Fourth of July Celebration** at Mystic Seaport with special ceremonies, a rowdy parade and old-fashioned games for the children. (888) SEAPORT; www.mysticseaport.org.

Mystic Seaport features boats built before the 1950s at the **Antique Classic Boat Rendezvous**. Other festivities of the day include arts and crafts and a parade. (888) SEAPORT; www.mysticseaport.org.

Olde Mistick Village is the setting for the **Mystic Carvers Club Show** where local woodcarvers exhibit their creations. Free admission. (860) 536-4941.

More than 60 pieces of local artwork and other auction items are available at the **Bid n' Buy Auction** fundraiser. (860) 536-7601.

Rooms by Design of Cheshire sponsors the **Annual Summer Dollhouse Show and Sale** at Best Western Sovereign Hotel. (203) 272-9102.

AUGUST
Greater Mystic Chamber of Commerce sponsors the **Mystic Outdoor Arts Festival** in historic downtown Mystic. More than 300 artists display and sell their wares in what is the oldest festival in the northeast. (860) 572-5098.

SEPTEMBER
Mystic Rowing Weekend is sponsored by the Greater Mystic Chamber of Commerce. (860) 572-9578.

OCTOBER
Chowderfest at Mystic Seaport features a variety of chowders. (888) SEAPORT.

NOVEMBER
Mystic Seaport Field Days take place the day after Thanksgiving and features wagon rides, children's games, food and songs pertaining to the sea. (888) SEAPORT; www.mysticseaport.org.

DECEMBER
Day-trippers attending **Lantern-Light Tours** at Mystic Seaport should reserve a spot early because tour group slots fill up quickly! This old-fashioned-styled event features a horse-drawn omnibus. (888) SEAPORT; www.mysticseaport.org.

Mystic Aquarium
See page 116

You never know who you'll run into!

SOUTHEAST CONNECTICUT
New London County
"Mystic Places"
Groton/New London/Old Lyme

West of Mystic, roughly halfway between New Haven and Providence, Rhode Island, Interstate Highway 95, one of the most traveled highways in America, crosses through Groton, New London and Old Lyme. The many public boat launches and optimum fishing spots along the Thames, Mystic and Connecticut Rivers lure water enthusiasts from everywhere.

In Groton, headquarters of Groton Long Point Yacht Club, day-trippers can tour and learn the history of the world's first nuclear-powered submarine. Most educators know the town through Project Oceanology, part of an environmental science organization that provides hands-on marine science instruction aboard 55- and 65-foot vessels—an experience also open to day-trippers of all ages.

In the adjacent city, New London's world-famous harbor, with its distinct lighthouse rumored to be haunted, is a major United States Navy submarine base. The core of New London's population also includes United States Coast Guard students, United States Naval Reserve recruits, commercial enterprise employees, civilian pleasure boaters and, of course, day-trippers! People from all over the world mark their annual calendars to attend the famous Yale-Harvard boat races held on the city's Thames River. Also in the summer, hear your flip-flops crack against the state's only wooden boardwalk at New London's Ocean Beach Park.

Landlubbers who prefer sightseeing have numerous tour options: celebrated houses once built by sea captains; two college campuses; a whaling museum; New London's revitalized downtown area; a historical state park and Monte Cristo Cottage, the childhood summer home of the town's most famous native son, Eugene O'Neill.

In the early 20th century, the charm of the countryside and tranquility of the shoreline drew artists to the town of Old Lyme and inspired a new movement in art. Today, the Florence Griswold Museum boasts one of the country's largest collections of American Impressionism.

Families searching for fun and couples who desire romance can visit an impressive list of restaurants, bed and breakfasts, museums and nature-related stopovers that will suit nearly every taste. No matter what age or interest, these places deserve a day's sojourn—at very least.

In 1781, what Connecticut town suffered casualties after General Benedict Arnold's (American traitor and native-born Norwich son) troops burned it to the ground?

What Connecticut town has earned the title, "Submarine Capital of the World"?

Smashingly Sub-Marvelous: **GROTON**

The hillsides and lush terrain inclining into the shoreline of what is modern-day Groton were infiltrated, like that of many surrounding territories (see **Mystic**; **New London** chapter), by the Pequot Tribe. The English title of what amounts to Groton today was secured nearly a decade after the English Puritan troops under the leadership of Captain John Mason and John Winthrop Jr., with the help of Mohegan and Narragansett allies, displaced the Pequot Tribe in 1637.

The early settlers called the land, situated at what is currently the mouth of Thames River, by its Indian name "Nameaug," (meaning, "fishing place") or "Pequot Plantation." By 1705, steady population growth east of the river persuaded the English General Court to allow the town's incorporation. Groton's name honors Groton Manor, part of the Winthrop Estate (owned by the family of founding father John Winthrop Jr.) in England.

The Battle of Groton Heights occurred on September 6, 1781, when troops, under the command of traitor and native-born Norwich son, Benedict Arnold attacked the American defenders and first burned New London's buildings, wharfs and ships (see **New London** chapter) before moving to assault Fort Griswold (see **Fort Griswold Battlefield State Park**, see below).

During the late 1700s and into the 1800s, stubborn, rocky soil prompted would-be farmers to initiate a seafaring heritage that included shipbuilding, whaling and maritime trade. The state established a navy yard at the mouth of Thames River in 1868, which government officials later designated as a World War I submarine base.

Groton earned its title, "Submarine Capital of the World," when the Electric Boat Division of General Dynamics, the world's leading producer of submarines, stationed 74 diesel submarines at the base during World War II. In 1954, USS Nautilus, the world's first nuclear-powered submarine, arrived on base. Now, a popular tourist attraction, it's permanently berthed at Goss Cove near the submarine base.

Totaling a residential population of just over 39,000, the 31-square-mile stretch, adjacent to Fisher's Island Sound, borders Thames River on the west and Mystic River on the east. Day trips with panache begin at the **U.S. Navy Submarine Force Museum**, home of the **USS Nautilus**, the only submarine museum operated by the United States Navy in the world. Museum roots sprouted in 1955, when the Electric Boat Division of General Dynamics Corporation established the Submarine Force Library and donated the collection to the navy in 1964. Today, the museum owns more than 33,000 artifacts—from a full-size model of David Bushnell's Turtle (see **Essex** chapter; **Westbrook** chapter), the first, ever submarine (used unsuccessfully) in the Revolutionary War, to modern submarines; plus, 20,000 historical documents and 30,000 photographs. Peer through one of three periscopes and witness simulated battles that occurred from World War I to present. The trip's highlight is poking inside the control and navigation room, the crew's quarters and the galley of the USS Nautilus. The decommissioned ship became a permanent museum exhibit in 1985 and has since been designated as a National Historic Landmark.

Less than three miles south at the Avery Point campus of the University of Connecticut, consider a summertime **Project Oceanology** cruise that goes into Long Island Sound aboard one of the U.S. Coast Guard-inspected, research vessels, Enviro-Lab, sponsored by various New England schools and universities. Professional marine scientists conduct the two-and-a-half hour, hands-on oceanographic cruises as well as expeditions to New London's legendary, (some say haunted!) **Ledge Lighthouse**. Wintertime day-trippers can join a Harbor Seal Watch offered by Project Oceanology.

The brick **Avery Point Lighthouse**, lit 1944 and the only lighthouse in America built as a memorial for lighthouse keepers, was extinguished in 1967 and was relit September 2005, thanks to the five-year restoration efforts of the Avery Point Lighthouse Society, University of Connecticut and the American Lighthouse Foundation.

Less than a half-mile northwest on Plant Street, golfers can head to the **Shennecossett Public Golf Course** (860-445-0262; www.town.groton.ct.us/depts/parksrec/shenny.asp). Also known as, the "Shenny," the course is most notable for its views of Thames River and sightings of occasional submarines passing by. One of summertime's best family-time pleasures is bringing the brood to experience the 18-hole course at **Great Brook Mini Golf** (860-448-0938).

History buffs should go east to Groton Center and visit the **Jabez Smith House**, deeded to the town in 1974. The circa 1783 Colonial farmhouse is one of the oldest houses in Groton. The house, unaltered in appearance, brims with authentic 18th- and 19th-century antiques.

Take a moment to contemplate the meaning behind the black marble Wall of Honor at the **U.S. Submarine World War II Veteran's Memorial** (860-399-8666) located between Bridge and Thames Streets, less than three miles north of the golf course. The monument includes a roster of WWII service members killed during submarine service as well as 52 memorial plaques listing sunken boats.

Southward, about three miles, day-trippers will espy fort ramparts of **Fort Griswold Battlefield State Park**. The story of the Revolutionary War massacre begins at the **Groton Monument**, commemorating the site of the 1781 massacre led by traitor Benedict Arnold in which British forces captured the fort, and continues inside the on-premises Revolutionary War museum. (Also note that east, within a mile; **Colonel Ledyard Cemetery** contains the tombstone, along with many other old graves, of the brave soldier [Ledyard] who gave up his life during the battle at Fort Griswold.) At the park, for some sensational shoreline and area views, day-trippers can ascend 166 stairs to reach the 135-foot-obelisk observation point. Don't forget to tour the **Ebenezer Avery House**, a circa 1750, center-chimney Colonial that served as a repository for wounded soldiers; it was restored and moved to the park from its original site on Thames Street in 1971.

Notable to naturalists is **Bluff Point Coastal Reserve** (860-444-7591; www.dep.state.ct.us/stateparks/parks/bluffpoint.htm), about three miles southeast on Depot Road, the last remaining, significant parcel of undeveloped land along the Connecticut coastline. The wooded peninsula juts out into waters of Long Island Sound and measures one and one-half miles long by one-mile wide, encompassing over 800 acres. Outdoorsy types will find hiking and mountain-biking trails and plenty of wildlife to watch. There is also a public boat launch and saltwater fishing and shell fishing opportunities. (Fishing permits are issued by the Town of Groton, 860-441-6600.) For additional hiking trails and excellent bird watching, try **Haley State Park** (http://dep.state.ct.us/stateparks/parks/haleyfarm.htm) on Brook Street, adjacent to the reserve.

Groton boasts many pizzerias and restaurants for casual-style dining. Noted for hands-on pizza making during children's birthday parties and field trips is the **Plum Tomato** (860-405-1630), open for lunch and dinner daily. Where else can you get red or white pizza going under such names as the Louie, the I.R.A. and F.B.I.? Kiss of Death pizza, anyone? At **Paul's Pasta Shop** (860-445-5276), 223 Thames Street, day-trippers can come for lunch and dinner, Tuesday through Sunday, as well as purchase fresh pasta to cook at home. Number 359, **Waterfront** (860-449-0074) offers seaside views and caters to families during lunch (Sunday brunch) and dinner daily. Back at the Shenny, **Par Four Restaurant** (860-446-9146), serving lunch and dinner daily, is a popular spot all year long.

To the east of Groton, the village of Noank is the setting of two award-winning eateries that are the epitome of the New England coast: **Abbott's Lobster in the Rough** (860-536-7719; www.abbotts-lobster.com), 117 Pearl Street, and **Costello's Clam Shack** (860-572-2779; www.costellosclamshack.com) in the Noank Shipyard; both open in season daily. Don't miss Noank's **Fisherman Restaurant** (860-536-1717; www.fishermanrestaurant.com/index.html), at 937 Groton Long Point Road, offering beautiful coastline views and a complete menu specializing in fresh seafood, open for lunch and dinner daily.

GETTING THERE:

Groton is within three hours or less from New Haven and Hartford, CT, Boston, MA, Providence, RI, and New York City; about seven miles west of Mystic. The region is easily accessible from Interstate Highway 95, which connects to I-84 and also from Massachusetts Turnpike, I-90, which connects to I-395.

TRANSPORTATION:

The Groton-New London Airport serves a growing demand of business commuters and leisure travelers in the southeastern Connecticut region. T.F. Green Airport in Warwick, Rhode Island, is approximately 47 miles northeast. The area is 61 miles southeast of Bradley International Airport in Windsor Locks. Groton is within three hours or less of major transportation centers in New Haven and Hartford, CT, Boston, MA, Providence, RI, and New York City. Southeast Area Transit (SEAT) bus service (860-886-2631) services Groton. In addition, two Amtrak (800-USA-RAIL) train stations are located in town.

ADDITIONAL INFORMATION:

U.S. NAVY SUBMARINE FORCE MUSEUM, HOME OF THE USS NAUTILUS.

Naval Submarine Base. Open all year, daily. The museum is handicapped accessible; wheelchairs are available on a first-come-first-serve basis. The library is also open all year, but a visit must be prearranged. General admission and parking are free. (860) 694-3174; (800) 343-0079; www.ussnautilus.org.

PROJECT OCEANOLOGY.

1084 Shennecossett Road, Avery Point. Cruises operate June through September. Harbor seal cruises operate February and March. Reservations are recommended since seating is limited to 50 on the research vessel. General admission ticket is $19.00 adults; $16 children. (860) 445-9007; (800) 364-8472; www.oceanology. org.

JABEZ SMITH HOUSE.

259 North Road. Open April through December, Saturday and Sunday. However, tours may be prearranged on other days throughout the year. Donations are accepted. (860) 445-6689.

FORT GRISWOLD BATTLEFIELD STATE PARK.
Between Monument Street & Park Avenue. Open all year from 8 a.m. to sunset, daily. The **Ebenezer Avery House** and museum are open Memorial Day through Labor Day, daily; weekends Labor Day through Columbus Day. General Admission is free. (860) 449-6877; http://dep.state.ct.us/stateparks/parks/fort_griswold.htm.

ACCOMMODATIONS:
While in the Groton area, for day-trippers extending their stay, a variety of hotel and motel options are available like **Hampton Inn Groton** (860-405-1585; www. hamptoninn.com/en/hp/hotels/index.jhtml?ctyhocn=GONCTHX) and the **Groton Inn & Suites** (860-445-9784; www.grotoninn.com).

FLAGSHIP INN & SUITES.
99 Gold Star Highway. Sixty (double and single) guestrooms and suites feature modern amenities including refrigerators, freezers, microwaves, coffeemakers; plus, free health club privileges at local Powerhouse Gym. Rates (including free continental breakfast): $59.99-$159.99. (888) 800-0770; (860) 445-7458.

THAMES INN & MARINA.
193 Thames Street. This property consists of 26 well-appointed guestrooms and is the only waterfront inn on the Thames River. Offering full, modern amenities, most rooms have water views, and all have full kitchens and stoves or built-in cooktops. Rates (inquire about boat-slip-and-room combination rates): $79-$159. (860) 445-8111.

ANNUAL FESTIVALS/EVENTS
Mystic Country/CONNECTICUT representing 42 communities, provides a gamut of tourism information, which includes seasonal events (800) 863-6569 or (860) 444-2206; www.ctquietcorner.com or www.mysticcountry.com. For additional festival and event information, contact the Chamber of Commerce of Eastern Connecticut, (860) 464-7373.

APRIL
Annual Shotokan Karate Do America Spring Championships are held at the UConn Avery Point Campus Gym. Admission for spectators is free. (860) 429-7067.

MAY
Groton's **Annual Kids Karnival**, featuring fun and games, is held at the Youth Center. (860) 694-3174; (800) 343-0079.

The Groton Public Library, Route 117, holds its **Annual Plant & Bake Sale**. (860) 441-6750.

JUNE
Groton's **Annual Air Festival** offers free plane rides and hot-air balloon rides for children ages 8 to 17. The day's activities include fire and police demonstrations, WWII fighter plane exhibits, a food court and live entertainment. (860) 572-9578.

Area high school valedictorians are invited to the Greater Mystic Chamber of Commerce, which co-hosts the **Annual Education Breakfast**; open to the general public. (860) 464-7373.

JULY

Spectators can't wait to see the multi-light and sound show at the **Annual Groton/ New London Mashantucket Pequot Thames River Fireworks** by the Grucci Family. Free entertainment and food prior to the event. (860) 443-3786.

SEPTEMBER

The **Annual Golf Ball** is an evening of festivities that include a cocktail party, live and silent auction and live jazz music. The event is held at the Branford House, Avery Point. (860) 442-2797.

U.S. Navy Submarine Force Museum
See page 123, 125

An all-year adventure.

Photos Courtesy of Eastern Regional Tourism District

During the Revolutionary War in 1781, what settlement
was set on fire under the leadership of traitor
(and native-born Norwich son) Benedict Arnold?

What Connecticut city boasts one of the
largest cultural renaissances in the state?

Rising Starfish of the Sea: **NEW LONDON**

Stretching along the western side of the Thames River, a watershed of Long Island Sound, New London or what the Native Americans called "Nameaug," meaning "fishing place," shares a part of Groton's early history (see **Groton** chapter). During the Revolutionary War in 1781, the British, under traitor Benedict Arnold's command, stormed New London's northern supply center and destroyed naval supplies and much of the colonial privateer fleet, which the British referred to as "rebel pirate ships." By the end of the battle, 143 buildings were destroyed by fire before the British proceeded to impose their wrath on neighboring Fort Griswold (see **Groton** chapter).

Massachusetts Bay Colonists, loyal to heritage, dubbed the area "New" London and officials incorporated the city in 1784. Historically, its deep, protected harbor spurred prosperous seafaring and maritime trade. Merchant traders exchanged flour, cured ham and pork for imports from the West Indies like sugar, molasses and rum. During the 19th century, New London also made nautical history when it served as a whaling port to as many as 80 whaling ships.

A summer playground for the rich and famous in the late 1800s, the young O'Neill family settled here before son Eugene became one of America's most beloved playwrights. The talk of the day then was, "Big things are going to happen to New London."

Whale Oil Row, 105-119 Huntington Street, reminds us of a wealthy maritime legacy. Whale oil merchants or sea captains lived in these four Greek Revival-style houses, nearly identical in appearance, built for them in the 1830s. The whale ships have long since departed, but what remains are busy waterways active with freighters, yachts, cruise ships, charter vessels and fishing boats. Ferry services, some operating throughout the year, including a high-speed service, depart New London and travel to such popular destinations as Orient Point and Fisher's Island, New York, and Block Island, Rhode Island.

These days, after a decade of economical decline and debates over possible incoming Indian-run casinos, residents have renewed faith that the 21st century will indeed bring "big things" to New London—this time for good! Especially, after Pfizer Global Development, employing more than 2,000 persons, built their headquarters alongside the Thames River in 2001.

The city, approximately 46 miles east of New Haven and 45 miles southeast of Hartford, has a population of more than 25,000 in a roughly six-square-mile land stretch, and is also home to sleek and modern Lawrence Memorial Hospital and, apart from the Coast Guard Academy, two outstanding colleges: Connecticut and Mitchell. Day trips with panache begin by strolling along **Waterfront Park at City Pier** (860-437-6346). This longtime transportation hub has recently had a 19-million-dollar makeover including a waterfront park expansion, opening up an inviting half-mile promenade and five piers to anglers, boaters and most certainly sightseers. Its fiber-optic lighted stage also creates a premier outdoor venue attracting bountiful crowds seeking music and live entertainment.

One of the best ways to get acquainted with New London Harbor and the Thames River is to board the **SeaPony** (860-440-2734; www.seapony.com), a 149-passenger boat offering sightseeing via various seasonal tours. Captain Claus F. Wolter leads day-trippers past such aquatic landmarks as the Coast Guard Academy, Connecticut College, Fort Trumbull, the obelisk at Groton's Fort Griswold and Pfizer's World Research Headquarters. Once into Long Island Sound, the 1909 **New London Ledge Light** appears; the fourth oldest lighthouse in the U.S. that is rumored by many spectators to be haunted. A view of the waterway's **Fisher's Island** also makes the journey memorable.

To accommodate sailors with sport fishing on his or her mind, boats are available from **Brothers Too Charters** (860-235-0965; 860-437-3491; www. brotherstoofishing.com), sailing from Crocker's Boatyard.

In this same vicinity, downtown New London, abuzz with nightclubs, theaters and art galleries, is chockfull of historical landmarks and impressive architecture. To help the day's peregrination, the **Trolley Information Center** (860-444-7264) at Eugene O'Neill Drive at the intersection of Golden Street, is open daily during high season. New London officials have transformed the onetime trolley-stop (operating until the mid-1930s) into a quaint, mustard-colored building that now houses a staff that aids tourists in their whereabouts. Off-season, look for outdoor racks stocked with brochures, maps and other tourism material.

For a nominal charge, day-trippers also have the option of boarding the **New London Heritage Shuttle Bus** (860-443-1209), operated by the New London County Historical Society, running throughout the summer, providing on-off access to some of the city's major landmarks.

Self-guided tours of downtown New London begin at the 1650 **Old Town Mill**, off Bank Street at 8 Mill Street. At the foot of State Street, notice the 1896 **Soldiers & Sailors Monument** and the 1888 **Union Railroad Station**. Within a two-block radius, view the circa 19th-century Greek Revival-style houses on Starr Street, now privately owned and no doubt prized possessions. Also across from the Union Railroad Station, the **Nathan Hale Schoolhouse** (1774-1775), a tiny one-room schoolhouse is where Connecticut's state hero once taught (he also taught in the schoolhouse located in East Haddam; see **East Haddam/Moodus/ Haddam** chapter). Operated and owned by the Connecticut Society of the Sons of the American Revolution, volunteers arrange occasional Saturday and Sunday afternoon tours.

At the top of State Street is the **New London Superior Courthouse**. Built in 1784, it is the oldest, continuously used courthouse in the country. Day-trippers can travel southwest onto Bank Street to the **Robert Mills U.S. Custom House and Museum**. Robert Mills, who also designed the Washington Monument and the U.S. Treasury Building, both in Washington D. C., designed the 1833 classic Greek Revival-style granite building. Once headquarters of the oldest, continuously operating customhouse in the country, the New London Maritime Society now operates the museum and provides day-trippers with a solid American maritime history while recounting the story behind the practice.

At the corner of Bank and Blinman Streets sits the 1756 **Shaw-Perkins Mansion** built in 1756 for Captain Nathaniel Shaw, a wealthy ship owner and trader. Home to the New London County Historical Society, the mansion previously served as

Connecticut's Naval Office during the Revolutionary War. George Washington *did* sleep in this house during one of his New London visits. The bed he slept in has disappeared, but the table he ate on is one of the assets out of a treasure trove of antiques, paintings, clothing and period pieces. In season, stroll the outdoor period gardens, see the old root cellar and admire the 1780 gazebo.

Less than one-half mile are the adjacent **Hempsted Houses**, both listed on the National Register of Historic Places. The earliest is the 1678 Joshua Hempsted House, the oldest house in town (all the more noteworthy for surviving the Revolutionary War fire set under Arnold's command). One of the oldest documented frame buildings in North America, the Antiquarian and Landmarks Society of Connecticut invites the public to experience what was also an Underground Railway stop and is on the Connecticut African-American Freedom Trail. Next to it stands the 1758 stone house built by Joshua Hempsted's grandson, Nathaniel, also owned and maintained by the society.

Downtown New London, between Hempstead and Huntington Streets is **Ye Antientist Burial Ground**. This is the final resting place of many early settlers including some of the oldest known graves of black colonists. During colonial times, settlers constructed many cemeteries, such as this one, on a hill to provide "scenic views for the dead souls." Legend has it that Benedict Arnold stood on its summit in 1781 watching his troops burn Fort Griswold.

Meanwhile, central downtown offers many cultural and artistic experiences. The **Garde Arts Center**, (888-444-7373; 860-437-2314; www.gardearts.org), 329 State Street, is a popular venue for live theater including Broadway-style shows, opera and other events. The center opened in 1926 as a movie palace/vaudeville theater and has been restored to its splendor.

The concentration of State Street art galleries; call for days and hours of operation, alone, includes: **Yah-Ta-Hey Gallery** (860-443-3204; www.yahtaheygallery.com), **Alva Gallery** (860-437-8664; www.alvagallery.com) and **Studio 33** (860-442-6355). **Hygienic Artist Cooperative and Galleries** (860 443-8001; www.hygienic. org) has a colorful past, housed in a building that New London officials almost tore down to accommodate a parking lot, but finally saved due to massive public protest. The latest additions to Hygienic are an outdoor art park, amphitheater and sculpture garden.

Call the **Griffis Art Center** (860-447-3431; www.griffisartcenter.com) for current exhibit information. The center hosts artists from the far-reaches of the world, so expect a broad spectrum of styles. At 123-131 Bank Street, day-trippers on an antiquing mission will surely accomplish their feat at the **New London Antiques Center** (860-444-7598), a cornucopia of more than 40 dealers, open daily in season.

The **Lyman Allyn Dolls and Toys** at Harris Place, 165 State Street, owned and managed by Connecticut College, a favorite area museum has, at press time, been closed. However, doll enthusiasts can still call the **Lyman Allyn Art Museum** in advance to ask if the curator can show the wonderland of dolls ranging from the mid-1800s to the 1960s, and doll-related displays that have been "closeted" until further funding is available.

The Lyman Allyn Art Museum resides on Connecticut College's campus at the northern outskirts of New London, along Route 32 and William Street. Within the impressive Neo-Classical building overlooking the U.S. Coast Guard headquarters are more than 15,000 objects that include paintings, sculpture, drawings, decorative arts and the like. This is one of the best places to study Connecticut Impressionism and see paintings by William Chadwick, William Metcalf and other members of the state's art colonies. Harriet Upson Allyn established the museum in 1926 in memory of her father Lyman Allyn, a prominent whaling merchant.

Day-trippers may amble across the street to the **United States Coast Guard Academy**, one of the nation's four major military installations, where the 2005 film remake *Yours, Mine & Ours* was filmed. Sprawled over 100 acres, among the classic red brick buildings are a visitor's center, gift shop and impressive museum. When not in use, the U.S. Coast Guard Cutter Eagle, a 295-foot historical barque training ship, is also open to visitors.

Moving in the opposite direction, pick up a self-guided walking tour brochure on Williams Street in front of the **Connecticut College Arboretum** (860-439-5020) and explore the grounds. The arboretum is for perfect warm weather outings, open daily from sunrise to sunset. Day-trippers also have the advantage of free, guided walking tours on Sunday (May to October) at 2 p.m.

Within the 750 acres of the arboretum is the **Science EpiCenter & DNA Learning Center**, 33 Gallows Lane. Hands-on, interactive exhibits exploring everything from sound waves to DNA science make learning fun. Other exhibits include live animals, reptiles and a marine touch tank.

Back downriver, **Fort Trumbull State Park** affords visitors panoramic views of New London Harbor. The Revolutionary War fort, named after Jonathan Trumbull, Governor of the Colony of Connecticut, contains, among other things, informative displays, a touchable cannon and artillery crew display.

A seasonal center for visitors also features state-of-the-art multimedia theaters, interactive exhibits, three-dimensional models and a variety of interesting displays that portray more than 225 years of military history. Day-trippers should not forget their fishing poles! Fort Trumbull offers an optimum fishing pier.

Take Pequot Avenue, adjacent to the park, and spend a few hours touring **Monte Cristo Cottage**. A National Historic Landmark, this perfect example of Victorian architecture sits back from the road, across the street from the river. Owned and operated by the Eugene O'Neill Theater Center in nearby Waterford, this was the boyhood home of the famous Eugene, the only United States playwright to win the Nobel Prize in addition to four Pulitzer Prizes. The life of this native New London son inspired city officials to rename Main Street in honor of him as well as erect a statue of Eugene as a boy perched on a rock overlooking New London Harbor, scribbling in his notepad. The house was purchased by O'Neill's actor father in 1884 with the money he earned from his title stage role, "The Count of Monte Cristo," hence its name.

Their cottage was the family's summer residence. The rest of the year, the clan toured with Mr. O'Neill's theater company. However, the playwright credited the cottage as "being the only home he ever knew." The cottage inspired two of his greatest works, *Ah! Wilderness* and his semi-autobiographical *Long Day's Journey into Night*. The summer abode gives the visitor a fascinating insight into a onetime troubled home that makes for a too-short journey into day.

On the southern edge of New London is **Ocean Beach Park**, a generous shore with well-groomed sand and the state's only wooden boardwalk, totaling half a mile. Other park amenities include special events and entertainment, a refurbished carousel, amusement-style rides and arcade, miniature golf course, a 50-meter Olympic-sized pool and waterslide, a convenient bathhouse and Sandbar Café and Lounge.

Saturday summer afternoons mean endless volleyball games on the beach. Saturday evenings, music from the **Summer Music at Harkness Memorial State Park** in Waterford (860-444-7373) wafts through the air. On a clear day, stand on the platform by the cove and spot the area lighthouses, Fisher's Island in Long Island and occasional wildlife sightings.

Before leaving the city, day-trippers with shopping in mind, may want to visit the **New London Mall** (860-443-4423) on North Frontage Road, open daily. Bank Street's **Greene's Books & Beans** (860-443-3312; www.greenesbooksandbeans.

com), open daily, is a bookstore that encourages community through art exhibits, special events, author signings and coffee bar. In the harvest months, make a note on the calendar to check out the **New London Farmers' Market** (860-440-2708), held Tuesday and Friday until early afternoon at the corner of Eugene O'Neill Drive and Pearl Street.

Shoppers or day-trippers of any kind needn't go hungry. For an in-season lunch or dinner daily, consider **Fred's Shanty** (860-447-1301; www.fredsshanty.com/ index.htm) and **Captain Scott's Lobster Dock Restaurant** (860-439-1741). At 158 State Street, **Les Papillons** (860-444-9489), serving French provincial cuisine, is open for lunch and dinner, Tuesday through Sunday. Patrons say the **Recovery Room** (860-443-2619) at 445 Ocean Avenue makes one of the best pizzas. The restaurant is open for lunch, Monday through Friday and dinner daily.

Bank Street Lobster House (860-447-9398), open for lunch and dinner, Tuesday through Saturday, ranks supreme when it comes to those crustaceous food sources. At number 64, in the summer, experience the outdoor dining at **Anastacia's** (860-437-8005). The Victorian atmosphere features lunch, Tuesday through Saturday, and dinner, Friday through Saturday.

Breakfast, lunch and dinner, with the exception of Sunday lunch, are served daily at the **Aqua Grill Restaurant at the Radisson New London/Mystic** (860-443-7000; see **Accommodations**). Legendary hotel-style dining is also featured at **Timothy's at Lighthouse Inn** (860-443-8411; see **Accommodations**), which is opened for lunch (Sunday brunch; no lunch Monday) and dinner daily.

GETTING THERE:
New London is within three hours of New Haven and Hartford, CT, Boston, MA, Providence, RI, and New York City; less than four miles west of Groton. The region is easily accessible from Interstate Highway 95, connecting to I-84 and also from Massachusetts Turnpike, I-90, which connects to I-395.

TRANSPORTATION:
The Groton-New London Airport, located in adjacent Groton, serves a growing demand of business commuters and leisure travelers in the southeastern Connecticut region. T.F. Green Airport in Warwick, Rhode Island, is approximately 49 miles northeast. The area is 59 miles southeast of Bradley International Airport in Windsor Locks. New London is within three hours or less of major transportation centers in New Haven and Hartford, CT, Boston, MA, Providence, RI, and New York City. Southeast Area Transit (SEAT) bus service (860-886-2631) services New London. Both Union Railroad Station Amtrak (800-872-7245) and Shoreline East (800-255-7433) are also located at the foot of State Street.

ADDITIONAL INFORMATION:
ROBERT MILLS U.S. CUSTOM HOUSE & MUSEUM.
150 Bank Street. Open May through October, Monday through Saturday. General admission is $5.00 adults; $3.00 seniors and free to children 12 and under. (860) 447-2501.

SHAW-PERKINS MANSION.
11 Blinman Street. Open all year, Wednesday through Sunday. General admission is $5.00 adults; $3.00 students/seniors; $1.00 children and free to children 5 and under and to museum members. (860) 443-1209.

HEMPSTED HOUSES.
11 Hempstead Street. The adjacent houses are open for public tours May through October, Thursday through Sunday. General admission is $5.00 adults; $3.00 seniors/students; $1.00 children and free to children 5 and under and to museum members. (860) 443-7949; (860) 247-8996; www.hartnet.org/als/alsprop.html.

LYMAN ALLYN MUSEUM OF ART AT CONNECTICUT COLLEGE.
625 Williams Street. Open all year, Tuesday through Sunday. A bookstore with gift items is also available for day-trippers as well as free programs included in admission price. General admission is $5.00 for adults; $4.00 seniors/students and free to children 7 and under and to museum members; free on the first Sunday of every month. (860) 443-2545; www.lymanallyn.org.

UNITED STATES COAST GUARD ACADEMY.
15 Mohegan Avenue. Open May through October, Wednesday through Sunday. General admission is free. For the academy, call (860) 444-8270. For U.S. Coast Guard band-concert information, call (860) 701-6826.

SCIENCE EPICENTER & DNA LEARNING CENTER.
33 Gallows Lane. The center and museum store are open all year, Tuesday through Sunday. General admission is $7.00 adults; $4.50 seniors/children under 12 and free to children 2 and under and to museum members. (860) 442-0391; www.science-epicenter.org.

FORT TRUMBULL STATE PARK.
Walbach Street. The park is open all year from sunrise to sunset, daily. The visitors' center and fort are open May 21 through Columbus Day, Wednesday through Sunday. General admission to the grounds is free; general admission to the visitors' center and fort is $5.00 adults; $2.00 children and free to children 4 and under and to Heritage Passport members (call 860-444-7160 for Heritage Passport membership information). (888) 287-2757; (860) 424-3200; http://dep.state.ct.us/stateparks/parks/fort_trumbull.htm.

MONTE CRISTO COTTAGE.
325 Pequot Avenue. Call for days and hours of operation and general admission prices. Call the Eugene O'Neill Theater Center in Waterford at (860) 443-7378 or the cottage at (860) 443-0051; www.oneilltheatercenter.org.

OCEAN BEACH PARK.
1225 Ocean Avenue. The park and boardwalk are open all year. Beach area and swimming pool are open the Saturday before Memorial Day through Labor Day, daily. Call for information about fees for day passes.

ACCOMMODATIONS:
LIGHTHOUSE INN RESORT.
6 Guthrie Place. Just past the classic white New London Lighthouse overlooking Long Island Sound, the inn has been in operation since 1927. This is the only hotel in the state designated by the National Trust for Historic Preservation as a Historic Hotel. The 27 guestrooms, brimming with antiques, offer full, modern amenities. The 23 guestrooms in the on-site carriage house are styled in a country-French

décor. A restaurant is also on premises (see above). Rates (including free continental breakfast): $99-$369. (888) 443-8411; (860) 443-8411; www.lighthouseinn-ct.com.

RADISSON NEW LONDON/MYSTIC.
35 Governor Winthrop Boulevard. New London's only downtown hotel, consisting of 120 guestrooms and four suites offering full, modern amenities. On premises, there are also an indoor pool, whirlpool, fitness center, on-site restaurant (see above) and casino shuttle. Rates: $89 to $189. (800) 333-3333; (860) 443-7000.

RED ROOF INN.
707 Colman Street. One hundred and eight guestrooms are equipped with full, modern amenities. Pets are also allowed. Rates: $44.99 to $99.99. (800) 843-7663; (860) 444-0001.

ANNUAL FESTIVALS/EVENTS
Mystic Country/CONNECTICUT representing 42 communities, provides a gamut of tourism information, which includes seasonal events (800) 863-6569 or (860) 444-2206; www.ctquietcorner.com or www.mysticcountry.com. For additional festival and event information, contact the Chamber of Commerce of Eastern Connecticut, (860) 464-7373. The New London Main Street Corporation also features numerous events and can be reached at (860) 444-CITY (2489).

New London Gazette, with a comprehensive listing of special events and other city-wide news, is available free at area sites like the Cross Island Ferry terminals, the railroad station and can be obtained online: www.newlondongazette.com.

JANUARY
Hygienic's Annual Art Show has been going strong for more than two decades. (860) 443-8001; www.hygienic.org.

Annual Night Kitchens is an event complementary to the art show with downtown restaurants staying open until midnight. (860) 464-7373.

FEBRUARY
Ever since New London was named *the 27th sweetest place in the country to live* by a poll conducted by Hershey Chocolates, the New London Main Street Corporation sponsors many **special events on Valentine's Day**. (860) 444-CITY (2489).

APRIL
Connecticut College becomes the grounds for the **Annual Connecticut Storytelling Festival**, marking a weekend of storytelling, special workshops and performances. (800) 863-6569.

MAY
The annual **Fine Wine & Food Festival** held at the Garde Arts Center includes an impressive wine list for test tasting. Portions of the proceeds benefit the cultural and educational programs at the Garde. (888) 444-7373; (860) 437-2314.

Artworks for Recovery Afternoon Tea and Exhibit is held at the Garde Arts Center and features a variety of tea, coffee and accompanying sweets and refreshments. The focal point is an exhibition by artists diagnosed with a range of psychiatric handicaps. The majority of proceeds benefits the artists. (888) 444-7373; (860) 437-2314.

JUNE
Harvard-Yale Regatta, more than 125 years old, is the largest and best-known city event that takes place in the downtown waterfront district. (800) 863-6569; (860) 444-2206.

Celebrate Regatta accompanies the races. Created by the New London Main Street Corporation, it is a city-wide celebration involving an observation train, food, entertainment and the opening of the Saturday Farmers' Market.

The **Hempsted Heritage Days** present an opportunity to tour the Hempsted Houses free. (860) 443-7949; (860) 247-8996.

JULY
The **Annual Groton/New London Mashantucket Pequot Thames River Fireworks** (the nation's largest!) by the Grucci Family are part of the annual **Sailfest** events, which feature numerous food venues and a variety of entertainment that includes live performances and an annual automotive show. Also look for Hygienic Art's Annual **Outdoor Bizarre/Bazaar** with more than 100 artisans and many special events on hand that coincide with the city-wide celebrations. (860) 443-3786.

Hourly **guided walking tours** begin at Fort Trumbull State Park. (860) 444-7591.

SEPTEMBER
Attend the annual **Labor Day Bash** (also inquire about other summer beach events) with entertainment, games and surprises for all ages at Ocean Beach Park. (860) 447-3031.

Fans of independent films should mark their calendars for the **Hygienic Filmworks Annual Filmfest** at the Hygienic Art Park. Participants can preview a variety of films, meet the filmmakers and learn new things partaking in filmmaking workshops. (860) 443-8001; www.hygienic.org.

There's nothing quite like this eclectic mix in the state: **Boats, Books & Brushes with Taste** is a literary, art, maritime and food festival with plenty of entertainment and action to keep everyone amused for the three full days that it is held on the New London waterfront. (888) 766-BBBT (2228); www.boatsbooksandbrushes.com.

DECEMBER
Celebration of Lights & Song by the Sea is the traditional tree-lighting ceremony in downtown New London and is accompanied by artists' open studios, ice-sculpture demonstrations and the arrival of Santa and Mrs. Claus. (800) 863-6569; (860) 444-2206.

---

*In the 19th century, what resort town of today was said
to have every house owned by a sea captain?*

*In what town did the most famous
Impressionist-artists' colony form?*

Coastline Masterpiece: **OLD LYME**

Old Lyme is nestled on Connecticut River's east bank, directly opposite Old
Saybrook on the west bank. Early on, a maritime history ensued and played an
integral part of the lower Connecticut valley development. Exactly when the first
settlers arrived is uncertain. On record, however, is that in 1665, what is today's
town of Lyme, which encompassed what we know as the present areas of Old Lyme
and part of East Lyme (the other part belonged to New London), was divided from
Old Saybrook, formerly East Saybrook. In 1667, settlers adopted the town's name,
first called South Lyme, from the seaside town of Lyme Regis, Dorsetshire.

In 1839, the Connecticut General Assembly made East Lyme into a separate
town. Old Lyme was not incorporated until 1855 and finally named Old Lyme in
1857.

Lyme and Old Lyme not only share a maritime trade and shipbuilding history, but
also in recent years were top-10 award winners in *Connecticut Magazine's* index of
the *Best Small Towns*. Apart from sharing similar natural resources—the shoreline,
tide marsh and inland wetlands—Lyme, unlike its neighbor, has squashed much
commercial development. With a population of about 1,900 yearlong residents,
Lyme totals 33 square miles and ranks number 19 out of the per capita income of
the 169 Connecticut towns. It goes down in history as being the first town in the
United States in 1977 in which doctors first recognized Lyme Disease spread to
humans by the bite of infected black-legged ticks.

In contrast, Old Lyme, extended over 27.1 square miles, has a population of about
7,400 that surges in the summer to approximately 16,000 people, many of whom
enjoy second homes that have been owned by the same families for generations.
Old Lyme ranks 31 on the per capita scale mentioned above.

Home to the Old Lyme Town Band, a 1975 incarnation of the original Old Lyme
Town Band that existed from 1886 to 1910, occasional summer performances waft
the atmosphere of Ferry Street's gazebo.

Today, the resort town of Old Lyme, which was said in the 19th century to have
a "sea captain in every house," has also been identified as an artists' colony for
more than a century. Day trips with panache constitute a one-mile jaunt down Lyme
Street, a charming stretch of shops, attractions, fine and casual restaurants. Begin
by surveying a National Historic Landmark, the **Florence Griswold Museum**.
The property's signature piece is what Miss Florence Griswold's sea captain father
built as a private home in 1817. After her inheritance of the late Georgian-style
mansion, she rented a room to artist Henry Ward Ranger in 1899. Impressionist
artist Childe Hassam's arrival signaled what by 1903 would become the most
famous Impressionist art colony in America.

Subsequent boarders seeking refuge from their New York City art studios and inspired by the now Bush-Holley House, another boardinghouse in the nearby art colony (see **Greenwich** chapter), included such artists as Matilda Browne, Willard Metcalf and William Chadwick. The 40 panels of artwork that the artists painted (sometimes in exchange for rent) on the dining room walls and doors in Miss Florence's house represent a unique legacy. By summer 2006, visitors can expect a complete restoration and refurnishing of the house representing a more thorough look into the significance of Miss Florence's allegiance with the artists.

One of the oldest North American art colonies stood on the principle that art represented locale. Day-trippers, today, not only have the opportunity to view the setting in which these early 20th-century artists lived and worked, but are also treated to a collection of art that exemplifies many historical representations of Old Lyme. For instance, compare William Metcalf's *Mountain Laurel,* to the "real" mountain laurel (Connecticut's official state flower) that blooms in the summer along the Lieutenant River, a lazy stretch located on the 11-acre property, where many artists, past and present, have set up their easels.

The museum offers one of the most impressive collections of Impressionist-style art in the world, totaling more than 400 paintings and 2,000 watercolors, prints and drawings. Complementing the main house is the **Robert and Nancy Krieble Gallery** on the riverfront, which accommodates changing-exhibition space and a museum shop. The **Kelly Bill and John W. Hartman Education Center** houses a 1,100-square-foot interior and provides a hands-on discovery classroom, studio and performance space. The **William Chadwick** (1879-1962) **Studio** is an artist's studio that has survived to this day. Day-trippers should visit the museum grounds at least once in the warmer months to experience the restored gardens that re-create a sense of Miss Florence's impeccable gardening skills.

Next door to the museum is the **Lyme Art Association**, a contemporary metamorphosis of the original Lyme Art Colony. At this other National Historic Landmark, the **Charles Platt Gallery** showcases many fine art exhibitions. Behind the Lyme Art Association building is the renowned **Lyme Academy College of Fine Arts** (860-434-5232; www.lymeacademy.edu). As part of New England's only fine arts college, the 1817 **Still House Gallery**, yet another National Historic Landmark, is open free Monday through Saturday for day-trippers to see changing exhibits that include works by students, faculty, alumni and notable artists.

Shoppers should not miss a stopover to **Lymes General Store** (860-434-9808), open Tuesday through Sunday, it sells more than 80 American-made crafts, gifts as well as antiques. Visitors can view an old photograph of the 1800s building, which once served as a general store and post office, at **Alice Rogers' Book and Gift Shop** at the same address as the general store. Tempt your sweet tooth at the **Chocolate Shell** (860-434-9727), 18 Lyme Street, open Monday through Saturday.

At 25 Lyme, the **Cooley Gallery** (860-434-8807; www.cooleygallery.com; call for days and hours of operation), housed in a tidy 19th-century building, invites day-trippers to explore 19th- and 20th-century American paintings, representing Impressionism, artwork from the Hudson River School and selections of contemporary realism.

Back across the street, premium, gourmet ice cream and fresh coffee call at the **Old Lyme Ice Cream Shoppe and Café** (860-434-6942). Early birds can eat breakfast, later in the day, lunch and light dinner. Near the end of the "Lyme Street mile" is the **First Congregational Church** (860-434-8686). Built in 1816, many artists have followed the lead of Impressionist artist Childe Hassam and today the church is often said to be "the most painted church in New England." The mile finishes at **Rooster Hall**, Old Lyme's only bed and breakfast establishment (see **Accommodations**, below).

Halls Road (Route 1), crossing Lyme Street, touts such shops as the **Happy Carrot** (860-434-0380), open Monday through Saturday and carries both used and new books, and the **Bowerbird** (860-434-3562), a gift store with an impressive toy selection, open daily. For the most unique quality, **E.F. Watermelon** (860-434-1600) is a cut above other jewelry stores.

Hungry day-trippers needn't leave the Lyme Street mile to experience two legendary restaurants. Next door to the Florence Griswold Museum at 100 Lyme Street, the **Bee and Thistle Inn** (860-434-1667; 800-622-4946; www.beeandthistleinn.com/dining.htm) is distinguished with its award-winning, fine dining American-style cuisine and historical guestrooms (see **Accommodations**); the restaurant is open for lunch (Sunday brunch) and dinner, Wednesday through Saturday; and breakfast and dinner, Monday and Tuesday.

Just across the street at number 85 is the **Old Lyme Inn Grill** (860-434-2600; 800-434-5352; www.oldlymeinn.com/dinner.htm), providing genteel guestrooms (see **Accommodations**) and award-winning contemporary cuisine that the staff serves for lunch and dinner daily; Sunday brunch.

For more casual fare near Lyme Street, consider the **Hideaway Restaurant & Pub** (860-434-3335) on Halls Road (Route 1), which is open for lunch and dinner daily. On Route 156, **Hallmark Drive-In** (860-434-1998), which serves lunch and dinner from April until November, has some of the freshest seafood and best homemade ice cream around.

It should be noted that Ferry Road, off Lyme Street, where the **Nut Museum** captured worldwide attention as a result of the efforts of curator and artist Elizabeth Tashjian, a zealot for the popular snack, was sold and liquidated due to Ms. Tashjian's ailing health.

With prior appointment, traveling northeast from Lyme Street, day-trippers can visit **McCulloch Farm** (860-434-7355; www.neinternet.com/whippoorwill), the oldest, continually operating (and one of the largest) Morgan horse-breeding farms in the state.

For summer day-trippers who do not have the convenience of a waterfront cottage, **Sound View Beach**, bordering the sound, with a parking lot on Hartford Avenue, permits nonresidents for a day fee. Boaters should note the two launching areas: the **Great Island**, Smith Neck Road and **Four Mile River**, Oak Ridge Drive.

Those with a penchant for hiking, swimming, fishing, hunting and the like, can check out **Nehantic State Forest** (860-526-2336; http://dep.state.ct.us/stateparks/forests/nehantic.htm), with more than 1,700 acres located farther northeast. By the shoreline is the state's acclaimed **Rocky Neck State Park** (860-739-5471; http://dep.state.ct.us/stateparks/parks/rockyneck.htm) in the neighboring town of Niantic, eight miles east. Offering a half-mile long crescent beach, windswept bluffs and camping sites, sports enthusiasts can swim, fish or scuba dive during the warm months; cross-country ski during the winter months.

"The (nearby) trains go to Boston and Washington, D.C. When a train goes by, the conductor blows his whistle and everyone in the train waves at you. Rocky Neck

has a crisp smell to it. You can taste the warm, salty sea. You can feel your hands sifting in the sand to make a sandcastle. The sand is so soft and there are no rocks!" Connecticut resident and frequent Rocky Neck beachcomber, Rachel Rosenberg, wrote these words as a fourth grader on her entry submitted to the Annual State Essay Contest sponsored by the Connecticut Office of Tourism and the Office of the Secretary of State.

GETTING THERE:
Old Lyme is within two and one-half hours or less from New Haven and Hartford, CT, Boston, MA, Providence, RI, and New York City; 16 miles west of New London. The region is easily accessible from Interstate Highway 95, connecting to I-84 and also from Massachusetts Turnpike, I-90, connecting to I-395.

TRANSPORTATION:
The Groton-New London Airport, located in Groton, is 17 miles in driving distance and serves a growing demand of business commuters and leisure travelers in the southeastern Connecticut region. T.F. Green Airport in Warwick, Rhode Island, is approximately 63 miles northeast. The area is approximately 56 miles south of Bradley International Airport in Windsor Locks. Old Lyme is within two and one-half hours or less of major transportation centers in New Haven and Hartford, CT, Boston, MA, Providence, RI, and New York City. Southeast Area Transit (SEAT) bus service (860-886-2631) is 16 miles away in New London. Both Union Railroad Station Amtrak (800-872-7245) and Shoreline East (800-255-7433) are also located 16 miles away in New London.

ADDITIONAL INFORMATION:
FLORENCE GRISWOLD MUSEUM.
96 Lyme Street. The house museum and other buildings are open all year, daily. Inquire about special family programs and seasonal events. General admission is $7.00 adults; $6.00 seniors/students; $4.00 children and free to children 5 and under and to museum members. (860) 434-5542; www.flogris.org.

LYME ART ASSOCIATION.
90 Lyme Street. The gallery is open all year, Tuesday through Sunday. Call to inquire about special events and workshops. General admission is $5.00 donation for adults. (860) 434-7802; www.lymeart.com/oldlyme/laa.

ACCOMMODATIONS:
OLD LYME INN.
85 Lyme Street. Across the street from the Florence Griswold Museum (see above), the elegant 1850s mansion offers 13 guestrooms with full, modern amenities, some with canopy beds and others with four-poster beds and provides a splash of antiques throughout and on-site restaurant (see above). The staff allows some pets. Summers mean lazing in a white wicker chair on the front porch. Rates (including country-continental breakfast): $135-$185. (860) 434-2600 or (800) 434-5352; www. oldlymeinn.com.

ROOSTER HALL.
2 Lyme Street. The owners of the Old Lyme Inn, Keith and Candy Green also own this, the only bed and breakfast on historic Lyme Street. It complements its parterre gardens with welcoming porches and terraces. The 1895, elegantly decorated home offers four guestrooms with full, modern amenities and a suite with kitchenette and whirlpool tub in the rear of the house. Guest amenities include a recreation center with fitness equipment, billiards and ping-pong table. Rates (including full, country breakfast): $175-$235. (860) 434-2600; (800) 434-2600; www.oldlymeinn.com.

BEE AND THISTLE INN.
100 Lyme Street. This 1756 yellow clapboard house situated along the Lieutenant River will spark the romance in just about any relationship. Outside are exquisite herb gardens and a sunken perennial garden. Inside there are 11 guestrooms, all with private baths and canopy and poster beds and on-site restaurant (see above). Children 12 years old and older are welcome. Rates (including full, country breakfast): $110-$219. (860) 434-1667; (800) 622-4946; www. beeandthistleinn.com.

PECK TAVERN HOUSE.
1 Still Lane. Across from the Still Lane Green, the tavern was built in 1680 (wow!) and is listed on the National Register of Historic Places. The historical ambiance includes beamed ceilings, wide-board floors, and the original, sturdy corner beams in the guestrooms. Two guestrooms with canopied four-poster beds and private baths. Rates: $100-$130. (860) 434-8896; www.pecktavern.com.

ANNUAL FESTIVALS/EVENTS
Mystic Country/CONNECTICUT representing 42 communities, provides a gamut of tourism information, which includes seasonal events (800) 863-6569 or (860) 444-2206; www.ctquietcorner.com or www.mysticcountry.com. For additional festival and event information, contact the town clerk's Office, (860) 434-1605.

MARCH
Held at the Lyme Academy College of Fine Arts and sponsored by the Chamber of Commerce, visit the **Taste of Old Lyme**, displaying food vendors and entertainment. (860) 434-1575.

MAY
McCulloch Farm offers free **Open Barn Visits**, call for exact dates and details. (860) 434-7355.

JUNE
Annual Garden Tours in the towns of Lyme and Old Lyme are self-guided tours of select private gardens and homes. (860) 442-2797.

JULY
Special programs and activities mean it's time for the **Annual Historic Gardens Day** held at the Florence Griswold Museum. (860) 434-5542.

The **Old Lyme Midsummer Festival** at the Florence Griswold Museum and throughout various town locations features a host of hands-on activities for children and outdoor markets offering everything from fresh grown Connecticut flowers to cheeses to specialty foods. (860) 434-5542; www.flogris.org.

AUGUST
More than 100 years old and going strong is the **Annual Hamburg Fair**. Held at the Grange Hall and Fairgrounds on Route 156 in Lyme, the day's activities include pony and horse-drawn rides, games, entertainment, amusement-style rides, special demonstrations and food concessions. (860) 434-1459; www.ctfairs.org.

SEPTEMBER
Morgan Horse Versatility Event is open free to the public at McCulloch Farm. (860) 434-7355.

OCTOBER
McCulloch Farm hosts **Fall Foals and Foliage Open Barn Days**. Call (860) 434-7355 for additional details.

DECEMBER
Old Lyme's **Annual Tree Lighting and Carol Sing** attracts celebrants from everywhere. (860) 434-1605.

Area map for preceding section appears on page 166

Lieutenant River
See page 137

*Old Lyme's famous river that once captivated the
imagination of many artists—and still does!
Tip: professional artist or not, bring your easel.*

SOUTHEAST CONNECTICUT
Middlesex County
"River Valley & Shoreline"
Old Saybrook/Essex/East Haddam/Moodus/Haddam

These southeastern river towns dotting the east and west banks of the mighty Connecticut are synonymous with summertime pleasures. Located less than 20 miles west of the Thames River, after Memorial Day, the general population swells with visiting fishermen and women, swimmers, boaters and those who simply seek respite on sandy shores.

Pristine miles of rolling hills and acres of natural woodlands, including Gillette Castle State Park in East Haddam and Fort Saybrook Monument Park, also vie for a day-tripper's attention during peak fall foliage. Two unique leaf-peeking adventures include those experienced from Essex's Steam Train and River Boat Ride. During the colder weather months, eagle watching takes precedence along the shores of East Haddam. From April to December, day-trippers who prefer indoor entertainment should not miss musical theater—or a backstage tour at the legendary Goodspeed Opera House in East Haddam. The month of May means that the shad (Connecticut's official state fish) appear in the Connecticut River, prized by gourmands worldwide, the fish is incorporated on Haddam's state seal.

A cluster of distinguished bed and breakfast accommodations and inns provides cozy dining and overnight quarters for romantic wintertime escapes or warmer-weather hideaways. One of the last surviving family resorts, Sunrise Resort in Moodus, open during the warmer months, has won many awards and much praise over the years.

At any season, these town gems, packed with history, unlock quaint villages brimming with charming architecture and streets abuzz with hundreds of antiques and specialty shops.

What Connecticut town served as the original site of Yale College, called the Collegiate School at the time, until officials relocated it to New Haven in 1716?

What Connecticut town contains the lighthouse that was the official model for the state of Connecticut's "Preserve the Sound" commemorative license plate?

Yachting Lollapalooza: OLD SAYBROOK

Situated near the mouth, and west of the Connecticut River at the confluence of Long Island Sound, Old Saybrook wasn't incorporated from Essex until 1854, but this modern-day town is still the oldest on the river. Under the leadership of English explorers Lord Saye and Lord Brooke (hence, its present-day name), a fort was established in 1635. Among its earliest English inhabitants were Colonel Fenwick and his wife Lady Alice. Visitors with a penchant to see ancient tombstones should find her grave in the historical **Cypress Cemetery**. The cemetery is located near Fort Saybrook Monument Park on College Street; Colonel Fenwick is buried in England.

Originally, the area called Saybrook Colony encompassed the seven towns we know as Lyme, Old Lyme, Chester, Deep River, Essex, Westbrook and Old Saybrook. Never a stranger to prosperity, many sea captains took permanent residence in Old Saybrook, which for a number of years was the only major railroad stop between New London and New Haven.

The original site of Yale College, then called the Collegiate School, was founded in 1701 in what we now call Old Saybrook and remained until it relocated to New Haven in 1716 (see **New Haven** chapter).

Since 1870, with the appearances of summer cottages along Saybrook Point, today, this quaint, exclusive community, identified as Connecticut's yachting capital, has also been a popular summertime resort, resulting in its residential population of 10,000 doubling in warmer months.

Day-trippers needn't turn off Route 1 to experience the ambiance of coastline tranquility. Although more commercially developed than Old Lyme, its neighbor across the Connecticut River, a large sandbar at Old Saybrook's estuary limits urbanization. For great water views and easy peddling, another option is to bicycle what is known as "the loop" in town. The closest shop for rentals, group tours and maps is in neighboring Clinton at **Rock 'n' Road** (860-388-1534).

On foot, day trips with panache start by exploring **Fort Saybrook Monument Park** at Saybrook Point. Route 154 leads into this 18-acre park commemorating the oldest fort in Connecticut. Void of historical remains, storyboards are displayed to help day-trippers envision 17th-century Saybrook Colony. This park is also a favorite place to bird watch. Additionally, the seawall is an excellent fishing perch. Incidentally, the park is reputed to have the area's most scenic, sweeping views of the Connecticut River.

For intimate river encounters—these charter boats seat no more than 27—consider experiencing one of the **Connecticut River Boat** (860-575-9888) cruises or ecology tours, which generally last less than two hours. They depart from Saybrook Point at Saybrook Point Inn's dock. Boaters should also note that public boat access is available north of the **North Cove** area. Water enthusiasts can also find a newer, wider boat access ramp at Ferry Road (beneath I-95).

Southward, hikers can embark on the trail leading into the exclusive **Fenwick** area, the onetime residence of the late actress Katharine Hepburn. Visitors can espy **Lynde Point Light**, overlooking the Connecticut River, from several places along the shore. This original 1802 wooden landmark has the distinction of being the second lighthouse erected in Connecticut (only to be rebuilt in stone in 1838), and is probably best viewed from the water since the road to the Lynde Point is closed to autos, but can be biked or hiked to.

Overlooking Long Island Sound, the 1886 **Saybrook Point Lighthouse** crowns the Lynde Point jetty. Again, best viewed from the water, this cast iron 40-foot conical, brick-lined tower was the official model for the State of Connecticut Commemorative *Preserve the Sound* license plate helping fund conservation efforts and can be purchased from the Department of Motor Vehicles.

For families on a budget, or day-trippers who prefer unadulterated fun, consider an hour well spent at **Saybrook Point Miniature Golf** (860-388-2407) at the Point, Route 154. Open Memorial Day through Labor Day, and weekends in September, the course is across the street from the Saybrook Point Inn (see **Accommodations**) and overlooks the river.

Across the causeway, serious golfers can take advantage of the nine-hole public course at **Old Saybrook Fenwick Golf Club** (860-388-3499). Make note, however, that the course is restricted to residents during July and August weekends.

Nonresidents pay a parking fee from July fourth to Labor Day for **Harvey's Beach** on Route 154; a true charmer with 100 yards of beach, seasonal concession stands and playground.

Over time, the original Fort Saybrook settlement migrated to what is now the Main Street commercial center. To help maneuver the area, near the top of Main Street (look for the gas-lit, lantern lights) is the **Old Saybrook Chamber of Commerce** (860-388-3266; www.oldsaybrookct.com). One of the chamber's best publications is a self-guided walking-tour brochure detailing the 17th- and 18th-century architecture along Main Street. This guide illustrates 37 historical sites beginning with the circa **1870 railroad station** and ending with what is referred to today as the **Millstones**, the remaining relics of a windmill built by early settlers in 1637, spanning 137 years of continuous operation. The chamber is open everyday but Saturday; however, day-trippers can riffle through at anytime travel brochures and area guides displayed outside the building's door.

Just beyond the town green where musicians perform Wednesday summer concerts on the gazebo, consider a tour at the **General William Hart House**, also the headquarters for the **Old Saybrook Historical Society**. This circa 1767, Georgian-style home belonged to merchant and Revolutionary War General William Hart. Docents offer guided tours of the fully restored home, period furnishings and costumes conveying the lifestyle of its previous affluent owners. Among the intriguing features is a fireplace in the library decorated with tiles imported from England, portraying Aesop's fables. Colonial-style gardens and a charming gift shop complement the journey.

Across the street is the **James Gallery and Soda Fountain** (860-395-1406; call for days and hours of operation), owned and operated by the same people who run the **Deacon Timothy Pratt Bed and Breakfast** (see **Accommodations**) located next door. Initially built as a general store in 1790, it surfaced as a pharmacy in 1917 and became most notable for employing Anna Louise James, Connecticut's first African-American woman pharmacist. Included on the National Historic Register and the Connecticut Freedom Trail, this is one of the few places where you will find antique apothecary artifacts. Peruse the gift shop and taste the nostalgia behind an ice cream soda from the original 1896 soda fountain before embarking on the remainder of the trip.

Over the years, Old Saybrook has established more than 400 specialty shops within a two-mile radius. At the train station hub, **Antiques Depot** (860-395-0595) unfolds 10,000 square feet, featuring more than 95 dealers displaying an array of antiques and collectibles. About five minutes by auto is **Essex-Saybrook Antiques Village** (860-388-0689) where more than 130 dealers sell everything from ephemera to clocks.

Not to be missed is **Emerson and Cook Book Company** (860-388-0686), a bookstore open daily and providing a gamut of adult and children's books as well as gift items, toys and coffee. For a unique gift or heirloom, consider an Irish import from the **Life of Riley** (860-388-6002; 800-404-7956; www.loririshimports. com), open daily, except for Sundays. *Canoe & Kayak* readers voted **North Cove Outfitters** (860-388-6585; www.northcove.com) *retailer of the year*. Specializing in adventure sports out-fittings, this 22,000-square-foot store, open daily, carries a complete range of equipment and apparel.

Most of the 20 or so restaurants operating in town are clustered on Main Street. At number 210, the casual quarters of **Paperback Café Coffeehouse & Eatery** (860-388-9718; www.pbcafe.com), where books are meant to be lingered over, breakfast (all day), lunch and dinner are served daily. Live jazz heats up the premises on Friday and Saturday nights and Sunday afternoon. A Tuesday afternoon tea party keeps the little ones occupied. **Bruehwiler's Bakery & Café** (860-388-0101), 247 Main Street, is a comfy place for a snack or light meal; closed Sunday and Monday.

Open for lunch and dinner daily and Sunday brunch, the **Cuckoo's Nest** (860-399-9060; www.cuckoosnest.biz) at 1712 Boston Post Road, has presented award-winning Mexican, Cajun and Creole food for more than 25 years. When patrons aren't streaming into **Penny Lane Pub** (860-388-9646), open daily for dinner and lunch, sinking their teeth into what some say are the finest burgers around, they are flocking to the premises in May to sample the fresh shad on the menu. (For visitors who want to buy some of the best shad and shad roe [the caviar of the New World] to bring home, make time to stop at **Atlantic Seafood**, 860-388-4527; call for days and hours of operation.)

Just off Main and Route 1 at 70 Mill Rock Road, **Pat's Kountry Kitchen** (860-388-4784), with an adjacent shop, **Pat's Kountry Kollectibles**, is another award-winning restaurant that's known for its signature clam hash. Closed Wednesday, the restaurant specializes in family-style dining for breakfast, lunch and dinner daily.

What has become a regional institution at Saybrook Point is **Dock & Dine** (860-388-4665; 800-362-DOCK), with its own marina for boaters. The house specialty is fresh seafood served for lunch and dinner daily. Soft rock entertainment is offered on Saturday nights. Another restaurant known for excellent seafood, **Saybrook Fish House** (860-388-4836), open for lunch, Monday through Saturday, and dinner daily, the casual atmosphere is family-perfect. Reservations are essential at this award winner, which has restaurant siblings in Canton and Rocky Hill.

At the **Saybrook Point Inn & Spa** (see **Accommodations**) is the **Terra Mar Grille**, (860-388-1111; www.saybrook.com/fine_dining.html), another highly acclaimed restaurant serving breakfast, lunch (Sunday brunch) and dinner daily.

GETTING THERE:

Old Saybrook is within two and one-half hours or less from New Haven, Hartford, Providence, RI, and New York City; four miles west of Old Lyme. The region is easily accessible from Interstate Highway 95, connecting to I-84 and also from Massachusetts Turnpike, I-90, which connects to I-395.

TRANSPORTATION:

The Groton-New London Airport, located in Groton, is about 21 miles in driving distance from Old Saybrook and serves a growing demand of business commuters and leisure travelers in the southeastern Connecticut region. T.F. Green Airport in Warwick, Rhode Island, is approximately 66 miles northeast. The area is approximately 55 miles southeast of Bradley International Airport in Windsor Locks. Old Saybrook is within two and one-half hours or less of major transportation centers in New Haven, Hartford, Providence, RI, and New York City.

DATTCO bus (800-229-4879) services the Old Saybrook/Madison/Guilford/ Branford and East Haven areas. Amtrak (800-872-7245) accommodates the town of Old Saybrook. Shoreline East (800-ALL-RIDE in CT; 203-777-7433) runs a commuter-connection train weekdays.

ADDITIONAL INFORMATION:
FORT SAYBROOK MONUMENT PARK.
Saybrook Point, Route 154. Open all year from sunrise to sunset, daily. (860) 395-3123; www.oldsaybrook.com/Attractions/.

GENERAL WILLIAM HART HOUSE.
350 Main Street. Open Memorial Day through Labor Day, Friday through Sunday. The on-site historical library is open all year, call for days and hours of operation. The on-site Frank Stevenson Archives building is open all year, call for days and hours of operation. General admission is by donation. (860) 388-2622.

ACCOMMODATIONS:
Old Saybrook features a variety of motor inns and national chain motels for lodgers to choose from.

DEACON TIMOTHY PRATT BED & BREAKFAST.
325 Main Street. This circa 1746 house, listed on the National Historic Register, attended to five generations of the Pratt family before it was converted into an award-winning bed and breakfast. Nine guestrooms and suites now attend to a traveler's needs with a Jacuzzi, whirlpool tub, four-poster or canopy bed, private bath and modern amenities. Rates (including full-candlelit breakfast): $110-$220. (800) 640-1195; (860) 395-1229; www.pratthouse.net.

SAYBROOK POINT INN & SPA.
Two Bridge Street. This property boasts panoramic waterfront views; the 80 guestrooms and suites exude an unsurpassed, European style and provide full, modern amenities. Additional amenities include full-service spa, an indoor and outdoor swimming pool, on-site restaurant (see above), health club and private marina. Rates: $229-$399. (860) 395-2000; (800) 243-0212; www.saybrook.com.

WHISKERS INN.
Providing purr-fect lodging for feline friends, this cats-only (yes, cats only) B & B has been operating since 1988. To make reservations (call for rates) or schedule a tour in person, call (860) 388-6565.

ANNUAL FESTIVALS/EVENTS

The Central Regional Tourism District, Connecticut's Heritage River Valley, representing 46 communities, provides a gamut of tourism information, including seasonal events (800) 793-4480 or (860) 244-8181; www.enjoycentralct.com/index.cfm. For additional festival and event information, contact the Old Saybrook Chamber of Commerce, (860) 388-3266.

FEBRUARY

Vote for your favorite recipe during the town-wide **Annual WinterFest and Chili Cooking Contest** on the town green, Main Street. Sponsored by the Old Saybrook Chamber of Commerce, food dishes are prepared by local restaurants, civic groups and organizations as well as town officials. (860) 388-3266.

MAY

For more than 50 years, planks have been used at the **Planked Shad Supper** to cook the fish. The process enables the natural oils to drain and helps seal in flavor. One of the most celebrated dinner events in the state; it is held at Fireman's Field and hosted by Siloam Lodge No. 32 of the Connecticut Freemasons. (860) 873-9525.

JUNE

Spectators are treated to exhibits and demonstrations of watercrafts including canoes, kayaks and cruisers at the **Old Saybrook Boat Show**, sponsored by the Old Saybrook Shopping Center. (860) 388-3266.

St. John's Carnival, 161 Main Street, is a weeklong event-filled amusement park-style extravaganza with rides, food concessions, white elephant sale, children's games and strawberry shortcake social. (800) 793-4480.

JULY

Annual Taste of Saybrook, sponsored by the Old Saybrook Chamber of Commerce, attracts many area restaurants to show off their specialties on the town green. (860) 388-3266.

Friends of Acton Library hold their **Annual Book and Bake Sale**, a major fundraiser in town. (800) 793-4480.

The Old Saybrook Chamber of Commerce sponsors the **Annual Arts & Crafts Show** held on the town green on Main Street. More than 200 local and national artisans exhibit their work. (860) 388-3266.

The Main Street Business Association organizes the **Annual Sidewalk Sale** on Main Street. (860) 388-3266.

AUGUST

The **Annual Saybrook Summer Pops** features entertainment, food and fireworks at Saybrook Point. (860) 388-3266.

SEPTEMBER

Old Saybrook **5-mile Road Race and Half-Mile Kid's Fun Run** is fun for all ages. (800) 793-4480.

OCTOBER

A day of activities for the entire family is the highlight of the **Annual Main Street Pumpkin Festival**, sponsored by the Main Street Business Association. (860) 388-3266.

The Old Saybrook Fire Department sponsors the **Annual Haunted Hayride**, organized at Fireman's Field, Elm Street. (800) 793-4480.

Apple Festival/Country Fair, held on the town green on Main Street, is a day commemorating the red fruit with food, games and special surprises. (860) 388-3266.

DECEMBER

The **Annual Saybrook Stroll** includes a day featuring hayrides, holiday caroling and visits with Santa Claus. (860) 388-3266.

Christmas Torchlight Parade, held at Main Street's town green, is one of the most popular celebrations of the year. The highlights include more than 40 fife and drum corps, colorful floats, antique cars, fire trucks and a town-wide carol sing. (860) 388-3266.

Old Saybrook

See pages 142-148

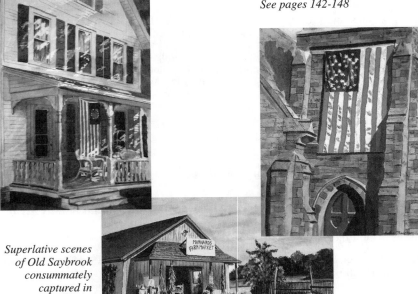

Superlative scenes of Old Saybrook consummately captured in watercolor by local artist Katie Beecher.

Watercolor paintings and photos courtesy of Katie Beecher,
www.beecherwatercolors.com

In what town's village did African ivory play the most significant role?

What Connecticut town has received international notoriety as being the "number one best small town in America"?

Day-Trippers' Bonanza:
ESSEX/CENTERBROOK/IVORYTON

Essex's Native American name, Potapoug, translates "bulging out of the land" and perfectly describes what amounts to modern-day Essex Village, which borders the Connecticut River and is a peninsula with two wide coves on either side. Families began settling near a fort in today's village as early as 1648, making it one of the oldest Connecticut settlements. In colonial times, the current town of Essex fell under the umbrella of Saybrook Colony, including what are known today as the towns of Chester, Deep River and Old Saybrook.

Essex's shipbuilding industry began on the Connecticut River in the late 1700s. During the War of 1812, British troops, in an attempt to destroy economic sovereignty, set ablaze 28 ships in the harbor. The incident did not deter business. What did affect and later squelch shipbuilding in town, however, was the emergence of riverboats, the preferred seafaring vessel in 1823. By the time shipbuilding completely diminished—more than 500 vessels had already been built in Essex.

In 1854, the State Legislature made Essex a separate town, its official name adopted after the English county of Essex. In 1859, the territories now known as Centerbrook, where the town's first meetinghouse was built, and Ivoryton later combined with Essex and are two other town villages today.

Fortunately, when shipbuilding declined, the region gained prominence through a piano key factory employing as many as 1,000 artisans who converted imported African ivory into piano keys. Up until the mid-1900s, the Connecticut village, appropriately designated Ivoryton, manufactured the keys on nearly every piano in the United States.

Today, the factory is long gone as are memories of steam trains transporting visitors who arrived for summer vacations. However, stately, tree-lined streets, along with inviting wooden benches and pastoral landscapes, help Essex retain a nostalgic appearance. In 1996, Norman Crampton's book, *100 Best Small Towns in America*, brought worldwide fame when it ranked Essex as *number one best small town in America*. In more recent years, Essex has repeatedly garnered a top-10 spot in *Connecticut Magazine's* index of the *Best Small Towns*.

About 20 minutes in distance to Middletown, the town of Essex stretches 12.2 square miles and has a population of approximately 5,890 residents. The town is primarily a residential community despite its summer resort town status (another thing that remains unchanged).

Day trips with panache are walker friendly in historic Essex Village along Main Street, running perpendicular to Pratt Street. Views of the Connecticut River, Middle Cove and North Cove stretch below the skyline as far as the eye can see. In warmer months, if you fancy an old-fashioned atmosphere where everyone seems like family, don't miss the shad bake or lobster bake, sponsored by the Rotary Club and Lion's Club, respectively. Visitors, many covered in straw hats, cool off from the season's heat by enjoying ice cream. **Essex Farmers' Market** features fresh fruits, vegetables, baked goods and other Connecticut specialties every Friday at Essex Town Park, beginning in June and running 'til the beginning of October.

At the foot of Main Street is **Steamboat Dock**. Listed on the National Register of Historic Places, this is an 1879 replacement of the village wharf, originally called Lay's, that dates back to 1650. The best interpretation of the Connecticut River Valley story is through the permanent and many changing exhibits, programs and activities at the **Connecticut River Museum**, located in two National Register Landmark buildings situated at the riverbank. The museum owns the only working, full-scale reproduction of Westbrook's native son David Bushnell's 1776 invention of the Turtle, America's first submarine (see **Groton** chapter; **Westbrook** chapter). Other displays include shipbuilding tools and ivory piano keys made in Ivoryton. (After the **Ivory Museum** closed in 1988, the artifacts were divvied up among local museums.)

Before embarking on the town (behind the museum is a public-parking area), consider an expedition on the **RiverQuest** (860-662-0577; www.ctriverexpeditions. org/default.asp), a 54-seat passenger vessel. In-season day cruises sail the Connecticut River and Essex Harbor and special discounts are available to Connecticut River Museum patrons. Approximately one hour in length, day tours are narrated and encompass historic, environmental and ecological information. For romantic, nighttime ventures, no-children cruises on the RiverQuest are also available.

There are two launch sites for canoes and kayaks. Enthusiasts have a good day's worth of waterways to peruse, including North Cove that reaches north of Essex Islands, taking travelers into Falls River, Middle and South Coves, behind the museum, going south of Essex down to Thatchbed Island.

There is also a **Connecticut River Estuary Canoe/Kayak Trail at Essex Town Park** (860-767-4348) on Main Street where nature lovers can spend downtime. The **Chandlery at Essex** (860-767-8287; www.chandleryatessex.com), located on the west side of the Connecticut River, welcomes transient boaters.

Landlubbers who like to shop have dozens of options in Essex and the surrounding area. Antique lovers have many choices in Essex Village. Centerbrook, about one mile west, is home to **Brush Factory Antiques** (860-767-0845; www. brushfactory.com), housed in an old mill, it features more than 30 dealers. One merchant, carrying more than 15,000 rare books (including autographed ones) is **Centerbridge Books** (860-767-8943). In Ivoryton, **Isobel's Gifts & Collectibles** (860-767-7911), adjacent to the Ivoryton Playhouse, sells items ranging from collectible lighthouses to wedding gifts. If you love Byers' Choice Christmas Carolers, Snoopy, Garfield or Charlie Brown, this is a blissful place where the motto is "Browsers are always welcome!"

Step into Isobel's after an Ivoryton Playhouse evening performance during the extended store hours. On your way out the door, grab a brochure with a 10-percent-off merchandise coupon for future purchases.

Back in Essex Village, a stroll down Main and Pratt invites browsers to relish in everything from clothing stores to arts and antiques. Near the harborside, 51 Main

Street is home to **Essex Coffee & Tea Company** (860-767-7804) for a pick-me-up snack, **Essex Mariner** (860-767-7805) for nautical gift items and **Sweet P's Ice Cream & Candy** (860-767-7805).

Moving down Main, Lilly Pulitzer dresses are the specialty at the **Yankee Palm** (860-767-9589). **Hattitudes!** (860-767-0775; www.hattitudes.com) carries just about any hat imaginable and the **Christmas Barn** (860-767-1181) brings Yuletide joy for all seasons. Classic toys, with brand names like Brio, Lego and Playmobile, lure visitors of all ages to **Toys Ahoy!** (860-767-2067). The **Essex Art Association** (860-767-8996) invites day-trippers to take a glimpse at original artworks inside its North Main Street gallery, open from May to September. At 12 North Main, relax with a good read at **Clipper Ship Bookshop** (860-767-1666). This independent bookstore is open daily and specializes in nautical and children's books.

The village of Essex also highlights more than 50 historical homes (many private residences) and sites; the **Essex Historical Society** (860-767-0681; www.essexhistory.org) makes available a detailed walking map. Occasionally during the summer months, the society also conducts town walking tours. A handful of houses are open to the public on a limited seasonal basis.

Next door to the Connecticut River Museum is the **Hayden Chandlery/Stevens Library**. In 1813, Richard Hayden had this Federal-style building constructed and it served as a chandlery and general store. Next door at number 59 is the **Robert Lay House**, circa 1730. It is thought to be the oldest surviving house in Essex Village.

Across the street from the museum is the **Dickinson Boathouse**. E.E. Dickinson, the famous witch hazel distiller constructed the small building in the early 1920s; before that time, it was the former site of a one-story warehouse that operated from 1753 until the town torn it down in 1918.

Farther up at 34 North Main, alongside Dickinson Lane, is the **E.E. Dickinson House**. It was built in 1842, purchased by the famous witch hazel distiller in 1888 and extensively remodeled to resemble the distinct Flagler Mansion in Palm Beach, Florida.

Once known as the 1766 Ship Tavern, now home to the **Dauntless Club**, across from the Dickinson Boathouse, it was the homestead and tavern of shipbuilder Uriah Hayden and his wife, Ann. In 1776, to the south of this building is where the first Connecticut warship *Oliver Cromwell* was built for the Connecticut Colony.

The only house open for the public to visit is the 1732 **Pratt House**, a short walk from Main Street on West Avenue. The Essex Historical Society operates this house, first built in 1701 for the descendents of Lieutenant William Pratt, one of the original founders of Essex, and subsequently enlarged over time due to prosperity. The interior contains 17th- to 19th-century furnishings and accessories. The barn at the rear of the house features changing exhibits pertaining to Essex's history as well as a collection of tools and other artifacts highlighting town life.

The historical society is headquartered at Prospect Street's **Hill's Academy Museum** (860-767-0681), a landmark that first supplemented the town's one-room schoolhouse, later becoming a prominent boarding house. Today, the renovated museum re-creates a yester-year country store, displaying artifacts like tools and items pertinent to the ivory industry. The society opens up the museum to day-trippers on an occasional basis and by appointment.

Across from the Pratt House, directly opposite the Essex Public Library, is approximately 16 acres consisting of 17 walking trails in a nature sanctuary known as **Cross Lots**. Outdoorsy types should also make note to visit **Turtle Creek Preserve**. On the Essex-Old Saybrook town line, these 93 acres are located north on Route 154 at Watrous Point Road. The preserve abuts a tidal estuary at South Cove.

Parade lovers should "about-face" to Ivoryton's **Museum of Fife & Drum**. The museum—the only one of its kind in the world—is operated by the Company of Fifers and Drummers, "a nonprofit, educational organization dedicated to preserving and promoting music of the 'ancient' fife and drum." Museum exhibits chronicle this beloved music form, beginning in the middle ages, to the fife and drum corps of today.

About a half-mile away at 103 Main Street is (remember, it's adjacent to Isobel's Gifts & Collectibles) **Ivoryton Playhouse** (860-767-8348; www. ivorytonplayhouse.com). Ivoryton Playhouse was first built in 1908 as a recreation hall for the employees of the Comstock-Cheney (ivory manufacturing) factory. In 1930, well-known actor and stage director Milton Stiefel transformed what had become an unused building into a renowned stage, and the Ivoryton Playhouse became the first self-supporting summer theater in the country, making it the oldest, professional theater of its kind today.

Owned and operated by the Ivoryton Playhouse Foundation, the playhouse has seen many stage stars, including Katharine Hepburn who started her luminary career here. The playhouse presents a gamut of yearlong evening and matinee productions as well as River Rep Summer Theater from drama to comedy to musicals to children's theater. For a cost-free day, stroll Ivoryton, enjoy the gazebo and small park, especially nice since motorists are few! When it's open, pop into the Ivoryton Playhouse, pick up a schedule and examine the rustic feel and walls plastered with photos of Hollywood icons. Sit a spell in the balcony, close your eyes and imagine the applause!

The most popular attraction for both old and young is outside Essex Village's main hub at **Essex Station**, another building listed in the National Register of Historic Places (off Saybrook Road at Railroad Avenue). The station is about 20 feet from the old **E.E. Dickinson Witch Hazel Building**, an operation that moved up river to Hampton.

Essex Steam Train and Riverboat Ride (860-767-0103; 800-377-3987; www.essexsteamtrain.com), operated by the Connecticut Valley Railroad, offers an approximate one-hour train ride on traditional vintage steam trains that make a scenic roundtrip to neighboring Chester. The train connects with an optional riverboat cruise at Deep River Landing. The riverboat glides past such sites as the majestic hills called Seven Sisters, housing East Haddam's Gillette Castle (see **East Haddam** chapter), built by America's famous actor who immortalized Sherlock Holmes on stage, and the majestic Goodspeed Opera House. East Haddam's swing bridge marks the cruise's finale.

Consider a five-course, elegant **dinner train** excursion. To make any dinner occasion special, Ivoryton's **Copper Beech Inn** (860-767-0330; 888-809-2056; www.copperbeechinn.com; see **Accommodations**) offers four distinctly appointed dining rooms with famed country-French accents. This four-star restaurant, housed in a stately 1890s country house, is open daily for lunch and dinner featuring French country-style cuisine and an award-winning wine list. The excellent food served, elegant setting and overall flawless dining experience have helped win it many annual *best of Connecticut* polls in local newspapers and magazines.

Back in Essex Village, the **Crow's Nest Gourmet Deli** (860-767-3288) is a favorite for breakfast and lunch daily (call for seasonal days and hours of operation).

Offering the only waterfront dining in town, wintertime means popular homemade soups.

If not experiencing a classic fare (shad and shad roe in season!), for lunch or dinner, served daily at the **Griswold Inn** (860-767-1776; www.griswoldinn.com/High_Index.htm), day-trippers should at least survey the interior of one of the oldest, continuously operating inns in America (see **Accommodations**) at 36 Main Street—and survivor of the town's burning during the War of 1812 (see beginning of chapter). Immediately behind the inn, but part of the main 1776 inn, is the taproom built in 1738 as an Essex schoolhouse. Supported on logs, it was moved by a team of oxen to this present location in 1865. A collection of Currier & Ives and Endicott & Company steamboat prints and temperance posters and paintings, an antique popcorn machine, a variety of Saturday night musical performances and 11 beers on tap have helped the taproom gain a whimsical, fun-loving reputation reaching beyond the state's borders.

Dining rooms include the Gun Room with its firearms collection dating back to the 15th century and the Steamboat Room, featuring a mural depicting a historically accurate Essex scene in which the river actually rocks (yes, in 3-D!). The Covered Bridge Room was constructed using wood from an abandoned New Hampshire covered bridge and later moved to this present location. The Sunday Hunt Breakfast is another distinct tradition at the "Gris." Its roots go back to the British when they temporarily occupied the Griswold Inn during the War of 1812.

Southwest of Essex Village, **Oliver's Taverne** (860-767-2633; www.oliverstavern.com) at 124 Westbrook Road, serving lunch and dinner daily, is well known for its steaks and burgers and lively pub-style atmosphere.

Back in Centerbrook, **Gabrielle's** (860-767-2440; www.gabrielles.net), located in the Victorian-era house at 78 Main Street, has been a local favorite since 1979. Fresh seafood and Italian-style dishes are the specialties for lunch, Tuesday through Friday and Sunday and dinner Tuesday through Sunday.

GETTING THERE:

Essex is within two and one-half hours or less from New Haven, Hartford, Providence, RI, and New York City; five miles north of Old Saybrook. The region is easily accessible from Interstate Highway 95 (Exit 69 at Old Saybrook to Route 9 North. Take Exit 3 to Essex); connecting to I-84 and also from Massachusetts Turnpike, I-90, connecting to I-395.

TRANSPORTATION:

The Groton-New London Airport, located in Groton, is about 23 miles in driving distance and serves a growing demand of business commuters and leisure travelers in the southeastern Connecticut region. The area is approximately 51 miles southeast of Bradley International Airport in Windsor Locks. Essex is within two and one-half hours or less of major transportation centers in New Haven, Hartford, Providence, RI, and New York City. DATTCO bus (800-229-4879) services the Old Saybrook/Madison/Guilford/Branford and East Haven areas. Amtrak (800-872-7245) accommodates the nearby town of Old Saybrook. Shoreline East (800-ALL-RIDE in CT; 203-777-7433) runs a commuter-connection train weekdays in Old Saybrook, also. Essex Limousine Service, (860) 767-2152 or (800) 864-2651, also services Essex and the surrounding area.

ADDITIONAL INFORMATION:
CONNECTICUT RIVER MUSEUM.
67 Main Street. Open all year, Tuesday through Sunday. General admission is $5.00 adults; $4.00 seniors; $3.00 students/children and free to children 3 and under and to museum members. (860) 767-8269; www.ctrivermuseum.org.

PRATT HOUSE.
19 West Avenue. The house and barn are open June through Labor Day, Saturday and Sunday and by appointment. General admission is $3.00 adults; $2.00 seniors; $2.00 students and free to children 12 and under and to museum members. (860) 767-1191; www.essexhistory.org.

MUSEUM OF FIFE & DRUM.
62 North Main Street. Open June through August, Saturday and Sunday and by appointment. Closed third weekend of July and fourth weekend of August. General donation is $3.00 adults; $2.00 seniors/children and free to children 12 and under and to museum members. (860) 767-2237; www.companyoffifeanddrum.org/museum.htm.

ACCOMMODATIONS:
GRISWOLD INN.
36 Main Street. Designated as the first three-story frame structure built in Connecticut (and the only overnight accommodation in Essex Village), its handsome quarters have availed themselves to sleepy travelers since 1776. Today, "the Gris" has 30 guestrooms ranging from standard to superior suites. Some with fireplaces, all feature period antiques and fine reproductions. Amenities include air-conditioning, classical music "piped" into the rooms and access to the historic Hayden House to watch television, read or just relax in front of one of the fireplaces; plus, classic on-site restaurant (see above). Rates (including continental breakfast): $100-$370. (860) 767-1776; www.griswoldinn.com/Pages/Inn.htm.

COPPER BEECH INN.
46 Main Street, Ivoryton. Look for the 200 or so year-old gargantuan copper beech tree and you will find the 1890s building restored and accessorized with period antiques, Oriental rugs and classic European-style sophistication. Amenities in the 13 guestrooms and luxury suites include air-conditioning, cable television, extra-firm mattresses, CD players and some offer Jacuzzis. There is an impeccably classic on-site restaurant on premises (see above). Rates (including full breakfast): $165-$335. (860) 767-0330; (888) 809-2056; www.copperbeechinn.com.

ANNUAL FESTIVALS/EVENTS
The Central Regional Tourism District, Connecticut's Heritage River Valley, representing 46 communities, provides a gamut of tourism information, including seasonal events (800) 793-4480 or (860) 244-8181; www.enjoycentralct.com/index.cfm.

FEBRUARY

Traditionally held the Sunday immediately following Ground Hog Day, the **Ground Hog Day Parade** is a town-wide celebration. (860) 767-4348.

The **Connecticut River Eagle Festival** is a two-day weekend event held at the Connecticut River Museum. The days' activities afford many excellent opportunities to view bald eagles in their natural habitat. There are also offerings of environmental lectures, children's nature programs and special presentations. (800) 714-7201; www.ctrivermuseum.org.

MARCH/APRIL

Youngsters shouldn't miss the **Easter Eggspress**, a traditional springtime excursion with the Easter bunny aboard the Essex Steam Train. (860) 767-0103; (800) 377-3987; www.essexsteamtrain.com.

MAY

The **Annual Shad Festival** celebrates the season with special demonstrations and activities at the Connecticut River Museum. (860) 767-8269; www.ctrivermuseum. org.

Each year the Essex community commemorates its rich maritime heritage with a tribute to the 1776 construction of *Oliver Cromwell*, Connecticut's first warship, with a **Burning of the Ships Parade** promenading down Main Street; a ceremony at Steamboat Dock concludes the day. (860) 767-4348.

Essex May Market is held at Essex Town Park and features gourmet specialties, plants, flowers and many varieties of Witch Hazel plants. (860) 767-2160.

JUNE

The Essex Rotary Club holds it annual **Shad Bake**, which has been going strong for more than 44 years! Location: Essex Elementary School, Centerbrook. www. essexrotary.com.

Essex Rotary Club's **Annual Golf Tournament** is held at the Clinton Country Club, Route 145 in Clinton. This is the club's fundraiser, attracting statewide participants and spectators. (860) 767-6024.

The Annual **Hot Steamed Jazz Festival** was started in 1992 by the Valley Railroad and to this day presents the highest quality in classic, jazz, swing and blues music. All proceeds benefit the Hole in the Wall Gang Camp. (800) 793-4480.

JUNE-AUGUST

Summer concerts are held at Essex Town Park or Ivoryton Town Park, Wednesday evenings. A schedule can be obtained by calling the Essex Town Hall at (860) 767-4348.

JULY

More than 35 restored wooden motorboats are displayed at the **Antique and Classic Boat Show** at the Connecticut River Museum floating docks. (860) 767-8269.

Friends of Acton Library hold their **Annual Book and Bake Sale**, a major fundraiser in town. (860) 767-4348.

AUGUST
The **Annual Lobster Bake** sponsored by the Essex Lion's Club is held at Main Street Park. (860) 767-4348.

OCTOBER
A town-wide **Halloween Parade** takes place in Essex Village. (860) 767-4348.

DECEMBER
Trees in the Rigging and Santa's Arrival by Boat is an event beginning with a lantern-light parade down Main Street, festivities at Pratt House, carol singing, Santa's arrival at the Connecticut River Museum and parade of lighted ships. (800) 714-7201; www.ctrivermuseum.org.

The Essex Steam Train features the **North Pole Express**, which is a nighttime steam-train ride highlighting a special appearance by Santa Claus, live readings of Christmas stories, sing-a-longs, and holiday surprises. (860) 767-0103; (800) 377-3987; www.essexsteamtrain.com.

Ivoryton Playhouse
See page 152

The oldest professional theater of its kind today.

Essex Rotary Club Shad Bake
See page 150

*What town is the only one in the state
bisected by the Connecticut River?*

*What town village first prospered from processing twine
and then from vacation resorts, earning it the title,
"Catskills of Connecticut"?*

Off-the-Beaten-Trek Sojourns:
EAST HADDAM/MOODUS/HADDAM

Migrating Wethersfield and Hartford settlers paid a meager amount, probably thirty coats (worth less than 100 dollars today), to the Native Americans for what comprises the currently named towns of Haddam and East Haddam. The territory was chartered in 1662 as the "Plantation at Thirty-Mile Island," because of its close proximity to the mouth of the Connecticut River.

This land parcel included the locality that the Native Americans—Pequot, Mohegan and Narragansett—called Machimoodus, meaning "place of strange noises." The tribes perceived the subterranean sounds, or mysterious vibrations in the earth's surface, which to this day are said to agitate the river and can be heard for miles, to be evil spirits. These noises—which are said to sound like anything from a ball cracking to thunder rumbling to bowling pins being smashed—are theorized to be the result of tiny earthquakes close to the earth's surface. Others reject such notions and, apart from lore and generations of legends, the noises have continued to be a subject of intrigue and speculation. What is absolute is that the name Moodus is a derivative of its Native American origin and refers to today's village of East Haddam housing a population of about 1,170, located northeast of both Haddam and East Haddam.

The town of Haddam was incorporated in 1668; its name believed to have been taken from the name Much Hadham, England. Adopting a geographically appropriate name, East Haddam did not officially separate from the town on its opposite west bank until 1754. Like other river towns, the Connecticut River has played an integral part of history in both East Haddam and Haddam. Haddam is unique in the sense that it is the only town in Connecticut bisected by the river. Early economy was based on river trade, shipbuilding and granite quarries. The first gristmill was built as early as 1668 and after that time, as many as four ferries serviced commerce based on textile, tannery and distillery businesses. Each spring, the area continues to boast an abundant shad migration.

The Moodus River in Moodus, draining into the eastern portion of Salmon Cove, also generated regional prosperity through as many as 15 water-powered mills working to process bales of cotton into twine between 1819 to 1865. Some of the mill foundations have remained and the community's future goal is to create an accompanying park, enhancing this area's historical value.

Historical significance also amounts to what was dubbed the "Catskills of Connecticut." The village of Moodus, especially, saw dozens of resorts, which resulted in the late 1800s and early 1900s, after village farmers were the first to rent out rooms to boarders. This phenomenon, peaking in the 1940s and 1950s, quadrupled East Haddam's summer population to some 20,000 vacationers who came primarily from Connecticut, but also from Massachusetts, New York and New Jersey. Although the area no longer accommodates such legendary hotels as the Machimoodus House and Carrier House, a scant number of survivors remain (see **Accommodations**).

Both Haddam and East Haddam are rural in nature, predominantly residential areas; and still a popular draw for tourists. Stretching 46.7 square miles, Haddam has a residential population of around 7,200. East Haddam with a residential population of 8,333 inhabits 56.6 square miles. Both towns are a testament to preserving the past. Sweeping views of old stonewalls, historical houses, farms with post-and-beam barns and ample open space dominate the countryside.

Northwest of New London, between the towns of Portland and Essex, East Haddam's most pronounced feature is the Route 82 swing bridge. Built in 1913, and resembling an 899-foot-long steel caterpillar, it's said to be the longest bridge of its kind in the world. When not ushering motorists in and out of town, the bridge swings open in order to accommodate oversized recreational and commercial river traffic.

With this swanky swing bridge hovering in the background, day trips with panache kick off in the heart of the historical village. Since being built in 1876 by tycoon shipbuilder, merchant, banker and lover of theater William Goodspeed, the **Goodspeed Opera House** has gone through many incarnations. Under the direction of the Goodspeed Opera House Foundation since 1959, its mission to preserve and advance musical theater, Goodspeed's accolades include numerous Tony Awards and the debut of various Broadway-bound productions. Day-trippers can catch a matinee, evening performance or a backstage tour at this Victorian marvel known as the birthplace of the American musical. Bravo to the fact that staff members create all the sets and costumes. Plus, all musical orchestrations are original. After considering relocating to a larger facility in neighboring Middletown, from all appearances, it looks like Goodspeed is here to stay—at least until the staff figures out how and where to expand its 800-square-foot stage to an anticipated 3,200-square-foot platform, as well as how to nearly double its current 398-seating capacity.

Serious scholars and students are invited to examine, by appointment, the collection of scores, sheet music, scripts, original-cast recordings, programs, photographs and theater memorabilia at the **Goodspeed Library of the Musical Theatre** (860-873-8664) at 20 Norwich Road.

Day-trippers who choose off-season jaunts December through mid-March should be on the lookout for eagles that winter along the river in search of fish. They soar in East Haddam's crisp wind, meander along the riverbanks and perch in trees—one favorite being a big sycamore draped over the river. In the town office parking lot, overlooking the north side of the swing bridge, there is even a designated eagle-viewing area.

Another favored spot to espy these majestic birds is farther north of the swing bridge on Route 149. On Main Street, peek inside **St. Stephen's Episcopal Church** (860-873-9547; www.ststeves.org). The *Guinness Book of Records* lists the belfry in this stone church as having the oldest bell in America, originally cast for a Spanish monastery in 815 A.D. before proceeding on its journey to the New World.

Outside, behind the church where the restored **Nathan Hale Schoolhouse** (see **New London** chapter) is located, day-trippers can not only get the best view of the bell, but also in season, see the eagles congregate in the trees and fly off the top of the hill. Anytime of year, this land parcel known as **Nathan Hale Schoolhouse Park**, containing 800 feet of riverfront, affords sweeping views of the village. The house itself, more than 200 years old, and named after the state's hero, is open for summer tours. Serving as a school from 1750 to 1799, 18-year-old Yale graduate Nathan Hale taught in the building for a five-month stint between the years 1773 and 1774. The Connecticut Society of the Sons of the American Revolution operates the museum, which was furnished by the Daughters of the American Revolution with period desks, tables and accessories and some of Hale's personal belongings. (A sculpture of Hale's bust at Main Street's Goodspeed Plaza marks the original sight of the schoolhouse.)

Southward down the river in the Hadlyme section of East Haddam is **Gillette Castle State Park**. The park's imposing granite structure built from local fieldstone looks like a throwback from medieval times and is reputed to be modeled after the Normandy fortress of Robert LeDiable, father of William the Conqueror. Hartford-native, actor William Gillette, who accumulated a considerable fortune from his best-known role as Sherlock Holmes, finished the castle in 1919. Complete with four-to-five-feet thick walls, a major restoration that includes a visitors' center has been unveiled and the castle sparkles down to its furnishings, paintings, woodwork and wall coverings. Be forewarned, that no castle is complete without secret passageways, hidden mirrors and hidden doors!

The castle, at a dizzying 200 feet above sea level, gives sightseers another optimum bird's-eye view of the valley, especially when standing outside on the castle's lookout terrace. The 184 acres outside lead to other serendipitous encounters (also masterminded by Mr. Gillette), such as stone-arch bridges, wooden trestles spanning up to 40 feet long, a vegetable garden, goldfish pond and many walking trails that follow over trestles and through a tunnel and the actor's three-mile long narrow gauge railroad tracks to accommodate his trains. If time restricts visiting the castle, have a picnic at the park. For day-trippers who prefer more to this already novel adventure, (from late May to Mid-November), board the **Chester-Hadlyme Ferry** (860-443-3856; www.chesterct.com/ferry.htm) at Route 148 from the town of Chester, cross the Connecticut River, and arrive to tour the castle from that route.

Within five miles of Gillette Castle State Park is another favorite state park for day tripping, the 860 acres of **Devil's Hopyard** (860-873-8566; http://dep. state.ct.us/stateparks/parks/devilshopyard.htm). The Connecticut Ornithological Association ranks this area as one of the top-10 bird-watching sites in the state. Additionally, the park's main feature is the 60-foot-high **Chapman Falls**; the second tallest in the state next to Kent Falls, listed in the *Eastern Waterfall Guide* as one of the top-10 waterfalls in Connecticut. Day-trippers can also take advantage of the park's 15 miles of hiking and mountain-biking trails and, in the winter, cross-country skiing and snowshoeing trails. **Eight Mile River** is a favorite among fly fishermen and women; wheelchair-accessible fishing platforms are also available. Across from the river is **Eight Mile Gardens**, now called **I-Park**, a garden park and artist's colony sponsoring many future art-related events.

A 21-site campground is located about 1,000 feet from the falls (see **Accommodations**) at Devil's Hopyard. A number of legends surround the actual park name, the most popular being that on one of his forays, the devil ran through the park and was so mad at getting his tail wet that he hopped around until his hooves burned holes in the rock, leaving permanent "potholes," which visitors can see today.

Just south of the state park is **Burnham Brook Preserve** on Dolbia Hill Road, owned and maintained by the Nature Conservancy. Visitors are welcome to walk the marked trail within these 1,000 acres of woodlands, swamps, meadows and brooks. The conservancy also owns **Chapman's Pond Nature Preserve** on River Road. Easiest to reach by canoe, visitors are also invited to hike marked trails on moderate and steep terrain and survey 600 acres of forests, marshes and a tidal pool. Day-trippers with boats or canoes should make note of the **Connecticut River Boat Launch** directly on Route 149. Located at the junction between Salmon and Connecticut Rivers, with or without a boat, this is another sightseeing option offering panoramic views.

About two miles away from the center of East Haddam at 69 Town Road, horse lovers should trot to **Allegra Farm** (860-537-8861; www.allegrafarm.com), a restored, 19th-century livery stable and coach house. Established in 1976, this 12-acre working farm provides a nostalgic glimpse into the past with its **Horse-Drawn Carriage & Sleigh Museum**, housing some 40 carriages and sleighs, including hearses and a U.S. mail wagon, open by appointment. The farm also features hay, sleigh and country-carriage rides, chuck-wagon dinner parties, educational programs and party facilities, complete with bonfires and marshmallow roasts.

The Antiquarian and Landmark Society owns and operates the **Amasa Day House**, Town Street, on the Moodus Green. This Federal-style home was built in 1816 and presents three generations of Day-family heirlooms; in addition to rare stairwell stenciling, toys and original floors and carpets. From the tour, visitors learn firsthand how the Industrial Revolution changed the lives of ordinary Americans.

While in the Moodus section, canoeing, boating and fishing enthusiasts have three lakes, **Bashan**, **Moodus Reservoir** and **Lake Hayward** at their disposal. The town of Haddam, bordered on the east by East Haddam and west by Killingworth and Durham, touts two additional state parks (860-663-2030): **Haddam Meadows** (http://dep.state.ct.us/stateparks/parks/haddammeadows.htm) and **Cockaponset** (http://dep.state.ct.us/stateparks/forests/cockaponset.htm). Overlooking the Connecticut River, Haddam Meadows, Route 154 (Saybrook Road), officially a Connecticut State Scenic Road, situated on 175 acres of uniquely flat terrain allows for boating, fishing and cross-country skiing. At 18 Ranger Road, Cockaponset, the second largest state forest in Connecticut, boasts 15,652 acres tailored for hiking, mountain biking, cross-country skiing, snowmobiling, swimming, fishing and hunting.

Past Haddam Meadows State Park, south on Route 154, the **Thankful Arnold House** at 14 Hayden Hill Road is the headquarters for the Haddam Historical Society, inviting day-trippers to visit the two-story, gambrel-roofed 1794 house. The tour provides a glimpse of 19th-century widow's life via Thankful Arnold (yes, that was her name). Period furnishings, Civil War correspondence of the Arnold family and a memorial garden featuring herbs, typical to the 18th and 19th centuries, flowers and vegetable varieties are some of the home's particulars.

To obtain the full flavor of Route 154, pick up a copy of *Scenic Route 154*, an excellent booklet (available at most attractions) describing the many historical stops, scenic views and natural preserves along this road running parallel to the Connecticut River. Off 154, another notable Haddam experience is **Camelot Cruises** (860-345-8591) at 1 Marine Park, which offer a climate-controlled, luxury ship seating up to 500 passengers. Join the other revelers in a murder-mystery dinner, brunch or matinee cruise or a host of other Connecticut River in-season adventures. For a bird's-eye perspective of the town, try a scenic ride on a three-passenger plane departing from **Goodspeed Airport Eagle Aviation** (800-564-2359; 860-873-8568).

Haddam is a locus of antiques shops including **Howard House** (860-873-9990), an antiques store specializing in miniatures; **Miller's Antiques** (860-873-8286) and **T.F. Vanderbeck Antiques** (860-526-3770).

Day-tripping golfers can hit a few rounds at **Fox Hopyard Golf Club** (860-434-6644; http://sandri.th.net/FoxHopyard/foxhopyard.htm) at 1 Hopyard Road, an 18-hole golf course. The club's restaurant, **On the Rocks** (860-434-6644), is open to the public for lunch and dinner daily.

In the town of Haddam and the surrounding area, there is a variety of dining options, including a good number of casual, fast-food and pizza-style restaurants. For river dining, the **Blue Oar** (860-345-2994), 16 Snyder, is a crowd-pleaser offering seafood specialties for lunch and dinner daily. Once a Haddam tradition, **Spencer's Shad Shack**, one of the state's last shad shacks, is now an abandoned roadside stand along Route 154 — but a great backdrop for photographs!

Speaking of shad, probably one of the quirkiest attractions in Connecticut is the **Haddam Shad Museum** (860-267-0388; www.kids.state.ct.us/shad/shadmuseum.htm), Route 154, behind Citgo Gas, open Sunday, mid-April until mid-June or by appointment. Connecticut residents (or those who want to familiarize themselves with true Yankee roots) need to speak "shad" and *the place* to learn the language fluently is none other than in the circa 1925 building that once operated (on Route 154) as **Maynard's Shad Shack** until 1960. Yes, the museum is a tiny herring in the sea of tourist attractions in the state, but standing amidst things like the original scale from Maynard's, newspaper clips lining the wall and audio recordings of former shad fishermen, it's near impossible not to catch the fervor, especially with the museum's brainchild and current director Joseph Rzaientz, a retired Haddam dentist, his devoted wife Fredda and Curator George Bernard nearby. Situated in a shopping complex that Dr. Rzaientz owns, the museum is free and receives anywhere from zero to 20 visitors on a given Sunday. **Haddam Shad Museum** is one museum that cannot be duplicated anywhere else!

Two other Route 154 quick stops serving lunch and dinner are the **Pilot House** (860-345-8333; call for days and hours of operation) and **Higgies** (860-345-4125; call for days and hours of operation). Configured after a ship pilot's house, the landmark roadside stand that advertises its homemade relish serves breakfast, lunch and dinner daily. The other roadside stand, Higgies, known for its ice cream, has also garnered a reputation for juicy, steamed cheeseburgers.

GETTING THERE:

East Haddam and Haddam are located northwest of New London between the towns of Portland and Essex. Both are less than two hours from Providence, Rhode Island; less than one hour from New Haven and Hartford. East Haddam and Haddam, just off Route 9, offer easy access to Interstate Highway 95; connecting to I-84 and also from Massachusetts Turnpike, I-90, connecting to I-395.

TRANSPORTATION:

The Groton-New London Airport, located in Groton, is about 34 miles in driving distance and serves a growing demand of business commuters and leisure travelers in the southeastern Connecticut region. The area is approximately 40 miles south of Bradley International Airport in Windsor Locks. Both towns are within two and one-half hours or less of major transportation centers in Providence, RI, New Haven, Hartford and New York City. The closest service is DATTCO bus (800-229-4879), which services the Old Saybrook/Madison/Guilford/Branford and East Haven areas. Amtrak (800-872-7245) accommodates the nearby town of Old Saybrook. Shoreline East (800-ALL-RIDE in CT; 203-777-7433) runs a commuter-connection train weekdays in Old Saybrook, also.

ADDITIONAL INFORMATION:

GOODSPEED OPERA HOUSE.

Goodspeed Landing, Route 82. The season runs April through December. Goodspeed, which produces three musicals a season on its main stage, is in conjunction with the Norma Terris Theatre in neighboring Chester, which produces new, first-time musicals. Tours of the opera house are conducted June through October on most Saturdays. Call for pricing information. (860) 873-8668; www.goodspeed.org.

NATHAN HALE SCHOOLHOUSE.

29 Main Street, Route 149. Open Memorial Day through Labor Day, Saturday and Sunday and on certain holidays and by appointment. General admission is by donation. (860) 873-3399.

GILLETTE CASTLE STATE PARK.

67 River Road. East Haddam. Open Memorial Day through Columbus Day, daily. Additionally, during the Christmas season. General admission is $5.00 adults; $3.00 students/children and free to children 3 and under. Admission to the park grounds is free. (860) 526-2336; http://dep.state.ct.us/stateparks/parks/gillettecastle.htm.

AMASA DAY HOUSE.

Town Street, Moodus Green. Open May through October, Sunday. General admission is $4.00 adults; $2.00 children and free to Antiquarian and Landmark Society members. (860) 247-8996; (860) 873-8144.

THANKFUL ARNOLD HOUSE.

Hayden Hill Road. Open Memorial Day through Columbus Day, Wednesday through Friday and Sunday. General admission is $4.00 for adults; $3.00 seniors; $2.00 children and free to children 5 and under. (860) 345-2400; www.haddamhistory.org.

ACCOMMODATIONS:

DEVIL'S HOPYARD STATE PARK.
Route 82 to Mount Parnassas/Millington Road to Hopyard Road, East Haddam. Reservations are accepted for the campsites, which are available in season. Call for pricing information. (877) 668-2267; (860) 873-8566; http://dep.state.ct.us/stateparks/parks/devilshopyard.htm.

SELDON ISLAND.
Gillette Castle State Park is in charge of camping at this island, which can only be reached by canoe. The riverside sites are primitive with fireplaces and are available from May 1 through September 30. The length of stay is limited to one night, only. Call for pricing information. (860) 526-2336.

BISHOPSGATE INN.
7 Norwich Road, East Haddam. A quaint inn built in 1818 as a shipbuilder's homestead. Four of the six guestrooms have fireplaces; the suite comes with sauna. Each accommodation has a private bath and air-conditioning in the summer. Rates (including continental breakfast): $110-$175. (860) 873-1677; www.bishopsgate.com.

KLAR CREST RESORT & INN.
11 Johnsonville Road, East Haddam. Twenty-one acres provide a country-resort atmosphere for 60 guestroom cottages, all offering private bath. Open June through October, this family-style hideaway boasts an Olympic-sized, outdoor swimming pool. Rates: $85. (860) 873-8649.

SUNRISE RESORT.
Route 151, Moodus. Whether families are looking for a game of tennis, a rubber-ducky race in a pool or a ride on an antique fire truck, this 400-acre resort, meandering by the eastern pocket of the Salmon River, has been accommodating a variety of family needs since its humble beginnings in 1916 as a lodge known as Elm Camp. Open Memorial Day through Labor Day, the all-inclusive resort also allows day-trippers who prefer to go home at night an option to book a day and take advantage of resort amenities and such favorites as outdoor barbeques. Room rates (which are all-inclusive and offer a variety of rooms [160]): $91 to $111, children under 14 receive discounts. (800) 225-9033; (860) 873-8681; www.sunriseresort.com.

ANNUAL FESTIVALS/EVENTS
The Central Regional Tourism District, Connecticut's Heritage River Valley, representing 46 communities, provides a gamut of tourism information, which includes seasonal events (800) 793-4480 or (860) 244-8181; www.ctbound.org. For additional festival and event information, contact the Haddam town office, (860) 873-5020.

FEBRUARY
The **Connecticut River Eagle Festival** complements the events held in Essex and along the lower Connecticut River Valley. East Haddam events include eagle watching, special demonstrations, lectures and a chowder cook-off. (860) 873-5020.

APRIL

The **Annual April Fool's 5 K Road Race and Children's Fun Run** is held; call for location. (860) 873-3206.

MAY

Friends of the Rathbun Library sponsor an **Annual Plant Sale**, with plants donated from local gardeners. (860) 873-5020.

The Moodus Sportsmen's Club holds its **Fishing Derby**. (860) 873-5020.

JUNE

The **Great Connecticut Cajun/Zydeco Festival** at Sunrise Resort features a generous array of musical entertainment, food and fun for all ages. (800) 468-3836; www.sunriseresort.com.

The Moodus Sportsmen's Club holds its **Annual Shad Bake**. (860) 873-5020.

JULY-AUGUST

National as well as local talent is featured at the **Summer Sounds at Chestelm** celebration, an annual series of free concerts held most Tuesdays on the lawn of Chestelm Health Care Center, 534 Town Street. (860) 873-1455.

JULY

The **Annual East Haddam Lion's Club's Auction/Tag Sale** is held at the Town Grange Hall on Town Street. Among the wares are antiques, collectibles, motor vehicles, books and unusual items. (860) 873-2980.

AUGUST

The **Great Connecticut Jazz Festival** held at Moodus's Sunrise Resort attracts thousands of patrons with a weekend featuring traditional jazz, Dixieland and swing. (800) 468-3836; www.sunriseresort.com.

Bring an appetite and enjoy the **Annual East Haddam Lion's Club Chicken Dinner**. (860) 873-5020.

SEPTEMBER

Friday through Monday during Labor Day weekend means the **Haddam Neck Fair** at the fairgrounds at Haddam Neck Road. Food, animal and special exhibits and entertainment for all ages are featured during this long-standing tradition. (860) 873-1930.

Festivities at the **Haddam River Days Celebration** range from arts and crafts, games and entertainment, food and a fireworks grand finale. (860) 873-5020.

OCTOBER

The **First Church Rug & Quilt Show**, at 499 Town Street, features quilts, needlepoint, cross-stitch, embroidery, hooked rugs and other forms of needle art on display and for sale. Refreshments are also available. (860) 873-9084.

DECEMBER

An **East Haddam Village Christmas** is hosted by the East Haddam Village merchants and held in the heart of the village. The day's activities include entertainment, seasonal décor, caroling, food vendors and a visit from Santa himself. (860) 873-5020.

Holiday Celebration on Moodus Green is another holiday event that is entertaining and fun for all ages. (860) 873-5020.

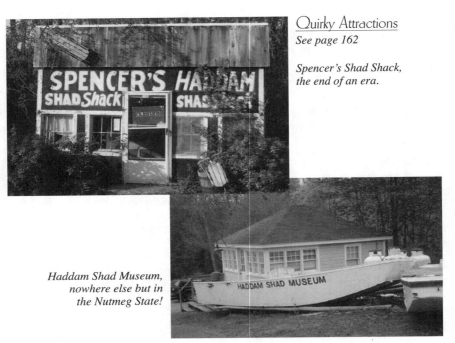

Quirky Attractions
See page 162

Spencer's Shad Shack, the end of an era.

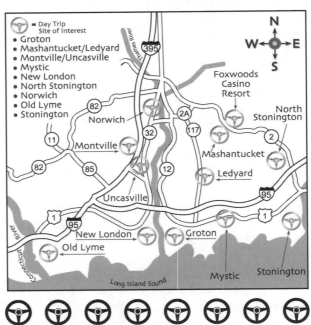

Haddam Shad Museum, nowhere else but in the Nutmeg State!

IV.
SOUTHERN CONNECTICUT
Middlesex County/New Haven County
"Heritage River Valley & Shoreline"
Westbrook/Madison/Branford

These coastline hamlets nestled by Long Island Sound southward, are located northeast of metropolitan New York and southwest of Boston, Massachusetts; within about a two-hour driving radius to either city. Situated on Route 1, in the summertime, the fine harbor marinas and sandy beaches become abuzz with swimmers, boaters and sun worshippers. Hammonasett State Park in Madison touts the largest beach in the state. Cruises to obtain a closer view of the Thimble Islands, Branford's archipelago, are one of the more novel summer experiences. Throughout the year, many naturalists, bird-watchers and hikers explore the area's public parks, rolling hills, open marshes and pristine woodlands that become ablaze in the fall.

Although an increasingly popular vacation spot, these towns hold steadfast to their small town charm apparent in their tidy town greens, preserved historical buildings, museums and amicable merchants who take idle chitchat seriously. Diners will find a variety of restaurant options that range from clam shacks to five-star dining experiences. Legendary Lenny & Joe's Fish Tale, for instance, has two restaurant locations: a family restaurant in Westbrook, and an eatery in Madison that boasts an authentic Dentzel Carousel in which the owners donate all proceeds to charity. On any given summer weekend, more than 10,000 diners are served at either restaurant location; quite a feat, considering the fact that both dining establishments metamorphosed from humble clam shacks! One of the most popular souvenirs at both locations is an inexpensive t-shirt that presents a new Fish Tale design each year.

Day-trippers who decide to stay the night will encounter many lodging selections including a range of cozy and attractive bed and breakfasts. Whatever the season, these coastline towns offer a relaxing getaway that is doable (and most advisable!) for all ages.

*In 1742, what Connecticut town was David Bushnell,
who would later change history with his invention
of the submarine, born in?*

*What Connecticut town is referred to as the
"boating capital of the state"?*

Boating Prince: WESTBROOK

The Middlesex County town that we know today as Westbrook was settled in 1638 as part of the Saybrook Colony, which also included the presently named towns of Old Saybrook, Chester, Deep River, Essex, Lyme and Old Lyme. The Native American name for Westbrook was Pochoug, meaning, "a place where a river divides." Settlers later differentiated the region from the surrounding area by dubbing it West Parish and decided on the derivative, Westbrook, in 1810 when it was incorporated as a town in that same year.

Boasting four miles of natural Long Island coastline and twin rivers, the Menunketesuck to the west and the Patchogue to the east, shipbuilding was the earliest and prime industry in settlement history. One of Westbrook's most famed sons, David Bushnell, born in 1742, a Revolutionary War patriot, later was recognized by the United States Navy as the inventor of the submarine. Called the American Turtle, the submersible, one-man contraption built from wood and steel resembled two large interlocking tortoise shells. It goes down in history as being involved in the first submarine attack in New York Harbor in 1776. However, during its mission, instead of destroying the HMS Eagle, flagship of the British fleet, with gunpowder, it became entangled in the ship and surfaced! (see **Groton** chapter; see **Essex** chapter). Later, during the War of 1812, Westbrook shipbuilders constructed a fleet of ships along the Patchogue River to help further the patriot's cause.

West of New London, situated between Clinton and Old Saybrook, Westbrook's public beach is one of the longest stretches of town-owned beaches in Connecticut. Yesteryears' coastline hotels, dance halls and casinos that likely inspired the original "tourists' traps," are mere memories. Although the 15.72-square-mile town (residential population, 5,714) is overshadowed by a seasonal tourism swell in neighboring Mystic and Essex, what is reputed as "the boating capital of the state," receives its own hefty wave of summer regulars, whether arriving by motor vehicle, motorboat, sailboat or yacht.

To create a day trip with panache to Westbrook, pick up maps, brochures and a variety of other tourism information at the **Westbrook Welcome Center**, located directly on Interstate 95.

From clothing fashions to home accessories, directly off Exit 65, serious shoppers can search for discounted, famous designer and national brand names at **Tanger Outlet Center** (866-655-8685; 860-399-8656). Housing 65 outlet stores with names like Timberland and Black and Decker, the center's design is reminiscent of a New England train station, complete with a restored 1902 cruising yawl and a 1930 steam engine. (Note: in Clinton, **Clinton Crossing Premium Outlets** is directly off Exit 63 [860-664-0700].)

Just north of Tanger Outlet Center on Route 153, the **Pink Sleigh** (860-399-6926) has been ringing in the Christmas spirit for more than 40 years, featuring brands like Byers' Choice Carolers and Old World Christmas and showcasing European glass ornaments by such makers as Radko and Slavic Treasures. The country barn setting extends a retail-shopping odyssey, open from July through December, filled with pinecone scents, more than 20-themed, decorated Christmas trees as well as Halloween and fall-harvest giftware and accessories.

Route 153 south travels into downtown Westbrook. Sightseers can look-see the many homes that were built before 1800. Spend at least an hour inspecting the nation's largest collection of American military uniforms at the **Military Historian's Museum**, North Main Street. An assortment of completely restored and operational military vehicles from World War II to a Desert Storm truck, complement the uniform collection.

The **Westbrook Historical Society** (860-399-7473), 1196 Boston Post Road, occasionally opens up its quarters to unveil area-related history exhibits. Those with a predisposition to history should be familiar with David Bushnell's circa 1678 home on South Main, built by his uncle. Resembling a Saltbox-style design, the "two-room with fireplace in between" architectural structure housed a museum in honor of Bushnell in the 1930s. Today, it is the headquarters for the **Museum of Early Engineering Technology**, chockfull of interesting gadgetry, which is open early Thursday evenings.

Just off US 1, open to the public, **West Beach** is Westbrook's largest beach complete with food concessions in season and the prime vantage point to espy Menunketesuck Island, Duck Island and Salt Island. **Pilot's Point Marina** (860-399-7906; www.byy.com/westbrook/index.cfm), the largest boating facility in the mid-Atlantic, is a mariner's beehive. Fishermen and women who desire a saltwater fishing experience filled with lots of potential prizes of frameable striped bass and bluefish, can be found aboard **Catch'em Charters** (860-223-1876; www.catchemcharters.com).

Captain Dick Siedzik (who's been sailing the Long Island waters for more than 35 years) and his crew will also retire the fishing gear in order to give more leisurely inclined day-trippers a cruise.

Note, Kayak rentals can be obtained at **Pier 76 Marina** (860-399-8531; www.pier76.com), billed as Westbrook's first marina, at 54 Old Boston Post Road behind Bill's Seafood Restaurant. **Salt Meadow National Wildlife Refuge** adjoins the marina. The 274 acres of natural surroundings attracting hikers, bird-watchers and appreciators of wildlife and open space, signify Connecticut's first National Wildlife Refuge. Today, part of the Stewart B. McKinney National Wildlife Refuge Program, Salt Meadow is one out of eight such units that form the 60-mile Connecticut coastline ribbon that stretches from Westbrook to the town of Norwalk.

Area restaurants, many of which are tried-and-true, don't let you down when you're out fishin' for fresh seafood. **Lenny & Joe's Fish Tale** (860-669-0767; www.ljfishtale.com) at 86 Boston Post Road, (see introduction, above) is an area institution open for lunch and dinner daily. For some unsurpassed views of the Patchogue River, dine at **Bill's Seafood Restaurant** (860-399-7224), another lunch and dinnertime favorite open daily. Where else can you find old-fashioned sing-a-longs on Sunday nights?

Steamers Grill (860-399-8000), known for its barbeque, serves breakfast, lunch and dinner daily. Those who have a yen for a lunch or dinner consisting of "healthy Mexican cuisine," should be familiar with the **Whole Enchilada** (860-399-1221), which is open daily. Carnivorous types should add **New Deal Steakhouse** (860-399-0015; www.culinarymenus.com/newdealsteakplace.htm) to their dinner plans, served daily (and Sunday lunch). A most bountiful feast of hot and cold menu items and everything in between is prepared fresh and colorful at the Sunday brunch featured at **Water's Edge Resort & Spa** (860-399-5901; 800-

222-5901; www.watersedge-resort.com). A smorgasbord haven; dieters beware. The brunch has won numerous accolades, including a string of *best of* categories in the annual readers' poll of restaurants conducted by *Connecticut Magazine*. Located in the historic Bill Hahn Lodge at Water's Edge (see **Accommodations**), the restaurant offers lunch and dinner daily.

GETTING THERE:
Westbrook is within two hours or less from New Haven and Hartford, CT, Boston, MA, Providence, RI, and New York City; is 21 miles south of Haddam. The region is easily accessible from Interstate Highway 95 (Exits 65 and 66); connecting to I-84 and also from Massachusetts Turnpike, I-90, connecting to I-395.

TRANSPORTATION:
The Groton-New London Airport, located in Groton, is about 24 miles in driving distance; Tweed New Haven Regional Airport is approximately 27 miles in driving distance. Both serve a growing demand of business commuters and leisure travelers in the southeastern Connecticut region. The area is approximately 55 miles south of Bradley International Airport in Windsor Locks. Westbrook is within two hours or less from major transportation centers in New Haven and Hartford, CT, Boston, MA, Providence, RI, and New York City.

DATTCO bus (800-229-4879) services the Old Saybrook/Madison/Guilford/ Branford and East Haven areas. Amtrak (800-872-7245) accommodates the towns of Old Saybrook and New Haven. Shoreline East (800-ALL-RIDE in CT; 203-777-7433) runs a commuter-connection train weekdays.

ADDITIONAL INFORMATION:
WESTBROOK WELCOME CENTER.
Located on I-95 northbound between exits 65 and 66. Open all year, daily; the building is staffed with personnel from Memorial Day through Columbus Day. (860) 399-8122.

MILITARY HISTORIAN'S MUSEUM.
North Main Street. Open all year, Tuesday through Friday, daily. General admission is free. (860) 399-9460.

ACCOMMODATIONS:
WESTBROOK INN.
976 Boston Post Road. Lovely gardens envelop the 1876 onetime sea captain's house brimming inside with period décor; no wonder a local magazine voted it as *the most elegant inn*. Nine guestrooms and a cottage, which sleeps four or more, with its own kitchen, offer private baths, full, modern amenities and a recently renovated spa facility. Rates (including full breakfast): $99-$309.90-plus. (800) 342-3162; (860) 399-4777; www.westbrookinn.com.

ANGEL'S WATCH INN BED & BREAKFAST.

976 Boston Post Road. The stately, elegant Federal-style mansion neighbors the Westbrook Inn and is one and one-half blocks away from West Beach. Five newly renovated guestrooms present a romantic ambiance with canopied beds, Vermont casting fireplaces and dual-person soaking pedestal tubs (Ooh la la!), plus full, modern amenities. Wellness packages and elopement/wedding events are what the B & B is known for. Rates (including full breakfast): $155-$195. (860) 399-8846; www.angelswatchinn.com.

CAPTAIN STANNARD HOUSE.

138 South Main Street. A former 19th-century sea captain's mansion, eight guestrooms, each with private bathrooms, furnished with antiques, exudes charm. Amenities include refrigerators and freezers, beach passes and telephones and television available in the common areas. Rates (including full breakfast): $125-$185. (860) 399-4634; www.stannardhouse.com.

WATER'S EDGE RESORT AND SPA.

1525 Boston Post Road. Situated on 15 acres of shoreline property, this sprawling turn-of-the-century New England-style estate complex extends 162 total guestrooms; which include luxury two-bedroom villa units in time-share buildings. Amenities include full-service spa, fitness center, business meeting center, tennis courts, indoor and outdoor swimming pools. Rates: $150-$340. (800) 222-5901; (860) 399-5901; www.watersedge-resort.com.

ANNUAL FESTIVALS/EVENTS

The Central Regional Tourism District, Connecticut's Heritage River Valley, representing 46 communities, provides a gamut of tourism information, which includes seasonal events (800) 793-4480 or (860) 244-8181; www.enjoycentralct. com. For additional festival and event information, contact the Westbrook Chamber of Commerce, (860) 388-3266.

FEBRUARY

Bargain hunters will find monumental savings at the **Annual President's Day Weekend Sales** at many of the Tanger Outlet stores. (860) 399-8656.

MARCH

The **Think Spring Soup-A-Ree** at St. Paul's Episcopal Church, Main Street, features a variety of soups, salads and desserts. (860) 669-7681.

APRIL

The Tanger Outlet Center provides the grounds for the **Morgan School Car Show**, highlighting more than 100 antique and classic automobiles and hot rods. (860) 399-8656.

Children of all ages can enjoy the **Tanger Outlet's Easter Egg Hunt** at Tanger Outlet Center. (860) 399-8656.

APRIL-OCTOBER

The **Westbrook Flea Market** at 110 Boston Post Road operates weekly, seasonally. (860) 347-0028.

JUNE
The **Westbrook Tag Sale** is a town-wide event. (860) 399-9239.

JULY
The Westbrook Town Green showcases the **Arts & Crafts Fair**. The juried show, highlighting all media, also features food vendors. (860) 669-0298.

JULY-AUGUST
Musical entertainment is provided at the Tanger Outlet Centers' courtyard Thursday evenings during the **Summer Entertainment Series**. (860) 399-8656.

AUGUST
More than 45 years old, the **Annual Westbrook Muster and Parade** is hosted by the Westbrook Drum Corps and is said to be one of the best parades providing wonderful musical entertainment. (860) 399-6436.

The **Annual Children's Scavenger Hunt** at Tanger Outlet Center allows children to search for back-to-school supplies from a list that is provided by store employees. (860) 399-8656.

SEPTEMBER
For a day of fun for all ages, check out the **Annual Westbrook Historical Society Day** on the green with visits to the society's special exhibits and outdoor booths featuring antiques, crafts, refreshments and a giant tag sale. (860) 399-7361.

DECEMBER
Tour Westbrook's finest B&Bs during the **Annual Historic Bed & Breakfast Christmas Tour** when the town's accommodations are decorated for the holidays. This free tour also provides refreshments at each participating establishment. (860) 342-3162.

Nautical Westbrook
See pages 9, 123, 143, 150, 167-172

"Knot" to be missed!

What Connecticut town was named after a
United States President?

What Connecticut town touts the
largest beach in the state?

Magnificent Marvel: **MADISON**

Reverend Henry Whitfield originally purchased Mohegan Indian-owned land in 1641 that would one day become Guilford and Madison. Declared a separate community in 1707, Madison was incorporated in 1826 and named after the fourth United States President James Madison (1809-1817). Maritime commerce that included a porpoise and whitefish fishery began in the late 1700s. From 1825 to 1890, Madison turned into a prosperous shipbuilding center. Since the 1860s, the sprawling-beach community has enticed throngs of summertime crowds.

Today, stretching 36.3 square miles, the New Haven County town accommodates nearly 18,000 residents. Long Island Sound cradles the town on the south while farms and woodlands occupy the northern region. Clinton lies east; Guilford, west and Durham, north.

For a custom-designed day trip with panache, step into the **Madison Visitor's Information Center** (203-245-5659). Open seasonally and headquartered in the quaint, yellow building called the Powder House, friendly volunteers provide personal insight as well as a comprehensive assortment of travel brochures, maps and other tourists' guides; impeccably clean restrooms are also on hand.

Across the way is the **Madison Town Green**, which is located within a National Register Historic District (west of the commercial district), and hosts a string of summertime concerts, art and antiques exhibits and drum corps and muster demonstrations (see **Annual Festivals/Events**). Stroll this meticulously maintained green. Many of the vintage houses date back more than 300 years and were once the residences of former sea captains and shipbuilders. The **First Congregational Church** (1838), an imposing Greek Revival-style building, located on a slight rise, is the green's centerpiece. The Madison Historical Society is housed at the **Allis-Bushnell House and Museum**, which borders the green. Inside the circa 1785 Saltbox, visitors will find 18th- and 19th-century furnishings and accessories indigenous to the original owner, Cornelius Bushnell, founder of the Union Pacific Railway and key financier of the Civil War ship USS Monitor, which was the first iron-clad war vessel.

In-season on Saturdays, the Madison Historical Society opens up **Lee Academy**, an 1821 schoolhouse that faces the green, to the public. Next to the green is the circa 1685 **Deacon John Grave House**, Madison's oldest home. The Deacon John Grave Foundation owns and operates the non-profit educational institution showcasing what was first built as a two-room dwelling, only to metamorphose into a New England Saltbox that (although the deacon's descendants inhabited it for more than 300 years) redefined itself in numerous ways including stints as a courthouse, a tavern and schoolhouse.

West of the green, **R. J. Julia Booksellers** (203-245-3959; 800-74-READS; www.rjjulia.com) at 768 Boston Post Road is an award-winning independent bookseller, including winner of the prestigious *Publisher's Weekly Bookseller of the Year* Award. Roost with a favorite book or catch a celebrity author's appearance, (owner Roxanne Coady and staff manage to reel in some literary super stars) free, but reservations required. Peruse the photo wall hangings of previous famous authors' visits.

One favorite shop along the drag is **Kirtland H. Crump Antique Clocks** (203-245-7573; www.crumpclocks.com/infodirect.html). Bargain hunters should take the day just to explore **Act II, the Madison ABC Thrift Shop** (203-245-2815; www.act2thrift.org) at 170 Boston Post Road. Staffed by volunteers, the store is a philanthropic endeavor in which all proceeds benefit charity; 2,200 square feet are chockfull of gently used clothing and accessories, furniture, antiques, sporting goods, bric-a-brac, seasonal decorations and lots more. The **Scranton Memorial Library** (203-245-7365; www.scrantonlibrary.com), 801 Boston Post Road, features a variety of special events and art gallery exhibits.

For a caffeine pick-me-up after sightseeing, Boston Post Road coffee bars include **Madison Gourmet Beanery** (203-245-1323); **R.J. Café** (203-318-0706), which shares the bookstore's quarters, but is a separate entity, and **Willoughby's Coffee & Tea** (203-245-1600).

Located on the southeastern edge of town, **Hammonasset State Park** is Connecticut's largest shoreline park with more than two miles of beach in the 930-acre park that includes 558 campsites (see **Accommodations**). With an overall park capacity to serve 16,000 people a day, about one-million people visit the park annually.

Daytime discoveries lead to a nearly one-mile-long boardwalk, fishing (saltwater) jetty, swimming, boating and crabbing opportunities, biking and hiking trails and food concessions. The on-site **Meigs Point Nature Center** offers occasional, interpretive programs. Interesting note: "Hammonasset" originates from the Woodland Indian (the region's original tribe) word meaning, "where we dig holes in the ground."

West of Route 79, south of Madison and Durham, **Rockland Preserve** is a serene setting for hikers and walkers; its history as interesting as its terrain featuring rocky hills, steep cliffs, lush woods and a pond. **The Shoreline Greenway Trail**, which spans from Madison to East Haven (see **Branford** chapter), currently under expansion and development, is another walkers' paradise.

Making a beeline south into Madison center, there is a concentration of dining opportunities in the Boston Post Road vicinity. At number 725, **Allegre Café** (www.allegrecafe.com), part of the Inn at Lafayette (see **Accommodations**), exudes an elegant and urbane atmosphere, complete with live piano performances Friday and Saturday, and specializes in Italian-style cuisine, serving lunch and dinner, Tuesday through Friday and dinner only on Saturday and Sunday. At number 885, **Perfect Parties** (203-245-0250; www.perfectparties.com/about.html) offers a gourmet-style breakfast, lunch and dinner, take-out service Tuesday through Saturday; the restaurant is open for dinner (Sunday brunch), Wednesday through Saturday. A large sign outside **Friends and Company** (203-245-0462), an area institution for nearly three decades, at 11 Boston Post Road, proclaims when shad is in season and featured on the menu, open for lunch, Monday through Friday, dinner (Sunday brunch) Sunday through Thursday.

Near Madison center at 45 Wall Street, for an extreme taste of British, the **British Shoppe** (203-245-4521; www.thefrontparlour.com) carries everything a chap needs. Bangers anyone? For a spot of tea and then some, the **Front Parlour Tea Room** occupying the same 1690 clapboard house, and open for lunch and tea Tuesday through Saturday, will trick you into believing that you have just crossed the Atlantic.

Off the Boston Post Road at 73 W. Wharf Road, in proximity to the Madison Country Club, the legendary **Dolly Madison Inn** (203-245-7377; www.bicoastal. com/dolly/menu.html; see **Accommodations**) restaurant offers lunch and dinner daily and breakfast on Sunday. At 94 West Wharf Road, the **Wharf at the Madison Beach Hotel** (203-245-0005; www.madisonbeachhotel.com/rest.html) is the only restaurant located on Long Island Sound in Madison and specializes in seafood served fresh for dinner daily. **Noodles** (203-421-5606), at the intersection of Routes 79 and 80, fills the bill for a super, family-friendly restaurant open for dinner Tuesday through Saturday.

GETTING THERE:

Madison is within two hours or less from Providence, Rhode Island and New York and 15 miles east of New Haven and 45 miles south of Hartford; nine miles west of Westbrook. Madison is easily accessible from Interstate Highway 95 (Exit 61); Routes 80 and 1 (Boston Post Road) intersect Madison eastward-westward; while Route 79 intersects Madison northward-southward.

TRANSPORTATION:

The Groton-New London Airport, located in Groton, is about 32 miles in driving distance; Tweed New Haven Regional Airport is approximately 15 miles in driving distance. Both serve a growing demand of business commuters and leisure travelers in the southeastern Connecticut region. The area is approximately 56 miles south of Bradley International Airport in Windsor Locks. Madison is within two hours or less from major transportation centers in Providence, Rhode Island and New York;15 miles east of New Haven and 45 miles south of Hartford. DATTCO bus (800-229-4879) services the Old Saybrook/Madison/Guilford/Branford and East Haven areas. Amtrak (800-872-7245) accommodates the towns of Old Saybrook and New Haven. Shoreline East (800-ALL-RIDE in CT; 203-777-7433) runs a commuter-connection train weekdays; other Metro-North and Amtrak connections are available from the New Haven Union Station.

ADDITIONAL INFORMATION:
ALLIS-BUSHNELL HOUSE AND MUSEUM.

853 Boston Post Road. Open from Memorial Day through September, Wednesday, Friday and Saturday or by appointment. General admission is by donation. (203) 245-4567.

DEACON JOHN GRAVE HOUSE.

581 Boston Post Road. Open mid-June through Labor Day, Wednesday through

Saturday; Labor Day through Columbus Day, Saturday and Sunday. General admission is $2.00 adults; $1.00 children and free to children 5 and under. (203) 245-4798.

HAMMONASSET STATE PARK.

Boston Post Road. The park is open Memorial Day through Labor Day, sunrise to sunset. **Meigs Point Nature Center** (www.friendsofhammonasset.org/naturecenter. html) is open late June to Labor Day, Tuesday through Saturday. For information about seasonal programs, call (203) 245-8743. Day fees per carload are weekends: $9.00 Connecticut registered vehicle; $14.00 out-of-state registered vehicle; weekdays: $7.00 Connecticut registered vehicle; $10.00 out-of-state registered vehicle. (203) 245-2785; http://dep.state.ct.us/stateparks/parks/hammonasset.htm.

ACCOMMODATIONS:
HAMMONASSET STATE PARK.

Boston Post Road. Reservations are accepted for the 558 campsites, which are available in season. Amenities include dump station, flush toilets, and showers; open May through October. Call for pricing information. (860) 424-3200.

TIDEWATER INN.

949 Boston Post Road. Once a former 1890s stagecoach stop, nine guestrooms (including one cottage suite), await the weary traveler, each with private baths and distinctly decorated in canopy beds and select antiques. Amenities also include summer beach passes (towels and chairs provided), cable television and Internet access. English gardens complement Tidewater Inn in the summertime. Rates (including full breakfast): $110-$200. (203) 245-8457; www.thetidewater.com.

DOLLY MADISON INN.

73 W. Wharf Road. The main building of this historical inn dates back to the turn of the 20th century. The setting is romanticized by the shoreline, 13 charming guestrooms boast fireplaces, terraces and balconies. On premises (see above) is a highly acclaimed restaurant. Rates: $145-$175. (203) 245-7377; www.bicoastal. com/dolly/welcome.html.

MADISON BEACH HOTEL.

94 W. Wharf Road. The hotel's roots can be traced back to the 1800s when shipbuilders rented out rooms in what was then a boarding house. These days, this Victorian charmer offers visitors 31 guestrooms and four suites, each overlooking the waterfront. Other features include private bathrooms, heat and air conditioning and cable television. Rates (including continental breakfast): $80-$250. (203) 245-1404; www.madisonbeachhotel.com/hotel.html.

INN AT LAFAYETTE.

725 Boston Post Road. Reminiscent of a European Manor house, this inn extends five guestrooms, each with private marble bathroom. Other amenities include cable television, plug-in computer and fax port, Egyptian-cotton linens and bathrobes; on-premises restaurant (see **Allegre Café** above). Rates: $95-$175. (203) 245-7773; www.allegrecafe.com/innatlafayette.htm.

ANNUAL FESTIVALS/EVENTS

Greater New Haven Convention & Visitor's Bureau, representing 19 communities, provides a gamut of tourism information, which includes seasonal events (800) 332-STAY or (203) 777-8550; www.newhavencvb.org/base/index.cfm. For additional festival and event information, contact the Madison Chamber of Commerce, 203-245-7394.

MARCH

More than 40 antiques dealers throughout the Northwest participate in the **Indoor Antiques Show** located at the Madison's town campus, Duck Hole Road. (888) 353-0552.

APRIL-JUNE

Spring Bird Walks are conducted at the Hammonasset State Park. (203) 245-9056.

MAY

Annual Rotary Antiques and Collectibles Show is held on the Madison Town Green, Route 1. (203) 245-1529.

Go fly a kite or sit back and watch the colorful display at the **Hammonasset Kite Festival** held on the park's grounds. (860) 424-3200.

The **Outdoor Antiques Show** highlights more than 100 distinguished antiques dealers. The event is held on the Madison Town Green, Route 1. (860) 685-3355.

JULY

The **Fourth of July Parade** begins in downtown Madison. The event is sponsored by the Exchange Club of Madison. (203) 421-1102.

JULY-AUGUST

Madison Concerts on the Green provide free musical entertainment ranging from jazz to pop. (203) 245-5623.

Bring a picnic and enjoy the outdoors while listening to the **Chestnut Hill Concerts**, which provide world-class chamber music. Held at the First Congregational Church of Madison, a light-refreshment reception follows the evening's entertainment along with an opportunity to meet the musicians. (203) 245-5736.

Madison Annual Sidewalk Sales sponsored by the Chamber of Commerce, in the downtown area, offer bargains for everyone. (203) 245-7394.

OCTOBER

Celebrating nature and Native American history and culture in form of music, dance and special exhibits, the **Hammonasset Festival** attracts patrons from everywhere. (203) 318-0517, Ext. 217; www.friendsofhammonasset.org/festival.htm.

---

*What Connecticut town did the colonists obtain in
exchange for winter coats?*

*What Connecticut town, located on the south central
shoreline, touts the largest population between
New Haven and New London?*

Summer Fun & Buccaneer Lore: **BRANFORD**

To the Mattabesec Tribe that occupied these gently rolling hills reposed by the shore, this land was "Totoket" (sometimes spelled "Totokett"), meaning "place of the tidal river." In 1638, New Haven Colony purchased the territory for, as record states, "eleven coats of trucking cloth and one coat of English cloth made in the English fashion." Wethersfield families first settled the region in 1644 and Branford's namesake was chosen in 1653 after Brentford in Middlesex, England. Along with a maritime history of shipbuilding and trade, industry began in 1655 when Connecticut's first iron furnace was established and operated at Lake Saltonstall, one of the most popular recreational areas for day-trippers today. In 1685, 10 ministers met and became official trustees to what marked the earliest beginnings of Yale College, first called the Collegiate School in 1701. (See **Old Saybrook** chapter; **New Haven** chapter.) Another Branford notable was that Revolutionary soldiers used the salt produced in town to preserve the troop's meat.

Railroad completion in 1852 jumpstarted industry and manufacturing and two manufacturing leaders were the Malleable Irons Fittings, founded in 1854, and the Branford Locks Works, founded in 1862.

The Branford Electric Railway opened in 1900 and served the community until 1947, making it the oldest, continuously operated trolley line in America and now listed on the National Register of Historic Places (see **New Haven** chapter).

Since the turn of the century, Branford's waterfront has attracted residents and visitors alike. Currently, the 27.9-square-mile town holds the record for the largest population, approximately 28,030 residents, located between New Haven and New London. Nineteen yacht clubs and marinas dot the waterfront; the Branford River alone is homeport for hundreds of boats docked at more than six marina facilities.

Day trips with panache in this mostly suburban community begin with exploring **Stony Creek**, a quaint (but busy in the summertime) Branford Village with 2,500 year-round residents. Immigrants once arrived here to quarry the area's unique pink granite that developers used in constructing such famous landmarks as New York's Brooklyn Bridge.

For firsthand encounters with the Branford and neighboring coastline of Guilford, adventure-sports enthusiasts can reserve a self-guided or group-organized kayaking tour via **Stony Creek Kayak** (203-481-6401). Novices can take lessons. A public boat launch is available for those who come equipped.

Legendary to these parts are the **Thimble Islands**—about 365 islands comprising a chain that the Mattabesec Indians called "the beautiful sea rocks." To get a closer look, consider a leisurely 45 minute or so in-season cruise, when weather permits, aboard one of the ferries: **Sea Mist Boats & Ferries** (203-488-8905; call for days and hours of operation and pricing information) or **Stony Creek Dock** (203-397-3921; call for days and hours of operation and pricing information).

Cruise captains spin fact, legend and lore. Listen to tales about the infamous Captain Kidd's hidden treasure—still unfound (if story holds true), a phenomenon that some believe gave "Money" Island its name. Hear trivia about the famous General Tom Thumb courting a petite woman and resident of Cut-in-Two Island. Relive horrors like how seven islanders drowned during the wicked 1938 hurricane.

Interesting, too, are present-day stories about the (some famous) lives of those who call these enchanting islands home. About 85, primarily Victorian-style houses, are built on 32 of the 365 islands, ranging in size from less than one-half acre to 12 acres. Fiercely guarded against outside visitors, the islands, once laden with thimbleberries, were named in honor of the fruit.

Spend part of the day trip on the idyllic Stony Creek walking-hiking paths. The village's own library, **Willoughby Wallace Memorial Library** (203-488-8702), offers a collection of trail maps. Additionally, the staff invites visitors to join one of their buoyant book discussions or enjoy a free Friday night movie. Don't forget to browse the changing artwork displays. Travelers with laptops in tow who want to surf the Internet, get a free cup of coffee, tea or hot chocolate at the library.

On-foot excursionists will likely uncover old trolley bridge remains by the waterfront, which also offers brilliant bird-watching terrain that includes scenic views of salt marsh flora and fauna. In the opposite direction, Thimble Island Road, embedded with Victorian-style houses and well-preserved barns, re-creates a picture of the past. Traveling east to Old Quarry Road, one of the most popular spots for natural expeditions is **Stony Creek Quarry**, interconnecting with Guilford's **West Wood Trail**. The myriad trails, ranging from easy to very difficult levels for hikers, unfold such delightful surprises as waterfalls, overhanging rocks and an abandoned quarry. Day-trippers should also keep the **Shoreline Greenway Trail**, spanning from Madison to East Haven (see **Madison** chapter) and currently under expansion and development, in mind for future haunts.

Before leaving the village, consider catching a show at **Puppet House Theater** (203-488-5752; www.puppethouse.org/index.htm). Since 1963, rare Sicilian, handmade puppets have entertained audiences. Situated within a theater that first premiered as a silent-movie house in the 1900s, today the renovated performing arts center presents a year-round variety of plays, puppet shows, children's programs and special events.

For a super-cool shopping experience in the **Branford Theatre Building**, a block from the historic **Branford Green** is the **Rock Garden** (203-488-6699; www.rockgarden.com/pages/location.html). What began as rock, mineral and jewelry shops has now expanded into a treasure chest brimming with thousands of magical items like beads, jewelry, rocks, minerals, fossils and lots more beads.

Hungry village visitors should note that **Stony Creek Marine & Cuisine** (203-488-8452), open all year, not only provides bait and fishing supplies, but also serves breakfast and lunch, Monday through Wednesday, and dinner Thursday through Sunday. For a special treat, consider reserving a lobster dinner Saturday or Sunday. **Stony Creek Market** (203-488-0145), which specializes in breakfast, lunch and dinner foods for take-out orders or dine in, is open daily, and also has available outdoor patio seating (wait 'til you see the scenic harbor view!).

The focal point of Branford's historical heritage is found in many well-preserved Colonial and Victorian-style buildings around the green in the town center. The best slice of history is at the 1724 Colonial Saltbox-styled **Harrison House** and adjacent barn. The Branford Historical Society maintains the clapboard house characterized by center chimney. A series of artifacts and memorabilia exhibitions depict Branford history; the barn is a backdrop for an interesting antique farm tool display. Outdoor herb gardens, maintained by the Branford Garden Club, flourish in the summer throughout the two-acre grounds.

After checking out a few quaint retail shops in and around the green, diners can choose from numerous fast-food, Chinese and pizza-style restaurants. Overlooking Branford Green, for pure romantic dining, remember **Le Petit Café** (203-483-9791). Open for dinner, Wednesday through Sunday, both the bistro atmosphere and the French cuisine served have won rave reviews from numerous critics. On the town green, for breakfast or lunch daily, try the **Waiting Station** (203-488-5176). For snacks, **Common Grounds** (203-488-2326), specializing in coffee, is just the place.

At the corner of North Main and Cherry Hill Road, **Jalapeno Heaven** (203-481-6759) cooks up fresh Mexican for lunch and dinner daily and so does **Su Casa** (203-481-5001), 400 East Main Street. Two exquisite seafood lunch and dinner choices, served daily, include **Lenny's Indian Head Inn** (203-488-1500) and **Chowder Pot III** (203-481-2356; www.usschowderpot.com). Another award-winning restaurant is **Parthenon Diner** (800-934-6379; 203-481-0333; www.parthenondiner.com), open 24 hours and specializing in Greek-style cuisine.

GETTING THERE:
Branford is less than two hours away from New York City; eight miles east of New Haven and 43 miles south of Hartford; 13 miles west of Madison. Branford is easily accessible from Interstate Highway 95 (Exits 53, 54, 55); as well as I-91 and Route 1.

TRANSPORTATION:
The Groton-New London Airport, located in Groton, is about 44 miles in driving distance; Tweed New Haven Regional Airport is approximately eight miles in driving distance. Both serve a growing demand of business commuters and leisure travelers in the southeastern Connecticut region. The area is approximately 59 miles south of Bradley International Airport in Windsor Locks. Branford is within two hours or less from major transportation centers in Providence, Rhode Island and New York City; 13 miles east of New Haven and 50 miles south of Hartford. DATTCO bus (800-229-4879) services the Old Saybrook/Madison/Guilford/Branford and East Haven areas. Amtrak (800-872-7245) accommodates the towns of Old Saybrook and New Haven. Shoreline East (800-ALL-RIDE in CT; 203-777-7433) runs a commuter-connection train weekdays; other Metro-North and Amtrak connections are available from the New Haven Union Station.

ADDITIONAL INFORMATION:
Branford offers more than 3,500 acres of open and undeveloped space. For a detailed map of public land, call the Branford Land Trust at (203) 483-5263.

HARRISON HOUSE.
124 Main Street. The house and barn are open from Memorial Day through September, Friday, Saturday and Sunday or by appointment only. General admission is by donation. (203) 488-4828.

ACCOMMODATIONS:

Branford has a number of chain-style hotels to choose from including **Days Inn & Conference Center** (203-488-8314); **Ramada Limited** (203-488-4991) and **Economy Inn** (203-488-4035).

BY THE SEA INN & SPA.

107 Montowese Street. This 19th-century, fully renovated mansion offers three guestrooms with private bathrooms and modern amenities. Extras include canopy beds piled with plush pillows and lace window treatments. Whether staying the evening or not, day-trippers may want to luxuriate at the inn for a few hours to experience the largest day spa in New Haven County. The award-winning spa is an odyssey of nine treatment rooms that provide a full range of beauty, skin and massage treatments. Shoppers should browse through By the Sea's own skin care line. Rates (including continental breakfast): $110-$200. (203) 483-3333; www.bytheseainnspa.com.

ABIGAIL'S B & B.

85 Cherry Hill Road. This updated, gracious 13 room, center-hall Colonial was built in the 1870's with local timber and extends three guestrooms. Period antiques as well as distinct features including bow windows, a window seat, marble fireplace, dentil moldings, chestnut paneling, wide plank oak flooring, two all-season porches, and terraced patio and glorious summer gardens accentuate the visit. Rates (including continental breakfast served during the week; full, country breakfast on weekends): $120-$200. (203) 483-1612.

ANNUAL FESTIVALS/EVENTS

Greater New Haven Convention & Visitor's Bureau, representing 19 communities, provides a gamut of tourism information, which includes seasonal events (800) 332-STAY or (203) 777-8550; www.newhavencvb.org/base/index.cfm. For additional festival and event information, contact the Branford Chamber of Commerce, 203-488-5500.

DECEMBER-EARLY MAY

Call Sea Mist Boats & Ferries (203) 488-8905 or Stony Creek Dock (203) 397-3921 about **Seal Watches** that allow visitors the opportunity to view migrating harbor seals.

JUNE

The **Branford Festival** at the town green is the largest of its kind in town. It features music, food, crafts, fireworks, special expeditions, the **Annual Branford Road Race**, car show and parade and more. (203) 488-8304; www.branfordfestival.com.

JULY

Catch the sights, sounds and bold colors at the **Fourth of July Fireworks** at Branford Harbor. (203) 488-5500.

JULY-AUGUST

A variety of talent is showcased at the **Branford Summer Concert Series** at town green. (203) 488-5500.

AUGUST

The **Annual Stony Creek Summer Art Show**, which is juried, is sponsored by the Friends of Willoughby Wallace Memorial Library. (203) 488-8702.

Church of Christ Congregational, 192 Thimble Island Road, Stony Creek, hosts the **Peach & Chowder Festival**. Highlights of the day include homemade peach shortcake, clam chowder and an assortment of other foods. All proceeds benefit the church. (203) 488-7827.

SEPTEMBER

Stargazers should make note of **Starry Nights at Young's Park**. The evening is hosted by the Astronomical Society of New Haven, and the park is located on Route 146. The event is free. (203) 468-0905.

OCTOBER

The **Annual Stony Creek Road Race** is a four-mile run through the scenic seascape and landscape. (203) 488-5500.

NOVEMBER

Branford's Annual Holiday Festival and Parade kicks off the upcoming season. (203) 488-5500.

Annual Open Studios by the Sound means that a variety of local artists in Branford and neighboring Guilford invites the public to examine their studio work. (203) 453-5034.

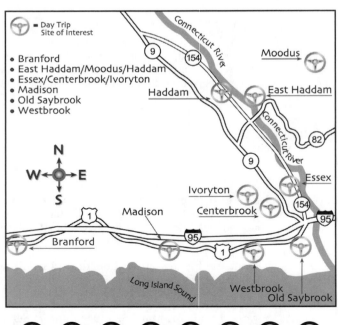

V.

SOUTH CENTRAL CONNECTICUT
New Haven County
Greater New Haven

New Haven is the third largest city in Connecticut, located where the West, Mill and Quinnipiac Rivers flow into New Haven Harbor on the northern coast of Long Island Sound. Generally classified as part of the Greater New York Metropolitan Area, it is home to Yale University as well as four other distinguished schools of higher learning and has rightly earned its reputation as a cultural mecca. In fact, day trips to New Haven can easily evolve into weeklong furloughs!

Scores of excellent museums explore infinite subjects ranging from the impressive collection at Yale University Art Gallery (the nation's oldest college art museum) to dinosaur specimens at Peabody Museum of Natural History to more than 1,000 musical instruments, artifacts and accessories at the Yale University Collection of Musical Instruments.

Award-winning theater companies produce traditional and experimental plays all year long for audiences of every age. Concerts, music and movies, employing nearly every form imaginable, abound. Also popular are the many free summer entertainment events like the July jazz concert series, the New Haven Symphony Orchestra shows and *Free Shakespeare in Edgerton Park* productions. Art organizations provide another vibrant feel to the community in addition to the sundry artists who regularly open their studios to the public.

Past the buzz of the city streets, which are chockablock with history, architecture, cultural heritage and cuisine, one need not go far to comprehend why this region is nicknamed the "Elm City." Sweeping country roads, lined with lauded elm trees, farmyards as well as a charming village green are virtually untouched by time; there's a foray of summertime festivals and fairs. Day-trip itinerary can include a seasonal boat or canoe ride or a trolley excursion at Shore Line Trolley Museum in West Haven, a neighboring town that shares a historical core with New Haven.

People who are more adventurous can—depending on the season—hike, bike, golf, ice-skate, cross-country ski or swim at Lighthouse Point Park, where no day's jaunt is complete without a spin on the old-fashioned carousel inside the pavilion. Sporting venues include intercollegiate, professional, amateur and youth association tournaments and championships and events that should appease every sports' fan. All these divergent interests in one city! Little wonder that New Haven possesses an impressive history, a strong present-day foundation and a celebrated future.

In 1640, in what Connecticut settlement did settlers plan the roads to correspond to nine-square blocks, denoted later as the first planned city in the country?

What city claims to have invented the hamburger and lollipop?

Supreme Oasis: **GREATER NEW HAVEN**

Shortly after Dutch explorer Adriaen Block's discovery of the region in 1614, Dutch entrepreneurs established a small post near the harbor and traded beaver pelts with the resident Quinnipiac Indian Tribe. For many decades, Native Americans had resided there, fishing and cultivating maize. Twenty-four years after the Dutchmen's brief stint, discontented by the Massachusetts Bay Colony's stringent religious practices, a few hundred Puritans led by Reverend John Davenport and former London merchant Theophilus Eaton, attracted by the rich resources, sailed into New Haven Harbor.

The timing was perfect. Fearing attack by its warring Pequot neighbors, the Quinnipiac Tribe willingly exchanged the property for the colonists' safeguard. In 1640, settlers changed the name "Quinnipiac," which meant "long water land," to New Haven from Newhaven on the south coast of Sussex, England.

In this same year, the enterprising settlers developed streets corresponding to a nine-square-block pattern that complemented the center green. To this day, the same street design represents the commercial mainstay of New Haven and the area goes down in history as being the first planned city in the country. What we know today as Guilford, Milford, Stamford, Branford and Southold (New York) joined New Haven Colony, until the King of England chartered the area to merge with Connecticut Colony in 1664. From 1701 to 1873, the township served alongside Hartford as co-capital of Connecticut.

The greatest change in New Haven occurred in 1716. A substantial benefaction from English merchant Elihu Yale helped relocate the Collegiate School to New Haven from Old Saybrook started there in 1701 (see **Old Saybrook** chapter), the rest, as they say, is history. Today, Yale University has some 11,000 undergraduate, graduate and professional students and more than 3,000 faculty members. Synonymous with New Haven, it ranks as the third oldest university in the United States and is one of the most prestigious institutions in the world (an alma mater of the last three presidents of the United States: George Bush Sr., Bill Clinton and George W. Bush).

New Haven was a hotbed of Revolutionary War activity, and Major General William Tryon (see **Norwalk** and **Danbury** chapters) led the most famous raid in 1779. Unlike other towns, the British spared New Haven and did not burn it. New Haven was incorporated as a city in 1784; East Haven became an independent entity in 1785; North Haven was incorporated in 1786 and West Haven was incorporated—the last Connecticut town (169th) to be established—from Orange in 1921; albeit West Haven was differentiated as the west parish of New Haven around 1720.

The city thrived in the late 18th century; thanks primarily to Yale graduate Eli Whitney. Not only did his cotton gin revolutionize the south, but he also established a major gun-manufacturing factory (where Samuel Colt would invent the automatic revolver in 1836) in the Whitneyville section of Hamden (north of New Haven).

One of the most important events in 1800s New Haven involved the famous trial of 50 illegally kidnapped Mendi tribesmen from Africa, who caused mutiny upon the slaveship La Amistad (see below, **Freedom Schooner Amistad**). Even former United States President John Quincy Adams got involved, ceasing his retirement long enough to ultimately win their freedom.

The American Industrial Revolution enticed immigrant factory workers into the city. By 1900, 28 percent of the population was foreign-born, with a concentration of Irish, Italian and Eastern European. By the mid-'50s, however, changes in consumer demand forced many factory closures and, in turn, New Haven dipped in population, economy and aesthetics. Fortunately, since then New Haven has undergone urban redevelopment. City revitalization efforts include Wooster Square, a slum in the 1950s, which today, enhanced by Yoshino cherry blooms in the spring is reminiscent of a turn-of-the-century park. Notable New Havenites include U.S. President George W. Bush; sibling singers and songwriters, Karen and Richard Carpenter; inventor of vulcanized rubber, Charles Goodyear and expert pediatrician and author Benjamin Spock.

New Haven, like that of Hartford, boasts many "firsts." To name some: the first planned city in the country; first plotted burial ground; first assembly line; first United States university art museum; first telephone switchboard; first pay phone; first hamburger; first American football game; first lollipop; first game of Frisbee (for fun, a group of Yale University students tossed around a pie tin from the Bridgeport-based Frisbee Pie Company); first held international figure skating championship and first pizza.

Compared to 4,487 residents in 1790, New Haven's approximate residential population today totals more than 124,000. Tied economically to its universities and renowned hospitals, one being Yale-New Haven Hospital, the city is also a leader in biomedical and pharmaceutical research. City revitalization efforts include the demolition of the old New Haven Coliseum (see below) and 200 million dollars worth of future projects like a new college campus for Gateway Community College and a new facility for Long Wharf Theatre (see below, **Long Wharf Theatre**). Additionally, the city plans to obtain private investments to fund a new hotel, conference center and retail and residential space.

Day trips with panache include the free **Yale University Campus Tour**. The architectural standard hovering above campus is **Harkness Tower** on High Street, a 201-foot-high, Gothic-style structure built in the early 1900s; St. Botolph's Tower in England served as its prototype. Tours commence at the **John Pierpont House** (1767), which houses the **Yale Visitor Information Center**. Inside, visitors can obtain *Yale Trail* brochures, which detail school history and provide a map with route suggestions. Note: historians document the Pierpont House (with central chimney, it exemplifies Georgian-style architecture) as being the oldest in the city.

Students lead the university tour emphasizing the history, architecture and traditions of **Old Campus**. (The tour's main draw is incoming freshmen and their families.) The tour's highlight is the **Beinecke Rare Book and Manuscript Library**. Its 1963 construction design incorporates more than 100 translucent marble slabs. Also recognized as a museum, the world-renowned facility houses more than 600,000 books and several million historical manuscripts. Complementing the annual changing exhibits, on permanent display is the Gutenberg Bible, one of only several in the United States and an original Audubon bird-print collection. A sunken sculpture garden provides a tranquil outdoor setting.

East of Yale campus is the **New Haven Town Green**. Its original nine-square design has stood unchanged since colonial times. During the warmer months, the green spills over with city concerts and festival revelers. Numerous historical organizations have cited the 16-acre rectangle as one of the country's most beautiful public spaces.

Out of the historic churches that line its north-south axis, the one of most interest to day-trippers is the **First Church of Christ**, also known as **Center Church**. The church's ancestors were Reverend Davenport and Mr. Eaton (see beginning of chapter), the original city settlers. Marvel at the famous (original) Tiffany window depicting the reverend delivering his first sermon. This Georgian-style building, being the fourth construction to house the church, was built in 1814 over a portion of an early cemetery. The public can tour the **New Haven Crypt**, located under the church, and see tombstones dating back to 1687. Researchers have identified 137 remains, while some believe that there are more than 1,000 additional unidentified remains. Famous remains include the city's early settlers and Benedict Arnold's first wife.

Across from the green at 165 Church Street, make note of the bronze, three-panel, 14-foot **Amistad Memorial**. The sculpture depicting Senghe (also spelled Sengbe) Pieh, known as Joseph Cinque, who led the Amistad slave revolt (see chapter's introduction; also see below, **Freedom Schooner Amistad**), represents the first commission of a public statue of an African in the United States. The monument, sculpted by Ed Hamilton, stands on the exact site where the jail that imprisoned the illegally kidnapped Africans, awaiting trial in 1839, stood.

The memorial is in front of New Haven City Hall. Built in 1861, the building is one of the country's earliest and finest examples of High Victorian-style architecture. Another famed resting place that piques a day-tripper's curiosity is the **New Haven Burying Ground/Grove Street Cemetery**. Historians believe that the cemetery behind the 1845 Egyptian Revival-style gates is the oldest cemetery in the country with this particular type of grid layout. Established in 1796, this National Historic Landmark was the first chartered burial ground in the United States. Amid the luminaries buried here: Eli Whitney; Noah Webster; Roger Sherman; Charles Goodyear; Walter Camp; nine former Yale University presidents and Samuel F.B. Morse, an early New Haven Colony leader and inventor of the Morse code.

Unsurprisingly, the Yale University campus is the backdrop for the kind of museums day-trippers love to visit. Two blocks west of the green, the **Yale University Art Gallery**, founded in 1832, is the country's oldest college art museum and carries more than 80,000 artworks spanning from Ancient Egypt to contemporary times. Some of the masterpiece artists include Vincent Van Gogh, Claude Monet, Edouard Manet, Wassily Kandinsky, Pablo Picasso and Georgia O'Keefe. View John Trumbull's (he was the son of Jonathan Trumbull, colonial Governor of Connecticut) famous American Revolutionary War paintings. Per the artist's request, officials buried his body beneath the museum!

Museum architecture combines a landmark Louis I. Kahn modernist structure with an Egerton Swarwout's Italian Gothic-style design. In the Swarwout building's store, hunt for art-related books, cards and gifts. Make note that a second **Yale Art Gallery Museum Store** is open at 46 High Street, serving as a focal point for contemporary art and design, home accessories and local and international artworks.

Conveniently across the street is the **Yale Center for British Art**. American architect Louis I. Kahn also designed this four-story concrete, steel and glass structure. The museum holdings, ranging from the 16th century to the present, include paintings, drawings, rare books and sculptures, constituting the most comprehensive art collection outside Great Britain. Founded in 1977, the museum was a gift from philanthropist Paul Mellon, Class of 1929.

About a mile-drive northeast is the **Yale Collection of Musical Instruments**. Three galleries brim with more than 1,000 American and European musical instruments that follow a timeline that begins in the 16th century and ends in the present.

One block north is the **Yale Peabody Museum of Natural History**, the only museum in Connecticut containing a permanent display of brontosaurus and other fossil dinosaurs, making it a popular sightseeing jaunt for all ages. The first original building that opened in 1876 was due to the combined efforts of Othniel C. Marsh, Yale University's first paleontology professor (the first of his kind in the country) and his uncle, philanthropist George Peabody. This present building replaced the old one in 1926, itself expanding over time. Today, museum holdings (space restrictions allow less than 1 percent to be displayed) total more than 11 million specimens and objects that include archeological and Native American artifacts as well as mammals, rare birds and minerals. What visitor can ever forget the breathtaking *Age of Reptiles*, a Pulitzer Prize-winning mural in the Great Hall (where the dinosaurs are displayed)? The more than four-year, laborious feat of artist Rudolph F. Zallinger, it measures 110-feet-long by 16-feet-high.

Impressively standing in the Colonial Revival-style building on the block between the Peabody Museum and the Collection of Musical Instruments is the **New Haven Colony Historical Society**. The society's permanent collection helps to portray the city's history from colonial times to present. A room is dedicated to Amistad-related artifacts and documents. Other exhibits showcase Eli Whitney's cotton gin and a collection of Winchester guns. Take time to peruse the gift shop.

Families with children up to 10 years old should visit the **Connecticut Children's Museum** near the town green; south of the historical society headquarters. Eight rooms feature hands-on, interactive exhibits that explore such subjects as mathematics and science while encouraging children to learn, but most of all have fun.

To show the city's ethnic gamut, the **St. Michael's Ukrainian Heritage Center**, southwest of the children's museum, opens its doors to seven exhibition rooms that present an outstanding collection of the culture through artistic artifacts, historical documents and photographs.

Driving northwards towards Southern Connecticut State College, serious researchers, scholars and interested day-trippers should call before stopping at the **Dixwell Avenue Museum and Research Center** (203-772-2665) at number 197, which owns the largest collection in the area devoted to local black history. For further ethnic culture, and approximately one and one-half miles in distance, is the **Ethnic Heritage Center**. A welcome addition on the campus of **Southern Connecticut State University**, this center represents 200 years of the city's Jewish, Afro-American, Irish, Italian and Ukrainian heritage. Also on campus, visitors can delve deeper into the theme of New Haven's Jewish communities and investigate an array of memorabilia and archives at the **Jewish Historical Society of Greater New Haven** (203-392-6125; call to schedule an appointment).

About five miles from the Southern Connecticut college campus and easily accessible to I-95, the **Knights of Columbus Museum** brims with archives, artifacts and changing exhibits that trace the history of the Knights of Columbus to present day. The family fraternal service organization was founded in New Haven in 1882 and, today, still headquartered in the city, it has 1.6 million members worldwide. Across the street, replacing the **New Haven Coliseum**, a former sports-entertainment facility that closed in 2002, will be the future site of **Long Wharf Theatre** (203-787-4282; www.longwharf.org). Day-trippers with a passion for live performances can choose from at least a dozen theaters. The Long Wharf is a Tony award-winning regional theater along with two others, **Yale Repertory Theatre** (203-432-1234; www.yale.edu/yalerep), and the **Shubert Performing Arts Center** (203-562-5666; 800-228-6622; www.capa.com/newhaven), where *My Fair Lady* and *The Sound of Music* premiered before their Broadway-runs.

Another day-tripping pleasure is the free **Tours of the Shubert Performing Arts Center** (203-624-1825) given by appointment at 247 College Street. Examine backstage areas, dressing rooms and novel "graffiti walls" with etched autographs of many previous performers. For those seeking a unique interpretation of the classics or a premiere work from the next Arthur Miller, reserve tickets for one of the area student productions: **Yale School of Drama** (203-432-1234; www.yale.edu/drama); **Summer Cabaret at Yale** (203-432-1567; www.yale.edu/summercabaret); Albertus Magnus College's **Act 2 Theatre** (203-773-8584) and **John Lyman Center for the Performing Arts at Southern Connecticut State University** (203-392-6154). Other theater venues include the **New Haven Ballet** (203-782-9038; www.newhavenballet.org), **Palace Theatre** (203-789-2120) and the **Irish-American Community Center** (203-469-3080; www.iacc-ct.com/announce.htm) in East Haven, debuting well-known works of Irish playwrights.

Musical culture in New Haven is similarly diverse. Day-trippers can be entertained by the **Yale University Chamber Music Society** (203-432-4158); **University Bands** (203-432-4111); **New Haven Symphony Orchestra** (203-562-5666; 888-736-2663; www.newhavensymphony.com) or **Connecticut Gay Men's Chorus** (800-644-CGMC). For an entertaining look at the less-serious side of Yale University, the expert revue of the Spizzwinks (?) (203-594-9024; www.yale.edu/spizzwin) is not to be missed. Originally formed in 1914, the underclassmen who join become part of the legacy that is categorized as America's oldest a cappella chorus. The other renowned campus a cappella group is the **Whiffenpoofs** (www.yale.edu/whiffenpoofs), Yale senior classmen.

For night hounds, evening entertainment, as one would expect in a college town, rocks. **Toad's Place** (203-624-TOAD; www.toadsplace.com), consecutively voted *Number One Nightclub in America* by numerous local and national publications, is a national treasure and has hosted musical performing stars from the Rolling Stones to Bob Dylan to Johnny Cash.

With the myriad art choices in the city, the **Arts Council of Greater New Haven** (203-772-2788; www.artscouncilgnh.org) helps eliminate the guesswork to the many exhibitions, workshops and special events. The council is located at 70 Audubon Street, a good starting point when it comes to art pursuits since the street denotes the **New Haven Arts District** and is home to such entities as the **Small Space Gallery** (203-772-2788); **Creative Arts Workshop** (203-562-4927; www.creativeartsworkshop.org) and the **Educational Center for the Arts** (203-777-5451). Call **ArtSpace** (203-772-2709) at 50 Orange, a street that runs off Audubon, for the latest dates for the annual festival of **City-Wide Open Studios** (see **Annual Festivals/Events**), in which more than 450 visual artists open up their studios to the public.

Since 2004, the **New Haven Cutters** baseball team in the Independent Northeast League, call Yale Field its home park. Other sporting options for day-trippers concentrate mostly on university-level activities, namely, **Yale University Sports** (203-432-YALE [9253]; www.yalebulldogs.collegesports.com), **Southern Connecticut State University Sports** (203-392-6004; www.southernowls.com) and the **University of New Haven Sports** (203-932-7025; www.newhaven.edu/athletics). The **Connecticut Tennis Center at Yale University** (203-776-7331) also holds a range of tournaments open to the public.

Shoppers who are keen on boutiques and specialty shops should not miss the retail opportunities on Chapel and College Streets and upper State Street, to name a few. At 450 Sargent Drive, **Ikea New Haven** (800-434-4532), an international conglomerate store, offers home furnishings and accessories that are "affordable solutions for better living." If you are interested in up-and-coming (mostly local) designers, New Haven's fashion buzz of the decade is **Lordz Fashion House** (203-785-1427) that joins the upscale Chapel Street boutiques. No mass merchandising here, thank you very much, and considering the exquisite array, a bang for the buck too!

Throughout the year, on Saturday and Sunday, bargain hunters can head to the **Boulevard Flea Market** (203-772-1447) at 500 Ella T. Grasso Boulevard.

Day-trippers who prefer hours of antiquing should add Whalley Avenue to the itinerary. Known as the Westville section, a few of the treasure haunts (many are closed Sundays; call for days and hours of operation) include: the **Antique Corner** (203-387-7200); **Antiques Market** (203-389-5440); **Sally Goodman, Ltd.** (203-387-5072) and **W. Chorney Antiques** (203-387-9707).

Greater New Haven has also gained a reputation for its booksellers; these establishments range from the **Yale Bookstore** (203-777-8440), offering—for starters—more than 170,000 book titles to **Book Haven** (203-787-2848), located next to Toad's Place. What are books without a hot (or iced) cup of java? **Atticus Book Café** (203-776-4040) combines both as does the **Book Trade Café** (203-787-6147), which specializes in used books. (Note: Yale Bookstore also has a café on premises). No bookstore list would be complete without adding the **Foundry Bookstore** (203-624-8282), which specializes in both children and adult selections. To name a few coffee houses (where you can bring your own book): the **Coffee Table Café** (203-777-7893); **Elm City Java** (203-776-2248); **Koffee Kitchen** (203-752-9414) and **Koffee?** (203-562-5454; www.koffeekoffee.com), which doubles as the city's live music venue Thursday through Saturday nights.

For further respite, indulge in a massage or other day spa treatment at **Amadeus Center for Health and Healing** (203-787-0869; www.amadeuscenter.com). There is also a guesthouse on premises, available for monthly rentals.

Beyond New Haven's city, there is country—in fact, 17 percent of the 21.2-square-mile region is designated park area. Two reddish sandstone "trap rocks," elevated in the northeast and the northwest section of the city, comprise two extensive parks. The first, **East Rock** (203-946-6086), located on the corner of Orange and Cold Springs Streets, is accessible from East Rock Road or from Davis Street in the bordering town of Hamden. The city's oldest park system as well as the largest (426 acres), includes 10 hiking trails with panoramic views of Long Island Sound and the harbor; playgrounds; recreational facilities; the **Trowbridge Environmental Center**; "giant steps" that take sojourners to the top of the rock's cliff; the distinct **Soldiers and Sailors Monument** set on the summit and ample winter cross-country skiing areas.

The second park, **West Rock Ridge State Park** (203-789-7498), in which the Wilbur Cross Parkway traverses from east to west, is located partly in the town of Hamden. Accessible from Wintergreen Avenue, the park rises as high as 627 feet above sea level, affording, at some points, up to 200 square miles of scenic views, including New Haven Harbor and Long Island Sound. West Rock (known as Three Judges Cave) was a historical hideout in 1661 for three famous regicides, Colonels Edward Whalley, William Goffe and Judge John Dixwell. Before their escape from England, they had signed a death warrant for the beheading of King Charles I of England; ultimately, causing them to flee from the vengeance of his son, King Charles II. (Three intersecting streets, Dixwell Avenue, Whalley Avenue and Goffe Street commemorate the three men.) History aside, day-trippers can also enjoy hiking, fishing, mountain biking and canoeing while at West Rock.

Fort Nathan Hale Park and **Black Rock Fort** (203-946-8790; www.fort-nathan-hale.org), Fort Hale Park Road, located along the New Haven Harbor, provides awe-inspiring views for tranquil walks. Those who have a penchant for history can examine the restored grounds that played a vital part in the Revolutionary War, War of 1812, as well as in the Civil War.

Farther north, **Lighthouse Point Park**, facing both New Haven Harbor and Long Island Sound, this 82-acre park, once designated as the last stop on the New Haven Trolley line, still bustles with action, especially in the summer when swimmers, naturalists and bird-watchers flock to its shores. No day trip is complete without a twirl on the early 1900s carousel, restored to its natural beauty and listed on the National Register of Historic Places.

Additionally, lighthouse aficionados have two objects of desire to feast their eyes on. The **New Haven Harbor Lighthouse** (1847), also known as **Five Mile Point Light**, is a 97-foot-tall design constructed of octagonal masonry that is painted white. Located directly in the park, it is five miles from downtown New Haven, hence its name. The **Southwest Ledge Light** (1877) is several hundred yards to the southwest. New Havenites exhibited the cast iron structure modeled in the Second Empire-style at the Centennial Exhibition in Philadelphia before attaching it permanently to its cast iron foundation.

Also located on New Haven Harbor is **Long Wharf Nature Preserve**, Long Wharf Drive. This 17-mile stretch along the shore includes a **Vietnam War Veterans Memorial**. Situated in the park is a **Visitor's Information Center**, which stocks brochures, maps and the like to help day-trippers and other tourists maneuver around the city.

Nearby, **Long Wharf Pier** is homeport to the famous (the replica was built in nearby Mystic) **Freedom Schooner Amistad** (203-495-1839; www.amistadamerica.org). The 1839 Freedom Schooner Amistad incident added New Haven (see chapter's introduction) as a modern-day tourist stop on the Connecticut Freedom Trail, dedicated to the history of African-Americans' struggle for freedom. The public take tours and sailing cruises when the schooner is docked at homeport.

One of the area's best-kept secrets is **Canoe New Haven** (203-946-8027; www.cityofnewhaven.com/parks/outdooradventure/#Canoeing), which conducts free canoeing and kayaking expeditions throughout the city's rivers and park systems. Other programs include river clean-ups, special demonstrations and nature walks. Boaters should note that most of the New Haven marinas are off the neighboring coastline town of Milford.

Opportunities for golfers are at the 18-hole **Allying Memorial Golf Course** (203-946-8014). The city's only municipal golf course is open all year (weather permitting) and offers a clubhouse, pro shop and restaurant. Winter enthusiasts should make note that the course also provides exquisite cross-country skiing.

While in the area, stop at **East Haven's Shore Line Trolley Museum**. Operated by the Branford Electric Railway Association, the trolley line has appeared in several Hollywood movies! Appointed as the oldest operating trolley museum in the country, visitors can peruse nearly 100 vintage vehicles, hands-on exhibits and other trolley-era artifacts and documents. The day's pièce de résistance is an actual three-mile roundtrip ride in a fully restored vintage trolley car along the tracks of the country's oldest, continuously operating suburban trolley line.

Restaurants and dining options, like everything else in and around the Greater New Haven area, offer a cornucopia of variety, ranging from deli-style to full-service elegance, with traditional American cuisine or nearly any ethnic-style fare available.

The Italian-style restaurants on Wooster Street have helped earn the area's reputation as New Haven's "Little Italy." To name a few establishments (call for days and hours of operation): **Parrott's** (203-624-4407); **Tree Scaling** (203-777-3373; with a sister restaurant, **Polo Grille** at 7 Elm Street; www.pologrille.com); **Consuelo's** (203-865-4489) and **Tony and Lucy's Little Italy** (203-787-1621).

In the heart of "Little Italy," as legend goes, a cook named Frank was the first ever to roll out dough, layer it with sauce and cheese and, essentially, duplicate an Old Country tradition in New Haven, U.S.A. in the 1900s. The rest is pizza-pie (which some swear are the best in the world) history at **Frank Pepe Pizzeria** (203-865-5762), open for lunch Friday, Saturday and Sunday; dinner, Wednesday through Monday. Consider ordering the legendary clam pizza. Next door, **Frank Pepe's the Spot** (203-865-7602), open for dinner Tuesday through Sunday; lunch on Sunday, is cousin to the first; many say the pizza is just as good, without a long wait. Rival of Pepe's is **Sally's Pizza** (203-624-5271), open for lunch and dinner, Tuesday through Sunday. Top the meal off with an Italian pastry or famed Liberator Italian Ice at **Libby's Italian Pastry Shop** (203-772-0380), open daily.

Closer to downtown, said to be the birthplace of the hamburger, is **Louis' Lunch** at 261 and 263 Crown Street (203-562-5507; www.louislunch.com), open for lunch, dinner and late night snack Tuesday through Sunday. No ketchup. No mustard. No roll. A slice of tomato, A-okay. Two slices of toasted bread, A-okay. Anything else would be like splattering an original Renoir with poster paint.

On the next block at 228 College Street, **Café Adulis** (203-777-5081), serving Eritrean and Ethiopian fare, is open for dinner daily. At nearby 1157 Chapel Street on the premises of Colony Inn (see **Accommodations**) is the **Lode Blue Public House** (800-458-8810; 203-776-1234), serving breakfast, lunch and dinner daily. Number 1104 Chapel Street, **Snooze Pretoria and Wine Bar** (203-776-8268), open for lunch and dinner daily, has won rave reviews for its Italian-style cuisine. At 1044, **Rumba** (203-562-7666), open for lunch, Tuesday through Friday, and dinner, Tuesday through Sunday, is a notable nuevo Latino restaurant. For Parisian flavor, try **Union League Café** (203-562-4299) at 1032 Chapel Street, which is open for lunch, Monday through Friday, and dinner, Monday through Saturday. A vegetarian favorite is at 1000 Chapel, legendary **Claire's Cornercopia** (203-562-3888; www.clairescornercopia.com), which is open for lunch and dinner daily.

GETTING THERE:

New Haven is approximately two hours away from New York City; 42 miles south of Hartford; eight miles west of Branford. New Haven is easily accessible from Interstate Highways 95 and 91; within the city, the Oak Street Connector/Route 34 intersects just south of the 95 and 91 interchange and runs northwest into downtown.

TRANSPORTATION:

Tweed New Haven Regional Airport is approximately five minutes driving distance from downtown and is located along the New Haven/East Haven border; it provides daily service to 126 cities. The area is approximately 53 miles south of Bradley International Airport in Windsor Locks. The three major New York City metro airports are Westchester County Airport, LaGuardia, JFK and Newark Airport in New Jersey.

CT Transit (203-624-0151) operates frequent commuter-connection buses from Union Station. New Haven Union Station provides Metro-North (800-METRO-INFO) trains to New York, Shore Line East commuter trains to Old Saybrook (800-ALL-RIDE in CT) and Amtrak (800-872-7245) to New York, Boston and Springfield, Massachusetts.

ADDITIONAL INFORMATION:

Information New Haven will answer questions related to New Haven tourism, call (203) 773-9494.

For further detailed information about shopping and dining options in the Greater New Haven area, the Small Business Council of Greater New Haven Chamber of Commerce publishes and distributes a free guide, *Greater New Haven Official Restaurant & Shopping Guide*, (203) 787-6735.

YALE VISITOR INFORMATION CENTER.

149 Elm Street. Open all year, daily. Free university campus tours conducted all year, daily; call to inquire about times. (203) 432-2300; www.yale.edu/visitor.

BEINECKE RARE BOOK AND MANUSCRIPT LIBRARY.

121 Wall Street. Open all year, Monday through Saturday. General admission is free. (203) 432-2977; www.library.yale.edu/beinecke.

NEW HAVEN CRYPT.

311 Temple Street. Free tours are conducted, April through October, Thursday and Saturday between 11 a.m. and 1 p.m. (203) 787-0121.

NEW HAVEN BURYING GROUND/GROVE STREET CEMETERY.

Corner of Grove and Prospect Streets. One-hour free tours, from late spring through October, meet at the cemetery's chapel building every Saturday at 11 a.m. (203) 787-1443.

YALE UNIVERSITY ART GALLERY.

1111 Chapel Street at York Street. Open all year, Tuesday through Sunday. Inquire about family programs offered throughout the year for a charge. General museum admission is free. (203) 432-0600; www.yale.edu/yuag.

YALE CENTER FOR BRITISH ART.

1080 Chapel Street. Open all year, Tuesday through Sunday. General museum admission is free. (203) 432-2800; www.yale.edu/ycba.

YALE UNIVERSITY COLLECTION OF MUSICAL INSTRUMENTS.

15 Hillhouse Avenue. Open September through June, Tuesday through Thursday. General admission is $2.00; free to Yale University community members. (203) 432-0822; www.yale.edu/musicalinstruments.

YALE PEABODY MUSEUM OF NATURAL HISTORY.

170 Whitney Avenue. Open all year, daily. The facility hosts many statewide school field trips; call to inquire about group rates and upcoming children's programs. General admission is $7.00 adults; $6.00 seniors, $5.00 students/children and free to children 2 and under and on Thursday afternoons from 2 p.m. to 5 p.m. and to museum members and members of the Yale University community with proper I.D. (203) 432-5050; www.peabody.yale.edu.

NEW HAVEN COLONY HISTORICAL SOCIETY.

114 Whitney Avenue. Open all year, Tuesday through Saturday. Whitney Library is also on site and open for research. General admission is $4.00 adults; $3.00 seniors; $2.00 students/children and free to children 6 and under. (203) 562-4183.

CONNECTICUT CHILDREN'S MUSEUM.

Open all year, Friday and Saturday. General admission is $5.00. (203) 562-5437.

ST. MICHAEL'S UKRAINIAN HERITAGE CENTER.

555 George Street. Open all year, Saturday and Sunday. General admission is by donation. (203) 787-3255.

ETHNIC HERITAGE CENTER.

270 Fitch Street. The center is open all year, Monday through Friday. General admission is by donation. (203) 392-6126.

KNIGHTS OF COLUMBUS MUSEUM.

1 State Street. Open all year, daily during the summer months and Wednesday through Sunday during the rest of the year. General admission is free. (203) 865-0400; www.kofc.org/index.cfm.

LIGHTHOUSE POINT PARK.

2 Lighthouse Road. Open all year from 8 a.m. to sunset, daily. Parking fees (call to inquire) apply from Memorial Day through Labor Day; New Haven residents park free with valid sticker. (203) 946-8790; www.cityofnewhaven.com/parks/parks/lighthousepoint.htm.

SHORE LINE TROLLEY MUSEUM.

17 River Street, East Haven. Open April through December; call for days and hours of operation. General admission is $6.00 adults; $5.00 seniors; $3.00 students/children and free to children 2 and under. (203) 467-6927; www.bera.org.

ACCOMMODATIONS:

COLONY INN.

1157 Chapel Street. Adjacent to the Yale University campus, and in the heart of downtown, 86 fully appointed guestrooms and suites offer European ambiance. Rooms are handicapped accessible. Restaurant on premises; see above. Rates: $95-$500. (800) 458-8810; (203) 776-1234.

FAIRFIELD INN BY MARRIOTT.

400 Sargent Drive. This renovated hotel, consisting of 154 guestrooms and suites, is bright, airy and full of warm colors. Conveniently located directly off I-95, amenities include a fitness center and outdoor pool; there are also handicapped-accessible rooms. Rates (including continental breakfast): $99-$129. (203) 562-1111.

OMNI NEW HAVEN HOTEL AT YALE.

155 Temple Street. Across the street from the green, the Omni chain of hotels has gained a solid reputation for its aesthetically designed guestrooms and modern amenities, down to the plush robes. Omni New Haven offers 306 guestrooms and also a health club on premises. Rates (including continental breakfast): $99-$209-plus. (800) THE-OMNI; (203) 772-6664.

THREE CHIMNEYS INN AT YALE UNIVERSITY.

1201 Chapel Street. Winner of numerous awards, this 1870s restored mansion is what the innkeeper describes as a "painted lady with a past." "She" comes with 11 deluxe guestrooms decked out in poster beds, Edwardian bed drapes, rich tapestries, Oriental rugs, full beds and is handicapped accessible. Rates (including full, gourmet breakfast): $195-$215. (203) 789-1201; (800) 443-1554 (outside Connecticut only); www.threechimneysinnct.com.

INN AT OYSTER POINT.

104 Howard Avenue. For nautical flavor, this former oysterman's residence is situated at New Haven Harbor, five minutes from downtown. Reserve one of the six impeccably decorated, thematic rooms or suites within this sunny, yellow-colored Victorian that is more than a century old. Rooms include fireplaces, soundproofing, whirlpools, TVs, air-conditioning and all modern amenities for the leisure and business traveler. Rates (including full breakfast): $89-$249. 1-86-OYSTERPT; (203) 773-3334; www.oysterpointinn.com.

THE HISTORIC MANSION INN.

600 Chapel Street. Located three blocks from the green, across from Wooster Square Park and near New Haven's Wooster Street restaurants, the 1842 Greek Revival-style inn was restored in 1999. The innkeepers have elegantly furnished the seven rooms with Queen Anne reproductions. Rooms include marble fireplaces, high ceilings, air-conditioning and private baths. Rates (including full breakfast): $139-$175. (888) 512-6278; (203) 865-8324; www.thehistoricmansioninn.com.

TOUCH OF IRELAND GUEST HOUSE.

670 Whitney Avenue. A wee bit of Irish friendliness and charm transcends into every nook and cranny in this 1920s Colonial, bordering Yale campus, from the innkeepers' hospitality to the muffins and breads baked fresh for guests to nosh all day. Three guestrooms, the Limerick Room, the Cork Room and the Armagh Room, offer full, modern amenities including Internet access and private baths.

Rates (including gourmet breakfast by candlelight): $95-$150. (203) 787-7997; (866) 787-7990; www.touchofirelandguesthouse.com.

ANNUAL FESTIVALS/EVENTS

Greater New Haven Convention & Visitor's Bureau, representing 19 communities, provides a gamut of tourism information, which includes seasonal events (800) 332-STAY or (203) 777-8550; www.newhavencvb.org/base/index.cfm. For additional festival and event information, contact Information New Haven, 203-488-5500.

JANUARY

Throughout the city, there are **Martin Luther King Day Celebrations** conducted at various locations. (203) 777-8550.

FEBRUARY

Throughout the city, there are **Freedom Trail Month Celebrations** conducted at various locations. (203) 777-8550.

APRIL

Film Fest New Haven features independent and innovative new films, shorts and screen works from around the world. Screenings take place at the Whitney Humanity Center at Yale and the Little Theatre. The roster of additional activities includes live-script readings and filmmakers' forums. (203) 776-6789; www.filmfest.org.

Join the **Cherry Blossom Festival** at Wooster Square, a celebration in honor of the trees as well as the neighborhood; food and fresh flowers for sale and musical performances further enhance the day. (203) 777-8550.

MAY

Hoards of spectators arrive to watch the **Freddie Fixer Parade**, which salutes the history and accomplishments of African Americans. It begins at Dixwell Avenue and Morse Street in Hamden and concludes at the city hall in New Haven. (203) 777-8550.

The **Tour of Connecticut** starts with a 70K road race around New Haven Green (see **Waterbury Annual Festivals/Events**). www.tourofct.com.

JUNE

The **International Festival of Arts & Ideas** in and around New Haven Green is a 16-day event featuring performing and visual artists that gather from around the world and present activities that range from theater to poetry to discussions. (203) 498-1212; (888) ART-IDEA; www.artidea.org.

The **Areyto Festival and Puerto Rican Parade** honors the culture, history and customs of Puerto Rico with two full days of events. (203) 776-3649.

The **Greater New Haven Pizza Fest** allows visitors to sample pizza and other foods from more than 80 area pizzerias while musical performers entertain the masses. (203) 787-2111.

JULY

Watch one of the state's largest fireworks shows at the **Annual July 4th Celebration** at Long Wharf Park. Live entertainment and a variety of activities are also on hand. (203) 946-7821.

Jazz in the Parks, part of the New Haven Jazz Festival, is a series of free performances in five of New Haven's parks, and runs consecutive Thursdays in July. (203) 946-7821.

The **Starry, Starry Saturday Night Concert** is part of a free series held on the green. (203) 782-4935.

The **Annual African-American Arts and Music Festival** presents art exhibits by local artists, music and special entertainment for children as well as poetry readings. (203) 230-1074, x1.

Fiesta de Loiza en Connecticut is a two-day event held at the Long Wharf Park. The days' activities include live Latino artists in concert, arts and crafts exhibits, informational booths and ethnic cuisine. (203) 777-8550.

AUGUST

New Haven Green has presented a pantheon of jazz artists since the **New Haven Jazz Festival** started there in 1982. Since then, this free Saturday night concert attracts approximately 40,000 finger-tapping audience members and has kicked off other local free jazz series at other outdoor venues that waft the summertime air. (203) 946-7821; www.newhavenjazz.com.

The **Annual Gauge Train Show**, held at Yale University, exhibits model trains. Vendors also sell a variety of trains and accessories and prizes; food items are also featured. (203) 777-8550.

The **Annual Pilot Pen Tennis Women's and Men's Championships**, at the Connecticut Tennis Center at Yale University, feature professional tennis with many of the best players in the world. Special events include "Kid's Day," live jazz concerts, which are part of the New Haven Jazz Festival, and interactive sports, plus daily prizes. (888) 99-PILOT.

Music lovers shouldn't miss the **Annual New Haven Carnival Luncheon** at Long Wharf, which is a free festival spotlighting steel-drum performances and food. (860) 818-0678.

SEPTEMBER

The **New Haven Folk Festival** is a three-day celebration of live folk music presented at different venues throughout the city. (203) 624-3559; 877-9-CTFOLK.

A long-standing tradition is the **North Haven Fair** at the Fairgrounds, Washington Avenue. A day of old-fashioned fun, highlights include a petting-zoo, oxen and pony pulls, pie-eating contests as well as food and musical entertainment. (203) 239-3700.

OCTOBER-APRIL

The **Annual Series of Concerts** presented by the Yale Collection of Musical Instruments Museum is one of the oldest and most distinguished of its kind. Call for upcoming schedule. (203) 432-0822.

OCTOBER

The **City Wide Open Studios**, the annual festival celebrating the visual arts in Greater New Haven, is a month-long event. (203) 772-2709.

East Haven's Shore Line Trolley Museum presents the **Pumpkin Patch**, a month-long celebration in which children are given trolley rides to the pumpkin patch, where they receive a free pumpkin (with paid admission). Refreshments are also on hand. (203) 467-6927.

NOVEMBER-DECEMBER
Children of all ages can climb on board to meet **Santa on the Trolley** at East Haven's Shore Line Trolley Museum. Refreshments and gifts for the children are also part of the price. (203) 467-6927.

UI Fantasy of Lights features outstanding holiday light displays at New Haven's Lighthouse Point Park. Visitors are charged by the carload. (203) 777-2000, ext. 269.

DECEMBER
New Haven's **Annual Kwanzaa celebration** takes place at Long Wharf Theatre with performances by local poets, dancers and musicians. (203) 787-4282.

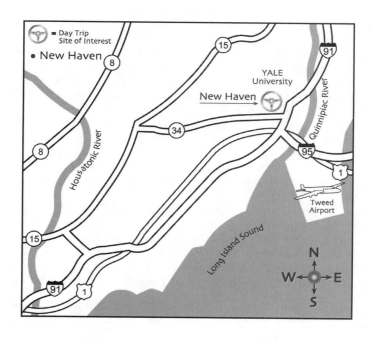

VI.

SOUTHWEST CONNECTICUT

Fairfield County

"Coastal Fairfield County"

Bridgeport/Black Rock/Westport/New Canaan/ Norwalk/South Norwalk/Stamford/Greenwich

Fairfield County's "Gold Coast" is a cluster of shoreline towns historically attracting a pantheon of wealthy residents; many of them neighboring New York City transplants who have left the urban hubbub in favor of country solitude. These calm bedroom communities, however, have turned of late into a mini-metropolis themselves, buzzing with residential and commercial developments, not to mention ever-increasing traffic jams. With real estate prices skyrocketing, generally, only a fortunate few can afford residences on the Gold Coast, namely in towns like Greenwich, Westport and villages like Riverside, Rowayton and Southport.

While the Gold Coast brings prestige to Fairfield County, the wealthiest county in the state, as well as one of the wealthiest in the country, disparity lies in its city of Bridgeport, the largest city in the state and also one of the poorest statewide and countrywide.

The county's diversity, however, is day-trippers' utopia. One can watch professional baseball and hockey teams compete in Bridgeport or a polo match in Greenwich. Encounter sharks or starfish at the nationally acclaimed Maritime Aquarium in Norwalk; wild birds at Westport's Earthplace or barnyard animals at Stamford's Nature Center.

Beyond the concrete cities like Stamford, acres of open space and unspoiled earth exist. The Audubon Center in Greenwich offers a 522-acre sanctuary with 15 miles of hiking trails. Thirty miles of Long Island Sound coastline accommodate serious water-sports zealots, not to mention the more laidback recreational types. Other aqua adventures may include viewing a lighthouse or taking a Norwalk Island tour, an educational eco-study cruise or a ferry ride from Bridgeport to Long Island, New York.

Day-trippers are likely to find festivals and special happenings any day of the year within this region, a cultural gem. There are art shows and theatrical performances to view. Parades to watch. Golf championships to attend. Oysters to eat. Regardless of what is on the agenda, bring the family; bring a friend; share the good times.

198

What territory did colonists purchase from the
Indians for a few bushels of corn and several blankets?

In what Connecticut city were the sewing machine,
horseless carriage, gramophone records, electric light
socket with pull chain and original Frisbee disc invented?

Let the Good Times Roll:
BRIDGEPORT/BLACK ROCK

During the 17th century, Pequonnock Indians sold the territory that would become the future city of Bridgeport for a few bushels of corn and several blankets. The buyers were settlers from Fairfield and Stratford, two towns that were incorporated in 1639. In 1800, officials incorporated the native region known as "Pequonnock" and renamed it Bridgeport in honor of the first drawbridge over the river.

Like other New England ports situated on a superior harbor, seafaring defined the town in the 18th and early 19th centuries. The opening of the railroad in 1840 jumpstarted an industrial center, producing such items as carriages, brass and cast iron fittings, sewing machines, tools and ammunition. The Industrial Revolution created, like that in Hartford and New Haven, a list of "firsts." Elias Howe invented the sewing machine. Innovators built the first horseless carriage in 1895. The city's American Gramophone Company manufactured the first records. Harvey Hubbell of Bridgeport patented the first electric light socket, complete with a pull chain, in 1896. Bridgeport's Frisbee Pie Company became most famous for its plate that would one day become the original Frisbee-playing disc (see **New Haven** chapter).

Of course, the city's greatest association was with Bethel-born Phineas Taylor Barnum, legendary P.T., the circus showman turned Bridgeport city mayor, who not only helped attract manufacturing to the city, but also in the 19th century brought the industrial hub worldwide repute. To this day, the "Park City," named as a tribute to its 1,300 park-land acres, bears his influence through his bequests of green space and creation of areas that include Mountain Grove Cemetery, where Barnum is buried. What is probably most remembered about the creator of the "Greatest Show on Earth" are his circus feats and public relation campaigns that memorialized the likes of Charles S. Stratton, most recognized as "General Tom Thumb" forever; so much so, in fact, that every year Barnum's memory lives on through the annual Barnum Festival events, the Jenny Lind Competition, and the Tom Thumb and Lavinia Warren Contest.

However, even Barnum's memory couldn't keep the city afloat when the onetime bustling urban port that boasted nearly 50 manufacturing firms in the 1930s, whose motto proclaimed "Industria Crecimus" (By Industry We Thrive), began to wane in the 1970s. Changes in consumer demand led to thousands of employees losing their manufacturing jobs. Soon it seemed that the most recognizable features of the city were gutted, crime-filled streets. However, between government and private, concerned-citizen efforts, things took an uphill change during the dawn of the millennium. Crime went down. Neighborhoods cleaned up; spiffed up with new city signs and outdoor lights as well as tree and flower plantings.

Despite endless debates regarding the pros and cons of possible future Native American-run gaming casinos in town, morale remains high. There is revived talk about converting Steel Point, the site of an electrical power plant until 1996, into a 50-acre waterfront tract beginning with one-billion dollars worth of retail stores, apartments and offices, and eventually, unveiling an amphitheater, boardwalk and hotel convention center.

For now, visitors will find this most populous Connecticut city with approximately 143,000 residents, home to the Pequonnock Yacht Club, which hit the 100-year-old mark in 2005, to be one of the best multi-generational and fun day trips in the state.

About 60 miles from New York City, situated as a port on Long Island Sound at the mouth of Pequonnock River, southwest in direction, is Black Rock Harbor. Day trips with panache begin by delving into Bridgeport's three and one-half miles of sandy beaches and nautical charm. Abutting the city's **University of Bridgeport**, Park Avenue heads to **Seaside Park** (203-576-7233). The **Perry Memorial Arch** leads the way to more than 200 acres; a land parcel donated by Barnum to the city.

View the 54-foot-high granite monument, dedicated in 1876, commemorating the Bridgeport men who died in the Civil War. Reflect upon a statue of Barnum, reposed near the seawall. To the background sounds of gulls, egrets and Canadian geese, summer day-trippers can swim and picnic; perhaps partake in an invigorating stroll from Barnum Boulevard and take in views of **Fayerweather Island** and its notable lighthouse. Constructed of wood and stone, the 47-foot-high structure, constructed in 1809 and rebuilt in 1823, was decommissioned in 1933.

Boaters have public access to Seaside Park at South Avenue. Other boat launches owned and operated by the city of Bridgeport are at the foot of Newfield Avenue and Brewster Street. A 1996 fire destroyed a 125-foot wooden bridge that connected visitors to **Pleasure Beach**, north of Seaside Park (from Seaview Avenue), a onetime island resort and amusement park. Currently, its fate remains in city officials' hands.

Captain's Cove (www.captainscoveseaport.com), One Bostwick Avenue, opened in 1982, which, today, attracting nearly 400,000 annual visitors, has made up a bit for Pleasure Beach's demise. Open seasonally from April through October, although there is no public swimming at the cove, day-trippers can hire a fishing boat charter; call Captain Bob Bociek, 203-615-0070; www.fishthesound.com. Leisurely harbor cruises (203-335-1433) with views of the **Fayerweather Island Lighthouse** and the town of Fairfield's **Penfield Lighthouse**, (rumored to be haunted by one of the former keepers), aboard the 40-foot navy launch, **Chief**, present about 40 nautically inspired minutes. Inland at Captain's Cove, peruse the retail shops—about 25—that resemble miniature Colonial and Victorian-style buildings along with a lighthouse replica that line the boardwalk along Black Rock Harbor.

Buy fresh fish and other seafood to take home and cook or dine on premises at the 400-seat **Titanic Restaurant** (203-368-3710). Rockers can catch lively rock 'n' roll music upstairs in the main bar, which is built from the wheelhouse of a 19th-century tugboat; additionally, the room features a 40-foot-model replica of the original RMS Titanic.

Occasionally on weekends, for a nominal fee, **Dundon House** (203-335-1433), an impressive Queen Anne-style Victorian at Captain's Cove, opens its doors and presents the area's maritime history through photographs, archives and even a collection of objects salvaged by divers from the bottom of Long Island Sound.

Another interesting feature at the end of the main dock at the cove is the **Gustave Whitehead Hanger** (203-335-1433). According to some experts, in 1901, 28 months before the first flight of the Wright Brothers at Kittyhawk, Gustave Whitehead, a German immigrant who moved to Bridgeport in 1900, built an aircraft that flew one-half mile over Long Island Sound. Witness a half-scale model replica of a Whitehead #21 aircraft, which at press time was on display in Germany, a country that considers Whitehead and not the Wright brothers first in flight.

In this same southwestern section of Bridgeport known as **Black Rock**, which had its own renaissance back in the 1980s, the main drag, Fairfield Avenue, presents an eclectic selection of boutiques and casual eateries. The **Black Rock Arts Center** (203-367-7917; www.internationalPerformingArts.com), 2838 Fairfield Avenue, is a lifeline to the creative chutzpah of "the Avenue." Located in a historic former bank building, the center presents a range of multi-cultural, visual and performing art shows performed by regional and national talent. Shows are geared for both children and adults. Day-trippers should also note **NEST** (North East Space Time; 203-847-3507), the collective art organization housed in a former factory at 512 Hancock. Curiosity seekers can expect art studio tours, slam poetry and a range of performances in the future.

What has added a crescendo to the artsy feel of the Avenue is the construction of **Bijou Square**. The anchor of this multi-million-dollar project is the renovation of the **Bijou Theater**, which will cater to independent film enthusiasts. Keep an eye out for film festivals and new restaurants and clubs that are expected to be a hotbed of live musical performances, poetry readings and book signings. The forerunner in Bijou Square at 269 Fairfield Avenue is **J.R.'s Bijou Café** (203-333-0055). Diners can feast on American-style specialties for lunch and dinner, Monday through Saturday, and dinner only Sunday. On the weekends, music makers rock the house down for the after-hours crowd.

While in Black Rock, motorists don't have to get out of their cars to enjoy **St. Mary's by the Sea** (203-576-7741). The wide, paved walkways that are handicapped accessible attract anglers, bird-watchers and power walkers. However, the rocky coastline prohibits swimming.

One of Bridgeport's most popular attractions, the **Bridgeport and Port Jefferson Steamboat Company** (203-335-2040; www.bpjferry.com) provides year-round daily 1,000-passenger ferry service offering picturesque views, such as the **Bridgeport Breakwater Lighthouse**, a 21-foot-tall landmark, known as "the bug." Located on Water Street in downtown Bridgeport by the city's main transportation hub, nosh in the snack bar or sip a cocktail in the Steamboat Lounge as the ferry makes the one-hour and fifteen-minute journey across Long Island Sound. Then spend the day perusing the charming shops and boutiques and dining in the quaint village of Port Jefferson on Long Island's North Shore.

Day-trippers who don't ride the ferry can likely catch a glimpse of the sleek vessel while sitting at the **Ballpark at Harbor Yard** at 500 Main Street, home to the **Bridgeport Bluefish** (203-345-4800; www.bridgeportbluefish.com), a professional baseball team that premiered in 1999. Of course, it's even more fun to watch while eating a hot dog, seeing the latest antics of the Bluefish mascot B.B., "a walking bluefish," and cheering on the game April through September. The facility has a seating capacity of 5,300, plus space for 200 standing-room-only fans for sold-out games.

As part of the revitalization of Bridgeport, the 19-million-dollar ballpark was built on the former site of the Jenkins Brothers Valve Company in the city's south end, which was the first integral part of a sports arena and transportation complex along the waterfront.

From October through April at the **Arena at Harbor Yard**, with a total 10,000-seat capacity, in the adjacent facility at 600 Main Street, the **Bridgeport Sound Tigers** (203-334-GOAL; www.soundtigers.com) of the American Hockey League (AHL), entertain fans. Then from May through August, the **Bridgeport Barrage** (203-345-4800) plays at the arena in the Major Lacrosse League. Throughout the year, the arena is a premiere entertainment venue that features concerts and a host of other special events.

About one minute north, the **Barnum Museum**, currently waiting for federal recognition as a National Historic Landmark, is the only museum in the world devoted to the life of P.T. Barnum. Just look for the lofty Romanesque Revival-style building capped off with a red-tiled dome. Inside, three floors memorialize the 18th-century life and times of one of the greatest showmen who has ever lived, beginning on the first floor with the Fejee Mermaid, Barnum's biggest hoax and ending on the third floor with *Barnum's American Circus* exhibit where, among other things, visitors can see the William R. Brinley miniature, model circus. Encompassing a million hand-carved animals, performers and circus equipment (much of it moving), the model took 42 years to complete. One of the most popular museum holdings is a 2,500-year-old mummy from Barnum's American Museum in New York City, believed to be the first Egyptian mummy ever exhibited in North America. Exhibits exploring the industrial history of the city are also part of the museum's theme.

Day-trippers with children should consider the ten-minute trip from Barnum Museum to another popular tourist attraction, the **Discovery Museum**. This ultimate hands-on arena touts three floors full of exhibits encouraging children to learn about science and art. Sign up for an unforgettable, simulated space adventure at the Challenger Learning Center. Enjoy a planetarium show. View the changing exhibits in the fine art gallery.

An off-the-beaten-track art scene is at the **Housatonic Museum of Art** (203-332-5052; www.hcc.commnet.edu/artmuseum) at Housatonic Community College, 900 Lafayette Boulevard. With a collection of more than 4,000 permanent pieces, including artwork by such artists as Pierre-Auguste Renoir, Henri Matisse and Pablo Picasso, the school possesses the largest art collection of any two-year college in the country. Best of all, the exhibits, which correspond to the school year calendar, are open to the public and free. Discover another impressive gallery collection at **City Lights Gallery** (203-334-7748; www.citylightsgallery.com) at 37 Markle Court in downtown Bridgeport. One of the gallery's missions is "to provide under-exposed regional artists" exhibition space. Exhibits, with pre-opening galas, change approximately every six weeks.

In north Bridgeport, near the town of Trumbull's border, are 52 acres belonging to **Beardsley Zoo**, inviting picnics and peaceful meanderings that have helped the city earn its "Park City" nickname. In 1878, the zoo's roots began with a 100-acre parcel that prominent cattle dealer James Beardsley donated to Bridgeport.

Before becoming the state's only zoo, Frederick Law Olmsted, creator of New York City's Central Park, designed **Beardsley Park**, where Barnum exercised his circus animals. In the 1920s, a zoo campaign initially funded today's accredited facility, one of the most popular Connecticut day trips, attracting approximately 250,000 visitors annually. Owned and maintained by the Connecticut Zoological Society, and based on a conservation mission and message, visitors can meet more than 300 animals representing about 125, primarily, North and South American species. Some of the endangered species include Siberian tigers, red wolves and ocelots.

A New England farmyard with animals and a South American rainforest exhibit with birds and monkeys, rouse the curiosity of all ages. Before exiting the zoo, take at least one spin on the exquisitely restored carousel, going strong for more than 80 years.

In the adjacent building, novice and advanced ice-skaters can take advantage of the four-season schedule at the renovated **Wonderland of Ice** (203-576-8110; www.wonderlandofice.com).

Bridgeport also affords theatergoers a variety of unique experiences. The renovated **Klein Memorial Auditorium** (203-345-4800 ext. 150), 910 Fairfield Avenue, home to the **Bridgeport Symphony** and **New England Ballet Company**, hosts a variety of dance, theater and fundraising performances. Call the **Downtown Cabaret Theater** (203-576-1636; www.dtcab.com) at 263 Golden Hill Street, for year-round show time premieres presented in an informal cabaret setting. Bring your own picnic and see first-rate, quality musicals and children's shows. Another four-season venue is **Playhouse on the Green** (203-345-4800) at 177 State Street. Located on McLevy Green, the present 228-seat, professional equity theater experience was the former Polka Dot Playhouse, the main stage at Pleasure Beach, until the bridge washed out.

After a day of theater or other pleasurable meanderings, hunger pangs are easy to satisfy in a town that boasts three classic diners: **Galaxy Diner** (203-372-8398); open daily until midnight, **Hi-Way Diner** (203-333-5269); open daily late night and **Frankie's Diner** (203-334-8971), open 24/7.

Two legendary classics that offer fast food prepared fresh and tasty and are a popular choice among University of Bridgeport students are **Conty's Drive-In** (203-333-2779), at 30 University Avenue, open for breakfast and lunch Monday through Friday and **Merritt Canteen** (203-372-1416), 4355 Main Street, open for breakfast, lunch and dinner, daily.

Next door to the Playhouse on the Green at 181 State Street, **High on the Hog BBQ Bistro** (203-332-0223) specializes in barbeque entrees and Italian-style cuisine. The restaurant serves lunch Monday through Friday with late night Friday dinner specials and live music.

Two Madison Avenue restaurants that extend a taste of Italy, prepared fresh, but offered at reasonable prices are **Tartaglia's Restaurant** (203-576-1281), open for lunch and dinner, Tuesday through Sunday, and **Testo's Restaurant** (203-367-4298), open for lunch and dinner, Monday through Friday; Saturday dinner, only.

Day-trippers don't have to go island hopping to find some of the finest Caribbean cuisine at 2004 Main Street. **McGhie's Caribbean Restaurant** (203-330-8854) serves lunch and dinner daily and breakfast Saturday.

Among the popular eateries in Black Rock are **Blackrock Castle** (203-336-3990), one of the best restaurants in the state specializing in Irish cuisine and entertainment and **Paddy Mac's** (203-367-5447), a steak and seafood restaurant; both serve lunch and dinner daily. Nearly everyone loves **Taco Loco** (203-335-8228), specializing in Mexican cuisine, lunch and dinner daily, which offers one of the most bountiful, but reasonably priced Sunday buffet brunches in the area. The happy hour and "birthday club" specials are other popular restaurant incentives. Keep an eye out for the new **Glimmerman Restaurant and Bar**, which at press time was being built in the former Arizona Flats building. Most seafood enthusiasts know about the fresh and reasonably priced lobsters served at **Dolphin's Cove Restaurant Marina** (203-335-3301) at 421 Seaview Avenue. Open all year for lunch and dinner, Tuesday through Sunday, mild weather means the deck is open to al fresco dining.

One of the most nationally known Bridgeport restaurants and an area institution is **Bloodroot** (203-576-9168) at 85 Ferris Street. Open for lunch and dinner Tuesday through Saturday and Sunday brunch, vegetarian cuisine has been the specialty for nearly three decades. The feminist bookstore on premises and outdoor dining make for an extraordinary experience. For tempting, homemade Italian ice and ice cream, try **Micalizzi Italian Ice** (203-366-2353; call for days and hours of operation), 712 Madison Avenue. No trip is complete without a spot of tea and the comradeship found at the **Soul of the World Tea Room** (203-362-2306; call for days and hours of operation) on Brewster Street. Just look for the door sign that says: "Good Karma in Every Cup."

GETTING THERE:

Bridgeport is approximately one and one-half hours away from New York City; 62 miles southwest of Hartford; 22 miles southwest of New Haven. Bridgeport is at the intersection of many major highways, which have greatly influenced its industrial past. The city is easily accessible from Interstate Highway 95; the Merritt Parkway (Route 15); Routes 8 and 25 and U.S. Route 1 (the Boston Post Road).

TRANSPORTATION:

Stratford's Sikorsky Memorial Airport is approximately four miles from Bridgeport. Tweed New Haven Regional Airport is approximately 22 miles driving distance, providing daily service to 126 cities through US Airways and Delta Airlines. The area is approximately 73 miles southwest of Bradley International Airport in Windsor Locks. The three major New York City metro airports are Westchester County Airport, LaGuardia, JFK and Newark Airport in New Jersey. CT Transit (203-624-0151) operates frequent commuter-connections. The Greater Bridgeport Transit District system (203-333-3031) operates frequent commuter-connection buses from and around the Bridgeport vicinity. The Bridgeport Transportation Terminal downtown provides Metro-North (800-METRO-INFO) trains to connecting cities as does Amtrak (800-872-7245). Both Metro-North station and Amtrak offer daily commuter service to New York City.

ADDITIONAL INFORMATION:

BARNUM MUSEUM.

820 Main Street. Open all year, Tuesday through Sunday. General admission is $5.00 adults; $4.00 seniors/students; $3.00 children and free to children 3 and under and to museum members. (203) 331-1104; www.barnum-museum.org.

DISCOVERY MUSEUM.
4450 Park Avenue. Open all year, Tuesday through Sunday. General admission is $8.50 adults; $7.00 seniors/students; $7.00 children and free to children 4 and under and to museum members. (203) 372-3521; www.discoverymuseum.org.

BEARDSLEY ZOOLOGICAL GARDENS.
1875 Noble Avenue. Open all year, daily. General admission is $8.00 adults; $6.00 seniors/students; $6.00 children and free to children 3 and under and to museum members. (203) 394-6565; www.beardsleyzoo.org.

ACCOMMODATIONS:
BRIDGEPORT HOLIDAY INN.
1070 Main Street. Recently updated and working hard at gaining a solid reputation for providing above-average banquets, meeting facilities and accommodations. Offering 234 guestrooms on nine floors, amenities include a business center, health club, indoor pool, fully handicapped-accessible premises and on-premises restaurant and lounge. Rates: $89.90-$149. (203) 334-1234.

ANNUAL FESTIVALS/EVENTS
The Coastal Fairfield County Convention & Visitor Bureau, representing 15 southwestern communities, provides a gamut of tourism information, which includes seasonal events (800) 866-7925 or (203) 853-7770; www.coastalct.com. For additional festival and event information, contact the Bridgeport Chamber of Commerce, 203-335-3800.

FEBRUARY
Dust off your dancing shoes and join the **Annual Sizzzzling Salsa Benefit Party** at Black Rock Arts Center, 2838 Fairfield Avenue. (203) 367-7917.

MARCH
For some foot-stomping entertainment, don't miss the acts that partake in the **Annual Black Rock Blues Festival** at Black Rock Arts Center, 2838 Fairfield Avenue. (203) 367-7917.

MAY
Barnum Festival's **Celebrate Bridgeport** attracts adults and children of all ages to the city for a day to experience many special entertainment events. Additionally, the city's museums and other attractions provide free admission for the day. (866) 867-8495; (203) 367-8495; www.celebratebridgeport.com.

JUNE
The Barnum Festival presents the **Greatest Car Show on Earth** with an array of live entertainment and trophy presentations. (866) 867-8495; (203) 367-8495; www.classicnights.com.

The **Annual Barnum Festival Jenny Lind ® Soprano Concert** features the newest American and Swedish Jenny Linds. Ticket price includes meeting the singers in person after the concert, recently held at Playhouse on the Green. (866) 867-8495; (203) 367-8495.

Catch one of the most colorful light shows in the state at the **Barnum Festival Fireworks Extravaganza** at Seaside Park. Ticket holders can also attend the **Skyblast Party**, which features buffet dining, DJ and musical entertainment prior to the fireworks. (866) 867-8495; (203) 367-8495.

Come watch more than 200 floats, bands and balloons at the **Annual Barnum Festival Great Street Parade**, which starts at Jackson Avenue and concludes at Harbor Yard. (866) 867-8495; (203) 367-8495.

Beardsley Park hosts the annual, ever-popular Barnum Festival's **Wing Ding Parade for Kids**. (866) 867-8495; (203) 367-8495.

JULY-AUGUST
Bridgeport Free Shakespeare Series presents numerous Shakespeare plays, staged outdoors under the moonlight at Bearsley Zoo, 1875 Noble Avenue, without charge. (203) 393-3213.

AUGUST
Join the excitement of the annual **Swim Across the Sound** in which the world's best marathon swimmers compete in a 17.5-mile swim from Port Jefferson, Long Island to Bridgeport's Captain's Cove. The money raised from pledges helps an innumerable range of cancer-related programs. (A series of "swim" events are held throughout the year.) For further information, contact St. Vincent's Medical Center Foundation. (203) 576-5451.

OCTOBER
Mark the calendar for the **Barnum Museum's Annual Gala** with special entertainment and a roster full of excitement. (203) 331-1104.

Black Rock
See pages 201; 204-205

Rocks!

---

*What Connecticut town became the chief onion supplier
to army troops during the Civil War?*

*What Connecticut town is known for attracting an
eclectic blend of immigrants, Hollywood celebrities
and homeless men once known as "tramps"?*

Go for the Gold: **WESTPORT**

Long before the beginning of colonial history, the Paugussett Indians named their homeland located along the banks of the river between what we know today as Fairfield and Norwalk, "Saugatuck," meaning "mouth of the river." Between 1639 and 1661, Massachusetts Bay Colony settlers divvied up that same territory purchased from the Native Americans. By 1711, the swell of inhabitants in the Bankside community (now known as Greens Farms), whose initial settlement had meshed in 1635 with what we today call Fairfield, split from its eastwardly neighbors and formed the Greens Farms Congregational Church. Currently, the church makes its home in a fourth meetinghouse, built in 1852.

By Revolutionary War times, Greens Farms (eventually to become a section of Westport) and the Saugatuck River settlements boasted wharves, warehouses, stores and taverns. A strong agricultural base, robust seafaring industry, legendary visits from George Washington and a famous Revolutionary War battle are part of Westport's history. The Battle of Compo Hill (taken from the Indian word, "Compaug," meaning "the bear's fishing ground") ignited in 1777.

Nearly 2,000 British soldiers anchored offshore stormed Compo Hill where outnumbered American troops could not halt the British who proceeded north to what is now present-day Danbury, burning homesteads, storehouses and barns along the way (see **Danbury** chapter). Four days later, upon the redcoats' return to their ships, they fought the Continental Army minutemen in a battle at Compo Hill. The replica cannons at Compo Beach and nearby minuteman statue commemorate the event. In fact, the bodies of colonists killed in battle are interred at Compo Beach Cemetery.

Here's some television trivia: the historic monument was the theme of *I Love Lucy's* episode of *The Ricardos Dedicate a Statue* in the famous sitcom that ran from 1951 until 1961. The zany redhead, who plays a Westport resident along with her husband Ricky (see below) during the final season of the show, accidentally breaks the town's new minuteman statue and attempts to conceal her blunder by impersonating the statue!

Westport settlers adopted the town's descriptive name and in 1835 incorporated from what is now modern-day Fairfield, Norwalk and Weston. Between 1861 and 1865, Westport, with a long agricultural history of growing vegetables, especially onions, became the principal onion supplier to the United States Army during the Civil War. Unfortunately, by the end of the 19th century, a cutworm plague had wiped out the industry. What remained, however, was a diverse blend of community including Irish, German and Italian immigrants; many of whom were initially onion industry workers and later laborers who helped construct the railroad.

Mills, factories and Kemper's Tannery (formerly located at the present Westport Country Playhouse) raised the standard of late 19th-century lifestyles. The town's robust economy attracted many prominent and business-minded individuals. On the other side of the economic spectrum—a disproportionate number of homeless men, known as tramps in search of handouts, infiltrated Westport where kindly housewives supplied them with meals. These men were later sheltered in the town's "poorhouse," possibly the first homeless shelter in the state.

Westport also became a magnet for intellectuals and freethinkers and its diversity grew even more evident, especially compared to its more Anglo-Saxon neighbors. During the first part of the 20th century, the start of the Famous Artist's School and Famous Writer's School generated talent from all over the country. Hoards of celebrities also infiltrated the vicinity. In the summer of 1920, F. Scott and Zelda Fitzgerald vacationed here. Many other luminary performers and entertainers would perform (as they still do!) at the venerable Westport Country Playhouse. Westport's reputation even earmarked TV-land. In the final season of *I Love Lucy* (see introduction above), the Ricardos move from New York City to Westport where Lucy proceeds to turn the suburban town upside down.

Residents like Paul Newman, Joanne Woodward, Michael Bolton, Linda Blair, Peter DeVries, Marlo Thomas, Phil Donohue and (on-and-off-again resident) Martha Stewart help bolster the town's tag line, "Beverly Hills of the East." Today, the town remains home to many famous artists and entertainment personalities (day-trippers should mind the unwritten laissez-faire policy towards celebrities and treat its famous residents accordingly); its 22.4-mile stretch is crowned with woodland hills on the north and graced by Long Island Sound on the south.

The town's posh landmarks include private country, yacht and hunt clubs, the town-owned Longshore Park and Country Club and Greens Farms Academy, an independent, K-12, co-educational day school. Author Sloan Wilson set his novel, *The Man in the Gray Flannel Suit*, in Westport and Mr. Newman started his philanthropic food company, Newman's Own, here. The town also touts its own community band that performs at a variety of area venues. Westport totals a population of nearly 27,000 residents. Only a bit more than an hour's drive from Manhattan, more than 2,200 out of the town's 14,000 workers commute to the city. Many residents are former New Yorkers who consider Westport, despite a recent surge in commercial and residential development and traffic congestion, pure country.

Day trips with panache fancy Westport's waterfront fanned with mansions, country estates and sprawling contemporary abodes, many bearing recognizable residents. One of the most popular aquatic rendezvous points (legend goes that it was Captain Kidd's favorite, too) is **Sherwood Island State Park**. The first designated state park, today, 234 acres of beach fronting Long Island Sound, uplands and salt marshes greet visitors at every turn. The **9-11 Living Memorial**, facing the Manhattan skyline, with its nine-foot granite, memorial stone and natural setting inspires peaceful contemplation.

Fishing, swimming, picnicking and just basking on the beach are summertime pastimes. In any season, hiking trails and walking trails entice sojourners. Off-season, dog owners and their companions have full rein of the setting that was named in honor of Robin Hood's Sherwood Forest. Handicapped day-trippers also have many points of access throughout the park.

Additionally, Sherwood Island is a Viewpoint Exhibit Host site. A joint effort of the Connecticut Commission on the Arts, the Connecticut Impressionist Art Trail and the Department of Environmental Protection, outdoor exhibits showcase 19th-century artworks and provide background information. At Sherwood Island, visitors should be on the lookout for Impressionist artist Edward Henry Potthast's representation of *Ocean Breezes*. This display plaque, one in a series throughout the state, denotes actual or representative Connecticut settings where American Impressionists painted (see **Kent** chapter).

Northward, adjacent to Sherwood Park, across from Greens Farms Academy, **Burying Hill and Wetlands** (203-341-1000; inquire about summer day fees) provide a more tranquil Long Island beachfront and prime location for swimming, fishing and crabbing. Some parts are handicapped accessible, and there is an abundant spectrum of birds and wildlife.

Day-trippers who make a beeline past Sherwood Island in the southwesterly direction will arrive at historical (see introduction above) **Compo Beach and Marina** (203-341-5090; inquire about summer day fees), a 29-acre oasis of summertime glee. Available activities include swimming, fishing, ice-skating, softball, basketball or volleyball. Kids can take advantage of one of the best wooden playscapes anywhere. After a day in the sun, community grills await the hungry.

Boaters have a boat launch ramp at Compo as well as westward at the **Saugatuck River Public Boat Launch** (203-341-5090). From either point, vessels can reach **Cockenoe Island** with its sandy beach and opportune surroundings for fishing, shellfishing, crabbing, bird and wildlife watching. Landlubbers at **Saugatuck River** will discover a boardwalk that stretches to downtown, ample fishing spots and handicapped accessibility. At 521-531 Riverside Avenue, the **Saugatuck River Rowing Club** (203-221-7475) extends three public-parking areas for visitors who can observe the members in action from a variety of vantage-point benches.

Tom Samose, owner of **Machias Adventures** (203-454-1243) in Westport, provides a full-range of canoe instruction for beginners, intermediate and advanced canoeists. Whether touring local favorites like the Saugatuck or Housatonic Rivers or partaking in out-of-town adventure trips, he is a delightful raconteur filled with a zeal for nature. One mile south of Saugatuck River, hourly rentals of sailboats and kayaks are available at the **Longshore Sailing School** (203-226-4646). Pre-registered day-trippers can also spend summer days learning to sail.

Nature lovers can head farther west, near the Norwalk town line, to experience a day at **Earthplace**, the Nature Discovery Center, boasting one of the largest wildlife rehabilitation programs in the state. Outdoors beckon visitors with five main walking trails, including handicapped and stroller-friendly access, on a 63-acre wildlife sanctuary. Youngsters can blow off hot air at the playground, while outdoor cages hosting such (rehabilitating) birds of prey as owls and vultures entertain children and adults of all ages.

Indoors at Earthplace means close encounters with creatures large and small down to a bee colony. Dilettantes should check out the ever-changing exhibition space. Before final departure, stop at the museum store to purchase a multiplicity of nature-themed gifts and collectibles.

History lovers should pencil in a day to spend at the Westport Historical Society-run **Wheeler House**. Built in 1795, today, this Victorian Italianate-style villa is a three-room showcase and listed on the National Register of Historic Places. Adjacent to the house, a cobblestone barn serves as an example of the only octagonal-roofed barn in Connecticut. Inside, day-trippers will find Westport history exhibits. History-related themed items are sold in the on-premises gift shop. To complement any day, the society also offers a variety of brochures describing self-guided walking tours to take through historical Westport and Greens Farms, many of the sites are marked by informative outdoor plaques.

A firsthand examination of the town's premiere art venue at the **Westport Arts Center and Gallery** (203-222-7070; www.westportartscenter.org), 51 Riverside Avenue, adds a hefty portion of appreciation to the town's cultural mecca. The center, highlighting a selection of artists' studios, extends yearlong activities that appease almost every interest—from visual art to chamber, folk, jazz and other musical venues to theater and film and special adult workshops and day camps for children.

Other Westport art galleries (call for days and hours of operation) that will tantalize the visual palate include: **Picture This** (203-227-6861); **Westport River Gallery** (203-226-6934; www.westportrivergallery.com); **Gallerie Je Reviens** (203-227-7716; www.galleriejereviens.com); **Amy Simon Fine Art** (203-226-8232) and **ARTredSPOT Gallery** (203-254-2698; www.artredspot.com), gallery of contemporary art. The **Westport Public Library** (203-291-4840; www.westportlibrary.org), a beehive of goings-on, nestled by the Saugatuck River, also showcases an eclectic blend of art in the **Great Hall Gallery**. Those seeking out-of-the-ordinary pleasures should visit **Kismet** (203-222-8880; www.kismetspace.com). The name means destiny and the Asian-themed art gallery and gift shop in Sconset Square—probably because of the friendly patrons and owner Tamson Hamrock's sweet demure—seems homier than home! Visitors can also attend art receptions and a variety of workshops.

Professional theater should be experienced at least once by sitting inside the ambiance of a 200-year-old converted barn designating the **Westport Country Playhouse** (203-227–4177; www.westportplayhouse.org). Opened in 1931, the walls showcase photographs of the celebrities who once performed here. Day-trippers can expect a newly renovated facility under the direction of artistic director (and Westport resident), Joanne Woodward, and an array of summer theater, holiday shows and theatrical productions throughout the year.

Theater patrons should also consider purchasing (very reasonably priced) evening or matinee tickets for one of the five yearly productions showcased in the **Westport Community Theater** (203-226-1983; www.westportcommunitytheatre.com) at the Westport Town Hall. New and experimental works, classic drama and comedy performances delight a range of audiences. Call for information about the next annual production presented by the **Music Theater of Connecticut, School of Performing Arts** (203-454-3883; www.musictheatreofct.com/aboutmtc.htm).

Surely, one of the finest summer spectaculars anywhere is at the **Levitt Pavilion for the Performing Arts** (203-226-7600; www.levittpavilion.com), an outdoor theater venue located by the banks of the Saugatuck River. Free performances range from rock to jazz to pop and classical music as well as dance ensembles and special children's shows. Benefit concerts by major name talents are also presented.

"Stargazers" have one other possibility: **Rolnick Observatory** (203-227-0925; www.was-ct.org/wasobs.htm). Public viewing at this astronomical observatory is open all year and is available Wednesday and Thursday nights beginning at 8 p.m. Before final departure, downtown Westport's retail establishments like **Lillian August** (203-454-1775; www.lillianaugust.com) with home design in mind and **Sundries** (203-226-6544), offering jewelry and gifts galore, shouldn't be overlooked. Join the knitting craze and enroll in a class at **Knitting Central** (203-454-4300; www.knittingcentral.com), 582 Post Road East. The town also lends itself to seasonal delights in such establishments as **Izzo & Son Country Gardens** (203-255-6429); **Geiger's Garden Center** (203-227-3811); **Gardener's Eden** (203-341-0855) and **Gilbertie's Herb Gardens** (203-227-4175; www.gilbertiesherbs.com). One not-to-be-missed jaunt is independently owned **Pymander Books and Gifts** (203-227-1715; www.pymanderbooks.com) carrying a comprehensive line of alternative and new age books and gifts.

Nearby downtown at 299 Post Road (Route 1) in Playhouse Square, no day is complete without downtime at **Derma Clinic** (203-27-0771; www.dermaclinicspa.com/index.html), a topnotch, full-service spa and salon that has been going strong for more than two decades and one of the earliest pioneers in the industry. The range of services includes consultation from Dr. Joseph B. O'Donnell, a highly reputable plastic and reconstruction surgeon. Shoppers should note that there is also a full-line of the spa's own products available for purchase to the public. Typically, founder and CEO Patricia O'Regan Brown greets visitors, ready and waiting with a hot cup of tea or lemon water.

One other outlet to consider for body-mind treatments is the **Aromatherapy Center of Connecticut** (203-226-2541), 231 Post Road East. These friendly folks carry a full range of sweet and poignant body lotions and other interesting merchandise.

After calling it a day, for casual fare try (call establishments for days and hours of operation): **Ben & Jerry's Ice Cream** (203-221-7443); **Chef's Table** (203-454-2433; 203-226-3663; www.chefstable.com); legendary **Oscar's Deli** (203-227-3705); **Gold's Deli** (203-227-0101) and **Calise's Food Market** (203-227-3257). Pure elegance, excellent service and family-owned for generations, don't miss **Three Bears Restaurant** (203-227-7219; www.threebearsrestaurant.com). Previously voted *Fairfield County's best restaurant* by *Connecticut Magazine*, the restaurant's history dates back two centuries and includes a stint as a stagecoach stop. Located at 333 Wilton Road (Route 33), it's open for lunch and dinner, Tuesday through Sunday; Sunday brunch is unmistakably fresh.

With Sunday brunch in mind, day-trippers who have a penchant for buffet-style cuisine should head to another old-time favorite on Route 33, the **Red Barn** (203-222-9549; www.redbarnrestaurant.com). Open for lunch and dinner daily, the "Friday Night Dinner Seafood Buffets" are another bodacious treat. Those hankering for seafood should visit the tried and true **Mansion Clam House** (203-454-7979). A restored 1800s onion shed neighboring the Saugatuck River sets the stage for lunch and dinner daily (no Sunday lunch).

Bombay Bar and Grill (203-226-0211) at 616 Post Road East also serves a monumental Sunday lunch buffet as well as weekday lunch buffets. Open for dinner nightly, the restaurant is another familiar fixture, rated number one Indian restaurant by local press.

A tiny establishment huge on flavor exploding with northern-Italian and southern French flavors is **Da Pietro's** (203-454-1213), open for dinner Monday through Saturday, 36 Riverside Drive. Chef-owner Pietro Scotti prepares the fresh, creative dishes served at this award-winning restaurant that's been rated *excellent* by the *New York Times*. **Tavern on the Main** (203-221-7222; www.tavernonmain.com) is another award-winning dining experience at 146 Main Street, open for lunch and dinner daily. Fresh American cuisine is the mainstay inside this 19th-century Colonial landmark. The Westport dining scene also surpasses ordinary Asian-themed restaurant cuisine. **Matsu Sushi** (203-341-9662; www.matsusushimenu.com) at 33 Jessup Road, serving lunch and dinner daily, is undeniably vegetarian friendly and seafood fresh. **Taipan** (203-227-7400), 376 Boston Post Road, specializes in Pan-

Asian cuisine. A unique ambiance including live Koi fish swimming underneath footbridges enhances dining pleasure, open for lunch and dinner daily. Taipan's youngest sibling, **Little Kitchen** (203-454-5540), is also open for lunch and dinner daily, serving amazingly fresh and super creative entrees.

GETTING THERE:
Westport is approximately 52 miles northeast of New York City, 29 miles southwest of New Haven and 68 miles southwest of Hartford. Westport is at the intersection of many major highways and roads. The city is easily accessible from Interstate Highway 95; the Merritt Parkway (Route 15); Route 7 and U.S. Route 1 (the Boston Post Road).

TRANSPORTATION:
Stratford's Sikorsky Memorial Airport is approximately 13 miles from Westport. Tweed New Haven Regional Airport is approximately 29 miles driving distance, providing daily service to 126 cities through US Airways and Delta Airlines. The area is approximately 77 miles southwest of Bradley International Airport in Windsor Locks. The three major New York City metro airports are Westchester County Airport, LaGuardia, JFK and Newark Airport in New Jersey. Danbury Municipal Airport, a small, private airport, is approximately 24 miles in driving distance. The CT Transit District (203-333-3031) and the Norwalk Transit District (203-852-0000) operate frequent commuter-connection buses from and around the Westport vicinity. The Westport Railroad Station, One Railroad Place, provides Metro-North (800-METRO-INFO) trains to connecting cities as does Amtrak (800-872-7245). Both Metro-North station and Amtrak offer daily commuter service to New York City.

ADDITIONAL INFORMATION:
SHERWOOD ISLAND STATE PARK.
Sherwood Island Connector. Open Memorial Day through Labor Day, 8 a.m. to sunset, daily. Day fees per carload are weekends/holidays: $9.00 Connecticut registered vehicle; $14.00 out-of-state registered vehicle; weekdays: $7.00 Connecticut registered vehicle; $10.00 out-of-state registered vehicle. (203) 341-1000; http://dep.state.ct.us/stateparks/parks/sherwood.htm.

EARTHPLACE, THE NATURE DISCOVERY CENTER.
10 Woodside Lane. The grounds are open all year from 7 a.m. to dusk, daily. The building is open all year, daily. Inquire about the special adult, children's and family programs and workshops. General admission is free, but donations accepted. (203) 227-7253; www.earthplace.org.

THE WHEELER HOUSE/WESTPORT HISTORICAL SOCIETY.
25 Avery Place. Open all year, Monday through Saturday. Inquire about special programs and events. General admission is by donation. (203) 222-1424; www. westporthistory.org/index.html.

ACCOMMODATIONS:

INN AT NATIONAL HALL.

2 Post Road West. Billed as "a historic, riverside, luxury hotel," elegance with a capital "E" exudes throughout the property—who would dream that in the 1800s this was the spot where Westport's famed onions and other produce were loaded for export? Listed on the National Register of Historic Places, the inn unveils eight guestrooms and eight suites with names as eclectic as its surroundings: "the India," "the Raindrop," "the Saugatuck" and "the Equestrian." The property offers full, modern amenities. Rates: $292.50-$715. (203) 221-1351. (800) 628-4255; www. innatnationalhall.com.

THE INN AT LONGSHORE.

260 Compo Road South. This venerable property built as a summer estate in the 1890s boasts 12 graciously appointed guestrooms and suites with full, modern amenities. Other guest services include outdoor pool, tennis, on-premises restaurant, 18-hole golf course and boating access. Call for rates. (203) 226-3316; www. innatlongshore.com.

WESTPORT INN.

1595 Post Road East. The 115 guestrooms with five suites provide full, modern amenities; on-premises pluses include sunlit atrium, indoor pool, Jacuzzi spa and fitness center and Spyglass, a new restaurant. Pets welcome! Rates: $149-$180. (203) 259-5236; (800) 446-8997; www.westportinn.com.

ANNUAL FESTIVALS/EVENTS

The Coastal Fairfield County Convention & Visitor Bureau, representing 15 southwestern communities, provides a gamut of tourism information, including seasonal events (800) 866-7925 or (203) 853-7770; www.coastalct.com. For additional festival and event information, contact the *Westport Magazine*, (203) 222-0600, and *Westport Now* (www.westportnow.com), a magazine on the web, providing excellent town news and related coverage to residents and visitors alike.

JANUARY

For a nominal charge, spectators can join **First Night Westport/Weston**, a town-wide New Year's Eve party for all ages, with venues throughout the town. Musicians, artists, and a variety of talented performers are featured throughout this non-alcoholic celebration. (203) 454-6699; www.firstnightww.com.

FEBRUARY

Annual Crossword Puzzle Contest is held at the Westport Library's McManus Room. (203) 291-4840.

MARCH

Near & Far Aid Spring Gala is held at Mitchell's of Westport, 670 Post Road East. Festivities include rare-wine tasting and auction, a fashion show, cocktails and dinner buffet. (800) 866-7925.

The Inn at Longshore sponsors an annual **Mardi Gras**, a New Orleans-style celebration including buffet dinner, open bar, silent and live auctions and dancing to live bands. The event benefits the performances at the Levitt Pavilion. (203) 226-7600.

APRIL
The Annual **Earth Day** celebration at Earthplace is filled with educational programs and fun for all. (203) 227-7253.

MAY
Sponsored by the Westport Young Woman's League, the **Annual Minute Man 5 K Race** congregates at the Compo Beach Pavilion. All proceeds benefit local charities. (203) 222-1388.

Another spring event sponsored by the Westport Young Woman's League is the **Doors of Westport**, in which day-trippers tour a variety of extraordinary residential homes. (203) 222-1388.

Memorial Day weekend means that it's time for the **Westport Craft Show** at Staples High School, 70 North Avenue. Listed among the country's top-100 craft shows and one of Connecticut's most prestigious events, more than 150 artisans across North America sell an array of contemporary and traditional handcrafts. (203) 227-7844; www.westportcraft.com.

JUNE
Westport Historical Society sponsors the **Annual Hidden Garden Tour** that takes sojourners into some of the most exquisite private properties in town. (203) 222-1424.

The long-running **Yankee Doodle Fair**, sponsored by the Westport Woman's Club, draws audiences of all ages to partake in four days of entertainment, raffles, amusement park rides and food; the on-premises Curio Cottage, open during the entire fair, is a must for bargain hunters. (203) 227-4240.

Southport-Westport Antiques Show, sponsored by Near and Far Aid and managed by the Antiques Council, is held annually on the grounds of Greens Farms Academy. (203) 227-9234.

JULY
Mid-summer means that the **Westport Fine Art Festival** will fill Main Street with music, entertainment, food and, yes, lots of artwork for sale. (203) 227-9234.

Any local can direct visitors to **Westport Festival Italiano**, one of the most famed and oldest ethnic festivals of its kind in the state. The week's events held in the Riverside Avenue section of town range from amusement park rides to food and entertainment. (203) 847-2818.

SEPTEMBER
Annual Soundkeeper Lighthouse to Lighthouse Race is held at Compo Beach. The 14-mile race is open to "all seaworthy human-powered vessels." (203) 846-9723.

OCTOBER

For those who would like to learn more about tropical fish or for those who just like to look at colorful, frolicking sea creatures, visit the **Annual Tropical Fish Show** held at Westport's Earthplace. Sponsored by the Norwalk Aquarium Society, there is an auction, special talks, exhibits and raffle prizes. (203) 227-7253.

More than 500 works of art by more than 100 artists grace the walls of Earthplace at the **Annual Art Show and Sale**, a benefit featuring a gala opening. (203) 227-7253.

The Westport/Weston Health District and the Westport/Weston YMCA both sponsor the **Annual Family Fun Walk** at Compo Beach. Their non-competitive event features a variety of sprint lengths. (203) 227-9234.

NOVEMBER

The **Westport Creative Arts Festival**, featuring everything from basketry to quilts and mixed media, takes place annually at Staples High School, 70 North Avenue. All proceeds from this highly praised show, sponsored by the Westport Young Woman's League, benefit a variety of charities. (203) 222-1388. www. wywl.com.

DECEMBER

The Westport Historical Society sponsors the annual **Holiday House Tour** offering participants a peek into an array of lovely abodes decorated for the season. (203) 222-1424.

Kismet
See page 210

One of the many Westport galleries and shops that give the town pizazz.

*What southwestern Connecticut town
claimed a biblical name as its own?*

*What Connecticut town's economy
was supplemented by shoemaking?*

Tony-Terrific Neighborhood: **NEW CANAAN**

The erected Ponus Monument on Ponus Ridge commemorates Chief Ponus, a Sagamore Indian from whom the land was purchased in 1640. It wasn't until 1731, however, borrowing the name of the biblical Promised Land of Canaan, that Congregationalists established a parish that occupied both colonial Norwalk and Stamford. Although the State Legislature recognized the settlement as a separate religious entity, depending on where they lived, community members were governed by either Norwalk or Stamford officials. Not until 1801 did the state incorporate the primarily agricultural town as the 108th town in the state, opting for the name, New Canaan, since the northwestern town of Canaan had already been established in 1739.

New Canaan was one of the few communities that did not have a central common (town green), a main street or town hall. After the Revolutionary War, apart from agriculture, shoemaking became New Canaan's backbone. As the industry gathered velocity—void of a village center—houses, mills and schools sprang up in regional clusters. Early residents created a number of districts, namely: Ponus Ridge, West Road, Oenoke Ridge, Smith Ridge, Talmadge Hill and Silvermine.

With the 1868 advent of New Canaan's railroad, many of nearby New York City's wealthy residents took advantage of the serene countryside, building summer estates. Eventually, many of these seasonal visitors settled year-round, commuting to city jobs and helping the Fairfield County town achieve its present status as one of the wealthiest suburbs in the state—where the median sale price for homes hovers just under one million dollars.

Today, New Canaan, with a 22.56-square-mile area, home to just over 19,000 residents, is a suburban enclave of Manhattan. The town boasts three private schools: St. Aloysius Regional Elementary, New Canaan Country Day School (pre-K through ninth) and St. Luke's School (grades five through 12). As far as day-trippers are concerned, rambling scenery, historical havens, restaurants donning rave reviews and art in the most surprising places; plus catching a performance of New Canaan's town band (the oldest, non-church, town musical group founded in 1831) during Fourth of July festivities or marching in the Memorial Day Parade, combine award-winning ingredients for any day trip with panache.

Historical votaries can conduct scavenger hunts to explore 42 houses that have existed for 100 years or more and are identified with New Canaan Historical Society plaques. The oldest, documented surviving house is the **Benedict-Eels-Thatcher House**, Carter Street, built in 1724. In total, 30 houses hold the sobriquet of the colonial-era **Drummond Visitation Homes**.

The historic district itself showcases 21 buildings along Main Street, Oenoke Ridge, Park Street and St. John's Place. The best way to embrace the essence of the district is with a self-guided walking tour following the New Canaan Historical Society's publication, *A Guide to God's Acre* (God's Acre designates a scenic area in the heart of the town).

The society also publishes a children's version entitled, *Child's Walking Tour of New Canaan*. The route begins at the historical society, heads down to Main Street, turns right onto Elm and then right onto Park, bringing participants back to the **New Canaan Historical Society**, its soigné grounds awaiting day-trippers of all ages. Visitors need to carve out enough time to examine the society's five buildings containing seven museums and a library housing more than 4,000 volumes of books covering subjects on genealogy and area history.

The **Hanford-Silliman House** is a 1764 Saltbox with center chimney, built as a tavern by colonial weaver Stephen Hanford, who was also the town's first licensed tavern keeper. Curiosity seekers marvel at the masterful architectural designs implemented by the Silliman family, the house's final occupants.

Other on-property must-sees are the **Town House**, originally built as New Canaan's first town hall in 1825 and acquired by the historical society from the Augustana Lutheran Church in 1963. Undergoing numerous renovations and additions since, the house accommodates the society's offices, a meeting room and extensive research library. Also inside, the **Clock Room** displays a 19th-century Connecticut clock collection and shelves of books written by New Canaan authors. The second floor's **Costume Museum** provides a foray through the many mannequins modeling 18th- and 19th-century clothing. The sculptures of artist John Rogers continue to be exhibited on the house's second floor until the renovation of the **John Rogers' Studio and Museum** is complete in summer 2006. Rogers, who achieved fame as "the people's sculptor," built the studio acquired by the historical society in 1878 and, now, registered as a National Historic Landmark. (The other National Historic Landmark building in New Canaan is architect Philip Johnson's Glass House, Ponus Ridge Road. The structure, currently a private residence, is made entirely of glass and is Johnson's most famous creation.)

Adjacent to the Town House, the **Cody Drug Store** allows sojourners to experience an 1845 drugstore brimming with original fixtures, store merchandise, apothecary jars and medicines once said to help nearly every ailment.

Also on premises, for an instructional (but fun!) time, learning about things like area carpentry and shoemaking, the **Tool Museum** leaves no leaf (or for that matter, tool) unturned. This is a combined exhibit with the **New Canaan Hand Press** affording spectators to witness a re-creation of a 19th-century printing office; a rare treat, considering that fewer than 30 hand-printing presses have survived in the United States today. Peek inside **Rock School**, another society acquisition. Built in 1799 as a one-room schoolhouse, the society saved the building from demolition and relocated it to its present grounds.

Although off premises, within three miles southeast on historic Carter Street, the **Little Red Schoolhouse**, built in 1865 and schooling kindergarteners through fifth graders until 1957, is another historical society property. The society opens it on special occasions; tours can be prearranged.

A few doors away from the historical society, the **New Canaan Nature Center** features one of the most diverse nature habitats around. Their 40-acre menagerie, formerly the estate of Miss Susan Dwight Bliss, a prominent area resident, includes meadows, woodlands, thickets, two ponds, herb, wildflower, bird and butterfly gardens and an old orchard. Two miles of trails invite hikers with the carrot being a 350-foot boardwalk and an observation tower overlooking a cattail marsh. The focal point at the visitor's center for day-trippers is the **Discovery Center**, boasting hands-on, natural science exhibits. The gift shop is a peregrination through a panoply of nature-related merchandise including books, toys, gardening accessories, maple syrup and local honey. A greenhouse, animal-care building, cider house, Audubon house and maple sugar shed are other campus buildings.

In all, New Canaan offers more than 400 acres of public space, parks and recreational facilities (203-594-3600). **Mead Park**, near the intersection of Mead and Park Streets, a 24-acre stretch, unravels horseshoe pits, tennis courts, a playground, pond fishing and four baseball fields. Pond skating at Mead as well as at **Mill Pond**, at the corner of East and Millport Avenues, is popular with winter enthusiasts. Summertime sojourns are not to be missed at **Kiwanis Park**, Old Norwalk Road. Day fees are charged from June through Labor Day for swimming in the large pond on this 12.6-acre property. Off-the-beaten-trek wanderings should include the enchanting three-acre woodlands that form the **Olive and George Lee Memorial Garden**, 89 Chichester Road.

The largest town park (containing the majestic Waveny House, a popular locale for weddings and special ceremonies) is the 300-acre **Waveny Park**, 677 South Avenue. Day-trippers can enjoy the approximate 3.5 miles of jogging and walking paths. Summer concerts waft the patio air outside Waveny House on Wednesday nights. Summer theater, including **Shakespeare at Waveny** and a variety of children's productions, are also performed outdoors.

Indoors, throughout the year, the **Town Players of New Canaan** perform live theater (at reasonable ticket prices) at **Waveny's Powerhouse Performing Art Center** (203-966-7371). The **Carriage Barn** (203-972-1895) hosts live concerts throughout the year, like those performed by the **Waveny Chamber Music Society**. The barn also accommodates the **Betty Barker Gallery**, holding several annual fine art exhibits open to the public from Tuesday through Sunday. Art encounters of changing exhibits can also happen at New Canaan Library's **Pelham Curtis Gallery** (203-594-5003). Note: library staff also facilitates some extraordinary writers and celebrities for public readings, talks and performances. Request an e-newsletter announcing upcoming library news and events at www. onlineref@newcanaanlibrary.org.

Another artsy venue that wins hands down with day-trippers began in the early 1900s as an art colony in the countryside. Artists gathered in a barn, identifying themselves as members of the Knockers Club, signifying that they generously dispensed criticism of each other's work! Herein lay the humble roots of the **Silvermine Guild Arts Center** (203-966-9700; www.silvermineart.org), 1037 Silvermine Road, one of the most respected institutions of its kind in the country. Deep in the verdant roads of the Silvermine District, five galleries offering changing exhibits by contemporary, professional artists are open Tuesday through Sunday. A variety of visual and fine art classes, workshops, and performances, including a chamber music series in the summer, are also available to interested parties.

If adventure is more your style, call upon **White Creek Expeditions** (203-966-0040), 99 Myanos Road. Their company provides year-round trips including canoeing, kayaking, whitewater rafting, hiking, camping, rock climbing and the like.

The Main Street commercial hub embracing quaint, upscale shops like **Talbot's**, boutiques and enticing restaurants is further characterized by brick-laid walkways. Whether searching for snuffboxes or English teacups, this is an antiques-haven lined with such shops as (call establishments for days and hours of operation): **Patricia Funt Antiques** (203-966-6139), **Evans-Leonard Antiques** (203-966-5657) and the **Silk Purse** (203-972-0898). Those in search of records or CDs should peruse Main Street's **Gramophone Shop** (203-972-0002). At 101 Main Street, the **Toy Chest of New Canaan** (203-972-0007) is the place for kids and adults to let loose. The **New Canaan Toy Store** (203-966-2424) at 127 Elm Street comes also packed with whimsical items that tickle the funny bone.

Other not-to-be-overlooked New Canaan shopping venues include two bookstores: **DandyTales** (203-966-7713), 13 South Avenue, open daily, carrying an impressive line of children's books for all ages. Parents rave about how the store emphasizes interactivity and special programs like writing contests. In addition, open daily, located at 175 Elm Street, **Elm Street Books** (203-966-4545; www.rjjulia.com), now collaborates with R.J. Julia Booksellers (see **Madison** chapter), and features a luminary mix of book signings. A knowledgeable staff, always willing to provide their thumbs-up on the latest good read, enhances the superior range of book subjects available.

For the finest department store cosmetics, plus superior fragrances and body products including Crabtree and Evelyn, step into family-owned **Lang's Pharmacy** (203-966-9593), open Monday through Saturday at 136 Elm Street.

Less than a half mile, **Next Station Needlepoint** (203-966-5613; www.needlept.com), 72 Grove Street, is a "needlepoint only" store open Tuesday through Saturday. The exquisite, artful selections can lure patrons to stay and gaze.

Shoppers interested in taking home fresh fruit, vegetables and baked goods should frequent **New Canaan's Farmers' Market**, held Saturday mornings until early afternoon from mid-June through mid-November at the Center School parking lot, corner of South Avenue and Maple Street. For a divine treat anytime of day, the **Canaan Parish Sweet Shoppe** (203-966-5432) at 4 South Avenue, open daily, has the answer.

For those ready to drop after they shop, consider a serene stopover. **Aetheria Relaxation Spa** (203-966-6650; www.aetheriaspa.com), located at 121 Cherry Street and situated in a Victorian home, is a full-service spa in which treatments include massage therapy and skin care. Open Tuesday through Saturday and also by appointment, all products, which are available for purchase, utilize pure, organic ingredients. Wrap the day up in a Thirsty Towel robe and meditate.

Another calmative experience for body, soul and spirit is certain to be had at **Garineh of New Canaan Unique Spa** (203-972-8488; call for days and hours of operation). This full-service spa facility at 36 Viti Street also offers a range of services including manicures and pedicures, reflexology, ear candling and yoga classes. On premises, day-trippers can also purchase an array of top-shelf facial and beauty products.

From East Avenue's **Best Wurst** (203-972-1233) to Elm Street's **Lemon Grass** (203-966-9891), both open daily, New Canaan accommodates numerous delis and specialty food establishments that will satisfy a variety of tastes and appetites. Pizzerias are also plentiful and range from **Joe's Pizzeria** (203-966-2226), open for lunch, Tuesday through Sunday at 23 Locust Avenue to **New Canaan Pizza** (203 966-3610; call for days and hours of operation), 53 East Avenue. An impressive league of restaurants present different cuisines, from regional favorites to international fare. Since it opened in 1998, **Ching's Table** (203-972-2830), with an Asian-style menu at 64 Main Street, has garnered numerous *best of Connecticut* restaurant awards and is open for lunch and dinner daily. Its sister restaurant, **Sushi 25** (203-966-2338) at 25 Elm Street, is also open for lunch and dinner daily. At 87 Main Street, **Thali Regional Cuisine of India** (203-927-8332) has received numerous accolades from patrons and professional restaurant reviewers alike. Open for lunch and dinner daily, a classic Indian food menu is presented in a distinct setting that was once a 1913 bank building and is now distinguished by an indoor cascading waterfall flowing from a sixty-foot long brook.

The unmistakable 19th-century wrought iron gates have led patrons into **Gates Restaurant** (203-966-8666), 10 Forest Street, for more than 20 years. West Brattleboro, Vermont artist Janet M. Picard's colorful murals along with the light and airy ambiance enhance the lunch (Sunday brunch) and dinner menu served daily. Specialties include seafood and homemade ravioli. Two other sister eateries: **Tequila Mockingbird** (203-966-2222) offers Mexican cuisine for dinner daily, and **Bistro Bonne Nuit** (203-966-5303) features a French menu for dinner, Tuesday through Sunday. **Cherrystreet East** (203-966-2100), open for lunch (Sunday brunch) and dinner daily, has a pub-like atmosphere, offering comfort foods including fresh cut fries, steaks and ribs.

Rated *excellent* by the *New York Times*, fine dining is offered at the venerable **Roger Sherman Inn** (203-966-4541; www.rogershermaninn.com; see **Accommodations**) at 185 Oenoke Ridge. Situated in the charm of a restored, 1740 Colonial-style landmark, various rooms look as good as they feel. Innkeeper Thomas Weilenmann, a typical fixture in the dining room, oversees every detail of fine dining and exudes European hospitality. Open for lunch, Tuesday through Sunday (Sunday brunch), and dinner daily, the menu features award-winning contemporary-continental cuisine, including seasonal and Swiss-style specialties and fresh seafood. Winter Sundays (January through March) mean fireplaces ablaze while noshing on Raclette and Fondue, the mainstay of "Cheese Nights."

GETTING THERE:
New Canaan is approximately 49 miles northeast of New York City, 37 miles southwest of New Haven and 75 miles southwest of Hartford. New Canaan is at the intersection of many major highways and roads. The city is easily accessible from Interstate Highway 95; the Merritt Parkway (Route 15); Routes 123, 124, 107 and 7 and U.S. Route 1 (the Boston Post Road). New Canaan is located north of Stamford, between Darien and the New York State line where Routes 124, 123 and 106 intersect.

TRANSPORTATION:
Stratford's Sikorsky Memorial Airport is approximately 23 miles from New Canaan. Tweed New Haven Regional Airport is approximately 37 miles driving distance, providing daily service to 126 cities through US Airways and Delta Airlines. The area is approximately 89 miles southwest of Bradley International Airport in Windsor Locks. The three major New York City metro airports are Westchester County Airport, LaGuardia, JFK and Newark Airport in New Jersey. Danbury Municipal Airport, a small, private airport, is approximately 22 miles in

driving distance. The CT Transit District (203-333-3031) and the Norwalk Transit District (203-852-0000) operate frequent commuter-connection buses from and around the New Canaan vicinity. New Canaan has two Metro-North railroad stations: Talmadge Hill and New Canaan Railroad Station, built in 1868 and boasting Gothic Revival architecture, it is one of the earliest surviving stations in Connecticut. (800) 638-7646.

ADDITIONAL INFORMATION:
NEW CANAAN HISTORICAL SOCIETY.
13 Oenoke Ridge. The house museum and its properties are open all year. Inquire about special performances and events. General admission is $3.00 adults; $3.00 seniors/children and free to children 5 and under and free on Tuesday. (203) 966-1776; www.nchistory.org.

NEW CANAAN NATURE CENTER.
144 Oenoke Ridge. The center and other buildings are open all year, Tuesday through Sunday. Trails are open all year, dawn to dusk, daily. Inquire about special events and programs, such as first aid certification, early morning bird watching, maple sugaring and horticultural classes. Additionally, live animal demonstrations are Saturdays at 3 p.m. General admission is free, but donations are appreciated. (203) 966-9577; www.newcanaannature.org.

ACCOMMODATIONS:
ROGER SHERMAN INN.
185 Oenoke Ridge. This 1783 landmark property, renovated in 1998, was once owned (1783-1806) by the niece of Roger Sherman, the famous lawyer and Connecticut delegate, signer of the Declaration of Independence and U.S. Constitution. Today, 17 tastefully decorated guestrooms welcome travelers into comfortable surroundings, whether in the main or carriage house, and each extend full, modern amenities and on-site restaurant (see above). Rates (including continental breakfast): $110-$350. (203) 966-4541; www.rogershermaninn.com.

MAPLES INN.
179 Oenoke Ridge. Directly next door to the Roger Sherman Inn (see above), the Maples Inn affords the comfort of turn-of-the-century, country-style quarters complete with fireplaces blazing in the winter months. In milder weather, a gracious assortment of wicker chairs spread throughout the wrap-around porch. The distinct décor in the 13 guestrooms, which provide full, modern amenities, includes four-poster, canopy beds and antiques. Rates (including continental breakfast): $105-$170. (203) 966-2927; www.maplesinnct.com/index.htm.

ANNUAL FESTIVALS/EVENTS
The Coastal Fairfield County Convention & Visitor Bureau, representing 15 southwestern communities, provides a gamut of tourism information, including seasonal events (800) 866-7925 or (203) 853-7770; www.coastalct.com. For additional festivals and events including a guide in the spring and fall, *100 Things*

to Do, published by Hersam Acorn's, *New Canaan Advertiser*, contact (203) 966-9541; www.acorn-online.com/100thing.htm; also the New Canaan Chamber of Commerce, (203) 966-2204.

FEBRUARY

The **Annual Maple Syrup Festival** at the New Canaan Nature Center is about everything maple, down to the syrup poured on the waffle dishes. Maple syrup demonstrations and other special activities tempt all ages. (203) 966-9577; www.newcanaannature.org.

Art lovers should attend the **Juried Photography Show** at the Betty Barker Gallery at the Carriage Barn Arts Center at Waveny Park. (203) 972-1895.

Another artsy venue is at the **Annual New Member Exhibition**, multimedia show featured at the Silvermine Guild Arts Center, 1037 Silvermine Road. (203) 966-9700.

APRIL

The Police Athletic League stocks Mill Pond at the corner of East and Millport Avenue for the **Annual Children's Fishing Derby**. (203) 966-0502.

MAY

The **May Fair** is an annual festival held on the property of St. Mark's Episcopal Church, 111 Oenoke Road. The day's activities revolve around a food court, vendors that sell wares including handicrafts, needlework, books and plants. A white elephant tent and carnival-style rides are also part of the fun. All proceeds benefit local charities. (203) 966-4515.

JUNE/JULY/AUGUST

Summer concerts in the open-air theater of Waveny House, South Avenue, are presented Wednesday nights. (203) 594-3600.

JUNE

There's nothing quite like cooling off at the **Annual Ice Cream Social** at the New Canaan Historical Society that attracts crowds from all over. The day is filled with special tours of on-premises properties and special activities for all ages. (203) 966-1776; www.nchistory.org.

JULY

Fourth of July at Waveny Park is a day of special activities and, of course, a spectacular display of fireworks. (203) 966-2204.

The **Annual Village Fair and Sidewalk Sale** is a block party formed by more than 100 merchants, restaurants and organizations in the downtown area (Elm and Forest Streets are closed to vehicles). The roster of events includes dancing and live entertainment, food and plenty of discount shopping. (203) 966-2204.

AUGUST

For a taste of art, consider attending the **Annual Faculty Exhibition** featured at the Silvermine Guild Arts Center, 1037 Silvermine Road. (203) 966-9700.

Also, savor the **Annual Members Show** at the Betty Barker Gallery at the Carriage Barn Arts Center in Waveny Park. (203) 972-1895.

OCTOBER

New Canaan Nature Center's **Fall Festival** buzzes with children's activities, hayrides and a variety of demonstrations with live animals. A half-mile run for preteens, walks for non-runners and seniors; as well as healing experts and trainers offer a variety of programs. (203) 966-9577; www.newcanaannature.org.

Everyone has fun during the **Annual Halloween Parade** that forms at Park Street parking lot (rain or shine). Balloons and gifts for the children are also on hand. (203) 966-2204.

DECEMBER

To mark the beginning of the holiday season, the first Monday after Thanksgiving is reserved for the **Annual Holiday Lighting of the Downtown Business District**, including Christmas caroling on God's Acre. (203) 966-2204.

The **Annual Open House** at the New Canaan Historical Society means many special events like Victorian tea and gingerbread house workshops. This is also a perfect opportunity to buy some unique New Canaan holiday gifts including town history books and holiday cards with an old-fashioned, artist's rendition of town. (203) 966-1776; www.nchistory.org.

Unique, handmade crafts for sale that include fresh centerpieces, green roping, wreaths, holiday plants, baked goods, holiday decorations and gently-used toys and stocking stuffers are just some of the features at the **Holiday Market** at the New Canaan Nature Center. (203) 966-9577; www.newcanaannature.org.

A biennial **Festival of Trees at Waveny Castle**, selling numerous holiday wares, is a major fundraiser hosted by the Garden Center of New Canaan. (203) 966-2204.

New Canaan
See pages 216-233

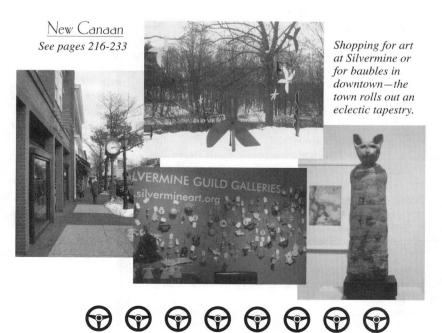

Shopping for art at Silvermine or for baubles in downtown—the town rolls out an eclectic tapestry.

What Connecticut city did settlers purchase from the
Indians for the price of 10 mirrors, 10 scissors, 10 hatches,
10 knives, 10 jewsharps (musical instruments),
10 hoes and a bundle of wampum?

In what Connecticut city did the earliest colonists
receive royal grants from the British Crown for their oysters?

Groovin': SOUTH NORWALK/NORWALK

In 1640, in exchange for land saddled on each side by a river, colonial leader and lawmaker Roger Ludlow gave Chief Mahackamo 10 mirrors, 10 scissors, 10 hatches, 10 knives, 10 jewsharps, 10 hoes and a bundle of wampum. Incorporated in 1651, making it the 14th town in the state, the city's modern-day name is a derivative from the Native American "Naramauke" or "Noyank," meaning "point of land."

During the Revolutionary War in 1779, 2,500 British troops invaded what we now call Calf Pasture Beach and, aided by the Tories, burned down the town. Many citizens who lost their homes during the infamous raid moved to the Western Reserve region, hence marking the earliest history of the city of Norwalk in the state of Ohio. Today, day-trippers can view a monument at the corner of East Avenue and Adams Avenue honoring the men who fought against the British.

In the 1700s, colonists received royal grants from the British Crown for their oysters. Oyster cultivation was a lustrous pearl in Norwalk's economy, and by the late 1800s, Long Island's Blue Points were one of the most prized culinary treats in the world. Continuing the tradition today, Connecticut is second only to Louisiana in oyster production. Tallmadge Brothers, a family-run business in South Norwalk since 1875, is one of the largest oyster cultivators of its kind; the company tends 24,000 acres of oyster beds.

In 1848, the train arrived in Norwalk and the town became an important industrial city, gaining a reputation second only to Danbury in hat production. By the 1960s, however, consumer demand waned. Many factories had closed their doors. Unemployment rates rose. Residents moved out of the city in search of other opportunities. Crime also rose, litter choked the streets, and the city's economy sank.

In the mid-1970s, city officials rooted the South Norwalk Revitalization Project by revamping and reinventing defunct buildings. Thirty-two properties were listed on the Register of Historic Places, thereby creating a historical district. What the community endearingly called "SoNo" was among one of the first American coastal cities that, after a serious economic plunge, got its groove back. Today, the vicinity's main drag, Washington Street, hosts business professionals, community members, sightseers and such lively personalities as Rick Glica, SoNo artist-in-residence, who signs his paintings: Zarzan. Just look for the man with the long, wooly beard, usually smoking a hefty cigar, reclined on a bench next to his paintings, bold in contemporary design, and softened with pastel hues.

Also, look for eclectic boutiques, international delis, bakeries, coffee shops and a robust nightlife (and rising real estate price tags!) in the sixth largest city in Connecticut. Situated between the Norwalk and Saugatuck Rivers and nestled along Long Island Sound, the city also attains a healthy base of businesses; to name a few: SoBe (the popular beverage), Virgin Atlantic Airways and priceline.com. Norwalk Community College and Merritt Seven Corporate Park located on busy Route 7, are two other examples that enhance the city's economy.

Norwalk's coastal enclave community, Rowayton, bordered by the Five Mile River on the east, Long Island Sound on the south and Wilson Cove on the west, is another ideal day-trip neighborhood defined by shops, restaurants, a historical society and a vibrant arts center. The city (population 82,951) is also headquarters for the **Coastal Fairfield County Convention & Visitor Bureau**; tourism plays a large part in the region's economy. A colorful resource that highlights the latest attractions and hotspots in town is www.lighthousemaps.com, also available for other Connecticut coastal areas.

Day trips with panache mean etching out at least two hours to survey what inducted SoNo and the surrounding region onto the tourism map: the **Maritime Aquarium**. In 1986, the aquarium began groundbreaking ceremonies at a former 1860s iron works factory site, an abandoned, brick building on the SoNo waterfront. This premiere aquarium is one of the few in the country solely devoted to one body of water, Long Island Sound. One of the largest attractions in Connecticut, annual attendance is around 525,000 visitors. The aquarium features more than 1,000 marine animals native to the sound. An unending spectrum of living creatures resides in the aquarium: oysters, seahorses, lobsters, jellyfish, nine-foot sharks (wow, wait 'til you see their 110,000-gallon tank home) and harbor seals, inhabiting indoor-outdoor tanks.

Everyone delights in viewing the resident seals — Susie, Polly, Leila, Tilly, Ariel and Rascal feed — they eat up to eight pounds of herring and capelin a day! None of them is camera-shy; they love to nestle up to the tank so visitors can get a close-up look! Not all sea life is under glass either. Devoted museum staff and volunteers invite day-trippers to touch sea stars, crabs, whelks and live rays (with stingers removed).

With the first major expansion project completed in 2001, the Maritime Aquarium unveiled a new 9.5-million-dollar Environmental Education Center encompassing classrooms and high-tech educational equipment, a loggerhead sea turtle exhibit addition, a new 180-seat food-service area and main entrance and gift shop expansion.

Day-trippers can also purchase a ticket to view the latest flick at the aquarium's (Connecticut's only and one of the few in the country) IMAX (image maximum) theater. The movie screen measures eight stories wide and six stories high. Whether the presentation involves an intricate examination of African lions or the people of Egypt or an infinite number of subjects relating to culture or nature, it is rare to attend a show without hearing patrons exclaim in awe at the cinematic magic presented.

Norwalk Harbor and River, steps away from the aquarium, lead to a number of water pursuits—especially considering this portion of Long Island Sound has been allotted more than 1,800 berthing spaces and 500 moorings for recreational boats. Norwalk Seaport Association, sharing the Tallmadge Brothers Building at 132 Water Street, operates the **Sheffield Island Lighthouse Cruises** (203-838-9444; 203-838-2898; www.seaport.org/default.htm), which consist of a 49-passenger, covered ferry vessel. Cruises, which begin Memorial Day weekend and run through Labor Day, meet at the ferry dock, between Maritime Aquarium's IMAX Theater and the Norwalk River Bridge. The ferry passes the Norwalk Islands, stretching into Sheffield Island Harbor, and docks at the three-acre-island park to tour the 1868 four-level, 10-room stone lighthouse adjacent to the Stewart B. McKinney U.S. Fish and Wildlife Sanctuary. While boating Norwalk's aquatic wonders, espy **Peck's Ledge Light** (1906), a cast iron, sparkplug-style tower, just off Norwalk Harbor's entrance and **Greens Ledge** (1900) in neighboring Rowayton, about a mile southwest from Sheffield Island.

Experience another up-close rendezvous of the waterway on a day's expedition touring with experts from the **Small Boat Shop** (203-854-5223; www. thesmallboatshop.com). Long before the kayaking trend, shop personnel have not only offered guided trips and hands-on instruction, but also the shop has continued to carry hundreds of makes and models of what else?—small boats.

Southeastward, nonresidents as well as residents can swim, sail and windsurf at 33-acre **Calf Pasture Beach** (203-854-7806; inquire about summer day fees), the area's largest beach. Landlubbers can espy the Norwalk Islands and Peck's Ledge Light, picnic or try their hand at a volleyball game or miniature golf. Also on the east Norwalk shores, **Veteran's Park** (site of the famed Annual Oyster Festival; see **Annual Festivals/Events**) affords a public boat launch. At the turn of the 20th century, city officials created the park from a former dump, naming it to honor all veterans. Lying partly in the Norwalk River watershed, **Cranbury Park**, towards the Norwalk/Wilton line, provides easy terrain for hiking and mountain biking amid 190 acres of tranquil surroundings including the former Gallagher Mansion, built in 1930 and currently rented out by the town for private parties and functions. Also noteworthy is **Norwalk State Heritage Park**, a waterfront development based around the estuary of the Norwalk River and unveiled in 2001. It is home to **Devon's Place**, a specially designed playground (thanks to myriad volunteer hours) accessible to all children, including those with special needs.

The playground is adjacent to the **Stepping Stones Children's Museum** at Mathews Park, one of the newest attractions, unveiling dozens of exhibits, workshops and programs geared for wee ones under 10 years old. Providing fun ways to learn about science, arts, culture and heritage, children can step into a real super-sized soap bubble or simulate climbing aboard a train, flying a helicopter or submerging in a submarine.

Next door, the **Lockwood-Mathews Mansion Museum** received Hollywood fanfare when producers used its setting for the 2004 remake of the classic film, *The Stepford Wives*. In return, Paramount Pictures restored many of the features in the 62-room Second Empire-style landmark, including the expansive rotunda. America's "first chateau" was built in 1868 at a cost of two million dollars. Today's market value: priceless. Attracting about 33,000 visitors annually, the museum is operated by its non-profit organization that subsequently squelched a proposed demolition of the property during the 1950s. The tour guides at the National

Historic Landmark spin a bittersweet tale of the people who once lived within its opulent, stenciled walls. Note that the Music Box Society International is responsible for the permanent, second-floor exhibit of antique music boxes that waft the premises with musical glee.

Before exiting Mathews Park, peruse some original prints and photographs at **The Center for Contemporary Printmaking**. Dwelling in a restored, 19th-century stone carriage house, the non-profit art gallery offers a variety of shows and workshops. Day-trippers should also jot down SoNo's **Norwalk Museum** on their "must-see" inventory. This two-story showcase, redefining the old city hall, highlights the industrial and manufacturing aspects of the city, including an impressive hat production exhibit. Other memorabilia include 19th-century Norwalk Pottery and Raggedy Ann and Andy Dolls memorializing their creator John Gruelle, who was born in Cleveland, Ohio, but later resided in Norwalk.

Day-trippers can call ahead to tour Norwalk's current **city hall** (203-866-0202) to examine WPA (Works Progress Administration, President Franklin Roosevelt's historic work relief program created to aid the Great Depression) murals from the 1930s and 1940s. Additional venues to view the city's WPA murals—nearly 50, said to be the largest surviving collection in the country, are at the **Norwalk Transit District** (203-852-0000), **Norwalk Community College** (203-857-7060; also inquire about changing art exhibits and student art shows), Maritime Aquarium and the **Norwalk Public Library** (203-899-2780; also inquire about programs open to the public).

In the Norwalk City Hall vicinity, the **SONO Switch Tower Museum** pays tribute to a range of the apparatus once used to switch trains from one track to another. The museum is located in the restored, 1896 Switch Tower building and operated by the Western Connecticut Chapter, National Railway Historical Society.

For those with a propensity for entertainment and culture, begin at the **Norwalk City Hall**, 125 East Avenue, which also doubles as a concert hall and features, among other acts, the **Norwalk Symphony Orchestra**, founded as a community volunteer organization in 1939. Call (203) 847-4850 for the latest schedule of public performances held at the **Ben Franklin Building**, Bayview Avenue, and presented by the **Crystal Theater**, an independent, non-profit performing arts school.

At 2 East Wall Street, from Memorial Day through Labor Day on Sunday afternoon, the Norwalk Historical Society leads tours at the **Mill Hill Historic Park and Museum** (203-846-0525). Free tours (donations welcome) at the complex include the 1835 Town House Museum, the circa 1740 Governor Thomas Fitch Law Office, the 1826 Little Red Schoolhouse and cemetery grounds.

Norwalk-based golfers may desire to tee off at the **Oak Hills Golf Course** (203-838-1015; www.oakhillsgc.com), an 18-hole course designed by Alfred Tull and located at 165 Fillow Street.

Shoppers can take advantage of the quaint SoNo gift shops and boutiques. For a taste of southwestern, Mexican and Native American-inspired gifts and collectibles, consider **Saga** (203-855-1900; www.shopsaga) at 119 Washington Street, open daily.

For a fine selection of American arts and crafts, the **Artists' Market** (203-846-2550), 163 Main Street, has gained a loyal following and is open daily. Norwalk is synonymous with **Stew Leonard's** (203-847-7213; www.stewleonards.com;

see **Danbury** chapter), which is listed in *Ripley's Believe It or Not!* as the *World's Largest Dairy Store*. This is an amusement park of a store, presenting such acts as singing bands of milk cartons, talking farm animals and other serendipitous mechanical creations.

Day-trippers can also eat on premises at Stew Leonard's. The Norwalk region lends itself to comestibles. In South Norwalk, savor fresh seafood at **Ocean Drive** (203-855-1665; www.oceandrivesono.com), open for lunch and dinner daily. Next door at 124 Washington Street, **Porterhouse Chophouse & Bar** (203-855-0441; porterhouserestaurant.com), open for lunch and dinner Monday through Saturday and dinner all day Sunday, is a carnivore's delight. At 86 Washington, **Relish Food & Wine** (203-854-5300), open daily with a focus on everything American, has mustered joy from the crackerjack patrons, including an *excellent* rating by the *New York Times*. Weekend party animals and patrons who want the "best burgers in town" should head to **Black Bear Saloon** (203-299-0711; www.blackbearsono. com), 80 Washington Street, serving lunch and dinner daily. If you have a yen for Mexican-style cuisine, add **Al Acapulco** (203-853-6217), 84 Washington, to the list.

Sono Seaport Restaurant & Market (203-854-9483) at 100 Water Street, provides a romantic view of Norwalk Harbor for lunch and dinner daily. For nearly 40 years, **Famous Pizza** (203-838-6100) at 23 North Main Street has proved to be a popular spot for lunch and dinner daily. Art, music and really neat stuff for sale complements the African and Caribbean food served in the tropical setting at **Shacojazz Art Café** (203-853-6124; www.shacojazz.com), 21 North Main, open for lunch and dinner daily. For barbeque and ribs, try **Jeff's Cuisine** (203-852-0041), 54 North Main, open for lunch and dinner daily.

At 70 North Main Street, serving from a "Cuban-chic" menu, **Habana** (203-852-9790), open for lunch and dinner daily, consistently wins rave reviews from diners and professional reviewers. Sample what consumers and connoisseurs have billed as the "best beer selection in SoNo" at the **Brewhouse Restaurant** (203-853-9110), 13 Marshall Street, serving lunch and dinner daily. At 24 Marshall, just look for the exterior bright sign posted outside of **Papaya Thai and Asian BBQ** (203-866-THAI [8424]), open for lunch and dinner daily. Before leaving SoNo, **Caffeine, Coffee & Chocolate Lounge** (203-857-4224), open daily, is the place to recline and brush up on people-watching skills.

In East Norwalk, the **Fat Cat Pie Company** (203-523-0389) has reaped numerous devotees with its amicable nighttime jazz and blues performances and lip smacking, thin-crust, brick oven pizza layered with organic toppings. Local newspaper reviews have praised the vegetarian cuisine served at the **Lime Restaurant** (203-846-9240; www.limerestaurant.com). First opened in 1979, boasting gourmet natural foods with limited meat selections, the restaurant is open for lunch and dinner daily. For breakfast, lunch and dinner daily, **Adam's Rib Restaurant** (800-303-0808; 203-838-5531; www.norwalkinn.com/restaurant/home.asp), located at the **Norwalk Inn & Conference Center**, has provided an American-style menu for more than 50 years. On the other side of town, be prepared to wait for lunch at **Swanky Frank's** (203-838-8969), 182 Connecticut Avenue, open daily and serving legendary hot dogs since the 1940s.

On the northern outskirts of Norwalk, for lunch, Monday through Saturday (closed Tuesday and closed on Monday from January through April); dinner on Wednesday through Saturday and an award-winning Sunday brunch; it always feels like a special occasion feasting at the **Silvermine Tavern Inn** (888-693-9967; 203- 847-4558; www.silverminetavern.com), 194 Perry Avenue. At this Colonial inn (see **Accommodations**), colder days are spent dining by the fireplace; milder weather means the patio is open. Day-trippers, who did not get their fill of shopping, can arrive Wednesday through Monday from 12 p.m. to 6 p.m. at the **Silvermine Country Store**; a browser's haven of New England foods and collectibles, not to mention a tempting array of old-fashioned candies. When cooking at home, consider purchasing fresh fish (shad from late April through May) at **Pagano's Seafood** (203-831-9670), 86 Scribner Avenue.

GETTING THERE:
Norwalk is approximately 48 miles northeast of New York City, 33 miles southwest of New Haven and 72 miles southwest of Hartford. Norwalk is at the intersection of many major highways and roads. The city is easily accessible from Interstate Highway 95; the Merritt Parkway (Route 15); Route 7 and U.S. Route 1 (the Boston Post Road).

TRANSPORTATION:
Stratford's Sikorsky Memorial Airport is approximately 17 miles from Norwalk. Tweed New Haven Regional Airport is approximately 33 miles driving distance, providing daily service to 126 cities through US Airways and Delta Airlines. The area is approximately 82 miles southwest of Bradley International Airport in Windsor Locks. The three major New York City metro airports are Westchester County Airport, LaGuardia, JFK and Newark Airport in New Jersey. Danbury Municipal Airport, a small, private airport, is approximately 23 miles in driving distance. The Norwalk Transit District (203-852-0000) operates frequent commuter-connection buses from and around the Norwalk vicinity. Both Metro-North stations (800-METRO-INFO) and Amtrak (800-872-7245) offer daily commuter service to New York City and New Haven. The four railroad stations are Rowayton, South Norwalk, East Norwalk and Merritt 7.

ADDITIONAL INFORMATION:
THE MARITIME AQUARIUM AT NORWALK.
10 North Water Street. Open all year, daily. Inquire about two and one-half hour Marine Life Study Cruises ($19.50 for adults and children) that run from mid-April through September. Off-season, check out fall foliage and winter creature cruises at the same price. General aquarium admission is $9.75 adults; $9.00 seniors; $7.75 children and free to children 1 and under and to museum members. (203) 852-0700; www.maritimeaquarium.org.

STEPPING STONES MUSEUM FOR CHILDREN.
303 West Avenue. The museum and on-premises café are open all year, Tuesday through Sunday. General admission is $7.00; free to children 1 and under and to museum members; also free on the last Thursday of every month from 5 p.m. to 8 p.m. (203) 899-0606; www.steppingstonesmuseum.org.

LOCKWOOD-MATHEWS MANSION MUSEUM.

295 West Avenue. Open mid-March to December, Wednesday through Sunday; or by appointment; call about gift shop hours. Inquire about the Music at the Mansion series and other special events. General admission is $8.00 adults; $5.00 seniors; $5.00 students; free to children 12 and under and to museum members. (203) 838-9799; www.lockwoodmathewsmansion.org.

THE CENTER FOR CONTEMPORARY PRINTMAKING.

299 West Avenue. Open all year, Monday through Saturday. Inquire about occasional Sunday receptions for art show openings. General admission is free. (203) 899-7999; www.contemprints.org.

NORWALK MUSEUM.

41 Main Street. Open all year, Wednesday through Sunday. General admission is free. (203) 866-0202.

SONO SWITCH TOWER MUSEUM.

77 Washington Street. Open May through October, Saturday and Sunday. General admission is free. (203) 246-6958; www.westctnrhs.org/tower.htm.

ACCOMMODATIONS:

Norwalk lodging includes **Clarion Hotel** (203-853-3477), **Courtyard by Marriott** (203-849-9111), **Four Points Hotel** (203-849-9828) and the new 266-guestroom **Doubletree Hotel** (203-853-3477; 203-222-TREE).

NORWALK INN & CONFERENCE CENTER.

99 East Avenue. The town's only family-owned and operated, full-service hotel, restaurant and lounge, it boasts 71 recently redecorated guestrooms; suites and on-site restaurant (see above). The inn also offers full, modern amenities, including full business-traveler services. Rates (including complimentary, full breakfast Monday through Friday): $79-$149. (800) 303-0808; (203) 838-5531; www.norwalkinn.com/the_hotel/home.asp.

SILVERMINE TAVERN INN.

194 Perry Avenue. The award-winning setting (reserve it for romantic occasions!) in this more than 200-year-old New England country inn, located by Silvermine River, invites weary travelers to experience its 11 comfortable guestrooms furnished with antiques complete with canopied beds; all with private baths. Cozy and private, guests who insist upon telephones and televisions can find them in the parlor; the on-premises restaurant is highly acclaimed (see above). Rates (including continental breakfast, featuring famed "Silvermine Honey Buns"; inquire about weekend packages and special events): $140-$185-plus. (888) 693-9967; (203) 847-4558; www.silverminetavern.com.

ANNUAL FESTIVALS/EVENTS

Norwalk's Coastal Fairfield County Convention & Visitor Bureau, representing 15 southwestern communities, provides a gamut of tourism information, including seasonal events (800) 866-7925 or (203) 853-7770; www.coastalct.com. Additionally, the Norwalk Parks Department provides a summer listing of outdoor concerts and will help visitors with other questions, (203) 854-7806.

APRIL

For a breath of spring, schedule a visit to Lockwood-Mathews Mansion Museum's breathtaking **Spring Garden Show**. Also, attend the gala preview party and Antiques Auto Show. (203) 838-9799.

JUNE-JULY

Shakespeare on the Sound provides free, professional, open-air productions of the plays of William Shakespeare. Join the performances held in Pinkney Park at Five Mile River in Rowayton. (203) 299-1300.

JUNE

The **Norwalk Harbor Splash Festival** features music and entertainment, food, boat races, parades and many other fun events and activities geared for all ages. Held on South Norwalk's Washington Street and created in 1995, the festival, among other things, promotes public awareness of Norwalk's need to protect and preserve the global water environment. (203) 853-7770; (800) 866-7925; www. norwalk.ws/splashfestival.

Music lovers should make note of the **Annual Spring Concert** performances by the Norwalk Community Chorale held at the Norwalk City Hall's Mary McCarthy Rehearsal Room, 125 East Avenue. (800) 866-7925.

JULY

Thousands of people attend the **Annual Round Hill Highland Scottish Games**, which not only features a gamut of fun, but also vendors and a variety of Celtic music and activities. (914) 242-0581.

AUGUST

Held in historic South Norwalk, the **SoNo Arts Festival** is a non-profit celebration to support original music, art and community spirit. Among the festivities are sculpture races and puppet parades. (800) 866-7925; (203) 853-7770.

SEPTEMBER

The **Oyster Festival** at Veteran's Park is one of the most recognizable and anticipated events in the state of Connecticut, drawing thousands of spectators. Vendors galore and many acclaimed musical bands set the stage for a day of food, drink and merriment. (203) 854-7806; www.seaport.org/default.htm.

The **International In-Water Boat Show** at Norwalk Cove Marina ranks as the largest boat show on the East Coast and attracts spectators from all corners of the world. Priced for every budget, displays include yachts, cruisers, sport fishers, performance boats, personal watercrafts and sailboats. (212) 984-7000; www. boatshownorwalk.com.

Lockwood-Mathews Mansion Museum offers its venerable **Annual Antiques Show** with pre-event annual gala and other festivities. (203) 838-9799; www. lockwoodmathewsmansion.org.

OCTOBER
Fall Foliage Cruises are some of the best ways to see Mother Nature's colors. Sponsored by the Maritime Aquarium, guides interpret the natural setting along the shores of Long Island Sound. (203) 852-0700; www.maritimeaquarium.org.

DECEMBER
Call the Lockwood-Mathews Mansion Museum staff to inquire about the annual **Victorian Christmas Celebration**. (203) 838-9799; www. lockwoodmathewsmansion.org.

Maritime Aquarium
See page 225

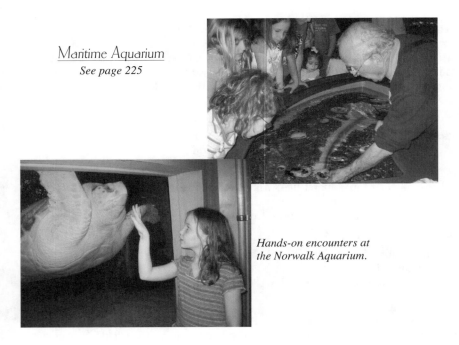

Hands-on encounters at the Norwalk Aquarium.

---

*In what Connecticut city's coastline can one attempt
to search for Captain Kidd's lost treasure?*

*What Connecticut city was home to producing
the famous elixir, Milk of Magnesia?*

Dream Boat: **STAMFORD**

In 1640, a fervid dispute caused irreversible friction, splitting the Church of Christ in Wethersfield. Although the exact cause of the disagreement is long forgotten, what resulted was what we now know as Stamford. By 1641, dissenters, probably some 30 families, including that of a minister's, under the coterie of the Wethersfield Company, began building their own meetinghouse after settling along the banks of what is present-day Long Island Sound, approximately 75 miles southwest from their Wethersfield roots.

Being the eleventh in order of colony settlements, settlers purchased the Indian territory of Rippowam, naming it Stamford in 1642, adopted from Stamford in Lincolnshire, England. The Revolutionary War brought two major enemies to town: loyalists and those known as skinner vandals who stole the community's provisions and sold them to the British and pirates. Pirates sequestered their vessels in the inlets of the coastline; legend states that the infamous Captain Kidd hid his (to this day unfound!) treasure somewhere in these coastways.

Stamford's transformation from an agricultural village of English Puritans to a bustling and diverse industrial hub started in 1848 after it became a regular New York, New Haven and Hartford train stop. Even before the onset of the Civil War, two manufacturing companies had established public fame. First, the Stamford Manufacturing Company became popular for selling sought-after dyes and licorice pastes, and then the Charles H. Phillips Company became famous for producing Milk of Magnesia.

The milieu drastically changed, however, when hundreds of impoverished Irish refugees, fleeing the potato famine of 1845, swelled the town's population, threatening the overtly Anglo-Saxon religion and culture. In turn, crime increased as a result of a new wave of anti-Catholicism. The Civil War was paradoxical in Stamford's history. Along with causing fatalities among residents who fought in the war, it helped ease relations with the Irish who enlisted as soldiers in record numbers.

Starting in the mid-1800s and continuing for the next two centuries, Stamford's primary market for exporting products like oats, fish and oysters by rail was New York City; although it did ship some goods as far as the West Indies. To meet the demands of urbanization, in 1893 a new entity was formed: the city of Stamford. By 1900, the population had reached 19,000. Today, boasting 120,000 people and 39 square miles, it is the fourth largest city in the state and the second largest in Fairfield County.

Located about 40 miles from New York City, companies such as Xerox, Pitney Bowes and GE Capital helped the city achieve its status as the third largest corporate headquarters community in the country.

Stamford residents as well as visitors have a cornucopia of attractions, including entertainment and shopping venues at their disposal in a city that also houses a branch of the University of Connecticut. Newfield Avenue's Italian Center of Stamford, featuring many special events throughout the year, is just one ingredient in the city's ethnic stew. Stamford's devotion to art is exemplified annually in its downtown streets. In the summer, in collaboration with the Stamford Downtown Special Services District, a collection of outdoor sculptures by a variety of talented artists is exhibited. At the end of the season, the sculptures hit the auction block and the proceeds are allotted to local charities.

Summer and early fall mean Stamford's **Downtown French Market** at West Park featuring Connecticut-grown produce. Likewise, to soften its urban image, the city possesses a roster of natural elements, namely two public golf courses, two public beaches and a well-maintained park system.

Day trips with panache roll up Stamford's green sleeve in the northern part of town to uncover the **Stamford Nature Center and Museum**. This 118-acre sprawl presents themes of history, agriculture and the arts among six nature trails of forests, rocky hillsides, bird and butterfly gardens, creeks and streams. Visitors can embark on the main Gothic-style building museum, hosting five themes: natural history of New England, 19th- and 20th-century American art, Native American art and culture, Early American and pre-World War II art and culture. Inside, stargazers, for a nominal fee, can explore the infinite worlds of outer space at the planetarium.

Leaving the museum, a jaunt past the totem pole guides visitors into Heckscher Farm, a 10-acre working farm that typifies New England. The country store brimming with neat gift ideas for all ages is perfect to complement the journey. Back outdoors, families shouldn't miss the playground, complete with a tree house.

Just off Scofieldtown Road, behind Heckscher Farm, those interested in firsthand celestial pursuits can scan the heavens at the **Observatory**. The Fairfield County Astronomical Society invites nighttime trippers Friday evenings throughout the year.

Abutting the Stamford Nature center is the 91-acre **Bartlett Arboretum and Gardens**. Whether bird watching, hiking or simply marveling at Mother Nature's artistry as the garden blooms, this is a seasonal oasis for all ages complete with boardwalk and marked ecology trails. Tour the visitor's center offering changing art exhibits and greenhouse.

Scofieldtown Road connects to Route 137, the location of the **Stamford Historical Society and History Center**. Founded in 1901, the facility presents a varied collection of exhibits documenting Stamford's historical significance in the state as well as in the country. On premises are also an extensive research library, book corner where patrons can purchase local history books and the **Shop Downstairs**, chockfull of used and new furniture, accessories, collectible and gift items; whereby all proceeds benefit the society.

Sometimes on weekends and during appointments only (203-329-1183; www. stamfordhistory.org), the Stamford Historical Society opens to the public the **Hoyt Barnum House** at 713 Bedford Street. Families of Stamford's first settlers built this post-1675, central-chimney, wooden structure. Hang out longer and enjoy a Thursday evening concert in July or August on the lawn, or in the event of rain, held in the Fellowship Hall of the **First Presbyterian Church**. The Avalon Bay Company at the church, featuring a carillon program followed by jazz-style music, sponsors these free concerts. Weekdays (call first, 203-324-9522), church officials welcome visitors to explore the unique fish-shaped edifice that inside, among other things, displays stained glass windows by Gabriel Loire of France and the largest mechanical action pipe organ in the state.

Those seeking aquatic adventure should make note of the **SoundWaters Community Center for Environmental Education**. Headquartered in the historic Holley House, the center features hands-on exhibits, special programs, workshops and jazz concerts in order to meet its mission of educating the public about Long Island Sound and protecting its watershed.

In the same vicinity, less than a mile in distance, two public beaches (call 203-977-4688 for information about fees for nonresident day passes and seasonal passes) **Cove Island Park** and **Cummings Park/West Beach** invite swimmers and sun worshippers in the warmer months. Open all year is the **Terry Conners Public Ice Rink at Cove Island Park** (203-977-4513, inquire about facility fees; days and hours of operation). Day-trippers at Cove Island Park will also discover more than 83 acres of fishing opportunities, playgrounds, a pavilion, in-season concessions and marina, picnic grounds and horseshoe pits.

Cummings Park/West Beach boasts 79-plus acres that include a boardwalk and fishing pier; marina; tennis, handball and basketball courts; pavilion and snack bar. Both parks offer public boat launch ramps and Cove Island Park is handicapped accessible. Stamford's **Southfield Park** is also open to nonresidents with a day pass. There is no swimming allowed, but fishing is permitted and tennis and basketball courts and a baseball field are provided.

Lighthouse lovers should keep an eye out for the **Stamford Harbor Lighthouse**, lit in 1882, 3,600 feet away from shore; it typifies the sparkplug-style tower. Surrounded by historical tales and tragic sagas, the best way to view the structure is by boat.

Nature lovers have hundreds of acres of green space to explore, from the 185-plus acres of sprawling nature trails at Westover Road's **Mianus River Park and Glen** to the charming six-acre **Chestnut Hill Bird Sanctuary**. The 18-hole **E. Gaynor Brennan Golf Course** (203-324-4185; www.ci.stamford.ct.us/EGaynorBrennanGolfCourse/default.asp), located close to downtown, is open to the public and extends a short (5,900 yard), but challenging course. Going north, at 1349 Newfield Avenue, the **Sterling Farms Public Golf Course** (203-461-9090; www.sterlingfarmsgc.com/sterlingfarms/outside_frame.asp) is an 18-hole, Brent-designed grass course built in 1971.

At this same Newfield Avenue address is **Curtain Call** (203-329-8207; www.curtaincallinc.com). The non-profit, community-based theater company presents a variety of productions at two Newfield Avenue sites: the **Kweskin Theatre** and **Dressing Room Theatre**.

A year-round school for the performing arts, **Stamford Theatre Works** (203-359-4414; www.stamfordtheatreworks.org), 200 Strawberry Hill Avenue, is an award-winning, professional theater that produces four shows (September through May) each season. The largest theatrical venue in Stamford is the **Palace Theatre and Rich Forum** (203-325-4466; www.onlyatsca.com) at 307 Atlantic Street, a premiere showcase of talent, operated by the Stamford Center for the Performing Arts, a not-for-profit organization. Both the Rich Forum and Palace Theatre present hundreds of performances, special events and workshops throughout the year, including those by top-name performers as well as local favorites: the **Stamford Symphony Orchestra**, the **Connecticut Grand Opera and Orchestra** and the **Ballet School of Stamford**. Dilettantes should be aware of the changing exhibits at **Sackler Gallery at the Palace Theatre** (203-325-4466). Consider, too, the

Stamford Art Association Townhouse Gallery (203-325-1139) for viewing changing art displays.

Day-trippers with shopping in mind can head for downtown's **Stamford Town Center** mall (203-324-0935; www.shopstamfordtowncenter.com), 100 Greyrock Place, which has more than 130 shops and restaurants. Opened in 1982, its multi-level complex received notoriety when actor Woody Allen and his crew filmed *Scenes from a Mall* (1991) there. About two miles north at 535 Hope Street, **United House Wrecking** (203-348-5371; www.unitedhousewrecking.com) started in 1954 as a family-operated demolition company and today sells nearly everything under the sun. Furniture and accessories spread over 35,000 square feet including two and one-half acres of outdoor displays.

Families seeking a pleasurable outing should visit **Fun for Kids and Grownups Too!** (203-326-5656; www.fun4kidsarcade.com), 370 West Main Street. This entertainment center unveils a cornucopia of video games and one of the largest, most sophisticated computerized laser tag arenas anywhere. Day passes can be had for indoor rock climbing at **Go Vertical** (203-358-8767; www.govertical.com), 727 Canal Street. Those who want to **Knit Together** (203-324-YARN [9276]) are advised to dangle into this community yarn shop. Located at 111 High Ridge Road, knitters will not only discover a ubiquitous supply of accessories, but also a knowledgeable staff ready to help with any project.

Throughout the year, there is always an opportune time to dine in Stamford. **Telluride** (203-357-7679; www.telluriderestaurant.com) at 245 Bedford Street, allows day-trippers to surround themselves in a rustic, yet elegant, country-farmhouse atmosphere filled with soft peach-colored walls and candlelight. An award-winning, contemporary-American menu is offered for lunch, Monday through Friday, and dinner daily. *Zagat* survey rated **Chez Jean-Pierre** (203-357-9526) at 188 Bedford Street *excellent*; it provides a bistro-type atmosphere for lunch and dinner, daily. Every Wednesday night, a visiting band performs in the cocktail lounge.

Another award-winner, **Ocean 211** (203-973-0494) at 211 Summer Street, boasts a signature oyster bar and seafood entrees and is open for lunch and dinner, Monday through Friday, Saturday dinner and Sunday brunch. **Zanghi** (203-327-3663), 201 Summer, open for dinner Monday through Saturday, serves a seasonal menu with French and Italian influences. An appealing wine list, homemade desserts and the chef-owner laboring in the kitchen have helped it earn a rating of *excellent* from the *New York Times* and it has been described by *Zagat* as *one of America's top restaurants*. At number 222, **Zinc Bistro and Bar** (203-252-2352), open for lunch Monday through Saturday and dinner, daily, has received much praise for its French and global-influenced menu.

At 21 Atlantic Street, near the Palace Theatre, **Wish Café** (203-961-0690), with its New American cuisine and Asian-inspired menu, is open for lunch Monday through Friday and dinner daily. Venerable **Long Ridge Tavern** (203-359-4747), 2635 Long Ridge Road, open Tuesday through Sunday, lunch and dinner, radiating with a rustic atmosphere that is warmed in the colder months with a firestone fireplace, twirls a wand of magic on the most ordinary occasion.

A legendary, family-owned and operated restaurant is **Columbus Park Trattoria** (203-962-9191; www.columbusparktrattoria.com), 205 Main Street, open for lunch Monday through Friday and dinner, Monday through Saturday. This Italian eatery is known for its homemade (and that means by hand!) pastas, loyal customers and devoted staff.

Patrons swear by the freshly prepared and substantial dishes served at **Bull's Head Diner** (203-961-1400), 43 High Ridge Road. Open 24/7 for breakfast, lunch and dinner, just look for its art deco, sleek exterior. **City Limits Diner** (203-348-7000), 135 Harvard Avenue, also open 24/7 for breakfast, lunch and dinner, provides another popular eating experience. In the mood for a sweet treat? The friendly folks at **Sunny Daes** (203-977-0661), 633 Shippan Avenue, offer some of the tastiest and creamiest homemade ice cream in the state, if not the world! Try the eggnog flavor in November and December and don't forget an extra doggie-size scoop for canine friends.

GETTING THERE:

Stamford is approximately 40 miles northeast of New York City, 41 miles southwest of New Haven and 81 miles southwest of Hartford. Stamford is at the intersection of many major highways and roads. The city is easily accessible from Interstate Highway 95; the Merritt Parkway (Route 15); Route 137 and U.S. Route 1 (the Boston Post Road).

TRANSPORTATION:

Stratford's Sikorsky Memorial Airport is approximately 26 miles from Stamford. Tweed New Haven Regional Airport is approximately 41 miles driving distance, providing daily service to 126 cities through US Airways and Delta Airlines. The area is approximately 92 miles southwest of Bradley International Airport in Windsor Locks. The three major New York City metro airports are Westchester County Airport, LaGuardia, JFK and Newark Airport in New Jersey. Danbury Municipal Airport, a small, private airport, is approximately 32 miles in driving distance. The CT Transit District (203-333-3031) and the Norwalk Transit District (203-852-0000) operate frequent commuter-connection buses from and around the Stamford vicinity. The Stamford Transportation Center, located at Station Place; between Washington Boulevard and Atlantic Street, provides Metro-North (800-METRO-INFO) trains to connecting cities as does Amtrak (800-872-7245). Both Metro-North station and Amtrak offer daily commuter service to New York City.

ADDITIONAL INFORMATION:
STAMFORD NATURE CENTER AND MUSEUM.

39 Scofieldtown Road. Open all year, daily; except for Mondays, call for off-season schedule. The facility is completely handicapped accessible and stroller friendly. General admission is $3.00 adults (Stamford residents); $6.00 adults (nonresidents); $2.00 seniors/children 14 and under (Stamford residents); $5.00 seniors/children 14 and under (nonresidents) and free to children 3 and under. General admission for the planetarium is $2.00 adults and $1.00 children 5 and under. General admission for the observatory is $3.00, which is open all year, Friday evenings. (203) 322-1646; www.stamfordmuseum.org/home.html.

BARTLETT ARBORETUM.

Brookdale Road. Open all year, from 8:30 a.m. to sunset, daily. Visitor's Center is open all year, Monday through Friday. Greenhouse is open weekday mornings (call first). General admission is free, but donations accepted. (203) 322-6971; www.bartlett.arboretum.uconn.edu/.

STAMFORD HISTORICAL SOCIETY AND HISTORY CENTER.
1508 High Ridge Road. Open all year, Tuesday through Saturday. The Shop Downstairs is open all year, Friday through Saturday. (203) 329-1183; www. stamfordhistory.org.

SOUNDWATERS, COMMUNITY CENTER FOR ENVIRONMENTAL EDUCATION.
Cove Island Park. 1281 Cove Road. Open all year, Tuesday through Saturday. The center is handicapped accessible. Preregistration is required for programs, workshops and daytime ecology and evening sunset sails; ships leave from Brewer Yacht Haven Marina. General admission to the center is free. Parking is free except from Memorial Day through Labor Day. Stamford residents must have a valid beach sticker to park at Cove Park; nonresidents are required to preregister for programs to obtain a SoundWaters parking pass. (203) 323-1978; www.soundwaters.org.

ACCOMMODATIONS:
Stamford's myriad lodging choices include the **Super 8 Motel** (203-324-8887), **Rodeway Inn** (203-324-8887) and **Holiday Inn Select** (203-358-8400).

HAMPTON INN AT MILL RIVER.
26 Mill River Street. Located on the waterfront, the guestrooms are elegant and offer full, modern amenities, including kitchen area with microwave and refrigerator. Rates (including continental breakfast): $159-$220. (203) 353-9855.

STAMFORD MARRIOTT HOTEL AND SPA.
Two Stamford Forum. Located in the heart of downtown, 506 guestrooms are available to day-trippers who decide to stay the night. There is an on-premises bar and restaurant, business center, health club and indoor and outdoor swimming pools and indoor golf range with instruction. Enjoy the new Agora full-service spa. Rates: $100-$279. (203) 357-9555; www.marriott.com/property/propertypage/STFCT.

WESTIN STAMFORD.
One First Stamford Place. Boasting a recent renovation, the 476 guestrooms and suites meet the traveler in full elegance and offer full, modern amenities. The lobby with its escalating atrium is a real showstopper; other hotel features include fitness room, outdoor tennis courts, dining room and lounge and the option to bring the family pet. Rates: $95–$369. (203) 967-2222.

ANNUAL FESTIVALS/EVENTS
The Coastal Fairfield County Convention & Visitor Bureau, representing 15 southwestern communities, provides a gamut of tourism information, including seasonal events (800) 866-7925 or (203) 853-7770; www.coastalct.com. For additional festival and event information, contact the Stamford Downtown Special Services District, (203) 348-5285.

MARCH
The nation's oldest and largest crossword competition is the **Annual American Crossword Puzzle Tournament** at the Stamford Marriott. Judges base scoring on accuracy and speed of solving eight crossword puzzles created specifically for

the event. Prizes are awarded in more than 20 categories, including a 4,000-dollar grand prize. Guest speakers and a wine and cheese reception are also part of the event. (203) 357-9555; www.crosswordtournament.com.

MAY

The Bartlett Arboretum's annual **Spring Plant Sale** offers visitors more than 250 species of perennials, shrubs and trees. Master gardeners are also on hand to answer questions. (203) 322-6971; www.bartlett.arboretum.uconn.edu.

Stamford Cherry Blossom Festival happens at Mill River Park, Washington Boulevard at Broad Street. Asian-style performances, including drumming circles, games, storytelling, origami crafts and more! (203) 348-5285.

JUNE/JULY

Join other spectators at the **Free Summer Concert Series**, headlining regional and national acts, held at Columbus Park in Stamford's downtown area. (203) 348-5285.

SoundWaters' Tall Ships Ball is a major fundraiser for the organization and features entertainment, dancing and a live auction at the Riverside Yacht Club. (203) 323-1978; www.soundwaters.org.

SEPTEMBER

The **Downtown Stamford Arts and Crafts Show** is a juried show displaying hundreds of wares. Held at Veteran's Park, treasures include paintings, jewelry, ceramics and many other items. (203) 348-5285.

The **Fall Plant Sale** held at the Bartlett Arboretum displays popular flowers, trees and shrubs as well as hard-to-find exotic plant types. Master gardeners are also on hand to answer questions. (203) 322-6971; (203) 322-6971; www.bartlett. arboretum.uconn.edu.

The Stamford Nature Center and Museum features a **Corny Harvest Day** celebrating America's number one field crop: corn. Everything corn-related, including contests and arts and crafts and food, is the call of the day. (203) 322-1646; www.stamfordmuseum.org/home.html.

Conservation Day is an annual celebration taking place at SoundWaters, Community Center for Environmental Education at Cove Island Park. Conservation-themed displays, family art projects, live animals and entertainment are just part of the day's festivities. (203) 323-1978; www.soundwaters.org.

Want to witness (or purchase) those renowned Ukrainian Easter eggs (called pysanky)? Schedule a visit to the **Ukrainian Day Festival**, one of the largest in the state, held at St. Basil College Seminary, 195 Glenbrook Road. Lots of food, crafts and entertainment make the day go by swiftly. Don't miss the on-premises museum (call first to prearrange a tour of the museum during the rest of the year). (203) 324-4578.

OCTOBER

Oktoberfest at the Stamford Museum and Nature Center is a day of food, music and traditional seasonal activities. (203) 322-1646; www.stamfordmuseum.org/ home.html.

NOVEMBER

Stamford's Balloon Parade is an annual Thanksgiving holiday extravaganza that draws more than 200,000 spectators from near and far. Featuring more than 20 giant helium balloons, it represents one of the largest events of its kind in the country. (203) 348-5285.

DECEMBER

The **Family Winter Festival** at the Bartlett Arboretum is a weekend celebration that includes a petting zoo and craft classes for children, special guided tours, presentations, music and food. (203) 322-6971.

Heights and Lights Rappelling Santa Claus and Colossal Tree-Lighting Ceremony is a not-to-be-missed holiday tradition in which Santa climbs, flips and flies 22 stories down downtown's tallest building at Landmark Square, and then leads the parade up Bedford Street to Latham Park for the annual lighting of the city's Christmas tree.

Pysanky
Page 239

Ukrainian Easter Eggs, just one of the many ethnic goodies that can be found at Stamford's Ukrainian Day Festival.

🛞 🛞 🛞 🛞 🛞 🛞 🛞 🛞

What Connecticut town did Indians
barter for 25 winter coats?

What town is known as the "Bel Air" of Connecticut?

Old Money, New-Fangled Treks: **GREENWICH**

In 1640, a handful of expanding New Haven colonists paid the Native Siwanoy Indians "twentie-five coates" (yes, warm winter coats!) in exchange for what today constitutes the Old Greenwich region. Ranking tenth, following the town of Fairfield in order of establishment, the Indian name "Patuqaupaen" was changed to Greenwich, named after Greenwich, Kent, England, located near London. Shortly thereafter, in an attempt to broaden territory, English and Dutch settlers massacred much of the tribe; only to wrangle with each other during the forthcoming years; until the rest of the land was completely surrendered to the English.

As the settlement spread to the east, west, and north and abutted the southern shoreline, so did crops of potatoes, grain and fruit. By 1730, the Mianus River was dotted with gristmills and ships. When the Revolutionary War ignited, Greenwich ended up playing the role of a garrison town and, thus, became prone to town raids. In 1779, British troops pillaged the town, and General Israel Putnam achieved his famous ride east to warn Stamford residents of approaching enemy forces.

The advent of the railroad in 1848 maximized town development. Hotels rose above the coastline to accommodate summer visitors leaving nearby New York City in search of summer pleasures. Greenwich lured prominent city families with surnames like Rockefeller, Milbank and Bruce. They, in turn, built vast estates, giving the town its "Bel Air" aura, at the same time creating the opulent neighborhoods of Belle Haven, Field Point Park, Byram Shore and Rock Ridge.

Today, with a residential population of 61,101 spanning over 50 square miles and bordering New York State, Greenwich along with neighboring Darien and New Canaan is the most expensive town to live in, not only in Connecticut, but in much of the country. To illustrate this point, in summer 2004, famous pop artist, resident, Diana Ross, just one of the famous town celebrities, held a charity concert to raise money for the teen center. The result: some 400 people paid between 250 to 1,000 dollars per ticket. Additionally, among Greenwich Country Day School's alumni is President George H.W. Bush. His boyhood address was 15 Grove Lane, a private residence today.

The town's 32 miles of shoreline and some other attractions have, historically, been guarded from nonresidents (unless they are guests of a Greenwich resident); examples include four-acre Island Beach—reached by the town-owned ferry (with terrific views of the 1868 Great Captain Island Lighthouse); the prestigious Griffith E. Harris Memorial Golf Course and the Dorothy Hamill Skating Rink, named after the Olympic gold medal figure skater who learned to skate at local Binney Park pond in the winter!

Ultra-exclusive Round Hill Club's walls have seen many of the nation's most rich and powerful. However, after a monumental Supreme Court case, launched by a Stamford-resident lawyer who sued the town, Greenwich was, at least, forced to amend its stringent beach-access policy.

With this in mind, summer day trips with panache can evolve with a blanket spread on the sands of **Greenwich Point** (203-622-7824; inquire about day fees between April 15 through November 14), also known as **Tod's Point**, a 147-acre beach property that is now open to out-of-towners. Picturesque coastline views of the Manhattan skyline set the stage for perfect picnic gatherings; in-season food concessions are available for day-trippers who arrive without edibles. Handicapped accessibility, areas for shell fishing and generous hiking trails aid other daytime pursuits.

Unlike the coastline, the town of Greenwich extends dozens of parks and recreational areas to nonresidents. On the Stamford border, adjacent to Stamford's **Rosa Hartman Park**, the 18 acres of **Laddins Rock Sanctuary** (203-622-7814) is located on Highmeadow Road in Old Greenwich. Desirable biking and walking trails are just one of the draws. All-season bird-watchers should look for migratory birds in May and September and the great horned owl in the winter months. Of greatest appeal, perhaps, is the legend behind the sanctuary that goes back to 1643. It is said that during Indian-settler warfare, a Dutchman named Cornelius Labden, later anglicized Laddin, escaped a raid in which his wife and daughter were scalped. He rode on horseback to the high ledge in what is today the sanctuary and made a daring leap, leaving him bruised, but alive. Folklore has it that only one Indian survived out of the tribe members who tried (but failed) to catch him by attempting the same feat.

Heading westward, back to town, **Putnam Cemetery**, 35 Parsonage Road, is an off-the-beaten-track, park-like escape for quiet walks or bike rides. Some of the luminary gravesites include the Milbank mausoleum, containing remains of the railroad magnate's family; elder President Bush's parents, and the infamous Martha Moxley, whose 1970s murder, spurring author Dominick Dunne to write the 1993 bestseller, *A Season in Purgatory*, continues to haunt the town today.

Traveling about three miles east from the cemetery, the non-profit **Garden Education Center** (203-869-9242) at 130 Bible Street, opens its library, gift shop, greenhouse and grounds to the public during the week. Outdoors, experience a spectacular collection of lush forestry, wildflowers and unusual specimen plantings in 102 acres called **Montgomery Pinetum**, a registered historic site and public park.

Heavily developed downtown contains three green treasures. **Roger Sherman Baldwin Park** (203-622-7814), home to municipal buildings including the ferry ticket terminal and teen center, with its sweeping views of Greenwich Harbor and Long Island Sound, invites daytime fishermen and fisherwomen. Serene walkways, colorful birds, including an occasional osprey, picnic benches veiled with weeping willows, all inspire romance. In the summer, a variety of musical concerts and performances echo through parts of its six-plus acres. (Greenwich Common on Greenwich Avenue, and Binney Park, south of the Post Road, are two other venues that present summer concerts.)

Grass Island, just off Shore Road, is the location of the **Greenwich Boat and Yacht Club**. This 14-acre property complete with grass marshes is open only to town residents; however, it contains a public marina. With water fountains, gazebo, ponds in which the largest one affords ice-skating in the winter, and a bit more than

60 acres wrapped in a multi-hued and rich-textured setting of natural terrain, **Bruce Memorial Park** is an eye-pleaser throughout the year. Spring, however, is probably the most beautiful when the landscape is a splash with deep-toned daffodils, azaleas and dogwoods; subsequently, summer arrives with blooms of brightly colored roses. Bird watching and fishing are optimum as are jogging or bicycling on the marked trails. Four-season people-watching is another option, especially in warmer weather months when the Greenwich Lawn Bowling Association competes on its bowling green. Don't hesitate to bring a lunch—picnic facilities are plentiful.

Bring the younger brood and enjoy FamilyLand, a fully equipped playground including handicapped-accessible equipment. The play area leads day-trippers to the western entrance of the **Bruce Museum of Arts and Science**. Opened in 1912, after Robert Moffat Bruce, a wealthy textile merchant, deeded to the public what was once his house and designated it to become a museum, a gift that included the surrounding park property. Museum grounds highlight an array of sculptures, including a 35-foot totem pole presented to commemorate the museum's 75th anniversary.

The Bruce contains about 15,000 items showcasing the fields of fine and decorative arts, natural history and anthropology. It also presents annually 14 changing exhibits of par excellence, while its permanent exhibitions include a mineral gallery, a marine tank with live animals and displays that teach visitors about the area's environmental and historical development.

Visit the on-premises gift shop featuring an exquisite selection of items ranging from jewelry to teapots and some of the most breathtaking decorative stones. Deirdre Jessica Stein, museum store buyer and manager, says it's not unusual for museum visitors who stop in the store first to have a hard time later pulling themselves out to view the exhibits!

In downtown Greenwich, shop—if funds allow (or window-shop)—Greenwich Avenue, known for its chic establishments (and svelte pedestrians) featuring everything from antiques to furnishings and collectibles. Easily compared to Rodeo Drive or Fifth Avenue, the district is also listed in the National Register of Historic Places and is further distinguished during the day with a traffic officer at each intersection directing traffic in place of traffic lights. Chain-retail stores include **the Gap**, **J. Crew**, **Waldenbooks** and **Saks Fifth Avenue**. Those with an eye for jewelry, look no farther than **Tiffany & Company** (203-661-7847).

Insomniacs may want to shop **Duxiana's** (203-637-2347; www.duxbeds.com) line of luxury mattresses and bedding at 15 West Putnam, just off the Avenue. If that doesn't do the trick, the Avenue's **Relax the Back** (203-629-2225) is a store full of therapeutic chairs to relieve the stress during the day.

At 11 East Putnam Avenue, the oldest bookstore in Greenwich offering a wide selection from children's to adult bestsellers, is **Just Books** (203-869-5023; www. justbooks.org/events). Its sibling **Just Books, too** (203-637-0707; www.justbooks. org/events), Arcadia Road, is another bibliophiles' dream.

Just off the Avenue, visit **Diane's Books** (203-869-1515), a family-owned store carrying a wide selection, also offers a cozy atmosphere. At 135 Mason Street, tucked in a strip mall, **Inspirations** (203-629-8473) is chockfull of religious and inspirational books and gifts. Consider ordering a gift-basket arrangement for anyone who needs some uplifting. For those who want to appreciate the range of fine art on the Avenue, try **Greenwich Gallery** (203-622-4494; www.greenwichgallery.com) and **Lois Richard's Galleries** (203-661-4441).

In the old town hall, 299 Greenwich Avenue, catch an art show or special performance at the **Bendheim Gallery** (203-622-3998; www.greenwicharts. org/index.asp), operated by the **Greenwich Arts Council**. Old Greenwich's **Discoveries in Art** (203-977-7800; www.discoveriesinart.com/index.htm) gallery shows provide a Latin-American and Caribbean bent. The **Flinn Gallery** at the **Greenwich Library** (203-622-7947; www.greenwichlibrary.org) consists of six art exhibits exuding a variety of styles a year. Friends of Greenwich Library volunteers, who have an unrivaled eye for top talent from local, national and international artists, coordinate the shows, running from September through June. Near the Flinn Gallery, bibliophiles can not only observe the **Beatrice M. Brittain Collection of Fine Book Design**, a chronicle of the 100-year period in book art production beginning in 1895, preserved under glass, but also request a personal examination of the books—utter ecstasy!

Art buffs as well as history buffs should visit the **Bush-Holley House** located in Cos Cob, a village of Greenwich. The house, a National Historic Landmark, and grounds inspired the birth of American Impressionism after the famed Cos Cob Art Colony formed in 1884. Maintained and operated by the Greenwich Historical Society, permanent and changing art displays in the 1200-square-foot Hegarty Gallery, housed in the visitor's center, complement the adjacent Bush-Holley House.

Built circa 1730, the main house, a tidy Saltbox, today serving as headquarters for the Greenwich Historical Society, accommodates eight period rooms; each very different in style. The impressive furnishings and art collection, including a selection of works by onetime artists-in-residence like Childe Hassam, Leonard Ochtman, Willard Metcalf, J. Alden Weir (who established another art colony in Wilton), Elmer Livingston MacRae and Theodore Robinson, center on the history of the house since its Revolutionary War beginnings.

About five miles southwest, day-trippers will notice the bright, red exterior of **Putnam Cottage**, circa 1700. The former Knapp Tavern hosted VIPs like Generals Israel Putnam and George Washington. Maintained and operated by the Daughters of the American Revolution, the house museum, containing an array of colonial artifacts, is the best starting point to learn about Putnam's legendary horseback escape from the British.

Just under nine miles in the northern Greenwich section, off Route 15 (the Merritt Parkway; one of the only roads listed on the National Register of Historic Places), experience 285 acres of woodlands, wetlands and meadows at the **Audubon Center of Greenwich**. A prime bird-viewing location, hikers and walkers have about 10 miles of trails to choose from. The visitor's center includes an art gallery and store brimming with nature-themed items.

Day-trippers who can't get enough Mother Earth can make the two-mile north jaunt from Route 15 to **Babcock Preserve** (203-622-7814). With a total of 297 acres, it represents the largest town park area, located between North Street and Lake Avenue. Trails attract four-season recreation including hiking, biking and cross-country skiing.

Music devotees should consider attending a performance held at the Dickerman Hollister Auditorium, Greenwich High School (203-625-8000), just off Putnam Avenue, to hear the **Greenwich Symphony Orchestra** (203-869-2664; www. greenwichsym.org). A volunteer board of directors manages this professional orchestra. Audiences can also catch a performance of the **Chamber Players of the Greenwich Symphony** (203-532-2895; 203-869-2664; www.greenwichsym. org/index.html), also typically held at the high school.

A great deal for seniors and students is the five-dollar matinee tickets available for the performances presented by the **Acting Company of Greenwich** (203-863-1919; www.tacog.org). Staging lesser-known works by a variety of playwrights, performances are held in the auditorium of the First Congregational Church, 108 Sound Beach Avenue.

During the summer, a day trip would not be complete in town without a Sunday spent watching a game at the **Greenwich Polo Club** (203-863-1213; www.greenwichpolo.com) at Conyers Farm, Hurlingham Drive, also off Route 15. (The grounds gained even more notoriety after television crews taped a segment of Donald Trump's series, *The Apprentice*.) Gates open at 1 p.m. for games starting at 3 p.m. Also during the summer months into the early fall season, the town is resplendent with the **Greenwich Farmers' Market** at Horse Neck commuter lot, Arch Street, held every Saturday until early afternoon.

Whether hankering to fill a slight hunger, ravenous appetite, or anything in between, Greenwich cooks up plenty of options. **Arcuri's Deli & Pizza** (203-637-1085) at 178 Sound Beach Avenue, Old Greenwich, and **Famous Pizza & Souvlaki Restaurant** (203-531-6887) at 10 North Water Street in Greenwich's Byram section are examples of two casual restaurants serving breakfast and lunch daily.

Hailed as *excellent* by the *New York Times* and described as one of the top-10 restaurants in Connecticut, **Baang** (203-637-2114), 1191 Putnam Avenue, specializes in modern-Asian cuisine. Open for lunch Friday and dinner daily, the atmosphere is as colorful as the meals served. **Rebeccas** (203-532-9270), 265 Glenville Road, among its many other accolades, also garnered a rating of *excellent* by the *New York Times*. Open for lunch Tuesday through Friday and dinner, Tuesday through Saturday, the establishment features a contemporary-American menu. Another highly praised restaurant, winning an *extraordinary* mark from *Connecticut Magazine* is **Gaia** (203-661-3443), at 253 Greenwich Avenue, open for lunch Monday through Friday with dinner daily. Most notable are Chef Frederic Kieffer's innovative American cuisine, cooked in glass jars to seal in flavor!

The Avenue's **Alta** (203-622-5138) also joins **Gaia** in achieving an *extraordinary* ranking from *Connecticut Magazine*. Open for lunch Monday through Friday and dinner, Monday through Saturday, a creative Scandinavian menu has reaped high praises among the culinary community and beyond. For romantic views in a historic mill overlooking a 30-foot waterfall, try **Centro at the Mill** (203-531-5514), 328 Pemberwick Road. Open for lunch Monday through Saturday and dinner daily, the restaurant not only delivers a memorable ambiance, but also fresh Italian cuisine. Greenwich Avenue's **Pasta Vera** (203-661-9705; www.pastavera.com) also offers flavorsome Italian cuisine and take-out service for lunch and dinner daily; Sunday, only dinner is served. Legendary among steak lovers is **Manero's** (203-622-9684; www.maneros-greenwichct.com), 559 Steamboat Road, open for lunch and dinner daily. At number 109 Steamboat Road, **Chola** (203-869-0700), open for dinner daily, sets an exquisite stage and presents a menu of fine classic and eclectic cuisine from India.

Restaurant Jean-Louis (203-622-8450; www.restaurantjeanlouis.com), 61 Lewis Street, specializes in classic nouvelle cuisine, serving lunch Monday through Friday and dinner, Monday through Saturday, has also been recognized by some of the toughest restaurant critics as one of the top restaurants in the state. **L'Escale** (203-661-4600), meaning "port of call" in French, presents a sophisticated ambiance, spacious lounge and outdoor terrace enhancing its menu focused on classic French entrees for breakfast, lunch and dinner daily. The 500 Steamboat Road restaurant shares dock space with Delmar Hotel (see **Accommodations**); both establishments welcome boaters. The chef by the same name at **Thomas Henkelmann**, (203-869-7500; www.homesteadinn.com) 420 Field Point Road, a restaurant located inside the Homestead Inn (see **Accommodations**), serves an award-winning, French-style menu for breakfast, lunch and dinner daily. In the mood for dessert? Open daily, **Darlene's Heavenly Desires** (203-622-7077), 397 East Putnam Road, is exactly what the name states!

GETTING THERE:

Greenwich is approximately 34 miles northeast of New York City, 47 miles southwest of New Haven and 87 miles southwest of Hartford. Greenwich is at the intersection of many major highways and roads. The city is easily accessible from Interstate Highway 95; the Merritt Parkway (Route 15); Route 7 and U.S. Route 1 (the Boston Post Road; also known as East or West Putnam Avenue).

TRANSPORTATION:

Stratford's Sikorsky Memorial Airport is approximately 31 miles from Greenwich. Tweed New Haven Regional Airport is approximately 47 miles driving distance, providing daily service to 126 cities through US Airways and Delta Airlines. Greenwich is approximately 98 miles southwest of Bradley International Airport in Windsor Locks. The three major New York City metro airports are Westchester County Airport, LaGuardia, JFK and Newark Airport in New Jersey. Danbury Municipal Airport, a small, private airport, is approximately 45 miles in driving distance. The CT Transit District shuttles (800-638-7646) service Putnam, Sound Beach and Greenwich Avenue. Both Metro-North New Haven Line (800-METRO-INFO) trains and Amtrak (800-872-7245) offer daily commuter service to New York City and New Haven bound. Metro-North provides rail service from four stations: Greenwich, Cos Cob, Riverside and Old Greenwich.

ADDITIONAL INFORMATION:
BRUCE MUSEUM OF ARTS AND SCIENCE.

One Museum Drive. Open all year, Tuesday through Sunday. The facility is completely handicapped accessible and stroller friendly. Inquire about special family programs and events, such as "Fridays in the Round," monthly gatherings that attract single adults to enjoy music and refreshments in the museum setting. General admission is $5.00 adults; $4.00 seniors/children and free to children 5 and under and free admission on Tuesday. (203) 869-0376; www.brucemuseum.org.

THE HISTORICAL SOCIETY OF THE TOWN OF GREENWICH & BUSH-HOLLEY HISTORIC SITE.

39 Strickland Road. The house and center are open all year, Tuesday through Sunday. General admission is $6.00 adults; $4.00 seniors/children and free to children 12 and under and to members. (203) 869-6899; www.hstg.org.

PUTNAM COTTAGE.

243 East Putnam Avenue. Open all year, Sunday afternoon and by appointment. General admission is $5; suggested donation for adults. (203) 869-9697; www. putnamcottage.org.

AUDUBON CENTER OF GREENWICH.

613 Riversville Road. The center and grounds are open all year, daily. General admission is $3 adults; $1.50 seniors/children and free to National Audubon Society members and to Friends of Audubon Center of Greenwich members. (203) 869-5272; greenwich.center.audubon.org.

ACCOMMODATIONS:

The many Greenwich lodging choices include the historic **Stanton House Inn** (203-357-9555; www.bbonline.com/ct/stanton), Old Greenwich's **Harbor House Inn** (203-637-0145; www.hhinn.com) and **Cos Cob Inn** (203-661-5845; www.coscobinn.com/main.htm).

HYATT REGENCY.

1800 E. Putnam Avenue. A luxurious, English Manor-style hotel located in the Old Greenwich section of town provides 373 fully appointed guestrooms. The hotel, in which some of the largest special events in the county are held in its 10,000-square-foot ballroom, is planning a major addition to its facility and currently offers full, modern amenities, including indoor swimming pool, complimentary use of fitness center; on-site lounge and restaurants. Rates: $139-$319. (203) 637-1234; www.greenwich.hyatt.com/property/index.jhtml.

HOMESTEAD INN.

420 Field Point Road. In the heart of Belle Haven stands a 1799 grand Italianate Gothic-style house, which opens the door to four-star luxury in the form of 19 European guestrooms and suites, accented with antiques and boasting a venerable on-site restaurant (see above). Each room contains full, modern amenities, sumptuous décor down to the lush linens and original artwork. Rates: $250-$495. (203) 869-7500; www.homesteadinn.com.

DELAMAR HOTEL.

500 Steamboat Road. This cozy, ultra-luxurious hotel, boasting 83 guestrooms, has the harbor's dock, which is shared with **L'Escale Restaurant** (see above), at its disposal. Each room is equipped and decorated to satisfy the high-demand business or leisure traveler. Rates: $315-$1,500. (203) 661-9800; (866) 335-2627; www.thedelamar.com.

ANNUAL FESTIVALS/EVENTS

The Coastal Fairfield County Convention & Visitor Bureau, representing 15 southwestern communities, provides a gamut of tourism information, including seasonal events (800) 866-7925 or (203) 853-7770; www.coastalct.com. For additional festival and event information, *Greenwich Magazine*, (203-869-0009), also prints a list of area-based events.

FEBRUARY

Thrilling old and young alike, the **Historic Reenactment of the Battle and Israel Putnam's Ride** is held annually at the Putnam Cottage grounds. (203) 869-9697; www.putnamcottage.org.

MARCH

Revel at the **Artist Preview Party,** held at the Greenwich Arts Center; the merriment proceeds to the Annual Art to the Avenue celebration. (203) 622-3998; www.greenwicharts.org.

MAY

The Greenwich Arts Council presents the **Annual Art to the Avenue**, a month-long event that transforms Greenwich Avenue into an art gallery with paintings, photographs, sculptures and art installations from local artists. (203) 622-3998.

The Greenwich Audubon hosts an all-day event called **Spring into Audubon Festival**. It begins with early morning bird walks, breakfast and then features programs for children and adults throughout the day. Activities include face painting, live tropical birds and guided hikes. (203) 869-5272; greenwich.center. audubon.org.

One of the most popular local gatherings is the **Outdoor Crafts Festival** held at the Bruce Museum featuring more than 75-juried artists and their crafts from around the country. Also slated for the day is a roster of entertainment, demonstrations and food. (203) 869-0376; www.brucemuseum.org.

JUNE

Don't miss the **Greenwich Concours D'Elegance**, a one-of-a-kind event held at Roger Sherman Baldwin Park. Spectators can enjoy viewing vintage powerboats, airplanes, motorcycles, post-World War II European cars and domestic cars from 1890 to 1942. Additionally, the two-day event features automotive books, art and memorabilia; workshops and demonstrations. (203) 618-0460; www. greenwichconcours.com.

The **Renaissance Ball of the Bruce Museum** is a major fundraiser for the organization and features entertainment and dancing to a live orchestra as well as live and silent auctions. The black-tie event is held annually under tents at a private Greenwich estate. (203) 869-0376; www.brucemuseum.org.

SEPTEMBER

Cooler weather signals the Greenwich Audubon to host the annual fall **Hawk Watch Festival** weekend. The roster of activities includes live birds of prey, children's programs, nature walks and more. (203) 869-5272; greenwich.center.audubon.org.

Catch a movie at the **Greenwich Film Festival**, a showcase of independent films, at various locations. www.greenwichfilmfestival.org.

OCTOBER

Greenwich Audubon's **Annual Run for Conservation and Holistic Wellness Morning** is a four-mile run through the center's Fairchild Wildflower Garden and country back roads. A half-mile kids' run for preteens, walks for non-runners and seniors; physical healing experts and trainers offer a variety of programs. (203) 869-5272; greenwich.center.audubon.org.

Every Columbus Day weekend, the **Outdoor Arts Festival** is held and features more than 75 artists from around the country displaying their work at the grounds of the Bruce Museum. Entertainment, demonstrations and food are other weekend highlights. (203) 869-0376.

248

Town Hall Tree-Lighting Ceremony takes place annually in front of the town hall. (203) 622-7821.

Multifaceted Bruce Museum

See pages 243, 246 & 248

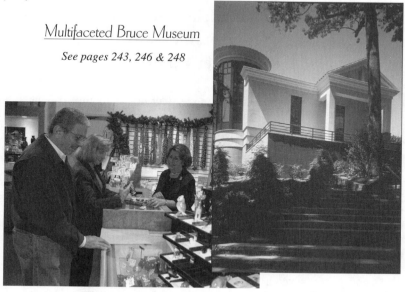

Photos courtesy of the Bruce Museum of Arts & Science

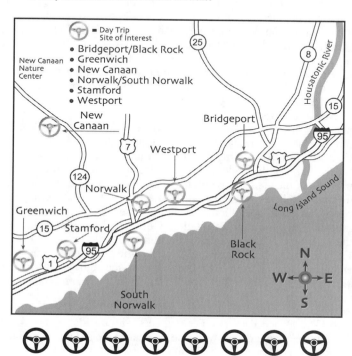

VII.
SOUTHEAST CONNECTICUT
Fairfield County
"Housatonic Valley"
Greater Danbury

Danbury is located in western Connecticut at the foothills of the Berkshire Mountains, 58 miles from Hartford and 69 miles from New York City. Just 40 minutes northeast of lower Westchester County, it is immediately east of the New York State line. Although Danbury is part of Fairfield County, the city falls under the jurisdiction of the Northwest Connecticut Convention & Visitor's Bureau, which promotes tourism in a total of 51 cities and towns.

Twenty or so years ago, Danbury was a stagnant little city. In the past few decades, however, the boom is measurable. In 2000, Danbury's growth reached 74,848, a 14-percent increase over 1990; compare this to an entire state population increase of 3.6 percent. A 2002 census estimate supplemented the population with 2,000 additional residents. Danbury's affordable real estate market, especially as compared to lower Fairfield County's real estate market, explains the growth factor.

Danbury, the seventh largest city in the state and the largest in western Connecticut, is home to Western Connecticut State University, Danbury Hospital and a sound industrial base of corporations including high-tech, publishing, pharmaceuticals, engineering and health care, not to mention the Danbury Federal Correctional Institute bordering the New Fairfield town line. The community takes pride in the fact that Meeker's Hardware, a family-operated business since 1883, is the only hardware store in America listed on the National Register of Historic Places. Other national accolades include being voted as *number one city to live in America* by *Money Magazine* in 1998, and, more recently, voted number eight (out of 331 United States metropolitan areas) as one of *America's best places to live* by Microsoft Network's House & Home poll.

Frequent day-trippers know the city's advantageous natural resources. Many visitors are, in fact, temporary residents renting cottages on Candlewood Lake, Connecticut's largest. Swimming, fishing, boating or plain relaxing are the call of the day at this artificially made marvel. Notice some of the area's oldest houses along the banks of the lake. Likewise, the Danbury Museum and Historical Society and the Danbury Railway Museum pay tribute to the city's rich heritage.

Shoppers can easily spend a day at the mall, set in a sparkling clean and airy building that houses more than 200 retailers. Golfers can tee off at Richter Park, rated among the top municipal golf courses in the country. Children, as well as adults, can race model cars at Danbury Raceway. The city offers an invigorating selection of theater and musical performances for both children and adults. Musicals by Richter, Connecticut's longest running, outdoor theater, for instance, presents the Fairy Tale Theater for children.

Those who seek nightlife have numerous possibilities like Tuxedo Junction Night Club (The Dance Factory). Day-trippers who decide to stay the night can choose from more than a dozen well-known chain hotels. Day or night, cooler or warmer months, day-trippers should visit Danbury anytime.

***What Connecticut town first earned the
nickname, "Beantown"?***

What city also earned the moniker, "Hat City"?

Booming: **GREATER DANBURY**

Bonny terrain and fertile soil, abundantly watered by the uppermost Still River, brought eight coastal families to the inland territory of what would become modern-day Danbury. In 1684, these newcomers established a wilderness outpost at Swampfield, central Danbury today. By 1687, the settlement purchased from the Paquioque Indians was decreed Danbury, named after a parish in Essex, England.

Incorporated in 1702, beans, along with other crops, helped Danbury become an inland trading center whose exportation center was Norwalk. The primary crop gave the town its earliest nickname, "Beantown."

It achieved prominence in the Revolutionary War serving as a storehouse for colonial commerce and a military supply depot for American troops. In 1777, Danbury's importance incensed the British; under Major General William Tryon, after the Battle of Compo Hill (see **Westport** chapter), the redcoats burned and looted the entire region. A central motto now on the Seal of the City of Danbury, appearing on every "Welcome to Danbury" road sign, is the Latin word: "restituimus," meaning, "we have restored," a reference to overcoming the Revolutionary War destruction caused by the British.

During the famous 1777 battle, enemy soldiers killed General David Wooster. In 1854, the community erected a monument to honor the valiant general and, today, history fans can view it at Wooster Cemetery's main entrance on Ellsworth Road. For those who cannot observe the Wooster Monument in person, they can notice it depicted on the lower left of the Danbury Seal.

A derby hat, also inscribed on the seal, salutes the city's hat manufacturing industry, spanning the 1800s and winding down in the 1950s, largely in part to diminishing couture demand, with the last factory closing in 1987. The world came to recognize Danbury as the "Hat City." In fact, some say that the first mass-produced man's hat in the United States started in that city. In 1780, the story goes that one Zadoc Benedict was the first to design and sell a hat. He opened a shop in town, selling an average of three hats a day, which kicked off a trend. Between 1808 and 1809, 56 hat shops sold headpieces ranging in price from six to 10 dollars. At the same time the small hat shops disappeared due to waning demand, however, a machine that created fur-felt hats appeared in 1849. This invention led factories to produce many of the world's hats for men, including the Stetson, which epitomized the American cowboy. These plants rose along the banks of the Still River, providing water for manufacture and, unfortunately, a dumping site for production waste.

In 1852, a railroad line was established, also playing a prominent part in history, it helped to accelerate city growth, and, likewise, is depicted on the Danbury Seal. Despite its substantial progress over the past few decades, the seventh largest city in the state, representing a melting pot of culture and language, encompassing a total 44.3 square miles, has maintained a homey feel through its preservation of historical and natural resources.

Visitors do not have to be vintage train buffs to feel the rush of excitement when first encountering the **Danbury Railway Museum**, delivering nothing less than a day trip with panache. In 1994, thousands of volunteer hours transformed the historic, but defunct, circa 1903 Union Station and rail yard in downtown Danbury, already a National Historic Landmark, into the museum.

Presently, the archives and artifacts in the station-building museum reflect the area railway history. Old and young alike, about 30,000 people saunter through its doors annually, delighting in pushing buttons, making model trains dating from the 1920s to 1960s (mostly donated) buzz around miniature towns. Outside, the railroad yard showcases an impressive, constantly growing collection of original and restored rolling stock—including locomotive, self-propelled vehicles, cabooses and passenger equipment—and opportunities for rail excursions and hands-on restoration volunteer work. Movie fans also feel energized here. Hollywood's camera crews filmed one of Alfred Hitchcock's finest suspense thrillers, *Strangers on a Train*, at the station in October 1950. This non-profit organization, staffed solely by volunteers, also maintains a gift shop boasting more than 500 train-related items ranging from books to train models.

Directly across the street, **Danbury Ice Arena** (203-794-1704; www.danburyice. com), 1 Independence Way, welcomes public skaters. Facilitators dub one of the most reasonably priced public skating deals throughout the state, "Lunch Skate," held from 11 a.m. to 2 p.m. during the week. For interested spectators, the **Danbury Trashers**, a United Hockey League team, has made Danbury home since 2004 with regularly scheduled games.

In the downtown vicinity, those who appreciate celestial bodies should experience the next free, public show and telescope viewing at **Western Connecticut State University Westside Observatory and Planetarium** (203-837-8672), located atop a five-acre hill on the university's Westside campus. One gaze into the 20-inch Ritchey-Chretien telescope, among the largest offered by any university in the state, and, if you aren't already, you will be hooked!

Danbury Museum and Historical Society, Main Street, wins hands down in accomplishing its mission to preserve and exhibit area history and highlight city heritage. Headquartered in Huntington Hall with its research library, a large portion of the collection exhibited in the modern-style exhibit gallery is the worldwide early 20th-century acquisitions of wealthy industrialist John Fanton and his second wife Laura Scott.

Through furnishings and accessories, the **John and Mary Rider House**, circa 1785, depicts Danbury's Revolutionary War efforts and the Rider family's multifaceted life from 1785 to 1830. In addition, on museum grounds, visit the **Dodd Hat Shop** (circa 1790); it represents onetime resident John Dodd's livelihood creating wood forms that facilitated the hat-making production. Additionally, a permanent exhibit at the shop pays homage to Danbury's hatting industry. The **Little Red Schoolhouse**, built from bricks salvaged from the old Balmforth Avenue School in the 1960s, is a reproduction of an Early American school in Danbury and is accessorized accordingly. In 1999, community members moved the **Marian Anderson Studio** to the Main Street location. Completely restored in 2004, the studio, listed on Connecticut's Black Freedom Trail, celebrates the life and accomplishments of famed opera singer Marian Anderson who lived in Danbury for more than 50 years.

Off the Main Street campus about one mile south, but also owned by the historical society, **Charles Ives' Birthplace** at 5 Mountainville Road touts furnishings and memorabilia in honor of Danbury's most beloved son, a Pulitzer Prize-winning composer, considered to be the father of American music. The most popular article in the parlor is his first piano.

While in the downtown area, day-trippers should carve extra time to roam around "**CityCenter**," a one-square-mile district inlay of restaurants, shops and other businesses perking with activity and special events throughout the year. The city's downtown revitalization program routinely upgrades the area with road and walkway improvements.

The Main Street stretch of eateries and restaurants includes **Good Taste Chinese Restaurant** (203-798-8978), open for lunch and dinner daily; **Clubhouse Deli** (203-739-0222), open for lunch and early dinner, Monday through Friday, and Saturday lunch; **Hat City Ale House** (203-790-4287), open for dinner daily and **Gusto Ristorante** (203-798-7233), open for lunch and dinner, Monday through Friday; Saturday dinner, only.

If kids are in tow, **Two Steps Downtown Grille** (203-794-0032) at 5 Ives Street, within the Main Street area, is open for lunch and dinner daily and located in a historic firehouse transformed into a restaurant—well, almost, a fire engine is the crown jewel on the second floor of the building. Within the vicinity, westward, some locals say **Cor's** (203-792-9999) at 65 West Street is the best place for breakfast, which along with lunch, is served daily.

While on the topic of food, **Ondine** (203-746-4900), 69 Pembroke Road, about five miles north of downtown, situated between Margerie Lake Reservoir and Candlewood Lake, has won its share of awards for French cuisine served in a romantic milieu of soft lighting, ornate fruitwood sideboards, Oriental rugs and white-jacketed waiters and waitresses. The five-course prix fixe menu changes seasonally, and the restaurant is open for dinner Wednesday through Sunday (Sunday brunch).

In a southeast direction about six miles, hungry day-trippers craving flavorful, spicy-hot food should remember **Bangkok Restaurant** (203-791-0640; www.bangkokrestaurant.com), 72 Newtown Road, open for lunch, Tuesday through Friday, and dinner, Tuesday through Sunday. The cuisine is as authentic as the traditional Thai-style costumes that servers wear—it should be: the family-owned establishment debuted in 1986 and bills itself as the oldest and best Thai restaurant in Connecticut and the tri-state area.

Heading south to number 52, **Dolce Vita** (203-746-0037) offers a northern Italian cuisine menu for lunch and dinner, Tuesday through Saturday, and Sunday dinner. Everything is fresh and handmade, including the pasta, aptly described by the *New York Times* as *made-to-order high quality*.

About five miles south at 100 Aunt Hack Road, **Café on the Green** (203-791-0369; www.cafeonthegreenrestaurant.com) serves breakfast, lunch and dinner daily; except when it is closed on Sunday, January 1 through March 1. The restaurant is tucked away on the green turf of the award-winning **Richter Park Golf Course** (203-792-2550; www.thegolfcourses.net/golfcourses/CT/7596.htm). *Golf Digest* rated the public course *fifth best* in the state among public and private courses. The par 72, 18-hole course on 160 acres lies near the New York State border.

Richter Park at the same address provides a scenic backdrop for the Arts Center Stage, **Musicals at Richter** (203-748-MUSE [6873]; www.musicalsatrichter.org). Operated entirely by a volunteer force, Fairfield County's longest-running outdoor summer theater produces shows for both adults and children.

Based in Danbury, **Connecticut Master Chorale** (203-743-0473; www.cmchorale.org/cmc/cmc.htm) comprises 55 professional singers performing seasonal concerts at a variety of venues throughout the state and nationally.

Berkshire Theatre at Western Connecticut State University, (203-837-8732), Osborne Street, presents a variety of musical theater productions throughout the year. **Charles Ives Center for the Arts** (203-837-9226; www.ivesconcertpark. com), on WCSU's Westside campus, offers myriad programs from jazz to pop to folk to classical at its outdoor performance facility.

For day-trippers who opt for a visual arts experience, about four miles south, in the vicinity of **Danbury Municipal Airport** at 73 Miry Brook Road, the **Wooster Community Art Center** (203-744-4825; www.woosterschool.org/community/woosterartcenter.php) focuses on presenting art classes and workshops in a variety of mediums. The small, fine art gallery generates notable artwork from regional professionals as well as students, and is open to the public, Monday through Friday.

About one minute northeast, **Danbury Fair Mall** (203-743-3247; www. danburyfairmall.com/controller/site) at 7 Backus Avenue, sits on the grounds where the famed Danbury State Fair, once the largest of all in the state, entertained and thrilled generations. The first Danbury State Fair was held in 1821 and by 1869, became a yearly event until its last fair in 1981.

Developers constructed the mall in 1987 and, today, there are about 225 stores, including such anchors as **Macy's**. Bring the young baseball stars to **Frozen Ropes** (203-205-0174; www.frozenropes.com) for baseball and softball training. (For *real* baseball action, catch a game of the **Danbury Westerners** (203-313-3024; www. danburywesterners.com/index.htm#), an all-volunteer, amateur hometown baseball team. In what other mall can you take a spin on a double-decker carousel (a part of which was salvaged from the actual state fair) and rekindle an old-fashioned pleasure?

Less than one mile northeast, '50s-style "cruise nights" showcasing hundreds of vintage cars and motorcycles add zest to any weekend at **Marcus Dairy Bar** (203-748-9427; www.marcusdairy.com/pages/about.html), 5 Sugar Hollow Road, serving breakfast, lunch and dinner, and, of course, legendary ice cream, daily. (Note that **Stew Leonard's Dairy** [203-790-8030; www.stewleonards.com], known as the "World's Largest Dairy Store," is located just off I-84 and US 7; this is the sister store to Stew Leonard's in Norwalk [see **Norwalk** chapter].)

Day-trippers should travel less than one mile northeast from Marcus to spend at least an hour visiting the **Military Museum of Southern New England**. This non-profit organization contains more than 10,000 military-related artifacts. Make time to scrutinize the outdoor exhibits featuring tanks, including a 1917 Renault, the first made in the United States, tank destroyers and a panoply of heavy equipment. The military vehicles and equipment date from World War I to Desert Storm in what comprises the largest collection of major military items in the region. Don't leave without exploring the life-size interior dioramas.

To illustrate the point of how Danbury accommodates a multi-generational crowd, young and old can race model cars at **Danbury Raceway** (203-778-3337), 60 Mill Plain Road, or pick their own produce at **Taylor Family Farm** (203-744-1798), 57 Great Plain Road; adults can dance the night away at **Tuxedo Junction**, 2 Ives Street, (203-748-2561; www.tuxedojunction.net).

In the summer months, day-trippers of all ages may just prefer to spend the daylight hours swimming, fishing, boating, kayaking or even diving at **Candlewood Lake**, Connecticut's largest. Covering 800 acres, Candlewood is the third largest fabricated lake in the world and the largest east of the Mississippi. In 1929, its 65-mile shoreline was artificially created where Wood Creek and Rocky River meet near the Housatonic River. The lake also extends into Brookfield and New Fairfield.

Currently, the Connecticut Light and Power Company operates Candlewood Lake as a hydroelectric power facility. A public boat launch, swimming area and hiking trails are available in the 11.1-acre **Danbury Candlewood Park** overlooking the water.

Nearby, another green space bordering the lake, located on Bear Mountain Road, just off Route 37, **Bear Mountain State Park** attracts hikers and picnickers to its 140 acres. River lovers can stroll through the Still River Greenway on the Housatonic River Trail situated on the lower section of the **Still River**, running through downtown, starting at the confluence of the river with Limekiln Brook; bring a canoe or boat! After years of enduring pollution and general neglect, in 1995 the city initiated the Still River Restoration Project, which included cleaning up the river and, throughout the trail, creating greater public access.

Another green encounter is the **Old Quarry Nature Center** on Maple Lane, adjacent to Rogers Park. Eighty acres of land contain two natural trails off Mountainville Road. The field house, offering special programs and nature-related exhibitions, is open to the public on the second Sunday of the month from 1 p.m. through 3 p.m.

Easily accessible from I-84, off Kenosia Boulevard, the 25 acres of Kenosia Park give day-trippers further opportunities to hike, swim, picnic, boat or ice-skate in the winter months on the pond. **Tarrywile Park** (203-744-3130; www.danbury.org/tarryterry; check out free guided hikes and special events), Tarrywile Lake Road, former estate of hat mogul Charles Darling, is a 654-acre retreat popular among day-trippers, with the mansion a favorite wedding venue. The park is open from dawn to dusk throughout the year, more than 21 miles of trails accommodate hikers and mountain bikers. In the summer months, try your skills at fishing; in the winter, cross-country skiing. A children's playground and garden modeled after Maurice Sendak's children's book, *Where the Wild Things Are*, complete any day trip. For a bit of respite, day-trippers can station themselves at the meditation garden next to the Tarrywile Gazebo. In the future, visitors can anticipate a new picnic area and environmental education facility.

Tour the 23-room, brown-shingled Victorian mansion listed on the National Historic Register, which has been incarnated as a community center open to the public. Pick up an interesting variety of self-guided tour brochures from *Mansion History* to *Tree Walk* available at the mansion office or from a park ranger.

GETTING THERE:

Danbury is approximately 69 miles northeast of New York City, 37 miles west of New Haven and 58 miles southwest of Hartford; Greenwich is 45 miles south. Danbury is easily accessible from the New York metro area and New England. The city is easily accessible from Interstate Highway 84, which connects to Interstates 684 and 287 and Saw Mill River Parkway in New York State; it is also accessible from the Merritt Parkway (Route 15); Route 7 intersects Danbury.

TRANSPORTATION:

Danbury Municipal Airport (203-743-3300; 203-797-4624), which serves the corporate and private sector, is adjacent to Danbury Fair Mall and is a tower-controlled facility with two runways. Stratford's Sikorsky Memorial Airport is approximately 33 miles from Danbury. Tweed New Haven Regional Airport is approximately 37 miles driving distance, providing daily service to 126 cities through

US Airways and Delta Airlines. The area is approximately 72 miles southwest of Bradley International Airport in Windsor Locks. The three major New York City metro airports are Westchester County Airport, LaGuardia, JFK and Newark Airport in New Jersey. Stewart International Airport in Newburgh, New York, is approximately 41 miles west of Danbury. The Housatonic Area Regional Transit system's (HART) buses (203-748-2034) service Danbury and the surrounding area. Metro-North (800-638-7646) offers commuter rail service to southern Connecticut and New York and all southern towns.

ADDITIONAL INFORMATION:
DANBURY RAILWAY MUSEUM.
120 White Street. The museum and railway yard are open all year, call for schedule. Inquire about special family programs and events, workshops and lectures. General admission is $6.00 adults; $5.00 seniors/children and free to children 4 and under and to museum members. (203) 778-8337; www.danbury.org/drm.

DANBURY MUSEUM & HISTORICAL SOCIETY.
42 Main Street. The museum and its properties, including the Charles Ives' Birthplace, are open for tours by appointment only, except, generally, in the months of December through April. Inquire about special programs and events. General admission is $6.00 adults; $5.00 seniors; $1.00 children and free to children 4 and under and to museum members. (203) 743-5200; www.danbury.org/drm.

MILITARY MUSEUM OF SOUTHERN NEW ENGLAND.
125 Park Avenue. Open all year, Tuesday through Sunday. Inquire about the open turret days held in summer and fall. General admission is $4.00 adults; $2.00 seniors/children and free to children 6 and under and to active-duty military personnel. (203) 790-9277; www.usmilitarymuseum.org.

ACCOMMODATIONS:
The many Danbury lodging facilities include: **Hilton Garden Inn** (203-205-2000; 800-445-8667) and for short-term or long-term stays, the **Residence Inn by Marriott** (800-331-3131; 203-797-1256).

WELLESLEY INN.
116 Newtown Road. Located off I-84, the property offers 183 guestrooms with complete, modern amenities. Guests can utilize a complimentary hotel van shuttle within a 10-mile radius. A large indoor and outdoor pool and an **Outback Steakhouse** are also on premises. Rates (including complimentary, continental breakfast buffet): $118-$319. (203) 792-3800; (800) 272-6232.

ETHAN ALLEN HOTEL.
21 Lake Avenue. This six-story hotel offers 138 suites and 57 guestrooms accented with traditional Ethan Allen furnishings. Just off I-84, guestrooms boast full, modern amenities. Enjoy a fitness center, spa tub and seasonal outdoor pool. Rates: $89-$132. (203) 744-1776; (800) 742-1776; www.ethanallenhotel.com.

ANNUAL FESTIVALS/EVENTS

The Northwest Connecticut Convention and Visitor's Bureau, representing a total of 51 communities in the northwestern region that includes Litchfield Hills, Housatonic Valley and the Waterbury region, provides a gamut of tourism information, which includes seasonal events (860) 567-5214; www.litchfieldhills.com. *Hat City Free Press* Newsletter ("working to create a citizens' medium for the open expression of perception and truth") detailing upcoming events and other interesting local tidbits, distributed free throughout the city, can be obtained at www.madhattersimc.org.

JANUARY

First Night Danbury is a city-wide New Year's Eve party for all ages, with entertainment and food courts throughout town. Musicians, artists and talented performers are featured during this non-alcoholic celebration. (203) 743-0546; www.firstnightdanbury.org.

Winterfest at Tarrywile is a day of entertainment including snowshoe and cross-country skiing demonstrations, vendors and food. (203) 744-3130;www.danbury.org/tarry.

Fly Fishing University's annual **World of Fly Fishing Show** is held at the O'Neill Center, conveniently located off I-84 East or West. One of America's finest fly-fishing shows, vendors, lectures and demonstrations are featured throughout the day. (203) 743-0546.

FEBRUARY

The **Annual Pool Classic Joss Northeast 9-Ball Tour** is an exciting competition that takes place at Danbury's Boston Billiard Club. (203) 743-0546; www.bostonbilliardclub.com/danbury.htm.

The **Eastern Scrabble ® Championship** is another exciting annual competition that takes Danbury by storm. (203) 743-0546.

MARCH

NCAA Division III National Tournament begins at the O'Neill Center, Western Connecticut State University. (203) 837-9015.

APRIL

Easter Bunny Rides are always a treat for the children—and adults, too! This annual train excursion with the Easter bunny takes place at the Danbury Railway Museum. (203) 778-8337; www.danbury.org/drm.

MAY

The **Train Show** and **RailFair** happen simultaneously at two locations: Western Connecticut State University and at the Danbury Railway Museum and rail yard. Along with special exhibits and vendors, they allow an opportunity to meet Metro-North railroad engineers, conductors, welders, machinists, track maintenance workers, and watch them compete in their specialized skills. (203) 778-8337; www.danbury.org/drm.

JUNE/JULY/AUGUST

Free **summer concerts** at the CityCenter Bandshell on the green, Ives Street, feature everything from jazz to folk to traveling children's theater. (203) 792-1711.

SEPTEMBER

Taste of Greater Danbury on the Danbury CityCenter Green, Ives Street, is an extravaganza of food, live entertainment and special activities for children. (203) 792-1711.

The **Gasball Arts and Music Festival** is a heralded tradition. Alternative music, eclectic artwork and vendors highlight the day. (203)) 743-0546.

OCTOBER

Ives Day is an annual celebration in honor of Charles Ives's birthday, culminating with a special concert presented by the Danbury Music Center. (203) 743-0546.

Train Rides to the Pumpkin Patch celebrates fall at the Danbury Railway Museum in which children get to pick their own pumpkins. (203) 778-8337; www.danbury. org/drm.

Participate in a haunted hayride at Tarrywile Park during the annual **Terror at Tarrywile** celebration. All proceeds benefit the Danbury Jaycees and the park. (203) 744-3130; www.danbury.org/tarry.

DECEMBER

The **Annual Holiday Lighting Program** kicks off the season at the CityCenter Green. (203) 743-0546.

All children who partake in the annual **Santa Train Rides** receive a free gift. There are also special visits with Mrs. Claus and Frosty the Snowman. (203) 778-8337; www.danbury.org/drm.

Danbury's Marcus Dairy
'50s-style "Cruise Night"
See page 254

Danbury Museum and Historical Society
See page 252

Grounds of the Danbury Museum and Historical Society.

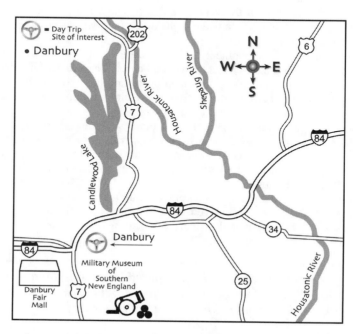

VIII.

WEST CENTRAL CONNECTICUT
New Haven County
"Housatonic Valley"
Greater Waterbury

Waterbury, total population approximately 107,000, is the fourth largest city in Connecticut. Part of New Haven County and located in the Housatonic Valley, it is categorized as a metropolitan center. About 22 miles north of New Haven and 30 miles southwest of Hartford, located at the junction of Route 8 and Interstate Highway 84, it inhabits a land area of 28.9 square miles. It is home to St. Mary's Hospital, a 347-bed, Catholic, teaching hospital and Teikyo Post University, a small business and liberal arts university established in 1890. Although, in the 1950s, the demand for plastics replaced metal consumer products ranging from clock parts to buttons, Waterbury remains tied to its "Brass City" moniker, proud of its brass-making heritage that once brought the city national notoriety.

Waterbury, still a center for hundreds of small manufacturing companies, is experiencing resurgence. Commercial developers are taking advantage of the attractive real estate prices and generous tax incentives. For instance, developers converted the site of one of the original brass mills into a mall, the Brass Mill Center. The resurrection of the venerable Palace Theater is part of the downtown renaissance. Since 1990, the famed Seven Angels Theater has attracted audiences far beyond the valley's reach.

One of the state's preeminent arts organizations, the Waterbury Symphony Orchestra, has mesmerized a generation of audiences. The Greater Waterbury Youth Symphony illustrates the city's long-standing commitment to budding musicians. The region's pride can also be discovered in two city museums: the Mattatuck and Timexpo.

A hodgepodge of ethnic neighborhoods, quaint shops and charming architecture are welcome accents to any 24 hours. Day-trippers do not have to journey far to find green expanses. One crown jewel in downtown, the Hayden Homestead Park, provides a sweet-scented carpet of activities during the annual Lilac Festival (see **Annual Festivals/Events**).

A roller-skating rink and two duckpin bowling alleys transform any day into a retro-type experience. Well-preserved historial districts, distinguished by Victorian-style houses built by wealthy industrialists and a string of monuments immortalizing a rich and diverse history are an intrinsic backdrop to any day's visit.

What Connecticut city prospered by making buttons
for Civil War uniforms, and how did this practice lead
to its being known as the "Brass City"?

What city also became famous for its clock and
watch-making industries?

What-ta-Wonderful: **WATERBURY**

The Indian name of today's Waterbury was "Matetacoke," later modified to "Mattatuck," meaning "poorly wooded area." In 1674, Farmington residents bought the tract of land for 38 British pounds. Gradually, the settlers' expansion succumbed to the acres of steep, hilly, rocky ground straddling what we know today as the Naugatuck River, located in the Naugatuck Valley.

In 1686, Waterbury became the 28th town established in Connecticut, so named after its abundant river location. Since the area's soil could not sustain an agricultural society, the town harnessed its water into mills. What led to Waterbury's brass-making empire was a button shop that materialized around 1750. In 1802, industrialists created the first, small brass rolling mill that supplied materials for the emerging button factories. By 1858, there were at least 10 factories in full operation. With the advent of the Civil War — and the uniforms that needed buttons — demand soared. Later, during World War II, Waterbury became a major producer of brass castings for artillery shells. By then, the country recognized Waterbury as a major business center.

The city's other illustrious industry was clock making. Resident James Harrison began manufacturing handmade, wooden clocks in 1790; soon other clockmakers followed suit. In 1857, the Waterbury Clock Company, the first to create brass clocks in quantity, was born, and by 1888, a day's work meant producing 1,500 pocket watches.

During the 1800s, the stagecoach and Naugatuck Railroad lines became signs of an industrial mecca. Sojourners can witness the imprints of this era in the city's grand scheme of architecture and private homes built by wealthy industrialists in the downtown Waterbury Green area. The statue of Father Michael J. McGivney, native son who founded the Knights of Columbus, the international Catholic fraternal order, is also in the vicinity. Venture by foot to historical downtown and experience a day trip with panache.

In the center of town, the **Hillside Historic District** is the oldest residential district in Waterbury, listed on the National Register of Historic Places. A prime example of historical grandeur, the architectural styles of the 300 historically significant buildings include Victorian, Tudor, Georgian, Cottage and other turn-of-the-century varieties.

Among the city rejuvenation efforts, the district's neighborhood association has spruced up **Hayden Homestead Park** with entrances off Grove Street and Glenridge Street. Bring a lunch and enjoy the downtown greenery or fall foliage.

Strolling southeast, at the foot of Bank Street, marvel at the **Apothecary Building**, built in the Renaissance Revival-style and trimmed with Venetian-style balconies. Halfway down Bank, the 17-foot tall **M.A. Green Clock** is a two-dial clock made by the Seth Thomas Company. It was relocated from its original 1920 Grand Street site to its present location in 1935 and dedicated to the city in 1993.

At the intersection of Bank Street and Main, the two-acre rectangular green, a popular political and cultural event gathering ground, holds an interesting assortment of historical monuments and trivia. Paul Lux of the Lux Clock Company designed the base and 15-foot granite tower of the **Clock-on-the-Green**. Charles Colley, Chamber of Commerce president from 1913 to 1917, won a heated debate regarding the question of its aesthetic presence on the green; secured its position, and to this day, community members refer to it as Colley's Clock.

Another distinct landmark on the green is the **Carrie Welton Fountain**. Its 2,500-pound statue memorializes Carrie's (who hailed from a prominent Waterbury family) black stallion, Knight, whom she routinely rode, rain or shine or snow, in the city streets. Upon her death in 1884, her will (which left a fortune to the ASPCA—even after an embittered family court battle) gave money to the city, and stipulated that the citizens memorialize her horse.

Renowned architectural firm, Cesar Pelli and Associates based in New Haven, designed the dramatic front entrance of the **Mattatuck Museum** on the northwest corner of the green, a mix of classic and contemporary styles. Maintained and operated by the Mattatuck Historical Society, the museum, housed since 1983 in the former Masonic Temple building, was established in 1911. The institution is the only one of its kind in the state committed to Connecticut artists and sculptors and depicts three centuries of industrial history.

Day-trippers can view exhibits embodying the fascinating period when the city was dubbed "brass capital of the world." Examine approximately 10,000 Waterbury-made buttons. An impressive artwork collection, ranging from the 18th to the 20th century, further enhances the day. Make a stopover in Mattatuck Museum's store offering a variety of books and signature gift items like greeting cards.

The museum's **Exhibition Café** (203-753-0381; www.mattatuckmuseum. org/cafestore/cafe/) is a distinct lunch experience specializing in "fresh nouveau California fusion cuisine with a twist." Art soup is one item available from the menu's selection of "food fit for a gallery." The café is open for lunch as well as afternoon coffee, tea and snacks, Tuesday through Saturday.

Note that for traditional pizza or Asian dishes, numerous restaurants located around the green and in the surrounding downtown area will satisfy such a yen. While in downtown, history buffs should not miss a lunch or dinner at **Drescher's Restaurant** (203-573-1743; www.dreschers.com), 25 Leavenworth. Established in 1868, Waterbury's oldest restaurant has an esoteric family history. In 1903, in order to save the building from demolition, preservationists relocated the 300-ton wood and brick structure at a cost of 130,000 dollars, 200 feet from its former Harrison Avenue address to its present location. Inside, under the old, metal ceiling, vintage photographs convey Waterbury's history. The menu specializes in German-styled entrees; lunch and dinner served, Monday through Friday, and Saturday dinner only.

Any day and anytime is good to eat (they're open 24 hours) at Connecticut's last surviving **Howard Johnson's Restaurant** (203-755-4910) at 2620 South Main Street. On Wednesdays and Fridays, the all-you-can-eat fried clam or fish fry dinner is a timeless tradition. The waitresses are probably the friendliest in the state— perhaps the universe!

Two miles north at 1230 Thomaston Avenue, **Baccos** (203-755-0635) is a 70-year-old institution. The classic Italian cuisine served for lunch and dinner, Tuesday through Friday, and Saturday and Sunday dinner only, begins with famous Italian bread baked fresh daily and continues with fresh pasta entrees.

Less than one mile east, **Carmen Anthony Steakhouse** (203-757-3040; www. carmenanthony.com), one of five such restaurant locations in the state, has won an impressive array of awards over the years. Located at 496 Chase Avenue, it is open for lunch, Monday through Friday, and dinner daily.

One cannot talk Waterbury food without a mention of **Frankie's Hotdogs**, a legendary restaurant that started back in the '30s, now with three Waterbury locations: Lakewood Road (203-756-2935), Watertown Avenue (203-753-2426) and Reidville Drive (203-757-9700); all open for lunch and dinner daily. For light appetites, the *Waterbury Observer's* reader's poll voted downtown's **Libero's Pizzeria** as *best pizza-by-the-slice* restaurant, open for lunch and dinner daily. Any sweet tooth will be satisfied at **Sweet Maria's** (203-755-3804; www.sweet-marias. com). Since 1990, the bakery features award-winning cakes and cookies—25 flavors of cookies and biscotti alone. Be forewarned: the whipped crème cake will break any diet!

Don't miss the rest of downtown's eminent architecture, most notably the *Waterbury Republican-American* building. The centerpiece of its structure was incarnated from the Union Station of the New York, New Haven and Hartford Railroad and is a 240-foot-high clock tower modeled after the Torre Del Mangia at Palazzo Publico (City Hall) in Siena, Italy. Between the traffic noise below and the great height of the tower bell installed in 1916, it is heard better on the city's nearby hills than at street level.

For a taste of Yankee integrity, stop in at 120-140 Bank Street. The **Connecticut Store** (203-753-4128; 800-4-SHOP-CT; www.ctstore.com) has been a Waterbury landmark since 1890, and the state's oldest department store. Open Tuesday through Saturday, the store carries only products made in Connecticut, such as Wiffle ® balls, Woodbury Pewter and many things related to Waterbury, including premium button souvenirs.

With shopping in mind, **Brass Mill Center & Commons** (203-755-5003; www. brassmillcenter.com), 495 Union Street, is visible from I-84, located in the building that was once the Scovill Manufacturing Company, one of Waterbury's famed brass mills. Shoppers have 125 retail shops at their disposal, including **Bath & Body Works**, **Eddie Bauer**, **Yankee Candle**, **GAP** and **GAP Kids**. Also on hand are some tried-and-true restaurants, including **Ruby Tuesday**, **T.G.I. Friday's** and **Hometown Buffet**. Catch a flick at **Hoyt's Cinemas** and a mouth-watering **Dippy's** (203-574-1609; also at a second location at 663 Lakewood Road) ice cream cone after the show.

Alternatively, for a fun, fascinating and funky learning experience, stroll over to the Brass Mill Commons section of the Brass Mill Center Mall, and visit the **Timexpo Museum**. (Day-trippers arriving via I-84 can't miss the 40-foot high, colorful Easter Island statue outside the building looking like an exotic medicine man.) When this long-awaited museum, sponsored by the Middlebury-based Timex Corporation, first opened in 2001, more than 700 spectators reveled in the celebration. To commemorate the event, staff and other enthusiastic time travelers buried a time capsule on museum grounds, including a selection of the year's hottest-selling Timex Watches.

Timexpo Museum explores Waterbury's Timex Watch tie-in, dating back to the assembly line, mass-produced timepieces manufactured by the Waterbury Clock Company in the 1850s, tracing Timex history until now. Magnificent timepieces and hands-on activities are also part of the experience.

On the opposite end of the Brass Mill Center, a 52-foot crucifix, a city landmark, especially to I-84 motorists, remains from **Holy Land USA**, accessible via Slocum Road. This onetime popular, religious destination consisting of an 18-acre park simulating a mini-Jerusalem, and in the 1960s and 1970s attracting some 50,000 pilgrims annually, has been marred by years of neglect; its future uncertain.

In Waterbury, golfers have a choice of two public 18-hole courses: **Western Hills** (203-756-1211) on Park Road and **East Mountain Golf Course** (203-753-1425). Water enthusiasts, who desire Naugatuck, Housatonic or Farmington River excursions, should call the Waterbury-based **Mountains Unlimited Adventures** (203-756-8218; 888-240-6976; www.adventuresports.com) for kayak and raft rentals. Note: the staff also provides rock- and ice-climbing lessons.

For an amusing day at reasonable cost, consider old-fashioned roller-skating at the **Waterbury Skating Center** (203-574-2118; www.sk8rollermagic.com), off South Main Street. Open to the public, benefits include special events, dramatic lighting and a large screen TV. You can't get anymore old-fashioned than duckpin bowling and Waterbury boasts, not one, but two outlets: **Danbury Lane** (203-744-4504) and **Perillo's Bowl-A-Drome** (203-754-7555).

For cultural affairs, **Seven Angels Theater** (203-757-4676; www.sevenangelstheater.org) is the only professional, equity theater in Waterbury. On its main stage, the audience can expect Broadway-quality shows highlighting a variety of playwrights' works throughout the year. Each season, Seven Angels also produces two community-based productions. Premium comedy acts are also highly acclaimed events.

History began at the famed **Palace Theater** (203-755-4700; www.palacetheaterct.org), 100 East Main Street, in 1920 when the doors opened on this Renaissance Revival-style building, constructed in a grand architectural mix and crowned with ornate dome ceilings. Until 1987, the theater brought great movies, theater, music and solid culture to the community. In 2004, after a complete renovation, the curtain rises again. Present-day audiences can anticipate a grand array of celebrity shows, theater productions, special events and a variety of musical and dance performances. Shows by the **Young People's Theater** (203-577-2377), a non-profit volunteer organization, allow families to watch popular children's theater at reasonable prices, held at J.F. Kennedy High School.

You can't mention culture without naming the **Waterbury Symphony Orchestra** (203-574-4283; www.waterburysymphony.org), located at 83 Bank Street, offering a season (September through April) of musical programs ranging from classical to pop as well as family concerts. The **Greater Waterbury Youth Symphony** (203-525-3939; www.gwys.org), comprised of youngsters ages six to 18, performs throughout the school year at a variety of venues including the mall. Day-trippers with a penchant for choral music, should hear a performance by the **Waterbury Chorale** (860-274-6088; www.waterburychorale.org), a congregation of both amateur and semi-professional singers who perform at a variety of locales.

The city's dance company, **Brass City Ballet** (203-573-9419), offers performances and dance education. After-hours, inquire about the public showings available from the **Mattatuck Astronomical Society** at Naugatuck Valley Community College (203-575-8236; www.mastransit.org/welcome.htm). One other exciting venue day-trippers should call to mind is **Artistic License** (203-568-6431), 1760 Watertown Avenue. The gallery, open Tuesday through Saturday, highlights both famous and up-and-coming local and international artists.

GETTING THERE:

Waterbury is approximately 38 miles east of Brewster, New York, 22 miles north of New Haven and 30 miles southwest of Hartford; Danbury is 28 miles west. Waterbury is easily accessible from the New York metro area and New England. The city is also accessible from Interstate Highway 84; connecting to Route 8.

TRANSPORTATION:

Waterbury-Oxford Airport (203-264-8010) is available for private, business and corporate aircrafts. Stratford's Sikorsky Memorial Airport is approximately 30 miles from Waterbury. Danbury Municipal Airport (203-743-3300; 203-797-4624), a tower-controlled facility with two runways, which serves the corporate and private sector, is approximately 30 miles driving distance from Waterbury. Tweed New Haven Regional Airport is approximately 22 miles driving distance, providing daily service to 126 cities through US Airways and Delta Airlines. The area is approximately 50 miles southwest of Bradley International Airport in Windsor Locks. The three major New York City metro airports are Westchester County Airport, LaGuardia, JFK and Newark Airport in New Jersey. Stewart International Airport in Newburgh, New York, is approximately 67 miles west of Waterbury. The CT Transit Waterbury District, operated by North East Transportation (203-753-2538 or 203-755-8242), services Waterbury. Metro-North (800-638-7646) offers connecting commuter rail service to Waterbury.

ADDITIONAL INFORMATION:

MATTATUCK.

144 West Main Street. The museum, research library and gift shop are open all year, Tuesday through Sunday. Inquire about special museum tours, children's programs, events, lectures and "First Thursdays," an ongoing, after-hours program held on the first Thursday of the month featuring live music, wine tasting, hors d' oeuvres and museum access. General admission is $4.00 adults; free to children 15 and under and to museum members. (203) 753-0381; www.mattatuckmuseum.org.

TIMEXPO MUSEUM.

Brass Mill Commons Mall, 175 Union Street. The museum and gift shop (brimming with Timex Watches) are open all year, Tuesday through Saturday. General admission is $6.00 adults; $5.00 seniors; $4.00 children and free to children 4 and under. (Museum admission includes 20-percent off all non-sale watches in the store.) (203) 755-TIME; 1-800-225-7742; www.timexpo.com.

ACCOMMODATIONS:

HOUSE ON THE HILL.

92 Woodlawn Terrace. This 1888 Queen Anne Victorian bed and breakfast, listed on the National Register of Historic Places, boasts three floors and 20 rooms, four of which are guestrooms. Amenities include balconies, terraces, refrigerators

and microwaves. Marianne Vandenburg hosts this distinctive "house on the hill," brimming with fine antiques and woodwork. Pets are welcome. Rates (including complimentary, full-gourmet New England breakfast): $125-$175. (203) 757-9901; www.houseonthehill.biz.

COURTYARD BY MARRIOTT.
63 Grand Street. There are 27 suites with Jacuzzis among the 200 guestrooms on premises. Rooms include coffeemakers, voice mail and free high-speed Internet access. A fitness center, indoor pool and sauna are also available for hotel guests. Rates: $99-$139. (203) 596-1000.

HOLIDAY INN EXPRESS.
88 Union Street. One hundred and four guestrooms offer in-room coffee, free local calls and Internet access. Other features include outdoor swimming pool, Jacuzzi tubs in king-sized bedrooms and free passes to Bally's Total Fitness. Rates (including Express Start Breakfast Bar): $109.95-$169.00.

CONNECTICUT GRAND HOTEL AND CONFERENCE CENTER.
3580 East Main Street. The largest hotel facility in Waterbury features nearly 300 guestrooms and suites. Amenities include over-sized indoor pool and whirlpool, fitness center with brand new cardio-vascular and weight training equipment, game room and video arcade and on-premises restaurant. Rates: $79-$175. (800) 446-1521.

ANNUAL FESTIVALS/EVENTS
The Northwest Connecticut Convention and Visitor's Bureau, representing a total of 51 communities, provides a gamut of tourism information, which includes seasonal events (860) 567-5214; www.litchfieldhills.com. For additional festival and event information, contact the Greater Waterbury Chamber of Commerce at 203-757-0701; www.waterburychamber.org.

MAY
Call (203) 757-0701 for information about the **Tour of Connecticut**, (see **New Haven Annual Festivals/Events**), a 70K road race that takes place in numerous state locales. www.tourofct.com

Many wonderfully sweet things happen during the **Lilac Festival** in Hayden Park, downtown, Waterbury Green. (203) 757-0701.

SEPTEMBER
The **Bi-Annual Juried Show** at the Mattatuck Museum represents a variety of artists and their works. (203) 753-0381; www.mattatuckmuseum.org.

OCTOBER
Yankee Invention Exposition is a two-day show that introduces inventors and their products not only to the public, but also to manufacturers, investors, venture capitalists and the like. Exhibitors include suppliers, marketing experts, patent attorneys, etc. Call about venues and pricing, (203) 575-8322; www.

yankeeinventionexpo.org.

NOVEMBER

The Mattatuck Museum sponsors an **Annual Frederic G. Mason Lecture**. The event is free, but those interested should reregister. (203) 753-0381; www. mattatuckmuseum.org.

NOVEMBER-DECEMBER

Festival of Traditions transforms the Mattatuck Museum into a holiday wonderland featuring glittering displays and dozens of trees decorated by businesses, local groups, organizations and volunteers. (203) 753-0381; www.mattatuckmuseum. org.

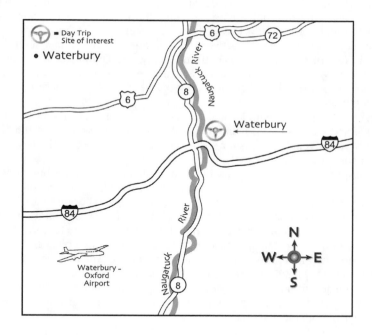

VIX.

CENTRAL CONNECTICUT
New Haven/Hartford County
"Greater New Haven & Heritage River Valley"
Cheshire/New Britain

Situated close to the heart of Connecticut, Cheshire and New Britain, separated by about 18 miles in driving distance, are positioned a smidgeon more westward than eastward. Cheshire falls under the umbrella of New Haven County and is located 16 miles north of New Haven, between Waterbury and Wallingford.

Located along Highway 6, between Farmington and Berlin and southwest of Hartford, New Britain belongs to Hartford County. The Quinnipiac River cascades through New Britain and Farmington and trickles southward 38 miles through numerous towns including Cheshire until it reaches New Haven Harbor, emptying into Long Island Sound.

Out of the five-town central Connecticut district (Cheshire, Southington, Berlin, Plainville and New Britain), which falls under the tourism efforts of the Greater New Haven Convention & Visitor's Bureau, New Britain boasts the largest area. Connecticut State University is the city's crown jewel.

Day-trippers will not only discover some diverse city neighborhoods with inviting restaurants and a flourishing downtown, but also vast sections of open space to be explored and historical homes and dwellings to be admired.

Hear the summertime sounds at Cheshire's Walnut Hill Park. Splurge on antiques and collectibles the last Saturday of the month when the Cheshire Historical Society holds its seasonal, merchandise sales. Between the two towns, ephemeral pleasures involve perusing one of the best museum collections of American art in the state, viewing hundreds of gadgets and gizmos at the New Britain Industrial Museum and spending unequaled hours at one of the most appealing and colorful Connecticut places of all—Barker Character, Comic and Cartoon Museum, an elixir to warm the heartstrings of both old and young.

What town did the Connecticut General Assembly designate
as the "Bedding-Plant Capital of Connecticut"?

In which town have officials created a historical park
out of the canal remains that include a restored lock,
the lone survivor out of the original 60?

Vim & Vigor: CHESHIRE

Once part of Wallingford, the first English settlers referred to the low range of hills that form modern-day Cheshire as "Ye Fresh Meadows," which later they called "West Farms on Mill River." Settled in 1694, colonist Thomas Brooks bestowed the town with its contemporary name in 1705, asserting that the region had resembled his homeland in Cheshire, England. The town's southern section identified today as "Brooksvale," bears a long-lasting tribute to him.

As the area grew to a whooping 2,015, the state legislature established it as a separate town in 1780. Marking the beginning of the 19th century, a stagecoach linking New Haven and Hartford helped accelerate further growth. By the mid-1800s, copper and barytes (barium sulfate) mining also influenced the town's economy. The native copper supply spurred such factories as the Cheshire Manufacturing Company, founded in 1850, it is still in existence today as the Ball and Socket Company.

Manufacturing-based businesses have remained the focal point in Cheshire's north end. The rest of town is eclectically proportioned with two state-prison facilities, one youth-correctional facility and the prestigious Cheshire Academy, a college-preparatory school. Additionally, townsfolk take pride in their high school football team, the Cheshire Rams.

Despite commercial and residential developments, it is a suburban hamlet, rural in nature. Thousands of open-space acres lace through the 32.91 square miles of land. Copious farmland remains in this town of some 28,000 residents; a telltale fact when fresh flower and vegetable harvests augment the countryside. In fact, the profusion of bedding-plant growers led the Connecticut General Assembly to designate Cheshire as the "Bedding-Plant Capital of Connecticut."

For a day trip with panache, transport your imagination back to the period between 1828 and 1848 and investigate the refurbished section of the Farmington Canal at **Lock 12 Historical Park**. Once a failed transportation system, today the expanse wins accolades from visitors seeking simple pleasures. In its heyday, before railroads made barge transport obsolete, the canal was the longest in New England.

Today, day-trippers can explore the remains of Lock 12, the lone survivor out of the original 60. A museum complements the grounds. Comprising part of the Farmington Canal Linear Park system, bikers, joggers, walkers, in-line skaters and cross-country skiers can embark upon the former five-mile canal path that runs the course of Cheshire to Hamden. Nosh in the designated picnic area.

While in a "green" frame of mind, about one mile north, across from the Cheshire High School on South Main (Route 10), experience community pride at **Bartlem Recreation Area** (203-272-2743). Adorned with a dazzling array of gardens, complete with the town's pool, take a stroll, bring a picnic, watch local baseball or let the kids blow-off steam at the playground or skateboard park.

For another resplendent act of nature, consider **Roaring Brook Falls**, about two miles north off Mountain Road (203-272-2743). The Cheshire Land Trust has preserved the natural beauty of this 80-foot-high waterfall—the highest single drop in the state. Day-trippers will find natural trails, an abundance of wildlife and wildflowers. Consider an impromptu visit in the spring after heavy rainfalls when the waterfall blasts in full gusto.

Farther north, about five miles on Notch Road, near the Cheshire/Prospect town line, the **Mixville Recreation Area** (203-272-2743), home to Mixville Pond, provides multi-seasonal activities for day-trippers that include swimming, fishing, ice skating and sledding. **Cheshire Park** (203-272-2743), Route 10, is the town's 75-acre treasure. In the summer, day-trippers should make note of free evening music concerts at the amphitheater.

Traveling north, less than 10 miles, is one of the most feel-good-all-over and unequaled places for both young and old anywhere—just look for the outdoor wooden caricatures like Lone Ranger and Tonto and family members from the Jetsons. Entering the **Barker Character, Comic and Cartoon Museum** is like taking a journey back to childhood—for children, the glee is magnified. Unfortunately, nothing out of the thousands of advertising, television character and comic-strip memorabilia acquisitions is for sale, but the most "unclutter bugs" may be inspired to begin amassing some sort of nostalgic collection of their own; the on-premises gift shop may just get them started.

Thousands of artifacts represent the collection that dates back to the early 20th century. Marvel at a rare 1900 Yellow Kid Pulver gum vending machine or 1904 Victor Talking Machine with a dancing man in the center. The museum's ceiling alone exhibits more than 300 vinyl, plastic and metal lunch boxes. Admire the ventriloquist cases that display Charlie McCarthy and Howdy Doody puppets. Imagine walls and display cases of PEZ dispensers, cowboy and western collectibles, more than 2,000 plastic cup collectibles and more than 600 Ty ® and Disney Beanies ®. Wait until you feast your eyes on a rare Superman and two Ronald McDonald telephones! And who can forget those California Raisin characters?

The impetus behind the museum is Herb and Gloria Barker's zeal for collecting toy memorabilia that started back in the '80s. So enthusiastic to share their passion and inspire others, especially kids, who the Barkers believe won't go wayward if they are kept busy with a hobby of collecting any kind of stuff (lots of it!), the couple offers day-trippers free admission to the museum. (They support the museum with proceeds from their separate merchandising and advertising businesses.) Museumgoers can also watch old cartoons in the theater. Before final departure, examine fine art and sculpture in the newest building on the grounds, the **Barker Animation Art Gallery**.

Spend a day, too, perusing idyllic downtown Cheshire. Weekdays, stop at 10 Main Street to view the latest display of artwork and photography at the **Kohn-Joseloff Gallery at Cheshire Academy** (203-272-5396). To help bring the feeling of respite home, with all the bargains, it is easy to find a relaxing read at **Buck-A-Book** (203-699-9902) at 961 Main Street. Within two miles southward, the last Saturday of the month, April through October, means the historical society is running its Antiques and Collectibles Sale at its headquarters, the **Hitchcock-Phillips House** (203-272-2574; www.cheshirehistory.org), located on the Cheshire Green at 43 Church Drive. Inquire about tours that members offer at the 1785 Georgian-style mansion, an experience heightened by period furnishings and historical exhibits. Shoppers should also call for operating hours for the society's **Boutique in the Shed,** located behind the house.

For a completely different perspective of the area, May through November, reserve a hot-air balloon ride from **Balloon Rides by Castle View** (203-272-6116; www.castleviewballoons.com). For year-round aerial adventures, call **Beaver Brook Hot-Air Balloon Services** (203-271-2004).

Back on the ground, in the downtown vicinity, out of the barrage of familiar franchise-type eateries, Cheshire boasts some popular spots that include **Tatzza's A Coffee Roaster** (203-250-7806), open for breakfast and lunch, Monday through Saturday; **Watch Factory Restaurant** (203-271-1717), open for lunch and dinner, Tuesday through Saturday; **Waverly Tavern** (203-272-5998), open for lunch and dinner, Tuesday through Sunday and **Victorian House Restaurant** (203-272-5743), open for lunch and dinner, daily.

Blackie's Hot Dog Stand (203-699-1819) has been a Waterbury Road legend since 1928, especially when it comes to its award-winning wieners and homemade relish. Highland Avenue favorites are **Paul's Restaurant** (203-271-3663), open for breakfast and lunch, daily, and **Brix Restaurant** (203-272-3584), open for lunch and dinner, Monday through Friday, and Saturday dinner. For lighter appetites and after-dinner treats, try **Scrooples Ice Cream** (203-699-8995), which is open daily in West Cheshire. Before leaving the area, make note that **Bishop Farms** (203-272-8243) and **Hickory Hill Orchards** (203-272-3824) are open during the good part of the year and sell produce and other seasonal, gourmet and specialty items. Any local can give directions to Academy Road's **Norton Brothers' Fruit Farm**; the family has rebuilt the 150-year-old, 50-by-100-foot barn, and expanded its retail operation that includes some of the freshest fruit and produce anyone can find.

GETTING THERE:

Cheshire is approximately 91 miles northeast of New York City, 16 miles north of New Haven, 27 miles south of Hartford and 13 miles east of Waterbury. Cheshire is at the intersection of many major highways and roads. Cheshire is easily accessible from Interstate Highways 91, 84, 691 and Routes 70, 68 and 10.

TRANSPORTATION:

Tweed New Haven Regional Airport is approximately 16 miles driving distance from Cheshire and provides daily service to 126 cities through US Airways and Delta Airlines. Additionally, Cheshire is approximately 39 miles east from Danbury's Municipal Airport (203-743-3300; 203-797-4624), a tower-controlled facility with two runways, which serves the general aviation user. The area is approximately 43 miles southwest of Bradley International Airport in Windsor Locks. Stewart International Airport in Newburgh, New York, is approximately 77 miles west in driving distance. The three major New York City metro airports are Westchester County Airport, LaGuardia, JFK and Newark Airport in New Jersey.

The CT Transit Waterbury District, operated by North East Transportation, services Cheshire, call (203) 753-2538 or (203) 755-8242. Waterbury also offers the closest city Metro-North commuter rail services, (800) 638-7646.

ADDITIONAL INFORMATION:
LOCK 12 HISTORICAL PARK.
487 North Brooksvale Road. Open daily from sunrise to sunset, March to November. Call for tour hours and days of operation at the canal museum. Also, inquire about lock and blacksmithing demonstrations. (203) 272-2743.

BARKER CHARACTER, COMIC & CARTOON MUSEUM.

1188 Highland Avenue. Open all year, Wednesday through Saturday. Tours by appointment, only. General admission is free. (203) 699-3822; www.barkeranimation.com/index.asp.

ACCOMMODATIONS:

CHESHIRE WELCOME INN.

1106 South Main Street. Centrally located, Welcome Inn offers 25 spacious and tastefully decorated units, including eight full-kitchen efficiencies. Guestrooms are equipped with full, modern amenities; some feature microwave ovens and two-person Jacuzzi tubs. Rates (including complimentary tea and coffee): $85-$100. (203) 272-3244.

ANNUAL FESTIVALS/EVENTS

Greater New Haven Convention & Visitor's Bureau, representing 19 communities, provides a gamut of tourism information about Cheshire, which includes seasonal events (800) 332-STAY or (203) 777-8550; www.newhavencvb.org/base/index.cfm. For additional festival and event information, contact the Parks and Recreation Department (203) 272-2743 or the Cheshire Chamber of Commerce (203) 272-2345.

MARCH

The **Annual Home, Garden & Business Expo** is held at Cheshire High School. Expo displays and workshops pertain to, among other things, home improvement and decorating and gardening. Children's activities and food and door prizes are also featured. (203) 272-2345.

JULY/AUGUST

Seasonal musical concerts, ranging from pop to swing to jazz, are part of the **Cheshire Summer Concert Series Under the Stars**. Concerts are free and held at the Cheshire Park Amphitheater, Stony Hill Road and Route 10. (203) 272-2743.

SEPTEMBER

The **Annual Craft Fair** on the Cheshire Green is a juried show with more than 120 artists and crafts. On hand will also be children's activities, raffles and refreshments. Free. (203) 271-1376.

Partake in a day full of exhibitors and vendors, carnival rides and pony rides, music, silent auction, classic car show and numerous other activities at the **Fall Festival and Marketplace** held at Bartlem Park. (203) 272-2345.

OCTOBER

Oktoberfest is an annual celebration brimming with German food, music and beer and is held at the Watch Factory Restaurant. (203) 272-2345.

NOVEMBER

The **Annual Craft Show & Bake Sale** takes place at Cheshire Lutheran Church, 660 W. Main Street. (203) 272-2345.

Cheshire High School, 525 S. Main Street, is the venue for the Cheshire **Jaycees Annual Fine Art & Crafts Fair**. (203) 272-2345.

Cheshire High School, 525 S. Main Street, is also the venue for the **Annual Model Train Show**. (203) 272-2345.

DECEMBER

Eavesdrop in a number of breathtaking homes, clad in their brightest holiday attire at the **Holiday House Tour** sponsored by the Church of Epiphany. (203) 272-4355.

An event that is well over 100 years old is the **Annual Christmas Fair** at the First Congregational Church, 111 Church Street. Visitors can expect homemade gifts, crafts, ornaments, wreaths, baked goods and gingerbread houses and a Christmas lunch featuring corn chowder. (203) 272-5323.

Barker Character, Comic and Cartoon Museum

See pages 268, 270

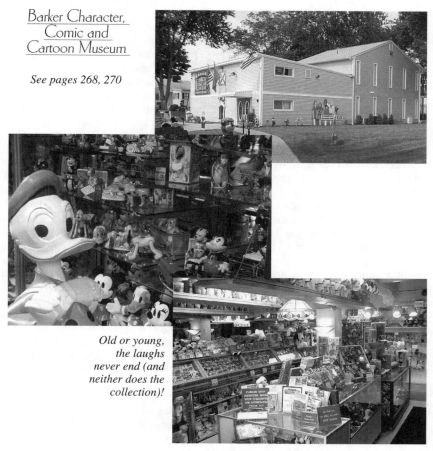

Old or young, the laughs never end (and neither does the collection)!

Photos Courtesy of Barker Character, Comic and Cartoon Museum

What Connecticut city became known as the
"Hardware Capital of the World"?

What municipality boasts the largest
Polish population in Connecticut?

Ethnic Pride: **NEW BRITAIN**

New Britain, an early agricultural community, was named in 1754 after Great Britain, and it was incorporated from the town of Berlin in 1850. In the early 1800s, industrialists produced small brass goods. During the first part of the 20th century, major hardware manufacturers like P. & F. Corbin, North & Judd Manufacturing Company and Stanley Works—still in existence today—flourished in the city and helped New Britain become known as the "Hardware Capital of the World." This industrial 19th-century city touted nearly 1,500 patent awards at one time. Job demand brought an influx of immigrants and commercial developments grew.

While plant relocations and closings affected New Britain's economy in the past decades, the city today is still a forerunner in manufacturing with an emerging strong technological base that has helped create economic revitalization. Downtown preserves an "old world flavor," accentuated with antique-style lighting, renovated streets and new walkways, and has capitalized on a new state-of-the-art regional courthouse, a new government center and new retail establishments.

The city, characterized by hilly terrain, spans a mere 13.2 square miles. With a total residential population hovering around 71,000, true to its immigrant roots, New Britain boasts the largest Polish population in Connecticut. Broad Street alone, with its many ethnic restaurants and retail stores, is a testimony to this fact. The city is also home to New Britain General Hospital, Central Connecticut State University, the oldest public university (1849), enrolling approximately 9,400 undergraduates and 2,730 graduates, not to mention its offspring, the Institute for Industrial and Engineering Technology.

In addition, a superb park system and strong involvement of grassroots art associations have made New Britain a popular day-trip destination. With a copy of the New Britain Chamber of Commerce's (860-225-5507; access online: www. newbritaindd.com/NBDDwalk.pdf) *New Britain Architectural Walking Tour* pamphlet in hand, day trips with panache escort the visitor through revitalized downtown. The must-see area is a mélange of restored monuments and imposing buildings, primarily constructed of granite, brownstone, limestone, brick terra cotta, boasting architectural detail; some encapsulated by gargoyles, many of which are National Historic Landmarks.

In the heart of downtown, in the Institute for Industrial and Engineering Technology building, the **New Britain Industrial Museum** tells the story of the "Hardware City's" industrial heyday. The collection, dating back to 1812, features changing exhibitions, highlighting manufacturing companies and the artifacts they created: hammers, screwdrivers, meat grinders, food choppers, eggbeaters, locks and keys and such. Explore the exhibit dedicated to Avery's Beverages (and then later in the day, grab a bottle of the real stuff [see below])—in a city that claims to have the best-tasting water in Connecticut.

Still in downtown, shoppers shouldn't miss **Amatos Department Store** (860-229-9069; www.hobbysurplus.com/AmatosToyAndHobby.htm). Open daily (double check seasonal schedule), the store has serviced customers since 1940 and is a legendary provider of toys, trains, arts and crafts and a complete scouting line.

Less than one mile westward, where quaint, old homes dot tree-lined streets, next to Walnut Hill Park, look for a 19th-century mansion housing the **New Britain Museum of American Art**. One of the top-10 American art museums in the country, the permanent collection is a treasure trove of more than 5,000 American artworks dating from 1740 to the present. Founded in 1903, it goes down in history as the first museum in the country to devote itself to American art. Headline artists include: Thomas Hart Benton, Mary Cassatt, Frederic Edwin Church, John Singer Sargent, James McNeill Whistler and Andrew Wyeth. In 2004, renovation and construction began. Expect the new facility to accommodate an additional 43,000 square feet of gallery space, an auditorium and café.

While in the vicinity, stroll through **Walnut Hill Park** (860-826-3360). Frederick Law Olmsted, most noted for masterminding New York's Central Park, designed the sprawling 90-acre grounds. In the summer, hear free musical performances from jazz to children's concerts. Jog, bicycle or walk the track. Try out the tennis courts. Take five in front of the World War I monument dedicated to New Britain's fallen soldiers.

Approximately two miles southeast is South Main's unrivaled **Willow Brook Park**, home to the New Britain Stadium hosting the **New Britain Rock Cats** (860-224-8383; www.rockcats.com), a member of the Eastern League AA professional baseball. Catch a game in season beginning in April and running through September.

North of Walnut Hill at High Street, children aren't the only ones sampling a taste of Connecticut history and culture at the **New Britain Youth Museum**, where exhibits range from paper toys to artifacts to memorabilia illustrating New Britain's past. Note: **Hungerford Park** (860-827-9064; www.newbritainyouthmuseum.org), adjacent to Willow Brook Park, in the Kensington section of Berlin, is the Youth Museum's "more natural" sibling, featuring a nature center complete with farm animals and a wildlife rehabilitation center.

Across from Central Connecticut State University, another popular outdoor venue is **Stanley Quarter Park** (860-826-3360). Bring the teens to its skate park, one of New England's largest skateboard parks. Stanley Pond also welcomes fishing poles, aqua cycles and paddleboats, not to mention sunbathers in the summer and ice-skaters in the winter.

To satisfy golf passions, the **Stanley Golf Course** (860-827-1362; www.stanleygolf.com), a public venue, is just northeast of the park. Before teeing off, don't forget a helping of "famous" buffalo wings at the on-site restaurant, **Zabbara** (860-229-7270).

Nightfall, journey to 1615 Stanley Street, CCSU's recently renovated **Copernican Observatory and Planetarium** (860-832-3399; 860-832-2950; www.ccsu.edu/astronomy). Call for a schedule of upcoming shows, special programs and scope out one of the largest, public telescopes in the United States.

Twenty-four hours, 365 days, the eternal flame burns at the **National Iwo Jima Monument**, east of the university at Ella Grasso Boulevard. This 40-foot, bronze monument depicts six soldiers raising a 48-star American flag. Both the flame and monument are perpetual reminders of World War II sacrifices accomplished in the name of freedom.

For those who seek art, theater and culture, one need not look far while visiting New Britain. A good starting point is the **Art League of New Britain** (860-229-1484; www.alnb.org), one of the oldest, continuously active American art leagues that presents public showings.

Visitors do not have to go farther than the university to experience other eclectic blends of expressions. At 1516 Stanley Street, check out the latest exhibition at the **Samuel S.T. Chen Fine Arts Center**, **University Galleries** (860-832-2633; call for schedule; www.art.ccsu.edu/Gallery.html).

Note that the **CCSU Music Department** (860-832-2912; www.music.ccsu.edu/concert.html) presents more than 40 annual recitals, a variety of concerts from jazz to pop by students, faculty and professional musicians, such as the **New Britain Symphony** (860-826-6344; www.newbritainsymphony.org), making its quarters in the Welte Auditorium at CCSU. Schedule additional dates to listen to some other professional musicians that make the town proud: **CONCORA/Connecticut Choral Artists** (860-224-7500; www.concora.org); **Connecticut Virtuosi Chamber Orchestra** (860-612-4371; www.thevirtuosi.org) and the **Greater New Britain Opera Association** (860-224-2466; www.newbritainarts.org).

The theater department at CCSU produces four to five faculty-directed productions ranging from classical to modern, showcasing student actors and stage crews. Most shows premiere at the intimate 100-seat **Black Box Theatre** (860-832-3152; www.theatre.ccsu.edu), 1615 Stanley Street.

For a taste of community theater, book a show, September through June, at the 261-seat **Repertory Theatre of New Britain** (860-223-3147; www.nbrep.org) at 23 Norden Street. Another idea to help obtain a dose of community culture is Main Street's **Hole in the Wall Theater** (860-229-3049; www.hitw.org). A neighborhood venue since 1972, it won the distinction of being *Hartford Advocate's best community theater* for numerous, consecutive years. Hole in the Wall presents a variety of six productions annually as well as special showcases.

Day-trippers who happen to be in New Britain the second Saturday of the month (September through April) can experience local and faraway excursions by viewing the monthly photographic travelogues the **New Britain Camera Club** presents at the library's community room, 20 High Street (860-224-3155; nbcameraclub.home.comcast.net).

Within three miles west of downtown, day trips are not complete without sampling why people "Always Ask for Avery's," as it says on the bottle of every Avery's soda, distributed in 12- and 32-ounce bottle containers. The main headquarters for **Avery's Beverages LLC** (860-224-0830; www.averysoda.com) has been in the same red barn on Corbin Avenue since Sherman F. Avery started testing his sweet recipes in 1904. Today, Avery's is one of the oldest soda bottling companies in New England. Primarily distributed throughout central Connecticut, there are more than 30 flavors available, including cream, birch beer, orange crème, lime, cola, pineapple, strawberry, black cherry, along with a diet-soda line. To top the day off with even more "bubbly," the staff is favorable to giving tours Tuesday through Friday between 11 a.m. and 4 p.m.

Whether it involves fast food, pizza, Chinese or more substantial meals, New Britain presents a comprehensive dining scene. For a breakfast, lunch or dinner, mosey into **Texas Lunch** (860-229-3000; no Saturday dinner and closed Sunday), 26 Main Street. Another option for breakfast or lunch, Monday through Friday, at 3 Main Street is **Anne's Gourmet Deli** (860-832-8200). As one would expect in New Britain, Polish cuisine rules, presenting options, such as South Main's **Fatherland Polish Restaurant** (860-224-3345), serving lunch and dinner daily; at 60 Broad

Street, **Cracovia** (860-223-4443), open for breakfast, lunch and dinner daily and at 252 Broad **Staropolska Restaurant** (860-860-612-1711), serving lunch and dinner daily. For those who have a yen for German cuisine, consider **East Side Restaurant** (860-223-1188) at 131 Dwight Street, open for lunch and dinner, Tuesday through Saturday; dinner is served beginning at noon Sunday.

No day in New Britain is complete without spending downtime at **Leaves & Pages** (860-224-4414), 59 West Main Street, open daily, except Sunday. Grab a (mostly used) book, recline and enjoy the local artwork on the walls; linger for a while over a cup of tea or coffee.

Consider shopping for fresh produce from July to November at **Urban Oaks Farmers' Market** (860-223-6200), 225 Oak Street, southwest of the university. (Inquire about the farm stand's year-round schedule at the same location.)

GETTING THERE:
New Britain is approximately 34 miles north of New Haven, 12 miles southwest of Hartford and 24 miles northeast of Waterbury. New Britain is easily accessible from Interstate Highways 91, 84 and Route 72, which cuts through the city's center.

TRANSPORTATION:
Tweed New Haven Regional Airport is approximately 34 miles driving distance from New Britain and provides daily service to 126 cities through US Airways and Delta Airlines. Additionally, New Britain is approximately 49 miles northeast from Danbury's Municipal Airport (203-743-3300; 203-797-4624), a tower-controlled facility with two runways, which serves the general aviation user. The area is approximately 26 miles south of Bradley International Airport in Windsor Locks. Stewart International Airport in Newburgh, New York, is approximately 90 miles west in driving distance. The three major New York City metro airports are Westchester County Airport, LaGuardia, JFK and Newark Airport in New Jersey. New Britain Transit services New Britain, call (860) 828-0512. Berlin, three miles away, offers Amtrak train service (800-872-7245).

Union Station Transportation Center, a multi-model transportation center in downtown Hartford, also provides scheduled Amtrak service (800-USA-RAIL). Nonstop bus transportation (860-247-5329) to every major northeast city also runs regularly to and from Union Station.

ADDITIONAL INFORMATION:
NEW BRITAIN INDUSTRIAL MUSEUM.
185 Main Street. Open all year, Monday through Friday. General admission is free. (860) 832-8654; www.nbim.org.

NEW BRITAIN MUSEUM OF AMERICAN ART.
56 Lexington Street. Open all year, Tuesday through Sunday. Inquire about children's programs, special events and lectures. General admission is $6.00 adults; $5.00 seniors; $4.00 students and free to children 12 and under and to museum members. (860) 229-0257; www.nbmaa.org.

NEW BRITAIN YOUTH MUSEUM.

30 High Street. Open all year, Tuesday through Saturday. Inquire about children's and family programs and special events. General admission is free. (General admission for the museum's sibling, Hungerford Park in the Kensington section of Berlin is $4.00 adults; $3.00 seniors; $2.00 students and free to children 2 and under and museum members.) New Britain Youth Museum: (860) 225-3020; www. newbritainyouthmuseum.org; Hungerford Park: (860) 827-9064.

ACCOMMODATIONS:

BRIANNA'S BED AND BREAKFAST.

32 Vine Street. Renovated to its original 1880 Victorian radiance, innkeeper Larry Knee named this B & B after his granddaughter. The four guestrooms extend gracious charm and guests can't help but relax in the comfortable common areas. Rates (including full, formal gourmet breakfast): $95 (additional rates for combined rooms). (860) 229-4262; www.briannasbnb.com.

DAYS INN.

65 Columbus Boulevard. Six floors accommodate 72 renovated guestrooms that offer full, modern amenities. The hotel is pet friendly, catering to both the pleasure and business traveler. Rates (including complimentary, continental breakfast): $59.99-$150.00. (860) 224-9161.

ANNUAL FESTIVALS/EVENTS

The Central Regional Tourism District, Connecticut's Heritage River Valley, representing a total of 46 communities, provides a gamut of tourism information, which includes seasonal events (800) 793-4480 or (860) 244-818; www. enjoycentralct.com. For additional festival and event information, contact the New Britain Chamber of Commerce at (860) 229-1665.

FEBRUARY

The **Annual Winterfest** is a free event held in Stanley Quarter Park. Activities include ice sculpture exhibits, ice skating, hayrides, live animals, helicopter rides, bonfires and food. (860) 826-3360.

APRIL

Approximately 100 singers from every faith in greater New Britain gather annually and present a music performance of the **New Britain Chorale**. Call for performance schedule and venue. (860) 229-3751; www.newbritainarts.org.

The Art League of New Britain presents to the public the **Annual Open Juried Spring Exhibition**, 30 Cedar Street. (860) 229-1484; www.alnb.org.

JUNE

Polish Pride is a weekend festival held at Veteran's Memorial Stadium. Festival features include soccer games, live musical entertainment and Polish food.

JULY/AUGUST

Seasonal musical concerts, ranging from pop to swing to jazz, are part of the **Walnut Hill Park Summer Music Festivals**. (860) 826-3360.

OCTOBER

The **Antique Auto Show** is a premiere family event held at Klingberg Family Center featuring automobiles that were manufactured before 1972. There are special displays, horse-drawn carriage rides, food, music and a DJ spinning oldies music. The many children's activities include a petting zoo and face painting. Parking with shuttle bus service is at Willow Brook Park. (860) 224-9113.

The opening of the **Annual Fall Carriage House Exhibit**, sponsored by the New Britain's Arts Alliance and the Art League, is popular with the art community as well as the community at large. (860) 229-1484; www.alnb.org.

NOVEMBER

Annual Autographed Book & Memorabilia Auction unveils hundreds of items and benefits the Youth Museum. (860) 225-3020.

Visit the **Joy of Art** program, an annual juried art show, presented at the Hospital for Special Care, 2150 Corbin Avenue. (860) 827-4774.

Annual Pedaling for Pathways Walkathon/Bikeathon, held at Walnut Hill Park, attracts participants and spectators of all ages. (860) 229-2776.

The **Annual Friendship Antiques & Collectibles Show** at the Special Care Community Center, Osgood and Corbin Avenues, is a shopper's delight and benefits a worthy cause. (860) 225-0211.

DECEMBER

Catch a free annual performance of **Handel's Messiah** at St. Jerome Church, 1010 Slater Road, by the New Britain Musical Club. (860) 224-2411.

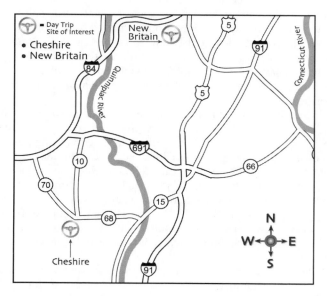

X.

NORTHWEST CONNECTICUT

Hartford County/Litchfield County

"Litchfield Hills"

Bristol/Litchfield/Washington/Kent

Known as Litchfield Hills, a 26-town cluster in northwestern Connecticut, nestled in the Berkshire foothills and sliced by the Housatonic River, the area is dotted with covered bridges, town greens, white clapboard houses, quaint inns, lush woodlands and endlessly rolling hills capturing the term "picture perfect." One of the best ways to experience this example of Mother Nature's grandeur is to motor along Routes 7, 41 and 272.

During fall, join hundreds of other leaf peepers on one- and two-lane roads set aglow with red, yellow and orange. Wintertime's wand paints the 100-year-old maples with sparkling white until they appear like spirited roadside ghosts. The colder weather in the Litchfield Hills in comparison to the rest of the state due to higher elevation doesn't hinder outdoor fun—ice boaters zip through the frigid shores and determined ice anglers, pole in hand, drill holes in the many lakes. Spring and summer signal nature's multi-colored floral canvases, deep green grasses and fresh breezes. Close to the New York State and Massachusetts borders, over the years, art colonies, eclectic boutiques, distinctive antiques shops, and fine-dining restaurants have paved the way for a number of celebrities, entertainers and prominent citizens to relocate themselves in these legendary hills where solitude meets sophistication.

Experience a day of fun at Lake Compounce, the country's oldest amusement park. Visit the Carousel Museum of New England touting one of the finest collections of antique carousels in the world. Be amazed viewing more than 3,000 timepieces on display at the American Clock and Watch Museum.

In Litchfield County, the towns of Litchfield and Kent are magnets for patrons who appreciate fine art, antiques and history. In fact, the entire center of Litchfield, with its 1828 Congregational Church and tidy examples of 18th- and 19th-century architecture, is designated a National Historic District. A hiker's favorite, Bull's Bridge in Kent leads to Macedonia Brook State Park and the Cobble Mountain Trail. Kent Falls State Park, with its cascading waterfalls, inspires both romantic and solitary moments.

One of the most sought-after restaurants in Litchfield County that provides a beautiful setting for intimate conversation is the Mayflower Inn, located in the hamlet of Washington. Day-trippers can encounter a simulated archaeological site at the Institute for American Indian Studies or simply experience the town's quiet countryside.

---

*What Connecticut city became the nation's capital
for the clock and watch industry?*

*What city is considered the birthplace of the
American metal spring?*

Bodacious: **BRISTOL**

Sharing part of Farmington's early history, Bristol was part of the 165-square-mile parcel west of Hartford that the native Tunxis Indians deeded to settlers in 1650. Possessing early agricultural roots, the city was originally comprised of small parishes known as New Cambridge and West Britain until it was incorporated from Farmington in 1785 and named after Bristol, England.

This small, central Connecticut city became the nation's capital for the clock and watch industry. Beginning in 1841, Theodore Terry, nephew of Eli Terry, an East Windsor-born clockmaker who mentored Seth Thomas, sparked the phenomenon. The younger Terry formed a partnership with Franklin C. Andrews, another clockmaker and their firm, Terry and Andrews, manufactured inexpensive, brass clocks. Although about 100 factories producing clocks appeared in Bristol, the Terry and Andrews company was the largest.

Bristol is also the birthplace of the American spring industry, and unlike the clock business, is still a large employer in town. Budding entreprenuers Albert and Edward Rockwell relocated to Bristol in 1888, taking advantage of its strong industrial climate. The two invented a spring-driven mechanism to ring doorbells, replacing the commonly used electric battery. Their company, New Departure Bell, became one of the largest bell factories in America giving Bristol its nickname, "Bell City."

Situated on the Pequabuck River, modern-day Bristol is still a hub for manufacturing, but best known today for housing the ESPN headquarters. It's also a leading chrysanthemum producer, thus the city's second nickname, "Mum City," and its annual celebration of the flower has gained a following well outside town borders.

In 1997, serious sports-minded citizens created the Bristol Sports Hall of Fame, and ever since have inducted annually the finest, local athletes into its roster. Hometown pride is also in the A. Bartlett Giamatti Little League Leadership Training Center, the eastern regional center for Little League Baseball, providing clinics, camps and special events throughout the year.

With a residential population of just over 60,000 covering 26.6 square miles, the city's downtown has been given a revitalized look, including aesthetic landscaping, new sidewalks, benches and street lighting. The historical jewel of the neighborhood, Federal Hill Green, located within the Federal Hill Historic District, rises above the town. Many fine examples of historically preserved buildings border this approximate one-acre triangular park.

Instrumental in conserving the past, the **Bristol Historical Society** (860-583-6309) is in the process of converting Bristol's former high school, initially opened in 1891, into a museum. Located at 98 Summer Street, at the corner of Center Street, day-trippers can look forward to a first-rate facility devoted to exhibits concentrating on area history. Bristol historians are doing a good job—the *ePodunk*

Historic Small Towns Index ranked Bristol as number four nationally and number one in Connecticut.

Wouldn't you know that the nation's oldest amusement park and one of the state's most popular attractions is **Lake Compounce**. In fact, Boulder Dash, one of the park's two wooden roller coasters recently garnered the *best of* vote from the *Golden Ticket Awards*, sponsored by *Amusement Today* magazine. Winner of numerous other *best of* awards given by regional publications, Lake Compounce has been in continuous operation since 1846 and has provided more than 150 years of day trips with panache.

Kennywood Entertainment in Pittsburgh currently owns this 325-acre park, situated by the lake of the same name. The park's other wooden roller coaster is the Wildcat, built in 1927. Don't miss a spin on the 1911 carousel, one of the oldest in the country, it showcases a menagerie of 49 horses, two chariots and one goat. Experience the Mark Twain sternwheeler, the Zoomerang sky ride or a legion of other amusements, including the 185-foot drop tower, Downtime, one of the park's newest additions. Another newcomer, sure to titillate audiences, is a 70-foot high swing named Thunder N' Lightning. Beat the heat at the water park featuring a 300-gallon water bucket, water cannons and slides. Don't leave the park without taking a ride on the C.P. Huntington Railroad Train, designed and built by actor William Gillette (see **Haddam** chapter) in 1943.

Throughout the operating season, catch free shows and entertainment geared to all interests and ages. During October, the main fall attraction is a haunted graveyard, an hour-long journey into a fantastically frightening array of spooky goblins!

Back toward the heart of Bristol, three miles northeast, the **New England Carousel Museum and Cultural Center** boasts more than 30,000 square feet of renovated display space within a defunct turn-of-the century factory building last producing hosiery. The highlight of this museum is 40 handcrafted horses, giraffes and other artisan carvings dating back to the 1800s.

Check out the new **Museum of Fire History**, 15,000 square feet displaying a 1936 American LaFrance "Invader" as well as hundreds of other fire-related items and memorabilia like firefighters' helmets and whistles. Carlyle F. (Hap) Barnes, who retired from the Barnes Group Foundation, a manufacturing company in Bristol, donated most of the items. His collection, amassed over a 50-year period, was started by his great, great grandfather, one of the founding members of the Bristol Fire Department, of which, Barnes, himself, served as commissioner for 50 years.

Additionally, the Cultural Center anticipates the opening of a satellite facility for the University of Connecticut at Storrs, emphasizing Greek history, culture and art. Still on the drawing board, a collection of artifacts and artwork, some owned by the university, will likely illustrate Greek society from ancient to modern times.

For day trips with kids, **Imagine Nation Museum** is within a half mile of the cultural center, traveling east. Parents and children don't have to go far to have fun. Instead, once inside, before checking out the museum's exhibits, they can slurp drinks at the old-fashioned soda fountain, a rescued object from old Redman's Dairy. However, upon entering all that Imagine Nation has to offer, it is likely patrons might not want to leave too soon. Home to the only teaching elevator in the world (thanks to the contribution from Otis Elevator), other hands-on exhibits include "competing" in sports' activities made possible by a high-tech display sponsored by Bristol-based ESPN. Get your hands dirty and learn about gardening and worldwide conservation at the greenhouse. Enjoy the outdoor scenery, complete with musical chimes.

Less than four miles northeast, the collection of mostly American timepieces dating from the 17th century to present, owned by the **American Clock and Watch Museum**, is one of the largest in the nation. One walk-through reinforces the museum's mission: "To preserve the history, artifacts and memorabilia of the clock manufacturing industry that had once been so vital to the town of Bristol." Housed inside the tidy 1801 Miles Lewis House, museum volunteer and ardent horologist, Tom Grimshaw, explains another key point of the museum: "This museum is all about the story of the American clock *and* the American Industrial Revolution, because the American Industrial Revolution started with the clockmakers. The first interchangeable parts, the first true factory, the first use of unskilled labor to make a very high-tolerance part—is what Eli Terry did. This is what ignited the productivity of the country."

Day-trippers should schedule time to view more than—some kept running and chiming—1,400 clocks and watches on display including grandfather clocks, shelf clocks, wall clocks, character watches, novelties, and an impressive assortment of unusual and rare pieces.

October day-trippers should schedule a visit for nominal cost to the **Silver Screen Museum and Archives** (860-583-8306; www.preservehollywood.org/home.htm; call for exact weekend dates and hours) at 90 Battle Street, approximately three miles northeast from the American Clock and Watch Museum. First debuting in 1966, this facility gives a fascinating behind-the-scenes look into classic fantasy and sci-fi moviemaking. Featured on CNN, the museum is also home to the *Witch's Dungeon*, an exhibit of highly life-like wax figures from horror and sci-fi classics. Visitors can view the life casts representing such actors as Boris Karloff, Bela Lugosi and Vincent Price. Additionally, some of the background sets, props and clothing were actually salvaged from the original films. Dioramas are simulated by recorded voice-overs from such personalities as Vincent Price and Mark Hamill.

Fundraising to transform the museum into a yearlong attraction includes saving the proceeds from **"Hollywood at the Bijou"** (860-583-8306; call for show times and dates), a weekly classic film series presented at the Forestville Theater, 815 Pine Street. Shows include film stars, such as Humphrey Bogart, Ingrid Bergman, Orson Welles and Vincent Price, all projected on the big screen.

For those seeking musical adventures, the **Bristol Symphony Orchestra** (860-567-4506) and the **Bristol Brass and Wind Ensemble** (860-567-4506; www.geocities.com/bristolbrass), two community-based organizations, perform free concerts at numerous town venues. Before leaving town, bowlers should make note of **Bristol Ten Pin** (860-583-1669). The facility offers public bowling at nominal prices, especially during weekdays. For a variety of Christian-based, live entertainment, call on the **Cup of Grace Coffeehouse** at the Grace Baptist Church (860-584-3840; www.grace-baptist.net).

The city offers 700 acres of parks and athletic fields, such as **DeWitt Page Park** (860-584-6160) in the Federal Hill section, providing residents and nonresidents, among other things, an outdoor swimming pool, playgrounds, five lighted tennis courts, a basketball court and a fishing lagoon available for children under16 years old. While in the outdoors frame of mind, catch a free summer concert at **Rockwell Park** (860-584-6160), Route 72.

About four miles north from downtown, the 70-acre sanctuary of the **Harry C. Barnes Memorial Nature Center** embodies one of the most popular sources for indoor and outdoor day trips. There are more than two miles of marked hiking trails. The nature center contains interpretive displays, animal exhibits, nature library and gift shop.

One needn't travel far to find foodstuff. Bristol extends a cornucopia of fast-food chains and a good selection of diners. Pizza restaurant selections win the vote for popularity; the following sample dining options are open daily for lunch and dinner: **LJs Pizza** (860-582-4115), 101 Maple Street; **Corner Pizza** (860-583-4672), 483 Farmington Avenue; **Centre Mall Pizza** (860-583-4000), 60 North Main Street; **Two Brothers Pizza** (860-314-1366), 962 Pine Street; **Mike's Pizza** (860-589-2566), 182 Pine Street and **MG Pizza and Wings** (860-583-9062), 90 Burlington Avenue. **Frankie's Hotdogs** (860-584-9826), 1195 Farmington Avenue, also open daily for lunch and dinner is as legendary here as it is in Waterbury (see **Waterbury** chapter) and at other locations.

GETTING THERE:
Bristol is approximately 19 miles west of Hartford, 43 miles north of New Haven and 12 miles north of Waterbury. Bristol is easily accessible from Interstate Highways 91 and 84 and Route 72, which cuts through the city's center.

TRANSPORTATION:
Tweed New Haven Regional Airport is approximately 43 miles driving distance from Bristol, providing daily service to 126 cities through US Airways and Delta Airlines. Additionally, Bristol is approximately 44 miles northeast from Danbury's Municipal Airport (203-743-3300; 203-797-4624), a tower-controlled facility with two runways, which serves the general aviation user. The area is approximately 33 miles southwest of Bradley International Airport in Windsor Locks. Stewart International Airport in Newburgh, New York, is approximately 87 miles west in driving distance. The three major New York City metro airports are Westchester County Airport, LaGuardia, JFK and Newark Airport in New Jersey. CT Transit (203-624-0151) operates frequent commuter-connections. New Britain Transit services Bristol, call (860) 828-0512. Berlin, about 14 miles away, offers Amtrak train service (800-872-7245). Union Station Transportation Center, a multi-model transportation center in downtown Hartford, also provides scheduled Amtrak service (800-USA-RAIL). Nonstop bus transportation (860-247-5329) to every major northeast city also runs regularly to and from Union Station.

ADDITIONAL INFORMATION:
LAKE COMPOUNCE THEME PARK.
822 Lake Avenue. Open April through October, inquire about hours and days of operation. General admission (price includes most rides) is $31.95 adults; $16.95 seniors; $22.95 juniors (under 52" tall) and free to children 3 and under. (860) 583-3300; www.lakecompounce.com.

NEW ENGLAND CAROUSEL MUSEUM AND CULTURAL CENTER.
95 Riverside Avenue. The museum, center and gift shop are open all year, daily. Inquire about changing fine art exhibitions, educational programs and special events. General admission is $4.00 adults; $4.00 seniors; $2.50 children, free to children 3 and under, and to museum members. (860) 585-5411; www.thecarouselmuseum. com.

IMAGINE NATION MUSEUM.
1 Pleasant Street. Open all year, Wednesday through Saturday. Inquire about children's and family programs, and special events. General admission is $4.00 per person (children must be accompanied by adults); free to children 1 and under and to museum members. (860) 314-1400; www.familycenter.org/ImagineNation.

AMERICAN CLOCK AND WATCH MUSEUM.
100 Maple Street. Open April 1 through November 30, daily. Inquire about children's programs, special events and gallery talks. General admission is $5.00 adults; $4.00 seniors/AAA members; $2.00 children up to 18 years old; free to children 8 and under and to museum members. (860) 583-6070; www.clockmuseum.org.

HARRY C. BARNES MEMORIAL NATURE CENTER.
175 Shrub Road. The trails are open all year during daylight hours in this 70-acre sanctuary. The center with interpretive displays is open all year, Wednesday through Sunday. General admission is by suggested donation. (860) 589-6082; www.elcct. org.

ACCOMMODATIONS:
CHIMNEY CREST MANOR.
5 Founders Drive. Within walking distance to the Carousel Museum, consider this spacious 32-room Tudor mansion, listed on the National Historic Register, as your next home away from home. The four guestrooms and private baths wrap the visitor with elegance; some rooms offer a fireplace and thermal spa. Other amenities include turndown service with pillow chocolates, fresh fruit, candy and tea for guests. Rates (including full, formal gourmet breakfast): $115-$185. (860) 582-4219; www.chimneycrest.com.

CLARION HOTEL.
42 Century Drive. Next door to ESPN, this 120-unit hotel offers full, modern amenities that include a business center and services, exercise room, gift shop, multilingual staff, sauna and indoor heated swimming pool. Rates (including all-American breakfast buffet): $116-plus. Super-value rates (without breakfast) $99. (860) 589-7766; www.choicehotels.com.

ANNUAL FESTIVALS/EVENTS
The Northwest Connecticut Convention and Visitor's Bureau, representing a total of 51 communities in the northwestern region that includes Litchfield Hills, Housatonic Valley and the Waterbury region, provides a gamut of tourism information, which includes seasonal events (860) 567-4506; www.northwestct.com. For additional festival and event information, contact the Greater Bristol Chamber of Commerce (860) 584-4718.

FEBRUARY
The **Greater Bristol Chamber of Commerce Home & Business Show** comes to the grounds of Bristol Eastern High School, 632 King Street. This three-day event

features a variety of vendors and exhibits of interest to homeowners, builders, and the like. (860) 584-4725.

APRIL-OCTOBER
Head out to see the **Bristol Auto Club's Cruise** Saturday nights at North Main's Bristol Center parking lot. Cruise nights are free and feature music, raffles and hula-hoop contests. (860) 584-4718.

JUNE/JULY/AUGUST
Rockwell Park's gazebo, Route 72, is the setting for free Tuesday night **Summer Concert Series** beginning at 7 p.m. (860) 584-6160.

AUGUST
The **Eastern Region Little League Baseball Tournament** takes place at Breen Field, A. Bartlett Giamatti Little League Center. (860) 585-4730.

SEPTEMBER
The **Carousel Lovers Convention** is a nearly weeklong event attracting participants from all over the map. Hosted by the New England Carousel Museum, on hand are vendors, discussions and special programs devoted to the art and history of carousels. (860) 585-5411; www.thecarouselmuseum.com.

One of the largest annual events in Bristol is the **Chrysanthemum Festival and Parade**. Included in the many days of activities are an antique car show; Bristol Heritage Festival and Family Farms Weekend. (860) 584-4718.

The **Annual Bristol Historical Society's Classic Clutter Tag Sale** is a three-day affair filled with bargain delights. Call for location, (860) 583-6309.

The Beals-Senior Community Center sponsors the **Great Teddy Bear Jamboree**, 240 Stafford Avenue. The call of the day includes exhibitors, hourly raffles and the Hungry Bear Snack Bar. (860) 584-7895.

OCTOBER
Limited to the first 200 people, the New England Carousel Museum and Cultural Center hosts the **Annual Halloween Party** for children. The evening features tricks, treats, games and children's costume party. The party admission fee for adults is nominal and free to children. (860) 585-5411; www.thecarouselmuseum.com.

NOVEMBER
Remember to mark the **Gloria Dei Holiday Fair** on your calendar, a day chockfull of crafts, "famous" apple pies, attic treasures, plants, books, children's items and the like. A holiday auction and health booth run by licensed nurses are also available for blood pressure and precautionary stroke screenings. Recharge the day with lunch. The Gloria Dei Lutheran Church sponsors the event at 355 Camp Street. (860) 582-0629.

The **Yankee Peddler Fair** at the United Methodist Church, 90 Church Avenue, features a country breakfast in the morning, plus holiday arts and crafts and baked goods sold throughout the day. (860) 584-0529.

The **Bristol Community Organization Annual Holiday Auction** is held at the St. Gregory Center, 1043 Stafford Avenue. Early holiday shoppers can purchase new donated items and gift certificates for goods and services. (860) 584-2725.

The **Bristol Sports Hall of Fame Induction Ceremony** includes a social hour and dinner. (860) 584-4725.

Sandy's Baton Studio at Chippens Hill Middle School presents the **Annual Miss Twirl Pageant**. (860) 584-4725.

DECEMBER

The Greater Bristol Visiting Nurse Association hosts an **Annual Wine Tasting Gala** at the New England Carousel Museum and Cultural Center. Tour the museum. Enjoy refreshments. (860) 585-5411; www.thecarouselmuseum.com.

The Greater Bristol Chamber of Commerce and the Children's Holiday Festival Committee sponsor a **Holiday Lighting Ceremony**. Live music and refreshments accompany turning on the holiday lights. (860) 584-4718.

Catch a performance of the **Annual Christmas Concert** performed by the Bristol String Orchestra at Liberty Baptist Church, 265 Maple Street. (860) 589-3724.

Sponsored by the Quota Club, the **Holiday House on the Hill Tour** takes a peek behind some of the most magnificent homes in Bristol. (860) 584-4725.

New England
Carousel Museum
See page 282

One of the most colorful stops in Connecticut.

Photos Courtesy of New England Carousel Museum

---

*In what Connecticut town was the first law school
in the United States established?*

*What town touted one of the first major
educational institutions for women?*

Transcendent Traverses: **LITCHFIELD**

Present-day Litchfield's lake, which happens to be Connecticut's largest natural body of water, pays homage to its native namesake: Bantam. Incorporated as the 50th town in Connecticut in 1719, its Litchfield name derives from Staffordshire, England. During the Revolutionary War, while the British occupied New York City and aimed attacks at many of Connecticut's coastal and river settlements, Litchfield's secluded location helped defer the enemy, and its strategic location (between what we recognize as modern-day Hudson River Valley and some prominent Connecticut settlements) helped further the patriot's cause. Today's Litchfield once served as a vital military supply depot; plus, its forefathers helped the revolution by acting as jailers for loyalist prisoners! Its most unique edge in history, however, took place in 1776, when the Sons of Liberty dissembled the lead statue of King George III that stood in Bowling Green, New York City. Afterwards, patriots rushed the pieces to Litchfield and mostly children and women melted the lead down and cast it into 42,000 bullets for soldiers to shoot against the British!

Tapping Reeve, a Litchfield judge with an odd-sounding name, greatly contributed to the town's growth when he coordinated and developed a series of law studies; thereby, establishing the first law school in the United States, the Litchfield Law School in 1784. By 1791, law school student Samuel Miles Hopkins's journal entry best described Litchfield's surging number of college-educated inhabitants: *hard, active, reading, thinking, intelligent men who may probably be set forth as a pattern of the finest community on earth.*

Subsequently, during its 60-year existence, approximately 1,100 men graduated from the law school including two United States Vice Presidents, Aaron Burr (Reeve married his sister, Sally) and John C. Calhoun, and 130 members of Congress.

Litchfield also receives an "A" for academics with Sarah Pierce's Litchfield Female Academy, one of the first, major educational institutions for women. Enrolling more than 2,000 students in its venerable 41-year span, Harriet Beecher Stowe was among the graduates. (Due to the proximity of the law school and the academy, marriages were inevitable!)

These Litchfield schools, along with a strong social, cultural and economic base, formed the town's golden age, between 1784 and 1834. By 1810, the town was the fourth largest settlement in the state with a population of 4,639, and the village, abuzz with successful merchants, included 125 houses and numerous shops and public buildings. However, by the 1840s, without abundant waterpower and railroad means, conceding industrial growth and manufacturing to other towns, Litchfield's popularity waned.

The creation of the 1872 Shepaug Railroad reawakened newcomers to the town's aesthetics, including its preserved and outstanding Colonial Revival-style architecture. Secondly, Bantam Lake's attractive surroundings incited construction of more than a dozen well-appointed hotels. Frequent vacationers, many wealthy New Yorkers seeking country escapes, added to the boom by building summer and vacation homes.

Located southwest of Torrington, in central Litchfield County, Litchfield's sprawling 57.3 square, mainly green miles accommodate about 9,000 residents and draw thousands of annual summer tourists seeking an antidote for ennui. Today, inns and bed and breakfasts have replaced the lakeside hotels, largely. The historic Borough of Litchfield, which includes the green, one of the country's largest, listed as a Historic District, hosts a Colonial-architecture stretch that includes the photogenic Congregational Church and the birthplace of Revolutionary War hero Ethan Allen. Abolitionist writer Harriet Beecher Stowe was also born in Litchfield, a town recently recognized in *Connecticut Magazine's* top-10 index of the *best small towns*. The Beecher House Society, a non-profit organization in town, rescued her homestead, known as the Wadsworth-Beecher home, from demolition. In conjunction with Yale University and University of Connecticut, the house was dismantled. Future day-trippers can expect the house's reconstruction in the University of Connecticut, Torrington campus vicinity.

The preserved Litchfield houses unfold a flattering historical, architectural scene, enhanced in the summer with a town-sponsored, free concert series and an invigorating holiday house tour in wintertime; efforts to launch a day trip with panache are nearly effortless. Litchfield Borough, the oldest such incorporated one in the state, is also the largest. (Note: additional town greens are located in the boroughs of: East Litchfield; Milton, east of the east branch of the Shepaug River; Morris, south of Litchfield Village and Northfield Green, located in the southern part of town.)

Of historical appeal is **Sheldon Tavern** on North Street, a 1760 Colonial-style mansion, now a private home. In its previous incarnation, it served as an inn that George Washington really did sleep in, en route from West Point to Hartford to meet ally General Rochambeau, commander of the French Army (both commanders would later plan the Battle of Yorktown, the final Revolutionary War battle). One other privately owned house of significance, the **Ludlow Bull House**, North Street, was built circa 1828; the L-shaped Colonial Revival-style house exemplifies the favored Litchfield architecture of the mid-20th century. Built by Leonard Goodwin, Mr. Bull purchased the house in 1925 as a weekend home. An Egyptologist with the Metropolitan Museum of Art in New York City, he presided over the unveiling of one of history's most spectacular discoveries—King Tutankhamen's Tomb. The Bull House is among the featured houses on the Holiday House Tour in December (see **Annual Festivals/Events**).

Located in the West Park of **Litchfield Green**, West Street (Route 202), the **Litchfield Hills Information Booth** supplies an array of booklets detailing neighborhood architecture and other tourism information from June through October.

Heading southward, the admission fee to the **Litchfield History Museum** also includes entrance to the **Tapping Reeve House and Law School**, both on South Street. At the first attraction, which is maintained and operated by the Litchfield Historical Society, visitors will encounter seven permanent galleries that showcase American art and artifacts from the 18th through the 21st centuries and their relation to the immediate region. The collection includes furniture and accessories, paintings, textiles, toys, ceramics, trade signs and fine and decorative arts.

Also run by the society, adjacent to the museum, journey through America's first law school at the Tapping Reeve House. Reeve, who originated from Long Island, New York, and moved to Litchfield in 1773, built the house. Law studies as its focal point, the house museum re-creates early 19th-century life through hands-on and interpretive exhibits. For Revolutionary War enthusiasts, the final resting place of Reeve is the **East Burying Ground**, which is located one-half mile east of the courthouse. (Ms. Stowe is buried at Andover Chapel Cemetery in Massachusetts; Ethan Allen is buried at Green Mount Cemetery in Burlington, Vermont.)

Looking for a perfect addition to an art collection? Browse the wide selection of original paintings, prints and sculpture by area artists at **P.S. Gallery** (860-567-1059; www.psgallery.com), open daily, on the green. Note: A *New York Times* journalist called gallery owner Pat Steier, *a pioneer in Litchfield's art boom*. The green affords many other shopping tarries including **Tina's Baskets** (860-567-0385; call for days and hours of operation), featuring handmade weaves and **Jeffrey Tillou Antiques** (860-567-9693; www.tillouantiques.com, call for days and hours of operation), a hodgepodge of 18th- and 19th-century American furniture, decorative accessories and paintings. Wait 'til you see the folk art! For the state's largest collection of antique and period jewelry (circa 1700 through circa 1950), **Bradford House Antiques** (860-567-0951; www.bradfordhouseantiques.com, call for days and hours of operation) is a glittering treasure trove.

About five miles southeast from Litchfield Borough, sometimes international wine connoisseurs travel to tour the facility and taste the award-winning flavors at **Haight Vineyard** (860-567-4045; www.haightvineyards.com), 29 Chestnut Hill Road. Open daily, don't leave "Connecticut's first established winery" showcased in a Swiss-style building, before perusing the gift shop brimming with wine-related foods, such as champagne mustards and wine-related gifts.

Traveling in the opposite direction, east, take time out to enjoy watching the gentle Morgan horses that call **Lee's Riding Stable** (860-567-0785; www.windfieldmorganfarm.com) home. Open daily, the farm offers a petting zoo; pony rides for wee ones, and provides one-hour horseback trail rides for all ages. The first right off Buell Road is the entrance to **Topsmead State Forest**, the setting of the English-Tudor cottage, gardens and grounds of the former summer estate of Miss Edith Morgan Chase, whose father was president of Chase Brass and Copper Company in Waterbury. When not taking advantage of the free, guided tours of the residence, visitors can picnic, bird watch, hike the relatively gentle terrain and cross-country ski in the wintertime.

Northeast about a mile from Topsmead, even non-Catholics can meditate in the tranquil milieu presented by the **Lourdes in Litchfield Shrine Grotto**, replicating the Lourdes Grotto in France. Build by the Montfort Missionaries, the 30-acre shrine was dedicated as a place of "peace, prayer and pilgrimage." Peruse the gift shop for religious articles and consider eating a reasonably priced, homemade lunch, offered during weekdays.

To enhance the meditative mood, visit the **Wisdom House Retreat and Conference Center** (860-567-3163; www.wisdomhouse.org), "an alternative space in an alternative place." You don't have to be a retreat participant to walk the outdoor labyrinth (Connecticut's first!) or view the latest art collection at the Marie Louise Trichet Gallery. Nearly 10 miles west, on 202, **Mount Tom State Park**, one of the oldest in the state park system, is named for the mountain within its boundaries. On the mountaintop, the stone tower is a favored destination among hikers, 1325 feet above sea level. The trail itself is a relatively easy climb, rising about 500 feet and amounting to less than one-mile long. Mount Tom Pond (860-868-2592; call for pricing information and call for days and hours of operation) affords swimming, scuba diving, fishing, canoeing and kayaking. Day-trippers can also bring picnics and leashed pets on the grounds, but pets are prohibited near the pond.

Another nature lover's paradise is about three miles east on Route 202 in Bantam Village. The state's largest preserve, the **White Memorial Foundation**, totaling 4,000 acres, was a 20th-century bequest from conservationist Alan and his sister Mary White, both descendents of wealthy hat manufacturers (see **Kent** chapter) and land contributors to other state park systems. A wildlife sanctuary with a mile-long boardwalk through wetland habitats and 35 acres of trails attract hikers, cross-country skiers, horseback riders, bird-watchers and four-season naturalists. Fishermen and women can cast their bait into **Bantam Lake** and **Bantam River**; both of which are accessible by a public boat launch. (Kayak as well as bicycle rentals can be had from the **Cycle Loft** [860-567-1713], 25 Commons Drive.) Also at the foundation, examine the newly expanded nature museum wherein exhibits focus upon the region's historical and natural resources. Whether day-trippers are in the market for field guides, compasses, binoculars or children's toys, patrons should not overlook the center's store.

While in the Bantam vicinity, athletic types can obtain day passes at the **Litchfield Athletic Club** (860-567-3510) at 599 Bantam Road. Open daily, the 10,000-square-foot health and fitness facility offers racquetball courts, nautilus strength training, massage therapy, yoga classes and a host of workshops. For a less rigorous day, opt for a treatment at the **Spa at Litchfield** (860-567-8575). Whether beginner or expert, golfers can play at **Stonybrook Golf Club** (860-567-9977), a nine-hole, public course that is open from April through December.

Bantam Road offers a gallimaufry of shops. To name a few (call individual stores for days and hours of operation): **Black Swan Antiques** (860-567-4429), **Linsley Antiques** (860-567-4245; 800-572-2360) and **Old Carriage Shop Antiques Center** (860-567-3234). For a spirit of community, music performances and poetry readings, check out the latest happenings at the **Chamaileon Gallery** (860-567-3988) on the second floor of the historic Old Switch Factory.

On Route 202, you can easily spend a day at the **Renaissance Center** (www. litchfieldart.com; call shops for days and hours of operation) where art rules in such magical surroundings as **Kil' n Time** (860-567-5400), paint-your-own pottery and mosaic studio and **Litchfield Doll Shop** (860-567-5402), complete with "doll hospital."

Also on 202, consider taking home fresh bread from the **Bantam Bread Company** (860-567-2737)—if you can exit without eating the loaf first! For a bit of European finesse, the **Dutch Epicure Shop** (860-567-5586; www.dutchepicure. com) carries breads, rolls, pastries and the like.

On Bantam Lake Road, **Bantam Cinema** (860-567-0006; call for upcoming show schedules), the oldest, continuously operating movie theater in the state, presents a variety of mainstream and also novel films. Just look for the red carriage barn.

Shoppers, who are also budding (or expert) horticulturalists, should be advised that there are numerous acclaimed nurseries and greenhouses to visit while in Litchfield. One of the most famous is the **White Flower Farm** (860-567-8789; www. whiteflowerfarm.com), directly on Route 63. Open in-season daily, the business, family-owned since 1950, maintains five acres of display gardens featuring many rare specimens.

If you'd like to try a hot-air ballooning adventure, click on www.aerblarney. com (or call 860-567-3448) for rates and information about **Aer Blarney Balloons**. Those searching for additional entertainment should make note that the **Litchfield**

Performing Arts (860-567-4162; www.litchfieldjazzfest.com) presents a spectrum of musical performances at a variety of venues throughout the year.

The Litchfield Green delivers many culinary surprises. Esteemed for homemade pasta and fresh seafood and steaks, the **Village Pub and Restaurant** (860-567-8307) renders fine dining for lunch and dinner daily. For years, the pub has won accolades among the locals and more recently from *Connecticut Magazine* readers who voted it, *best bar in Litchfield County*. Award-winning **West Street Grill** (860-567-3885), another fine-dining experience that has appeared in such magazines as *Bon Appetit*, serves lunch daily and, Wednesday through Sunday, dinner. The menu at **Aspen Garden Restaurant**, 51 West Street, (860-567-9477; www.aspengarden.com), open for lunch and dinner daily, features Mediterranean flavors and Greek specialties.

Across from the green is one of the trendiest dining experiences for lunch and dinner daily: **3W & the blue bar** (860-567-1742; www.3wandthebluebar.com). The seafood, fresh; the sushi, serious and the atmosphere? Strictly playful. Located about three miles from the green, serving lunch and dinner, Wednesday through Saturday, and Sunday dinner, the **Tollgate Hill Inn and Restaurant** (860-567-1233; see **Accommodations**) at 571 Torrington Road, has been a traveler's favorite since 1745. Notable for fine-dining fare, reserve an evening to attend a jazz performance.

Next door to Bantam Cinema, **Woods Pit** (860-567-9869), 123 Bantam Lake Road, is open for lunch and dinner daily; where patrons order authentic pit barbeque, southwestern and Mexican food. The **Bistro East at Litchfield Inn** (860-567-9040; www.bistroparty.com; see **Accommodations**), 432 Bantam Road, is a venerable milieu, open for lunch and dinner daily (Sunday brunch) for fine dining and signature seasonal menu items. **La Cupola** (860-567-3326; www.lacupolaristorante.com), 637 Bantam Road, open Tuesday through Sunday, conjures up a creative Italian-style menu. The setting—a converted stone house overlooking Bantam Lake—enhances the memorable dining experience.

At 810 Bantam Road, **Bantam Inn Restaurant** (860-567-1770), serving American-style cuisine, fresh seafood, homemade pasta and desserts for lunch and dinner daily, is one of the oldest, continuously operating restaurants in Connecticut. **Zini's Ristorante** (860-567-1613), 938 Bantam Road, serves courses of perfected Italian dinner specialties daily. Heading toward Torrington, families (and nearly everyone else) love the homemade goodness and reasonable prices offered at **Main Course Family Restaurant** (860-482-6246), open for breakfast, lunch and dinner daily.

To cool off anytime of year, **Peaches 'N Cream** (860-496-7536), Route 202, near the Torrington line, carries more than 50 homemade ice cream flavors and is open daily. Open in-season daily, beginning March, try **Max's Ice Cream** (860-567-7775), located on the Village Green and **Popey's Ice Cream** (860-567-0504), located on Route 109 in Morris, which is open March through October, daily. Yum!

GETTING THERE:

Litchfield is approximately 35 miles west of Hartford, 40 miles north of New Haven and 17 miles north of Waterbury. Litchfield is easily accessible from Interstate Highways 91 and 84 and Route 8, and by Routes 63, 254 and 202, which intersect with Litchfield Green.

TRANSPORTATION:

Tweed New Haven Regional Airport is approximately 40 miles driving distance from Litchfield and provides daily service to 126 cities through US Airways and Delta Airlines. Additionally, Litchfield is approximately 49 miles north from Danbury's Municipal Airport (203-743-3300; 203-797-4624), a tower-controlled facility with two runways, which serves the general aviation user. The area is approximately 41 miles west of Bradley International Airport in Windsor Locks. Stewart International Airport in Newburgh, New York, is approximately 89 miles west in driving distance. The three major New York City metro airports are Westchester County Airport, LaGuardia, JFK and Newark Airport in New Jersey. CT Transit (203-624-0151) operates frequent commuter-connections. Northwestern Connecticut Transit District (860-489-2535) provides service throughout the area; also New Britain Transit provides area services, call (860) 828-0512. Metro-North (800-638-7646) in Waterbury offers connecting commuter rail service. Berlin, about 30 miles away, offers Amtrak train service (800-872-7245). Union Station Transportation Center, a multi-model transportation center in downtown Hartford, also provides scheduled Amtrak service (800-USA-RAIL). Nonstop bus transportation (860-247-5329) to every major northeast city also runs regularly to and from Union Station.

ADDITIONAL INFORMATION:
LITCHFIELD HISTORY MUSEUM.

7 South Street. Open mid-April through November, Tuesday through Sunday. Inquire about changing exhibits, special events, colonial culture and history lectures and *Litchfield on Foot*, a walking tour of South Street sponsored by the Litchfield Historical Society. General admission (includes admission to Tapping Reeve House) is $5.00 adults; $3.00 seniors; $3.00 students and free to children 14 and under and free to law school students. Additionally, on premises, the **Ingraham Memorial Research Library** is open all year, Tuesday through Friday, and Saturday by appointment. (860) 567-4501; www.litchfieldhistoricalsociety.org.

TAPPING REEVE HOUSE AND LAW SCHOOL.

82 South Street. Open mid-April through November, Tuesday through Sunday. Inquire about workshops and special programs. General admission (includes admission to Litchfield History Museum) is $5.00 adults; $3.00 seniors; $3.00 students and free to children 14 and under and free to law school students. (860) 567-4501; www.litchfieldhistoricalsociety.org.

TOPSMEAD STATE FOREST.

Chase Road. The forest recreation areas are open from 8 a.m. through sunset, daily. Pets are permitted on the grounds. There is no parking fee or entrance fees charged weekends or weekdays to enter the state park. Additionally, free guided tours, June through October, are conducted on the second and fourth weekends of each month. (860) 567-5694.

LOURDES IN LITCHFIELD SHRINE GROTTO.

East Litchfield Road. The grounds are open from dawn to dusk, daily. Pilgrimage season is May through October. Sunday Mass in the grotto is at 11:30 a.m. and afternoon prayers and devotions are 3 p.m., daily. (860) 567-1041; www.lourdesinlitchfield.org.

WHITE MEMORIAL FOUNDATION AND CONSERVATION CENTER.

71 Whitehall Road. The trails are open all year, during daylight hours. The

Environmental Education Center, nature museum and nature store are open all year, daily. Inquire about special programs and events for all ages and also about concert series dates that take place at the Carriage House at White Memorial. General admission is by donation. (860) 567-0857; www.whitememorialcc.org.

ACCOMMODATIONS:

LITCHFIELD INN.
432 Bantam Road. An elegantly furnished and accessorized Colonial inn and restaurant (see above) that features 32 guestrooms, many with four-poster, canopied beds; all with private bathrooms and modern amenities. Inquire about special spa weekend packages and other specials. Pet friendly to boot! Rates (including continental breakfast): $140-$230-plus. (860) 567-4503; www.litchfieldinnct.com.

TOLLGATE HILL INN.
571 Torrington Road. The main 1745 inn is listed as Captain William Bull Tavern (see above) on the National Register of Historic Places. The tavern itself offers six guestrooms with complete, modern amenities. The Captain William Bull House, a separate building, extends 10 guestrooms and suites with full, modern amenities. The Schoolhouse building, was the oldest schoolhouse in Berlin, Connecticut, and was moved to the current premises in 1920. Today, it offers four charming private rooms that conveniently connect to accommodate larger families. There is also a restaurant on premises (see above). Rates (including continental breakfast): $95-$195. (860) 567-1233; (888) 567-1233; www.tollgatehillinn.com.

LILAC HEDGES.
40 East Litchfield Road. If privacy is preferred, the two well-furnished apartment rentals come complete with private living room, bath and wood-burning stove; plus private entrance will not leave you wanting for more. The units have transformed a 200-year-old dairy barn into a notable hideaway. Call for pricing information. (860) 567-8839.

ABEL DARLING BED AND BREAKFAST.
102 West Street. This 1782 Colonial home overlooks the green. The two guestrooms, named the Laura Ashley and the Queen Room, each with private bathrooms, are distinguished with wide floorboards, exposed beams and antique décor. The hand stenciling and antiques further enhance the house. Rates (including continental breakfast): $85-$125-plus. (860) 567-0384.

COUNTRY BED AND BREAKFAST.
74 Marsh Road. Three miles from town, one large guestroom is available with a private bath and separate entrance. Rates (including continental breakfast served in the greenhouse): $90-plus. (860) 567-4056.

HEMLOCK HILL CAMP RESORT.
Hemlock Hill Road. Litchfield's only resort-style campground offers large pine-shaded sites and a seasonal variety of rental units. Grounds include two pools and whirlpool spa. Rates: call for seasonal pricing information. (860) 567-2267; www.hemlockhillcamp.com.

LOOKING GLASS HILL CAMPGROUND.

Route 202. Forty-five sites with hookups are available at this family campground. Rates: call for seasonal pricing information. (860) 567-2050.

POINT FOLLY/WINDMILL HILL.

71 Whitehall Road. The White Memorial Foundation operates both campgrounds; Windmill Hill is situated in a wooded area while Point Folly is nearby Bantam Lake. Rates: call for seasonal pricing information. (860) 567-0857.

ANNUAL FESTIVALS/EVENTS

The Northwest Connecticut Convention and Visitor's Bureau, representing a total of 51 communities in the northwestern region that includes Litchfield Hills, Housatonic Valley and the Waterbury region, provides a gamut of tourism information, which includes seasonal events (860) 567-4506; www.northwestct. com. For additional festival and event information, contact the Litchfield Park and Recreation Department (860) 567-7569.

MARCH

The **Annual Barrel Tasting of the New Vintage** is a long-standing Haight Vineyard tradition, in which guests sample soon-to-be-released wines. (860) 567-4045; www. haightvineyards.com.

Visit the **Connecticut Antiquarian Book Fair**, Litchfield Community Center, Route 202. (860) 567-8302.

MAY

Hear the roar of the motorcycles as the Montford Missionary priests perform the **Blessing of the Motorcycles** at Lourdes Shrine. (860) 567-1041; www. lourdesinlitchfield.org.

JUNE/JULY/AUGUST

Free Wednesday night **summer concert series** are held beginning at 7 p.m. on the Litchfield Green. (860) 567-7569.

JUNE

The **Annual Taste of Litchfield Hills** is a two-day affair featuring more than 20 restaurants offering some of their best entrée selections. Live music, wine and beer garden and winery tours are also on hand. (860) 567-4045.

Patrons from all over the region participate in the **Block Dance**, featured on the Litchfield Town Green. (800) 663-1273

The **Annual Gallery on the Green**, held at Litchfield Green, presents more than 100 artists and craft people exhibiting and selling their wares. The host of items ranges from jewelry to paintings and leather goods. (860) 567-8298.

Come see the impressive assortment of wares at the **Greater Litchfield Summer Antiques Show**. All proceeds benefit the Greenwoods Counseling Service; call for venue location. (800) 663-1273.

The **Litchfield Hills Road Race** begins on Litchfield's Village Green. (800) 663-1273.

JULY

Area homes of historic and architectural significance are opened to the public at the **Litchfield Open House Tour**, which benefits the Connecticut Junior Republic. A luncheon is included in the day's activities. (860) 567-9423.

The **Annual Summer Carnival** of the Bantam Fire Department is a fundraising event held at 92 Doyle Road. (860) 567-5198.

AUGUST

Litchfield Jazz Festival at Goshen Fairgrounds is a three-day event with an impressive line-up of world-renowned musicians, plus a substantial list of arts and crafts and food vendors. (860) 567-4162; www.litchfieldjazzfest.com.

The **Annual Sandy Beach Triathlon** is a .5- mile swim, 10-mile bike and 3.1-mile run at Sandy Beach on Bantam Lake, Morris. (860) 567-7569.

SEPTEMBER

One of the most anticipated events in Litchfield is the **Annual Harvest Festival** held at the Haight Vineyards. The harvest fair includes a range of artisans and their for-sale wares, children's games, hayrides and pony rides. (860) 567-4045; www. haightvineyards.com.

OCTOBER

The focus of the **Antique Carriage Rally**, held at the White Memorial Conservation Center, is riding competitions and there is a costume competition as well. (860) 775-3223; www.whitememorialcc.org.

Held on the Litchfield Green at the Litchfield Congregational Church is the **Annual Fall Festival**. The jubilant day features a German-style luncheon, silent auction, baked items and bargain shopping galore, plus activities for all ages. (860) 567-8705.

DECEMBER

Attend the **Litchfield Carol Sing** to get into the spirit of the holidays. The old-fashioned Christmas gathering assembling on the Litchfield Green is complemented with hayrides, music and outdoor ice-skating, weather permitting. (860) 567-7569.

Litchfield Performing Arts sponsors its annual **Holiday House Tour**, which features a handful of interesting houses dressed in their holiday best. (860) 567-4162.

The annual **Litchfield Cross-Country Challenge 5K Road Race** gathers at the White Memorial Foundation and follows the outdoor trails. (860) 567-7569.

The **Jingle Bell Run** is an annual run that starts and finishes at Litchfield High School. (860) 567-7569.

What town was the first in the country to take the namesake of the first president of the United States?

What town was the temporary home of the famous Rolling Stones Band?

Wow: WASHINGTON

Washington, first settled in 1734, was eventually separated from the towns that we know today as Litchfield, Kent, New Milford and Woodbury and incorporated in 1779. Honoring one of its most famous visitors by adopting his namesake, the town was the first in the country to be named after Revolutionary War hero and first president of the United States. Records indicate that General George Washington slept for one night in the northeast room of North Street's Sheldon Tavern, currently a private home (see **Litchfield** chapter).

Probably the town's other most famous citizens were the Rolling Stones, the famed rock band that resided in town during the first part of the 21st century, just long enough to set up and work in a recording studio converted from a barn.

Early on, the hilly terrain situated high above the Shepaug River Valley limited agriculture. However, the town prospered with industries that included ironworks, quarries, small-scale mills and factories that utilized waterpower from both the Shepaug and Aspetuck Rivers. Today, the factories as well as many of the farms have disappeared. However, the Washington Grange that was started in 1875, continues to hold regular meetings for agricultural-minded members.

Summer vacationers flocked into town beginning in 1872 on the new Shepaug Railroad. Today, largely a residential community and still a weekend escape for some; the land area embodies 38.7 square miles and tallies a population of about 4,000. A good core of artists, writers, musicians and "freethinkers" make up this town.

Home to Washington Golf Club, a private association and two public schools and five private schools, Washington is located about 10 miles from the upstate New York border. The town claims four villages, each with its own zip code: Washington, Washington Depot, Marbledale and New Preston. Protected and governed by the town's Historic District Commission, Washington Green is probably the most popular out of the three designated historic districts. Folded into the Berkshire Mountain foothills, natural scenery is everywhere. On an occasional summer evening, Bryan Memorial Town Hall, mid-way between Washington and Washington Depot, hosts free concerts on the lawn where local celebrity Papa Joe sells his famous hot dogs off his cart.

Day trips with panache dig deep into the town's Yankee roots at the historic district of **Washington Green** where many of Washington's first and most prominent families settled. Nearby, the **Gunn Memorial Library and Museum** furnishes library services as well as preserves the town's earliest history. Named for abolitionist and Gunnery School founder Frederick William and his wife, Abigail Brinsmade Gunn, the library's main building was dedicated in 1908. Expanded in 1994, day-trippers should inquire about the roster of special events like piano recitals and lectures.

If anything, stop in to see an architecturally detailed building, accented with dramatic murals. The upper level of the library, displaying the original rooms, is the **Stairwell Gallery**, where approximately every six weeks local artists headline new shows. Genealogists and professional and neophyte historians can reserve an hour or more of time in the **Connecticut Room** to mull over the local- and state-history resources including photograph albums, family histories, town histories, church records and books written by local authors.

The library's museum headquarters are in the circa 1781 **Willis House**, donated to the town by June Willis in 1964. Hosting three visiting exhibits a year, five rooms accommodate permanent exhibits. You don't have to be under 21 years old to fall in love with the turn-of-the-century dollhouses in the children's history room. Visitors can also view many traditional-style decorative antiques, practical and glamorous textiles, wardrobe selections and plain oddities, such as a longhorn chair once owned by P.T. Barnum and a commemorative wreath made of human hair in a museum assortment that spans some 200 years.

Within a two-mile radius of the library, volunteers occasionally, during the summer months, conduct Washington Depot historical tours. In the warmer months, hikers (with or without leashed pets) should experience the **Shepaug Greenway** (860-868-1519; www. washingtonct.org/greenway.html), a 3.3 mile-long trail that connects **Steep Rock Reservation** and **Hidden Valley Reserve**. The town hall, Hickory Stick Bookstore and the Gunn Library distribute trail maps to day-trippers. The Greenway meanders along part of the **Shepaug River**, which can be paddled in canoes or kayaks especially in the spring; during other months, day-trippers typically encounter low-water levels. (Washington residents have had a longtime battle with Waterbury officials who siphon river supply to feed their dam.)

Depot visitors can peruse the changing art shows featured at the gallery in the **Washington Art Association** (860-868-2878; www.washingtonart.org). Do not leave the premises without browsing the association's gift shop offering handmade gifts and other artwork created by members.

About three miles from the depot, just off Route 199, the **Institute for American Indian Studies** invites patrons of all ages to explore Native American tradition through arts and artifacts dating back 10,000 years. Outdoors, an authentically constructed, Algonkian village, consisting of two wigwams, dugout canoe, longhouse and seasonal garden, is open to day-trippers. Additionally, occasional outdoor simulated archaeology digs and actual archaeological excursions off premises enrich the experience. Bring the dog and enjoy the easy walking trail. Shoppers note, the store contains a large variety of unique native-made jewelry, handicrafts and books.

North, about eight miles away from the museum, **H.O.R.S.E. of Connecticut** will tug on the heartstrings of young and old alike. The non-profit rescue and rehabilitation facility for abused and neglected horses is open to the public daily. Call for advance tours, (860) 868-1960; www.horseofct.org. Don't be surprised if you adopt one of these equine miracles.

To tote home a piece of Washington, remember that the depot is a treasure trove of charming shops. The **Tulip Tree Collection** (860-868-2802; www.tuliptreecollection. com), open daily, Route 47, unfolds 3,000 square feet of showroom with home accessories that include antique and reproduction furnishings, upholstery and all things beautiful for the home. The Colonial-style house that highlights **Seraphim Boutique** (860-868-1674; call for days and hours of operation), 2 Titus Road, brims with exemplary fashions and gifts. Selections include formal and informal dresses; skirt, lace and crocheted jackets; shawls; jewelry and lingerie. While in the depot, not to be missed is the **Hickory Stick Bookshop** (860-868-0525; www. hickorystickbookshop.com), an independent bookseller that has been an area legend for more than 50 years. Specialists in a variety of genres including mainstream and children's books, the store also carries greeting cards, book accessories and toys. Special orders are welcome. Coordinate a day trip to meet a favorite author and purchase his or her signed book.

While in the shopping mode, consider in-season (until around December), fresh produce and jellies from area farms like **Averill Farms** (860-868-2777) and **Starberry Peach Farm** (860-868-2863), about two miles from the depot and located on Kielwasser Road. Back towards the green, 20 East Street, another favorite for fresh-grown goods is **Waldingfield Farm and Organic Vegetables** (860-868-7270; www.waldingfieldfarm.com).

Any day trip can be transformed into a special occasion when dining inside the **Mayflower Inn** (see **Accommodations**), 118 Woodbury Road, (860-868-9466; www.mayflowerinn.com/dining), an English-style country inn that is open for breakfast, lunch and dinner daily. The award-winning restaurant features an American, continental menu, impeccable service and surroundings, including a summer terrace. Another award-winning establishment, **The Pantry** (860-868-0258; www.litchfieldcty.com/dining/pantry.html) is a favorite noshing spot in the depot that serves continental breakfast, lunch and afternoon tea and home-baked goods. Open Tuesday through Saturday, the interesting hideaway merits time to browse in the on-premises store brimming with imported and domestic giftware and gourmet and specialty foods. Another advisable choice for special celebration dining is three miles north at **G.W. Tavern** (860-868-6633; www.gwtavern.com), 20 Bee Brook Road (Route 47). Styled after a tavern complete with wood-burning firestone fireplace, patrons can eat lunch (Sunday brunch) or dinner daily. In the summer months, consider terrace dining, which overlooks the Shepaug River.

GETTING THERE:

Washington is approximately 40 miles west of Hartford, 35 miles northwest of New Haven and 14 miles south of Litchfield. Washington is easily accessible from Interstate Highways 91 and 84 and by Routes 47, 199 and 109.

TRANSPORTATION:

Tweed New Haven Regional Airport is approximately 35 miles driving distance from Washington and provides daily service to 126 cities through US Airways and Delta Airlines. Additionally, Washington is approximately 24 miles north from Danbury's Municipal Airport (203-743-3300; 203-797-4624), a tower-controlled facility with two runways, which serves the general aviation user. The area is approximately 54 miles west of Bradley International Airport in Windsor Locks. Stewart International Airport in Newburgh, New York, is approximately 64 miles west in driving distance. The three major New York City metro airports are Westchester County Airport, LaGuardia, JFK and Newark Airport in New Jersey. Northwestern Connecticut Transit District (860-489-2535) provides service throughout the area. Metro-North (800-638-7646) in Waterbury offers connecting commuter rail service.

ADDITIONAL INFORMATION:

GUNN MEMORIAL LIBRARY AND MUSEUM.

5 Wykeham Road. Call for library and museum days and hours of operation. General museum admission is free (donation suggested). (860) 868-7756; www. gunnlibrary.org.

INSTITUTE FOR AMERICAN INDIAN STUDIES.

38 Curtis Road. Open all year, daily. There is an on-site library open for researchers, students and scholars. Inquire about family programs, special demonstrations and events. General admission is $4.00 adults; $3.50 seniors, $2.00 students and free to children five and under. (860) 868-0518; www.birdstone.org.

ACCOMMODATIONS:

MAYFLOWER INN.

118 Woodbury Road. Through its somewhat erratic history, beginning in 1920, this Colonial-style inn has retained a reputation for being a refuge for some of the world's most prominent citizens. Three buildings named Mayflower, Speedwell and Standish unveil 25 exquisitely accoutered guestrooms and suites, replete with four-poster, canopy beds and fireplaces. Full, modern amenities include the Mayflower's signature shampoos, body lotions and conditioners. Guests can also use the state-of-the-art fitness club, tennis court and, in seasonal weather, an outdoor heated pool and pool house. Additionally, the knot gardens of boxwood and red barberry and wildflowers solicit peaceful summer respite. Hikers can experience acres of private property that lead to the foot of the Shepaug River. Rates: $420-$1,350. (860) 868-9466; www.mayflowerinn.com/lodging.

POPPLE VIEW BED AND BREAKFAST.

191 Popple Swamp Road. Off Route 202, a circa 1780 barn has been restored into a charming guest suite (converted over an auto garage) that accommodates up to four people and includes a kitchen and one bath. The 500-square-foot suite also offers full, modern amenities and overlooks cornfields and perennial gardens. Rates (including full breakfast): $150. (860) 868-7177.

ANNUAL FESTIVALS/EVENTS

The Northwest Connecticut Convention and Visitor's Bureau, representing a total of 51 communities in the northwestern region that includes Litchfield Hills, Housatonic Valley and the Waterbury region, provides a gamut of tourism information, which includes seasonal events (860) 567-4506; www.litchfieldhills. com. For additional festival and event information, contact the Washington Parks and Recreation Department at (860) 567-7569.

MARCH

Everyone knows it must be spring when the **Maple Syrup Festival** at the Institute for American Indian Studies takes place. Visitors learn—besides everything related to maple syrup—Native American culture through demonstrations, music and dance. Food and special activities for children are also on hand. (860) 868-0518; www.birdstone.org.

JUNE

The **St. John's Annual Tag Sale** is a daylong bargain-hunting excursion. The Episcopal Church is located at 78 Green Hill Road (Route 47). (860) 868-2527.

JULY

The **Fourth of July Road Race** is a 5K run/walk that congregates at the horse rink at Steep Rock. (860) 868-1519.

For an old-fashioned, good time, attend the **Green Fair** sponsored by the First Congregational Church, 6 Kirby Road on the green, an affair that appeases all ages with food, entertainment and silent auction. (860) 868-0569.

AUGUST

Don't forget your wallet when attending the **Indian Market** at the Institute for American Indian Studies. It is an all-day event with a focus on authentic native arts and crafts for sale. (860) 868-0518; www.birdstone.org.

OCTOBER

For more than two decades, the **Washington Antiques Show** has attracted audiences throughout the state and beyond. A preview party takes place to kick-off the three-day celebration. (800) 663-1273; (860) 567-4506.

Columbus Day Weekend in Washington means it's time for the **Annual Book Sale** at Gunn Memorial Library. The major fundraiser features hundreds of books representing nearly all genres including mainstream fiction, children's literature and non-fiction titles. (860) 868-7756; www.gunnlibrary.org.

NOVEMBER

Participants of all faiths join the **Spirit of Washington**, which is a community-worship service and thanksgiving held at the First Congregational Church on the green. (860) 868-0569.

The **Storytelling Festival** at the Institute for American Indian Studies features a day of drama with performances by Native American storytellers. (860) 868-0518; www.birdstone.org.

The community invites the public to view a variety of artwork featured at the **Washington Art Association Student Show**, 4 Bryan Plaza. Held every two years, more than 150 pieces involve many mediums, and include original two-dimensional work, arts and crafts, jewelry and sculpture that range from contemporary to traditional. (860) 868-2878; www.washingtonart.org.

DECEMBER

The annual **Festival of Trees** debuts at the Gunn Memorial Library and Museum. The evening's events include a cocktail party, raffle and the sale of holiday-decorated trees. (860) 868-7586; www.gunnlibrary.org.

Another popular Gunn Library and Museum holiday event is the annual **Holiday Sale** that features a giftware boutique in which many items are reasonably priced enough for children to purchase. Gift wrapping services are also available. (860) 868-7586; www.gunnlibrary.org.

*During Revolutionary times, in what Connecticut settlement
did a Native American Tribe aid the colonists in their
fight against the British?*

*In what Connecticut town were all the trees used to power furnaces
that fueled the bustling iron industry?*

Artsy, Funky & So Soulful: **KENT**

The present-day, Kent-based Schaghticoke Indian Reservation sprawling over 400 acres on the left bank of the Housatonic River represents the region's remaining tribe. Whether spelled Schaghticoke or Scatacook or by any other variation, the name means "fork in the river" and conceivably referred to the confluence of the Housatonic and Ten Mile Rivers, where Bull's Bridge is today. In the early 1700s, colonists purchased most of the tribe's land that at the time spread through much of what is modern-day Litchfield County, northern Fairfield County, and beyond the New York border.

Settlers replaced the Schaghticoke Indian name and named the area after Kent, England, in 1738. Interestingly, the Schaghticokes later aided Kent's settlers in their war efforts against the British during the Revolutionary War by operating a hand-signal system along the river valley peaks. Incorporated as the 62nd town in Connecticut in 1739, settlers established a strong agricultural base. Cider, grist and sawmills appeared west of the Housatonic River, in what would become known as the Macedonia region. During the Industrial Age, the iron industry played a prominent role. The business of iron ore mining and smelting required workers to build towering stone furnaces along both the Housatonic River and what is presently Route 7. It is hard to imagine Kent's lush, hilly landscape today completely barren, but naked it was, back in 1848, after the furnaces ate every stick of timber! Consequently, the town formed a committee to prevent wood waste; this fact, coupled with the encumbering competition from larger Pennsylvania mines, retired the furnaces.

Kent reemerged as a leader in the field of education. Today, this northwestern town boasts three acclaimed private preparatory schools: Kent School, Marvelwood and South Kent School. During the last century, an influx of artists (along with prominent New Yorkers seeking country respite) influenced a large concentration of world-famous art galleries to appear in town, most of them in the Route 7 vicinity. North or south, Route 7 guides day-trippers along copious main arteries that snake and meander beside the scenic vistas of the Housatonic River.

One of the route's most favorite stops is the 110-foot-long Bull's Bridge. Originally built by resident Jacob Bull in 1760 (the first of at least five bridges that covered the rock-strewn gorge), what travelers currently see is the last bridge built in 1842 that connects the two riverbanks of the Housatonic. Out of a handful of covered bridges in the state, Bull's Bridge is only one of two open to motorists. (The other covered bridge open to motorists is the West Cornwall Bridge, several miles up U.S. 7 in West Cornwall.)

One rumor that has lasted for generations is that George Washington's horse slipped from the bridge into the river in 1781. (Fortunately, George, who was on route to Newport, Rhode Island, was not riding his furry companion during the accident and saved the horse's life.)

Adjacent to the New York State border, Kent stretches 49.5 square miles. Hovering somewhere around 3,000 residents, this small town ushers in visitors with its acclaimed restaurants, select bed and breakfasts, interesting antiques shops, eminent art galleries and Mother Nature's overly generous helping of greenery and abundant water sources. Peepers (a tiny frog) peep in spring. Bullfrogs bellow in the summer. The Saturday morning farmer's market on the green sells out early. June unveils the Annual Volunteer Fire Department's Ball. One year, as the ball began, the siren rang and the volunteers had to leave and rescue a car that had careened into the Housatonic River. Fortunately, the heroes made it back to the shindig in time to feast on the roast beef dinner. Regardless of the season, day trips with panache cater to all levels of sport adventures. Sometimes after the annual Christmas tree-lighting on the green, accumulated snowfall invites cross-country skiers to test the **Appalachian Trail** (866-287-2757) that runs along the western bank of the Housatonic River. (About 12 miles northeast at Mohawk Mountain in Cornwall [800-895-5222; www.mohawkmtn.com], Connecticut's largest mountain with an elevation of 1,600 feet and a 640-foot-vertical drop, offers downhill skiing complete with lights for night skiing.)

A national scenic route that totals 2,155 miles, the Appalachian Trail begins in Mount Katahdin, Maine, and moves south ending in Springer Mountain, Georgia. The best access to the trail from the center of town (only 56 miles weave through northwest Connecticut) is Route 341 West, near Kent School. Located on Appalachian Trail, **Backcountry Outfitters** (860-927-3377; 888-549-3377; www. bcoutfitters.com), 8 Old Barn Road, just off Route 7, provides trail maps and ski rentals. The 7,000-square-foot specialty shop is the largest outdoor outfitter in western New England. The store's most popular selling items include camping gear and cross-country skis, ice-skates and snowshoe rentals.

Four miles north off Route 341, **Macedonia Brook State Park**, another bequest (see **Litchfield** chapter) from hat-manufacturing scions, Alan and his sister Mary White, benefactors of the White Memorial Foundation in Litchfield, offers challenging cross-country skiing terrain. During milder weather, zealous hikers can jack up the Blue Trail across Cobble Mountain to experience panoramic views that include the Catskill and Taconic Mountains in New York State. Explorers will espy iron-furnace remains leftover from the Kent Iron Company in the southern end of the park. Additionally, fishermen and fisherwomen should bring equipment to spend the day stream fishing. In season, a campground invites weary souls (see **Accommodations**).

Located in the northeastern section of town and a favorite subject of many magazine and newspaper features, the cascading waterfall that meets the Housatonic River at **Kent Falls State Park** with a 70-foot drop is the centerpiece in this 1919 gift to the town of 200 acres also bestowed by the White family (see above). Today, the park attracts more than 100,000 visitors annually. Heavy foot traffic has prompted state officials to consider resurfacing the existing rustic trails with concrete, which has caused some debate with environmentalists.

An awesome sight during any season, the water cascades heaviest in the spring after winter's thaw. One of 11 designated "trout" parks in the state, officials stock the brook each April. Hikers who climb up the quarter-mile trail adjacent to the falls have a quarter-mile vantage point.

Additionally, Kent Falls State Park is a Viewpoint Exhibit Host Site. A joint effort of the Connecticut Commission on the Arts, the Connecticut Impressionist Art Trail and the Department of Environmental Protection, outdoor exhibits showcase works of 19th-century artwork and provide background information. At the park, visitors should look for Impressionist artist Willard Metcalf's (1858–1925) representation of "November Mosaic" (1922). The outdoor display plaque, one in a series throughout the state (see **Westport** chapter), also denotes actual or representative Connecticut settings where American Impressionists worked.

Left of the plaque, traditionally, amateur and professional photographers attempt to capture the romantic mood cast by the **Kent Falls Covered Bridge**, a 37-foot, lattice truss bridge, built over the park's brook in 1974.

Near the falls, curious day-trippers pull over to view Denis Curtiss's welded steel or bronze sculptures of dancers, gymnasts and wild and domestic animals (www.deniscurtisssculptor.com). A friendly, outgoing chap, the local native is happy to extend visitors a peek inside his studio. What animal figure do Connecticut residents prefer most in outdoor sculpture? Elephants! Don't forget to ask Denis to point out one of the oldest maple trees in the state. A knobby monolith to say the least—its circumference alone measures more than 19 feet, making it the largest maple in Connecticut.

Denis's wife Barbara is proprietor of the **Dog Show** (860-927-4599; www.thedogshow.biz), 3 Carter Road, one of the most consummate stores for dog lovers. The three-story barn, packed with everything (and then some) dog-related—paintings, housewares, rugs, stained glass, greeting cards, weathervanes— is a show within itself. Tip: one of the best gift ideas for dog owners is the family canine hand painted by Barbara on a decorative pillow.

Back to naturalist's activities, in south Kent just below the well-known covered bridge, **Bull's Bridge** (yet another popular passion with photographers), the white waters from the river tempt only the most skilled rafters and kayakers. From March through December, day-trippers can rent a kayak, canoe or raft from **Clarke Outdoors** (860-672-6365), Route 7, in the adjacent town of West Cornwall. Cycling enthusiasts should call in reservations at the **Bicycle Tour Company** (860-927-1742; 888-711-KENT; www.bicycletours.com), 9 Bridge Street, which organizes expeditions for all levels through Kent and its surroundings.

Motoring on South Main Street (going Route 7 northbound), gardeners should heed to **Kent Greenhouse and Gardens** (860-927-3480), open seasonally (call for days and hours of operation), which has been carrying a full line of quality floral sensations, including Christmas trees for more than 32 years. A few doors down, at 22 South Main, **R.T. Facts Antiques** (860-927-1700; www.rtfacts.com) specializes in ornamental garden and architectural antiques, decorative objects, statuary, gates, urns, indoor and outdoor furniture and lighting and 20th-century "eccentricities," and is open weekends or by appointment.

In the same vicinity, the **Kent Art Association's** (860-927-3989; www.kentart. org) fine art galleries are housed in a two-story, Colonial-style building. New York-based artists established the association in 1923 and the members currently present changing exhibits Thursday through Sunday in season.

For additional antique haunts, at Main Street's Kent Station Square, the **Antiques Center** (860-927-3313) is an eight-dealer hodgepodge, showcasing 18th- to 20th-century antiques and collectibles. Just look for the 19th-century farmhouse by the railroad depot. The center is open daily in season and during the winter open Friday through Monday. Any bon vivant can direct day-trippers to **Paris-New York-Kent Gallery** (860-927-3357), open in-season daily; the shop goes down in Kent history as being the first (with presentations of the most discriminating artwork) to entice the other art galleries to town. Just look for the old Pullman car.

The descendents of Thomas Judd who came from England to America in 1633 were the previous owners of the Judd House, an early 1800s farmhouse, idyllically nestled across from Bull's Bridge in South Kent and today the residence of the **American Heritage Shop** (860-927-3749; www.americanheritageshop.com). Proprietors sell a unique line of primitive-style home furnishings, accessories and giftware.

Back in the center of Kent, **Bachelier-Cardonsky Gallery** (860-927-3129), open weekends in season and by appointment, presents distinctive local and American contemporary art. Sharing the same number 10 North Main Street address, the **House of Books** (860-927-4104; www.hobooks.com; call for days and hours of operation) is an upscale bookstore that also carries greeting cards, music and gift-giving accessories. Directly on the Appalachian Trail, consider picking up trail guides and maps.

Out of 7,000 used, rare and out-of-print books covering all subjects, shoppers are bound to find something at **Richard J. Lindsey, Bookseller** (860-927-3025; call for days and hours of operation) at 15 North Main Street.

At 16 North Main, the **Heron American Craft Gallery** (860-927-4804; call for days and hours of operation) commands two floors of contemporary crafts including hand-blown glass, fine ceramics and jewelry. For the most exquisite selection of estate jewelry, including some by fine designers like Tiffany & Company and Cartier, experience **Pauline's Place** (860-927-4475; call for days and hours of operation), 79 N. Main Street.

Near Main at 8 Barn Road, **Northwest Corner Artisans**, formerly the Cosmic Hippo (860-927-3069), displays the work of more than 50 regional artisans including jewelry, fine art, stained glass and furniture.

At 99A North Main Street, next to the First Congregational Church, bargain hunters should carve out time to rummage through the **Quality Thrift Shop** (860-927-3287; call for days and hours of operation), operated by church volunteers. Various charities are the recipients of all proceeds from sales, and the staff welcomes day-trippers to donate household goods.

Directly on Route 341, for a bit of respite, walk the labyrinth and admire the outdoor sculptures on the property of **Gidion's Center for Health and the Arts** (860-927-1970). Indoors, the shop, open Wednesday through Sunday, is a new age mecca filled with candles, crystals and "intuitive" counseling services.

Visitors who arrive between Memorial Day and Labor Day should note the numerous attractions that are located about one mile north of the village. Open weekends in the **Seven Hearths** historical house, built 1754, the **Kent Historical Society** (860-927-4587; www.kenthistoricalsociety.org) invites the public to peruse their art gallery/local history museum.

Visitors can also trace the town's prosperity derived from iron production during the 18th century at the **Sloane-Stanley Museum and Kent Furnace**. Dating from the 17th century, many of the hand tools on display were used to build homes in northwestern Connecticut. On the grounds, herein also lie the remnants of the Kent Iron Furnace, which operated from 1826 to 1829. The final stop is a reproduction of Eric Sloane's studio, the museum's benefactor, tool collector and artist who depicted old barns, homes and tools in his rural New England paintings and wrote books about colonial America.

Adjacent to the Sloane-Stanley Museum (actually sharing the same driveway), is the **Connecticut Antique Machinery Association**. Its mission, as illustrated in its many fine pieces, is the preservation, restoration and demonstration of antique machinery from Kent's industrial and agricultural past. The **Connecticut Museum of Mining and Mineral Science**, in which exhibits explore Connecticut mining enterprises, runs in conjunction with the machinery museum.

Before heading out of town, note that the **Brook Run Farm** (860-927-4639), 161 Macedonia Road, invites the public to roam through its horse farm (call first), a popular choice for riding lessons.

Day-trippers always have the option of simply people-watching (and joining the many others who do) at two main hubs: **Kent Coffee and Chocolate Company** (860-927-1445; www.kentcoffee.com) and **Stosh's Ice Cream** (860-927-4495; call for seasonal days and hours of operation), both open daily. With 100 varieties of coffees and teas and great hot chocolate, the cup is bottomless and the assorted hand-dipped truffles, fudges and chocolates are divinely addictive.

For chocolates as well as pastries with a European flair, consider **Belgique Patisserie and Chocolatier** (860-927-3681; "belgique," by the way, means Belgium in French) at the corner of Routes 7 and 341, open Thursday through Sunday. (Winter should not be called winter without sipping the signature hot chocolate.) Open for dinner Thursday through Sunday (with champagne-Sunday brunch buffet), sister restaurant at the same address, the **Salon de Belgique** (860-927-3681) has won prominent dining reviews by food critics including those from the *Hartford Courant* and *Yankee Magazine Travel Guide*. Queen Anne Victorian décor, more than 150 wines, Belgian beers and prized cognacs, provide pure romance for any occasion.

A reasonably priced restaurant that's always popular with the locals, **the Villager** (860-927-3945), on North Main Street, serves American-style, casual fare for breakfast and lunch daily. Two other popular and easy-on-the-budget food choices open for lunch and dinner daily are **Paisan'**s (860-927-3774) at the town green and **Kent Pizza Garden** (860-927-3733) at the railroad station.

Two Asian restaurants on the green and open for lunch and dinner daily are **Shanghi Chinese** (860-927-4809) and **Wasabi Japanese** (860-927-0048). Out-of-town patrons make a specific trip to visit the distinguishable, rustic setting of the **Fife 'N Drum Restaurant and Inn** (860-927-3509; www.fifendrum.com; see **Accommodations**), 53 North Main Street. Family-owned since 1972, the restaurant is open for lunch (Sunday brunch), dinner and makes available a taproom menu, Wednesday through Monday and offers continental cuisine selections. Next door, between meals, stop by the **Fife 'N Drum Gift Shop** (860-927-3618) that features a fanciful gift-giving assortment including candles and bath products.

Another Kent favorite is **Restaurant Moosilauke** (860-927-4145), 23 Maple Street, that features an engaging New American menu integrating local farm-area poultry and produce. Open for dinner, Tuesday through Sunday, inquire about the daily, seasonal market specials.

In South Kent, **Bull's Bridge Inn**, (860-927-1000; www.bullsbridge.com), 333 Kent Road, provides traditional American fare, notable steaks and grilled seafood. Open for dinner daily, experience the charming ambiance that Jacob and Mary Bull created when they were the inn's first proprietors, running it after they were married in 1762!

GETTING THERE:

Kent is approximately 56 miles west of Hartford, 64 miles northwest of New Haven and 20 miles east of Litchfield. Kent is easily accessible from Interstate Highways 91 and 84 and located directly on Route 7 North-South; intersected by Route 341.

TRANSPORTATION:

Tweed New Haven Regional Airport is approximately 64 miles driving distance from Kent and provides daily service to 126 cities through US Airways and Delta Airlines. Additionally, Kent is approximately 27 miles north from Danbury's Municipal Airport (203-743-3300; 203-797-4624), a tower-controlled facility with two runways, which serves the general aviation user. The area is approximately 60 miles west of Bradley International Airport in Windsor Locks. Stewart International Airport in Newburgh, New York, is approximately 43 miles southwest in driving distance. The three major New York City metro airports are Westchester County Airport, LaGuardia, JFK and Newark Airport in New Jersey.

Northwestern Connecticut Transit District (860-489-2535) provides service throughout the area; also New Britain Transit provides area services, call (860) 828-0512. Metro-North (800-638-7646) in Waterbury offers connecting commuter rail service. Berlin, about 53 miles away, offers AMTRAK train service (800-872-7245). One option, about 41 miles east is the CT Transit Waterbury District, operated by North East Transportation (203-753-2538 or 203-755-8242), which services Waterbury. Metro-North (800-638-7646) also offers connecting commuter rail service to Waterbury.

Another option is nearby Bristol, which is serviced by New Britain Transit (860-828-0512). In addition, Union Station Transportation Center, a multi-model transportation center in downtown Hartford, provides scheduled Amtrak service and nonstop bus transportation to every major Northeast city and also runs regularly to and from Union Station, call (860) 247-5329.

ADDITIONAL INFORMATION:

MACEDONIA BROOK STATE PARK.
159 Macedonia Brook Road. The park is open all year, 8 a.m. to sunset, daily. Leashed dogs are permitted in the picnic area and on the hiking trails. There are no parking or entrance fees charged weekends or weekdays (also see **Accommodations**). (860) 927-3238; http://dep.state.ct.us/stateparks/parks/macedonia.htm.

KENT FALLS STATE PARK.
Route 7. The park is open all year, 8 a.m. to sunset, daily. Leashed dogs are permitted in the picnic area and on the hiking trails. Trails and other areas in the park are handicapped accessible. Day fees per carload are weekends: $7.00 Connecticut registered vehicle; $10.00 out-of-state registered vehicle; weekdays: no parking or entrance fees. (860) 927-3238; http://dep.state.ct.us/stateparks/parks/kentfalls.htm.

SLOANE-STANLEY MUSEUM AND KENT FURNACE.
Route 7. Open mid-May through October 31, Wednesday through Sunday. General admission is $3.50 adults; $2.50 seniors; $2.00 children and free to children 5 and under. (860) 927-3849.

CONNECTICUT ANTIQUE MACHINERY ASSOCIATION/ MUSEUM OF MINING AND MINERAL SCIENCE.
Route 7. Open mid-May through October 31, or by special appointment, Wednesday through Sunday. General admission is by donation. (860) 927-0050; www. ctamachinery.com.

ACCOMMODATIONS:

FIFE 'N DRUM RESTAURANT AND INN.
59 North Main Street. The inn raises the bar with its eight guestrooms, decorated in a genteel ambiance. All rooms are designated as non-smoking and each with private bath; one handicapped-accessible room is located on the ground floor. Amenities include ceiling fans, on-site restaurant (see above), complimentary juice and coffee and Gilchrist & Soames bath products. Rates: $110-$140. (860) 927-3509; www. fifendrum.com.

STARBUCK INN.
88 North Main Street. Formerly known as the Chaucer House, the center-hall Colonial has been renovated and presents five rooms with private baths and full, modern amenities. In the heart of Kent, tea is served in the mid-afternoon. Rates (including full breakfast): $175-$250. (860) 927-1788; www.starbuckinn.com.

THE INN AT KENT FALLS.
107 Kent Cornwall Road. The two-plus-acre award-winning inn with swimming pool unveils six guestrooms, each with full, modern amenities. The historical home was built in 1741 and is located in the charming Flanders Historic District, located between the village of Kent and Kent Falls State Park. Rates (including continental breakfast): $155-$325. (860) 927-3197; www.theinnatkentfalls.com.

MACEDONIA BROOK STATE PARK.

159 Macedonia Brook Road. In season (see **Additional Information**), the rustic campground offers 83 sites beginning mid-April and ends September 30. No dogs are allowed in the campgrounds. Some campgrounds are set by the brook. The Appalachian Trail also passes through the property. Rates: $11/night. (860) 927-3238; http://dep.state.ct.us/stateparks/parks/macedonia.htm.

CLUB GETAWAY.

Berkshire Mountains. Open May through October, a sports resort nestled on 300 acres in the Berkshire Mountains, offers all-inclusive vacations and features 84 comfortable cabins, plus handicapped accessible. Modeled after Club Med, sporting activities include water-skiing, swimming and sailing on a private lake, mountain biking, archery, in-line skating and rock climbing. Club Getaway is an award-winning resort for singles as well as married couples (and permits families with children one weekend a year). Inquire about theme weekend events. Rates (all-inclusive): $250-$399. (800) 6-GETAWAY; (860) 927-3664; www.clubgetaway.com.

ANNUAL FESTIVALS/EVENTS

The Northwest Connecticut Convention and Visitor's Bureau, representing a total of 51 communities in the northwestern region that includes Litchfield Hills, Housatonic Valley and the Waterbury region, provides a gamut of tourism information, which includes seasonal events (860) 567-4506; www.litchfieldhills.com. For additional festival and event information, contact the Kent Chamber of Commerce at (860) 927-1463.

AUGUST

Annual Paint-Out Auction at the Kent Art Association building is open to the public and features an array of artwork. (860) 927-3989.

SEPTEMBER

One of the most popular events in Kent that happens on the last Saturday and Sunday of the month and draws spectators from near and far is the **Fall Festival of the Connecticut Antique Machinery Association** on Route 7. There is a nominal charge to enter the museum grounds, watch "live" engines and machine demonstrations, and take a ride on the locomotive engine. A featured specialty among food vendors is CAMA's "Engineer's Vegetable Beef Soup." (860) 927-0050; www.ctamachinery.com.

The **Annual Fall Show**, a month-long event at the Kent Art Association building, is open to the public and features an array of juried artwork. (860) 927-3989.

Crowds gather to watch the annual **Crew Races** that take place on the Housatonic River by champion Kent School rowers. (860) 927-6047.

OCTOBER

The **Annual Pumpkin Run** begins and ends on the town green adjacent to the Kent Town Hall and features cash prizes for the top winners. After-race refreshments include a "famous" pumpkin soup. (860) 927-1463.

DECEMBER

Attend the **Annual Tree-Lighting Ceremony** that begins inside the Fife 'N Drum at the piano and sing Christmas Carols led by the local group known as the Kent Singers. Tree lighting takes place at the green. Check out the businesses that remain open late and before leaving, purchase cookies that benefit the Kent Volunteer Fire Department fundraiser. (860) 927-1463.

The Many Faces of Kent

Just some of the bow-WOW! things at "The Dog Show."
See page 304

Kent artist, Denis Curtiss, sitting amidst his sculptures.
See page 304

The state's largest maple tree grows in Kent.
See page 304

Additional Faces of Kent

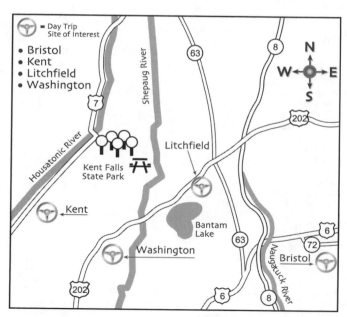

INDEX

Consummate Connecticut

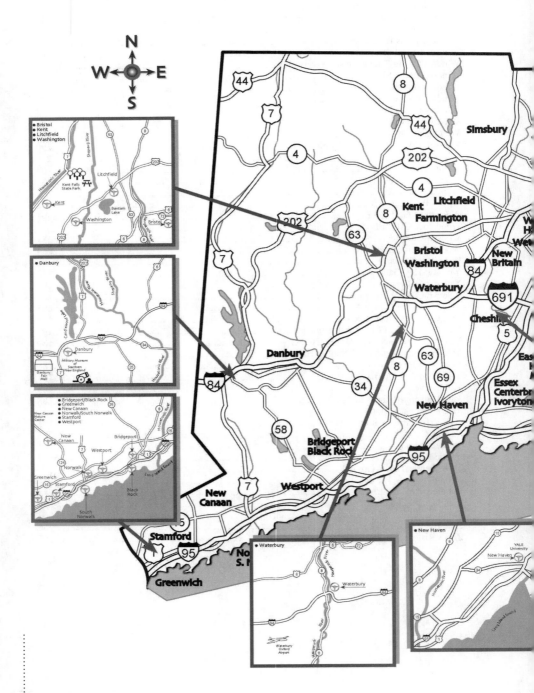

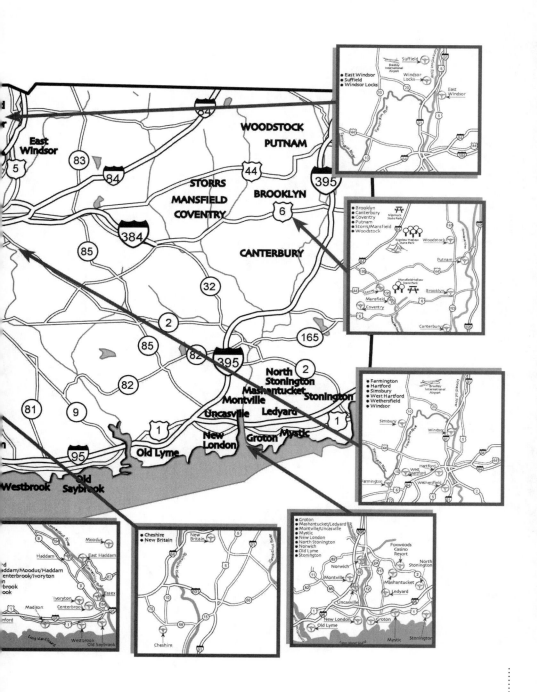